Dan Rutten

A CARTOGRAPH
SHOWING EARLY HISTORICAL LANDMARKS OF
GOLETA
the Good Land

DRAWN BY ROBERT L. DILLON, ARCHITECT

Goleta: The Good Land

HISTORICAL BOOKS BY THE AUTHOR
Santa Barbara Past and Present
California's Wonderful Corner
Santa Barbara's Royal Rancho
California Editor (co-author)
Little Giant of Signal Hill
Old Spanish Santa Barbara
Santa Barbara Yesterdays
Stearns Wharf Centennial
Fourteen at the Table
Goleta: the Good Land
Mattei's Tavern

Endorsed by
Santa Barbara
American Revolution
Bicentennial Committee

GOLETA
the Good Land

by Walker A. Tompkins

Published as a Community Service by
Goleta Amvets Post No. 55
Goleta, California
Co-sponsored by Santa Barbara News-Press

© Copyright 1966 by Goleta Amvets Post 55
Library of Congress Catalog Card Number: 66-23873

First printing, May 1966
Second printing, June 1966
Bicentennial edition, July 1976

MANUFACTURED IN THE UNITED STATES OF AMERICA
PIONEER PUBLISHING CO.
8 East Olive Avenue
Fresno, CA 93728

To my family and friends
who remember the Good Land when
it was more sylvan than suburban

AUTHOR'S ACKNOWLEDGEMENTS

Fifty years ago, G. M. Gidney published his two-volume history of the Tri Counties. Only one of its 456 pages dealt with the Goleta Valley. Gidney explained this thin treatment as follows:

> The quiet and prosperous contentment of the Goleta district and the absence of important happenings there give point to the epigram "Happy is that people who have no history."

If this epigram were true, the people of Goleta would be miserable; for their historic heritage is jam-packed with drama over a 400-year period, as we hope the following pages will demonstrate.

Geographically, this book defines the Goleta Valley as extending from the General Hospital to Dos Pueblos Canyon and, as the old Mexican *diseños* so poetically phrased it, "from the sierra to the sea."

One problem in writing this book was how to orient vanished landmarks with today's rapidly-changing surroundings. Whenever possible current street numbers and permanent (?) geographical features have been used, but in this bulldozer age, even they are ephemeral.

It would obviously have been impossible to include *every* family which settled in the Goleta Valley during the last century. Nor has the author attempted to trace the leading pioneer families beyond the third generation. To have included even partial genealogies would have transformed these pages into a dry recital of names as dull as the Biblical "begats" in *First Chronicles*.

... Many persons have contributed to this volume. It all began on New Year's Day, 1965, when Virginia and Ed Peirce of El Encanto Heights called on their friend and neighbor Steve Sullivan, who was the Goleta Bureau chief of the Santa Barbara *News-Press*. The Peirces expressed a wish that a Goleta Valley history could be produced, similar in format to the Sexton family's booklet *Fourteen at the Table*.

Author's Acknowledgements

Sullivan saw possibilities for a full-dress, hard-cover book instead. Taking the Peirces' idea, Sullivan within a week's time had engaged the go-getting Goleta Amvets Post 55 to underwrite the publication of such a book, with the *News-Press* handling promotion as co-sponsors. The undersigned was commissioned to do the research and writing—which he considered a high honor and privilege—and he officially began work on April 26, 1965.

The sponsors staged a county-wide contest to select a title for the book. Winners with *"Goleta: the Good Land"* were Miss Marcia Sepulveda and Mrs. Ross K. Nielson, both of Goleta. The Goleta branch of Security First National Bank, Gordon T. McEachran manager, donated safety vault space for the storage of valuable documents and pictures. Margaret and Sam Mosher graciously made available to the author a secluded studio at their home on Austin Road, More Mesa, which served as a convenient base of operations during the preparation of the book.

Many Valley pioneers cooperated, but special thanks go to these six for editorial counsel: Horace A. Sexton, Jim Smith, Judge W. T. Lillard, Miss Nellie Langman, Mrs. Ida Catlett Chamberlain, and Mrs. John B. Pico. Their ages total to more than 517 years.

Work on previous books dealing with Goleta—*Santa Barbara's Royal Rancho, Santa Barbara Yesterdays, Little Giant of Signal Hill* and *Fourteen at the Table*—resulted in the borrowing of material gleaned from the following persons now deceased:

Harry Arthur, Mrs. Frank Birabent, Nels Brown, Leo Carrillo, Yris Covarrubias, Rose Sexton Dearborn, Dr. William Ellison, Mike Farren, Frank F. Flournoy, Gail Harrison, J. J. Hollister Sr., Sen. Jack Hollister, Jane Kimberley, Tom and Mary Kinevan, Ysabella Den Monroe, John Pagliotti, Frank Price Sr., Annie Roberts, Gregg Reay, Herb Roberts, Jessie Rutherford, Mary Sexton, Ethel Hollister Strain, John K. Wade, A. B. Watkins, George Willey, Florence and James G. Williams.

A very deep debt of gratitude is owed to the following persons who contributed personal interviews, photographs, clippings and other assistance in the compilation of this community history:

Amelia Acres, Frank Acres, James Allison, James Anderson, Ray C. Ault, Dr. Frances Baker, Carrie Begg, Della Beguhl, Bruce Benedict, Marshall Bond Jr., Isaac A. Bonilla, Joy Bonilla, Dick Borden, Dorothy Boynton, Laura Borgaro, Angelo Bottiani, Nina Bottiani, Andy Brydon, Christian Brun, Mary Bueneman, Richard Buffum, Jessie Bundy,

Author's Acknowledgements

Mrs. George Canatsy, Granvel B. Caster, Coto Cavalletto;

Jack D. Cavalletto, Joe Cavaletto, George Cavalletto, Louis Cavalletto, Dr. Vernon Cheadle, Mary Chrisman, Ida Churchill, Lee H. Cornell, Dr. Ian Crow, Arthur Cummings, Dr. John Cushing, John Dell, Dr. Alfred A. J. Den, Joe Dominy, John Doty, Russel Doty, Mike Durbiano, Evelyn Durham, Helen Cooper Erickson, Frank Emigh, Norval C. Fast, Wilberta Finley, Elizabeth Baker Ford, Benny Gates;

Fr. Maynard Geiger O.F.M.; Laura Giorgi, John Gorin, George Goman, Grace C. Greenwell, Sylvia Griffiths, Edwin and Andriette Gledhill, Ruth Culver Hammond, Glen Hancock, Mrs. William Hanssen, John Harlan, Ben Hartman, Julius Hatlen, Kate Manchester Hendryx, Seth Hicks, Clifford Hill, Kathryn Hollister, Mary Irvine, Don P. Johnston, Leonard Kellogg, Ida Towne Klett;

Myrtle Klenk, Larry Lane, Nellie Langman, Rowena Sturges Lawrence, Jim Layne, Elizabeth Linquest, Paul H. Manchester, Myra Manfrina, Rita M. Marshall, Edward McCaffery, Leroy Metz, Maude P. Meyers, Margaret Miratti, Frank A. Morgan, Samuel B. Mosher, George Obern, J. W. O'Brien, Owen H. O'Neill, Phil C. Orr, Roger C. Owen, Virginia S. Peirce, Mima Lane Pickett, Dee Pomatto, Dominic Pomatto, Henry Roades;

Chester Rich, Robert Rich, Norman and Betty Rowe, Robert Rowe, Russell Ruiz, J. Monroe Rutherford, William Rutherford, Al Sandal, Dr. Norman Scharer, Jack Schwartz, John H. Senter, Marion Sepulveda, Eugene Sexton, Mary Shaw, James Silver, Mr. and Mrs. Henry Simpson, Allen Singleton, Charles Smith, Clifton Smith, Floyd Smith, Frank Smith, Jim Smith, Joseph Smith, Stanley Smith, Sydney Smith, Virginia Rose Smith, Donald L. Stillman;

Edward S. Spaulding, William Steinmetz, Pearl Stevens, Lola Lane Stevens, Thomas M. Storke, Charles A. Storke II, Mabel Hughes Strawn, James M. Stubchaer, Garrett Van Horne, Donald Welch, Robert E. Welling, Benjamin Wells, Richard Whitehead, Mrs. Oliver Wilson, and Phyllis Wind.

The author received splendid cooperation from the Amvets' History Project Committee, composed of James C. Durham, chairman; Jack W. James, Albert A. Irvine, Charles W. Begg and Commander Jack Hicks, Post 55. Project secretary Evelyn Begg Durham was kept busy keeping records on pre-publication orders. *News-Press* executives Stuart C. Taylor and Paul Veblen were most cooperative. Publicity and promotion were capably handled all year by the book's "father", Steve Sullivan.

Research assistants Finis Haskins and Edward H. Peirce spent many laborious days tracing Goleta land titles in the files of the Santa Barbara office of Title Insurance & Trust Company, which were provided without cost through the courtesy of Joseph Watson.

Also due special thanks are the reference librarians at the *News-Press*, UCSB Special Collections, UCLA Special Collections, Santa Barbara Public Library, Santa Barbara Museum of Natural History, Santa Barbara Historical Society, Bancroft Library in Berkeley, Huntington Library in San Marino, and the Santa Barbara County Law Library.

Unfailing cooperation in research phases came from the office staffs of County Supervisor Daniel G. Grant; the Santa Barbara County clerk, recorder, district attorney, sheriff, surveyor, road, planning and engineering, flood control; the State Highway department at San Luis Obispo; and secretary Gene Sexton of the Goleta Valley Chamber of Commerce.

Architect Robert Dillon contributed the endpaper cartograph of early landmarks. Penfield & Smith allowed the use of their copyrighted 1965 map of the Goleta Valley, with historical additions by the author. The dust jacket was designed by *News-Press* artist Richard Smith.

If the final manuscript went to the printers reasonably free of errors in spelling, grammar and punctuation, credit must go to the meticulous and merciless proofreading skills of Phyllis Wind, Steve Sullivan and William J. McNally, whose comprehension of these technical mysteries lies far beyond the author's ken. The latter must, however, assume responsibility for any errors of fact or interpretation.

When at last the composition and revision were completed, this fact dawned on the author: what he had created was an obituary to a way of life that is forever gone, a requiem for a sylvan Valley caught in a ferment of change known as "Progress." He submits *Goleta: the Good Land* for the appraisal of the reader with the distinct feeling that this book, whether good, bad or indifferent, was written in the nick of time; for the last dim traces of Goleta's pioneer past are disappearing with each passing day.

WALKER A. TOMPKINS

Table of Contents

I.	The Mystery of Mescalitán Island	1
II.	A Schooner Stranded on a Sandspit	10
III.	Yankee Don from Boston: Daniel A. Hill	21
IV.	Nicolás A. Den, Don of Dos Pueblos	30
V.	When Frémont Came Over the Mountain	39
VI.	Goleta Beef Feeds the 'Forty-Niners	49
VII.	Deluge and Death, Drought and Death	59
VIII.	1868: Goleta Valley Subdividing Begins	70
IX.	W. W. Hollister, Squire of Glen Annie	80
X.	Homesteading in the Goleta Foothills	92
XI.	The Twin Villages: Goleta and La Patera	101
XII.	Ellwood Cooper, the Olive-Oil King	113
XIII.	Sherman P. Stow Pioneers Irrigation	123
XIV.	Stagecoach Days in the Goleta Valley	131
XV.	Trouble Ahead—A Sinking Water Table	142
XVI.	"King John", the Monarch of More Mesa	150
XVII.	The Den Estate Sues Colonel Hollister	160
XVIII.	Glasgow to Goleta: The Scottish Exodus	171

XIX.	How Glen Annie Became the Bishop Ranch	179
XX.	The Booming Eighties Bring a Railroad	189
XXI.	Genoa to Goleta: Exodus Italian Style	203
XXII.	Vanished Industries of the 19th Century	214
XXIII.	Sexton's Hall: Symbol of the Gay Nineties	224
XXIV.	Hello, Central? Get Me the Auto Garage!	239
XXV.	Better Roads, County Parks, and Disaster	250
XXVI.	The Fabulous Campbell and Walora Ranches	261
XXVII.	Black Gold Bonanza at Ellwood Oil Field	273
XXVIII.	The Depression Years: Airports and Avocados	285
XXIX.	Strange Interlude: Sub Attack at Ellwood!	295
XXX.	From Marine Base to State University	307
XXXI.	Cachuma Triggers a Population Explosion	317
XXXII.	Progress: From Mescalitán to Megalopolis	330
	Index	343

Illustrations follow pages 36, 68, 100, 164, 196, 260, 292, and 312.

CHAPTER I

The Mystery of Mescalitán Island

Back in 1891, a Goleta rancher named Aventino Cavalletto was grubbing liveoaks from a bean field which is now the University campus. One evening after work, his crew went row-boating in the Slough—and stumbled across an amazing and unique discovery.

An outgoing tide stranded their skiff, forcing them to push it back to the landing. Midway along the mudflats below the mesa bluffs, one of the woodchoppers stubbed his toe on a big iron ring which lay half-buried in the ooze. It was attached to some immovable object.

Could it be a pirate treasure chest? With feverish haste the men started digging. They unearthed a wrought-iron anchor, eight feet long, thick with the rust of centuries. Its archaic design dated it to the Sixteenth Century—the era of Columbus and Cabrillo!

Cavalletto loaded the relic on his wagon and hauled it to his home, using it as a hitching post for sixty years. The anchor is still in the possession of the Cavalletto family.

Several theories have been advanced to explain how the anchor got so far inland. Romanticists speculate that perhaps it came from the wrecked schooner which, legend has it, gave Goleta its name. (The word derives from the Arabic *galata*, a North African coastal vessel, called *geolet* in French or *goleta* in Spanish.)

History relates how Captain Juan Perez, of Father Serra's supply ship *San Antonio*, sailed north in search of Portolá and his men in 1769. He "lost an anchor somewhere along the Santa Bárbara Channel" and had to return to San Diego. Could this have been Perez's anchor?

Another theory was that the anchor had been used in kedging the tiny flagship of Juan Rodríguez Cabrillo into the Goleta harborage in 1543. This was based on a local Indian legend concerning a corpse, answering Cabrillo's description, said to have been buried by his shipmates on Goleta's Mescalitán Island in the remote past....

The anchor was hidden by its present claimant to ownership but came to light in 1965 during the research on this book. Its origin may never be learned. It is doubtful if the mystery of Mescalitán Island will be resolved, either, for Cabrillo's log book disappeared in Mexico some four centuries ago.

Most historians agree that the first white man to lay eyes on the Goleta area did so from the crow's-nest of Cabrillo's flagship when it made its landfall on Monday, October 16, 1542. While Fiesta parades feature a float labeled "Cabrillo's Landing in Santa Barbara," the Spaniards did not come ashore in that area, but continued sailing up the coast until night overtook them off two Indian *rancherias* which Cabrillo logged as "Los Dos Pueblos," the name which the site bears more than 400 years later.

The old records say Cabrillo suffered a broken arm on San Miguel Island later in October, and died of blood poisoning on January 3, 1543. Most writers have taken for granted the *conquistador* was buried where he died. Which island that was, however, has long been a subject of debate in learned circles, for different names were applied to the same islands in old Spanish journals and charts.

Aborigines dwelling along the coast in 1542 called themselves *Cuabaijai*. The word *Chumash* now refers to their language group, the word *Canaliño*, meaning Channel-Dweller, to their cultural group.

It is an historical fact that Indians residing in the Goleta Valley in the mid-1500s started a legend—which was repeated by Canaliño lips in the hearing of persons alive when this book was written—that long ago, two sailing vessels anchored inside Goleta Slough, which was a deep-water port in ancient times, and their crews went ashore on Mescalitán Island to bury their dead leader.

While this legend cannot be authenticated by existing evidence, there are reasons to believe its salient details could be true. Consider that in 1543, the Goleta Slough area was the most heavily-populated place found by the Spaniards in Baja or Alta California.

The Mystery of Mescalitán Island

Consider that its estuary offered seafarers the only navigable landlocked anchorage between San Diego Bay and the as-yet unknown San Francisco Bay. It is therefore plausible that Cabrillo's men, faced with a winter's sojourn on windswept San Miguel Island, might have welcomed the snug haven of Goleta's harbor. If they returned to the mainland, they might have brought Cabrillo's remains along for burial.

There are skeptics who point out that no devout Catholic crew would bury their Catholic captain in unconsecrated soil already profaned by pagan burials, as was the case at Mescalitán Island. However, the same objection is equally valid at San Miguel.

Even if we assume the truth of the Goleta Indian legend, by now Cabrillo's bones would be lost beyond recall. Generations of pothunters, scientific excavators, oil well drillers, and the massive earthmoving operations at the outset of World War II, have disturbed hundreds of human skeletons on Mescalitán Island. Many Goletans are under the impression the name is "Skeleton Island," in fact.

History books will probably never recognize Goleta as the long-lost resting place of Cabrillo. May the explorer's dust *requiescat in pace* while we set aside the intriguing mystery of Mescalitán Island and the antique anchor. We must thumb through the weathered pages of time for another two and a quarter centuries—the period during which Spain neglected her California provinces—before we can plant our feet on the solid ground of documented facts.

Thus we find that the first white men to set foot on the soil of the Goleta Valley did so on Sunday morning, August 20, 1769. The cavalcade, numbering 67 Spaniards and their Indian retinue, comprised Governor Gaspar de Portolá's overland expedition from Loreto, seeking the lost *ensenada* of Monterey which Vizcaíno had described in 1602.

The advance scout and trailblazer for the party, Sergeant Jose Francisco de Ortega, was probably the first white man to actually ride over the coastal plain which we today inaccurately call the Goleta "Valley." He was a buxom, jolly Mexican career soldier from Guanajuato, then in his 35th year, who was destined to play a major rôle in the development of the Santa Barbara region.

Portolá's second in command was Lt. Pedro Fages, a future Governor of the Californias. There were two grayfriars of the Franciscan Order, Juan Crespí and Francisco Gomez; and a military engineer, Miguel Costansó.

Portolá and his leather-jacket bodyguards got their first glimpse of the lush Goleta Valley through eyes bloodshot from lack of rest in recent days and nights. All the way along the Channel Coast north of Malibu, the Indians had felt obliged to entertain their white guests night and day. To escape the non-stop entertainment program scheduled at Santa Barbara, the Spaniards had sought asylum in the brushy defile of Arroyo Burro.

From that canyon, after an early morning Mass, the column approached the Goleta Valley by way of an ancient Indian trail which meandered along the northern edge of the Cieniguitas swamps, passing the future sites of St. Vincent's School and the General Hospital, to link up with the route of Hollister Avenue in the vicinity of the present San Marcos High School.

In 1769, the Goleta Valley was verdant with live oak groves, thickets of willow and alders, sycamores and Castilian roses. So impressed was diarist Juan Crespí that he wrote this first appraisal of the Goleta Valley by a white man:

> *This is all a Good Land . . .*

In the two centuries following, successive generations of visitors and settlers have re-echoed Fr. Crespí's sentiments.

He went on to record in his diary:

> We came in sight of a long bare point of land [Pelican or Goleta Point, on the UCSB campus] . . . a large Estuary enters by two different mouths, distant half a league from each other. The Estuary is bordered . . . by a good piece of land [Mescalitán Island] of moderate extent, entirely isolated. On that island, which is very green and covered with trees, we saw a large town, in which were counted more than a hundred houses.
>
> This Estuary spreads out to the West, forming many marshes and lagoons, upon whose banks were other towns. . . . The whole country . . . is extremely delightful . . . giving signs of its being very fertile land, capable of producing whatever one might wish to plant.

The Franciscan priest was quick to discern the agricultural potential of what he called "the Good Land" (the name "Goleta" was not to appear for another half a hundred years). Crespí would have been astonished had he known the topsoil was 300 feet deep in some areas.

Portolá himself, with other diarists in his party, concurred with Fr. Crespí's rhapsodic appraisal of the Goleta Valley, but from different viewpoints. Costansó, the engineer, had only a limited knowledge of North American geography, so he was not aware that the mountains behind the Goleta Valley were one of only two ranges on the continent with an east-west traverse. But he did know that because the mountain wall faced the sun all day long, this stretch of east-west shoreline had a semi-tropical climate rivalling that of the French Mediterranean coast. The mountains, rising from 2,250 feet at San Marcos Pass to a maximum of 4,292 feet at Santa Ynez Peak, shielded the valley from cold weather fronts incubated in Alaska, while the sprawling Channel Islands on the south horizon protected the valley from ocean storms.

Sergeant Ortega's opinion of the Goleta Valley was influenced by the fact that it was his responsibility to blaze a trail for the expedition across *terra incognita*. Ortega had to choose each night's campground, close to wood and water. In his eyes, therefore, the sprawling Goleta Slough was an obstacle he must detour.

The Goleta Slough was vastly more extensive in Ortega's day than it is now. It sent thrusting tentacles of seawater north of Hollister Avenue almost to Stow (Los Carneros) Lake. One arm formerly extended westward to link up with the lagoon on the Devereux Ranch at Coal Oil Point. Salt beds from evaporated tidewater indicate that the Goleta Slough's prehistoric eastern arm reached into the flats south of the Goleta Cemetery, almost to the General Hospital site.

The Slough was diluted by pure mountain water sluicing in from nine streams, rising in a quadrant of deep canyons to converge fanwise onto the tidelands. All nine of these unnamed creeks teemed with steelhead trout until comparatively recent times; due to a depleted watershed and a sinking water table, the creeks are bone-dry now, except in the rainy season.

Human beings are known to have inhabited the Goleta Slough region as early as 5,000 years before the birth of Christ. In May,

1963, a group of UCSB students under Prof. Roger C. Owen obtained four shell samples from a middenheap near Highway 101, at the mouth of Glen Annie Canyon, and submitted them to UCLA laboratories for radiocarbon dating. The tests showed the shell samples ranged from 6,380 to 7,270 years old, making Goleta's Indians the earliest documented inhabitants found to date on the California mainland. Only 40 miles southwest, on Santa Rosa Island, radiocarbon dating tests indicate human habitation as early as 10,000 years ago. Scientists are confident they will match or surpass this age in the Goleta Valley, since Santa Rosa and the other Channel Islands were once part of the mainland.

David Banks Rogers of the Santa Barbara Museum of Natural History, in the middle Twenties, plotted the sites of 38 prehistoric Indian *rancherias* in the area bounded by the foothills and the beach between Hope Ranch and Dos Pueblos.

The two Franciscan priests with Portolá saw the Goleta Valley from yet another viewpoint—that of an ideal location for a future Santa Barbara Mission. They so recommended the valley in their reports to the Viceroy. They made a census of hundreds of brush huts and *temescals*, or sweat houses, each hut housing one or more Indian families, clustered around the edges of the Slough like insect eggs clotting the veins on the underside of a leaf. Such a concentration of Stone Age heathens promised a rich crop of souls for redemption by Christianity.

During the day, Portolá's explorers concluded there were actually four separate towns, bearing the Indian names of Saspili, Geliec, Alcajch and Heló, the latter being the largest, located on the north side of Mescalitán Island where the Goleta sewage disposal plant is found today. (The island itself has been reduced to a quarter of its original dimensions in order to obtain fill dirt for the airport runways.)

Fr. Crespí estimated that more than a thousand heathens lived on the 62-acre island. Among them was a squaw with an extremely dirty face. Her presence gave rise to the romantic fiction that an Indian "queen" or "princess" ruled the Goleta Valley. She did, however, contribute to the naming of Mescalitán Island, the second oldest place-name in the Goleta area (Dos Pueblos being the oldest).

A dirty-faced female figured in an ancient Aztec myth which Portolá's men had heard in the western coastal provinces of Mexico, from which most of them came. The dwelling place of the Aztec gods, according to this myth, was an island in the center of a sacred lake in Nayarit Province, between Mazatlán and Guadalajara. The island was called Mescaltitlán, meaning "the place where mescal grows." (Mescal is a species of cactus from which Mexicans brew their national drink, tequila. Mescal does not grow north of San Diego.)

According to this Aztec myth, when the great god Huitzilopochtli set forth to conquer the world in ancient times, his queen mother swore not to wash her face until he returned victorious. This took a century or two, so by the time her son got home from the wars the Aztec goddess who lived on the island of Mescaltitlán had a face as grimy as that of the squaw the Spanish soldiers found in 1769 on the island at the mouth of the Goleta Slough.

This prompted them to give the name Mescaltitlán not only to the island, but to the roundabout Indian villages and the valley and mountains as well. All the early Spanish charts of Alta California labeled the Goleta Valley "Mescaltitlán."

The official landmark-christener on the expedition was supposed to be Fr. Crespí. He naturally favored saint's names, and dubbed Mescaltitlán Island "Santa Margarita de Cortona." His choice failed to catch on. Neither did his polysyllabic religious titles for other geographical sites along the line of march, most of which today bear the simpler names given them by Portolá's soldiers. Examples would be Carpintería, carpenter shop; or Gaviota, seagull.

Sergeant Ortega, scouting ahead of the main column, picked the next camping spot near the fork of a creek, north and west of the Hollister-Fairview intersection, occupied in 1966 by a drive-in movie theater.

Once again, as all along the coast of recent weeks, the Indians overwhelmed the Spaniards with hospitality. They came bearing gifts of seafood, acorn meal, watertight baskets, and steatite bowls. Then they proceeded to stage a non-stop concert of singing and dancing to ear-splitting percussion accompaniment.

The priest, Fr. Crespí, complained that this 1769 version of a rock 'n' roll hootenanny was "an infernal noise . . . sufficient to rip our eardrums to pieces." The soldier, Lt. Fages, wrote in a more tolerant vein in his diary that night:

> The liberality and festivity with which these poor people received us cannot be adequately described. Our arrival was for them a motive of public rejoicing, in which there was no stint of music and dancing, which were not badly performed, after their fashion.

So enthusiastic were the childlike Goleta Valley pagans in their desire to give the bearded foreigners a warm welcome that around midnight, an exhausted Captain Portolá was forced to threaten punishment if they did not go away and let his jaded men and animals get some sleep.

The environs of the Goleta Valley looked somewhat different in 1769 than they do today. Fages refers to "dense oak groves" all the way to Dos Pueblos Canyon and back to Santa Barbara. Other early writers agree that the mesa which encompasses UCSB, Isla Vista and the Devereux Ranch was a solid jungle of oaks.

The three most common weeds growing in the valley today were unknown when Portolá arrived. They include the giant black mustard, *Brassica nigra*, the 12-foot stalks of which were to astonish Yankee settlers 100 years later; malva or cheeseweed, *Parviflora*; and the ubiquitous alfileria or *Erodium circutarium*. These plants are all native to the Mediterranean shores of Spain and France. They came accidentally to the New World prior to 1824, as seeds in the wool of sheep or in the straw packing of freight crates aboard ships. Falling in fertile soil half a world away, the seeds germinated and foliated up and down the California coast within a decade or two.

The wild life which Portolá witnessed in the Goleta Valley was infinitely more numerous than today. Incredibly large flocks of ducks and wild geese followed primeval flyways to landings in the *patera* and tidal bayous of Goleta Slough. The stirrup-high wild grasses abounded with quail, doves, and grouse. Buzzards, some with wing spreads rivaling those of their cousins the California condor (numerous in 1769, nearing extinction in 1966) soared in at eventide to roost in the taller sycamore trees along the creeks. Shrikes, almost non-existent now, hung lizards to dry on thorny bushes. Fish teemed in the creeks. The night sky hummed to a wingbeat symphony of owls and bats foraging for mosquitoes—an insect unhappily still with us.

Deer, elk, the giant California grizzly which is now an extinct species, and mountain lions mixed their spoor at creeks and waterholes with raccoon, skunk, rat, mouse and gopher tracks. The Good Land was almost over-ripe with wildlife, for the Canaliños were primarily seafood eaters, not hunters.

The mountain range in 1769 showed considerably more timber and less exposed bedrock than now, especially above Winchester, Ellwood, and Glen Annie Canyons. Earthquakes, floods, wind erosion, rainfall and periodic forest fires have resulted in the exposure of new cliffs, outcrops, scarps and ledges.

... At two o'clock the next afternoon, August 21, 1769, Portolá broke camp and marched westward through continuous oak groves to the next camp Ortega had selected. It was beside an *estero* at the mouth of a large canyon between two populous Indian villages, the same that Cabrillo had noted in his logbook as Los Dos Pueblos some 227 years earlier.

Once again, the Spaniards were dismayed to see preparations being made by the heathen to give them an all-night talent show. The Indians' spirits would have sobered had they recognized the white men for what they were—harbingers of the early doom of their race. Within 36 years both Goleta and Dos Pueblos would be extinct as Indian centers; and only 183 years would elapse before the last full-blooded Canaliño Indian would die, a pauper, in the Santa Barbara General Hospital, the ultimate decimal of a doomed people.

CHAPTER II

A Schooner Stranded on a Sandspit

Santa Barbara might be located where Goleta is today, had there been a few more loose boulders lying around, and a larger stream of water flowing down the creeks, when Governor Felipe de Neve made his second inspection of the Valley in 1782.

Five years previously, while moving his official residence from Loreto to Monterey, Governor Neve was under orders to scout the Channel Coast for the best site to locate a presidio to protect a mission which Padre Serra wanted to establish in the region. Neve chose Mescaltitlán (the Goleta Slough vicinity) because "it was an open place, and held a dominant position."

As a military man, Governor Neve knew a presidio should be built on ground which commanded the surrounding terrain. In Mescalitán Island, with its salt water moat, he had an ideal defensive site. The lay of the Goleta Valley was perfect, with level open space and fertile soil for the *milpas* and vegetable gardens of the future presidio's personnel. The western end of More Mesa was an ideal place for Santa Barbara Mission. Furthermore, Goleta Slough would offer an excellent all-year, all-weather port for the supply ships which were California's lifeline from San Blas.

But when Felipe de Neve was ready to actually establish Santa Barbara's Royal Presidio, in 1782, he was forced to change his mind about Mescalitán. A dependable water supply was the first essential for a mission-presidio community in this semi-arid climate, and Goleta's creeks were almost bone-dry in 1782. Neve's engineers also pointed out that there was not an adequate supply of rocks available for constructing a fort, or even a mission edifice.

Two leagues down the coast, the alluvial fan sprawling from the maw of Arroyo Pedregoso (now Mission Canyon) was impregnated with massive sandstone boulders, which could be easily dressed by unskilled Indian stonemasons. Equally important, Mission Creek was a major stream, even in drought years. A dam could be built to provide a year-round supply of water for the future mission and presidio.

So, on August 26, 1782, Governor Neve made his explanation of the change of site in a letter to Viceroy de Croix, which mission archivist Fr. Maynard Geiger O.F.M. discovered in Guadalajara while doing the research for his book *Mission Santa Barbara 1782-1965*. In this letter, Felipe de Neve said:

> This place [Santa Barbara] was preferable to the site of Mescaltitlán, two leagues distant, because Santa Barbara rather than Mescaltitlán had better advantages for pasture, land, wood, stone, and water, the three latter of which are lacking at Mescaltitlán.

Thus the Good Land missed becoming the locale of one of the world's most noted resort cities. . . .

Padre Junipero Serra, the Majorcan priest who was El Presidente of the California Missions, strung the first bead on his mission rosary at San Diego in 1769, the year of the Portolá expedition. He followed it in 1770 with a second mission at Monterey. Linking these two seaports by land was a mule trail which bore the grandiloquent name of El Camino Real, the King's Highway.

El Camino Real, now memorialized by U. S. Highway 101, spanned the Goleta Valley from end to end. The original Spanish trail followed existing Indian routes as far as Point Concepción and turned northward. Not until the year 1804 did it cross the mountain range at Refugio Pass, as a result of the building of Mission Santa Inés (on the outskirts of modern Solvang).

Father Serra's first overland journey across the Goleta Valley occurred in September, 1772, when he and Pedro Fages were riding muleback from Monterey to San Gabriel Mission.

In 1774, the Goleta Valley had another distinguished visitor in the person of Captain Juan Bautista de Anza, who was making a survey of a direct route from Mexico City to Monterey by way of Sonora. His journalist, Fr. Pedro Font, made the first mention in history of the gobs of natural asphaltum which littered the ocean beach between the Goleta Sandspit and Dos Pueblos. He also commented on the strong odor exuding from the oil slicks in the vicinity of what is still called Coal Oil Point, a southward-jutting promontory on the Devereux Ranch.

During 1776, the year an infant American nation on the Atlantic seaboard was declaring its independence from the British Crown, both Anza and Serra paid return visits to the Goleta Valley.

Six more years were to elapse before work actually began on a Royal Presidio at Santa Bárbara. Fr. Serra, together with Governor Felipe de Neve, dedicated the presidio on April 21, 1782. Serra's dream of establishing a mission at Santa Bárbara at this time was dashed when the governor ordered work on the mission delayed until the presidio was completed.

The task of erecting the Santa Bárbara Presidio's first temporary barracks, chapel and fortifications was assigned to Jose Francisco de Ortega, formerly Portolá's scout, now promoted to lieutenant. He remained as comandante of the presidio for two years, when he was replaced by a Basque soldier, Lt. Felipe de Goycoechea.

In 1784, word came from Monterey that Padre Serra had died, and that his successor as El Presidente of the California mission chain would be Padre Fermín Lasuén, O.F.M.

By decree of King Carlos III, each presidio town or pueblo was allotted four square leagues of land, while each mission was given dominion over the lands under its ecclesiastical jurisdiction, to hold in sacred trust for the Indians. Since the mission and presidio at Santa Bárbara would be in close juxtaposition, an agreement over land allotments had to be reached at an early date, or frictions would be sure to develop.

Therefore, the first thing Fr. Lasuén did upon arriving in Santa Bárbara to found a mission was to arrange a conference with Lt. Goycoechea at the Presidio, to decide on an equitable division of lands for the respective use of the church and the military. Their negotiations had a far-reaching effect on the destiny of the Goleta Valley, which fell under the control of the mission, rather than becoming a part of the Presidio's pueblo lands.

The division point between the two was in the vicinity of Tucker's Grove County Park. The coastal strip running easterly through

Santa Bárbara, Montecito, Summerland and Carpintería was designated Pueblo Lands; everything west of Tucker's Grove, both north and south of the Santa Ynez Mountains and as far up the coast as the Santa Maria River, fell into the orbit of the Franciscan fathers.

From the mission lands was carved what were loosely known as "royal ranchos." Santa Bárbara's main royal ranchos were Los Dos Pueblos, comprising the Goleta Valley; San Marcos, north of the mountains; and San Julian, in the green hills between Gaviota and the Lompoc Valley.

On Saint Barbara's Day, December 4, 1876, Fr. Lasuén dedicated the brush *ramada* which was the first Mission Santa Bárbara. From that moment forward, for sixty years into the future, the history of the Goleta Valley was inextricably bound to that of Santa Bárbara Mission. The padres converted more neophytes from Goleta than from any other district between Gaviota and the Rincon, including the numerous Indians dwelling on the various Channel Islands, which were also a part of the Santa Barbara Mission parish.

For many years an adobe ruin between Fairview Avenue and La Patera Lane was said to have been the remains of an *asistencia*, or branch chapel of the Mission, where the Goleta Indians who did not live at Santa Barbara's neophyte village could worship. Vague references to this Goleta chapel appear in the writings of pioneers; but in all probability the only local *asistencia* was the one built by the padres in 1803, near El Sueno railroad cut, to minister to the Indians clustered around the Cieniguitas swamps.

It was at no time compulsory for a Canaliño to leave his native village and move to the Mission. The great majority of the Good Land's Indian population rejected the regimentation of neophyte life, and lived happily in paganism at their own *rancherias*. Mission records indicate that out of an estimated 1,500 Canaliños living around the Goleta Slough when the white man came, only 575 accepted Christianity. At Dos Pueblos, with 1,000 Indians, the friars baptized only 352. This conversion ratio was greater than at any of the other Indian centers along the South Coast, however.

Some unknown calamity or exodus emptied the Goleta Valley of its native population between 1790 and 1804. By the latter date, only a handful of Indians remained, including one family in Maria Ygnacia Canyon.

What became of the two out of three Goleta Valley Canaliños who preferred paganism to life in the neophyte village at Santa Barbara? Perhaps an epidemic decimated the valley Indians; there was a scourge of smallpox and measles in the year 1801 which caused a sharp increase of Mission baptisms *in extremis,* and an unusually heavy number of entries in the Mission and presidio burial registers.

It was during this early mission period that the Goleta Valley received its earliest geographical place-names. The mountains, originally called the Mescaltitlán range, became the Santa Ynez after Santa Inés Mission was founded in 1804. The creeks flowing into the Slough, and out of the arroyos to the west, were named as follows, from east to west:

Cieniguitas (the marshes); Atascadero (the swamps); San Antonio (St. Anthony); Maria Ygnacia, the name of an Indian family residing at the Mission's Indian Orchard on that creek; San Jose (St. Joseph); Las Vegas (the green meadows); San Pedro (St. Peter); Los Carneros (the sheep, the rams); Tecolotito, an Indian word meaning small owl (in Glen Annie canyon); Los Armitos (the weapons), which includes Bell, Ellwood and Winchester creeks; Tecolote (the owl); Aguila (the eagle); and Los Dos Pueblos (the two towns).

During the years following the establishment of Santa Bárbara Mission and the unexplained disappearance of the Indians from the Goleta Valley, the Good Land was the stage for an ever-accelerating pageant of historical events.

One of the key players in the drama was Lt. Jose Francisco de Ortega. By 1791 he had become so obese he could not continue his military duties, so he was retired with the brevet rank of El Capitan, a promotion which is memorialized in the name of El Capitan State Park, a few miles up the coast west of Goleta.*

When he left military service, Ortega was the *habilitado* or accounting officer, at army headquarters in Loreto. He was evidently a better warrior than he was a clerk, for he left his accounts in a

---

* A word of explanation to the reader: whenever a compass direction appears in this book, it refers to a precise direction, not local usage. For generations, Goleta people have referred to anything on the way to San Francisco as being "north" and anything in the direction of Los Angeles being "south." Actually, such places as Ellwood, Dos Pueblos or Refugio are west of Goleta; Hope Ranch, Santa Barbara and Montecito are east of Goleta.

hopeless mess. In fact, he owed the government a sizeable sum of money he could not account for. In order to pay back this debt, Captain Ortega petitioned the Viceroy to grant him a piece of land, preferably in the Goleta Valley near Santa Bárbara, where he could raise sheep and cattle and thus pay his obligations.

Perhaps in deference to the fact that Ortega had served His Majesty in New Spain for 36 years, during which time he had built missions at San Buenaventura and San Juan Capistrano and the presidio at Santa Bárbara, the vice regal government made an exception to its rigid rule against granting land to private individuals, and notified *El gran Capitan* that he could select six square leagues of land on the Channel Coast, subject to mission regulations, and enjoy grazing rights, if not actual title, thereon.

The mission fathers vigorously protested this precedent of having an army veteran move onto mission-controlled land belonging to the Indians, especially when they learned that Ortega coveted their prize royal rancho, Los Dos Pueblos. Rather than quarrel with the Church, Ortega moved on up the coast a few leagues and took out grazing rights on a strip of land two leagues wide, extending from Refugio Bay to Cojo Canyon, in the lee of Point Concepción. To this 26,529-acre rancho Ortega bestowed the pious name of Nuestra Señora del Refugio, Our Lady of Refuge. Fr. Lasuén reminded Ortega in no uncertain terms that he could be evicted at any time the Mission took a notion to run its own cattle on the Refugio rancho.

Ortega built himself and his sons an adobe *casa grande* a mile and a half inland from Refugio Beach, the site of which was known for many years as the George Rutherford place, and moved in with his wife, the former Maria Antonia Victoria Carrillo, and their children.

El Capitan Ortega was making a good start toward settling his muddled accounts with the Mexican army at Loreto when, on February 3, 1798, tragedy struck. He was riding through the Indian village of Casíl, at the mouth of Refugio Canyon, on his way to Santa Bárbara to visit a son on duty at the presidio, when he was stricken with a heart attack and fell lifeless from his stirrups.

Ortega was buried with high honors in the *campo santo* of Mission Santa Barbara—his bones later being dug up and tossed into a charnel house to make room for new burials in consecrated soil—

and his son, Jose Maria, took over operation of the Refugio Rancho.

Very soon after Jose Maria Ortega moved into the *hacienda*, he began inviting trade with foreign smuggling vessels. Spain's harsh Laws of the Indies forbade any commerce whatever with ships other than those flying Spanish colors. It was about this time that the word reached Yankee ears at the Long Wharf, in far-off Boston, that Chinese mandarins would pay almost any price for the fur of the Pacific sea otter, when delivered to the hongs and godowns of Canton.

Thus the first Americans to go after the lucrative profits in the otter-poaching business were the first Americans to lay eyes on the Goleta Valley. This they did in about the year 1796, from the decks of anonymous otter-poaching ships. It did not matter a whit to the intrepid mariners from Massachusetts that the King of Spain claimed the Pacific Ocean as his private lake, demanding a monopoly on otter pelts for the Chinese trade. Ships flying the Stars and Stripes began to appear with increasing frequency on the placid waters of Santa Bárbara Channel in the early 1800s, since the offshore islands were a favorite breeding place for otter and sea lions.

These first Americans dared not come ashore at Santa Bárbara. Nor could they ride out a sou'easter or careen a ship on the mudflats of Goleta Slough while they scraped barnacles from her bottom, for the reason that California's Governor Pablo Sola was determined to stamp out otter poaching and had ordered the presidio comandante at Santa Bárbara to seize any foreign vessel foolish enough to sail close to the Channel coast.

The Yankees were not long in finding out that a Spanish grandee named Ortega was welcoming foreign-flag ships in the sheltered cove fronting his ranch at Refugio Canyon. Here the Ortegas were delighted to swap otter skins for the drygoods, tools, medicines and other unobtainable commodities which the Americans brought around the Horn. Eventually even gray-robed fathers from the three Channel Missions, Purísima, Santa Inés and Santa Bárbara, began coming clandestinely to Refugio to barter with the maritime smugglers.

Whenever word reached the zealous comandante at Santa Bárbara Presidio that a foreign ship had anchored in Refugio Bay by moonlight, he would dispatch a platoon of cavalry across the Goleta

Valley to pounce on the smugglers, if possible, and bring them back to the presidio for incarceration and the eventual confiscation of their ship and cargo.

On December 21, 1812, a devastating earthquake totally destroyed the three Channel Missions, and heavily damaged Santa Bárbara's Royal Presidio. The only damage reported in the Goleta Valley was the demolition of an adobe which an Indian family had built in upper Maria Ygnacia Canyon. The temblors dumped heavy earthslides down the mountain slopes overlooking the valley, and permanently altered the courses of many streams.

In 1815, a new comandante reported for duty at Santa Barbara Presidio, a dedicated Spanish blueblood named José de la Guerra. He was determined to eradicate the smuggling operations at Refugio Bay, and as a result was a frequent rider to and fro along the Goleta Valley trails.

Disaster struck Ortega's contraband business in 1818, however, when a French admiral named Hippolyte de Bouchard anchored his two black frigates in Refugio Bay and sent a cutlass-wielding party of freebooters ashore to sack and burn Refugio Rancho. Bouchard was technically not a pirate; he was a mercenary in the employ of Argentina, then fighting for its independence from Spanish tyranny. He was, therefore, legitimately harassing Spanish shipping and ports.

Scouts from Purísima Mission spied the approach of Bouchard's ships from a lookout post on Mount Tranquillon, thus enabling Captain de la Guerra to have a platoon of lancers waiting at Refugio Canyon when the raiders landed. They captured three of Bouchard's men and held them hostage, releasing them only when Bouchard agreed not to attack Santa Bárbara. The famous Yankee, Joseph Chapman, escaped from Bouchard's crew to Mission Santa Inés during the raid on Refugio, and later became a prominent American settler in Southern California.

Don Jose de la Guerra, unlike most professional soldiers in New Spain, was a rich man. He owned a *goleta*, or two-masted schooner, named *La Joven Angustias* after one of his daughters. De la Guerra sailed up and down the coast in this vessel on business junkets. Since the open roadstead at Santa Barbara was vulnerable to southeast storms, De la Guerra kept his schooner in the shelter of Goleta

Slough between voyages. Unfortunately, *La Joven Angustias* ran aground while attempting to enter the narrow inlet between Goleta Sandspit and the More Mesa bluffs in 1819, and was given up as a total loss.

It is quite possible that De la Guerra's wrecked schooner is the one which gave Goleta its name. The writer confesses to failure in finding conclusive proof to verify this premise. It is certain, however, that in Spanish times the Californians referred to the slough district as "the place of the *goleta*," or schooner. The name was firmly established long before June, 1846, when it first appeared on official documents.

Bouchard's raid ended the smuggling era at Refugio Bay, leaving De la Guerra with little police work to occupy him. Knowing the day was approaching when he would no longer be comandante of the presidio, and therefore would become ineligible to reside in the *comandancia* there, in 1819 De la Guerra started construction of an elaborate residence facing the town plaza, two blocks west of the presidio walls. He was building the Casa de la Guerra with Indian labor, and instructed them to strip any hardwood or hardware they needed from the wreck of *La Joven Angustias* which lay awaiting break-up by the winter storms on the Goleta Sandspit.

A young English sea captain happened to be in Santa Bárbara at the time, having lost his own coastal trading vessel in a storm. He paid Don Jose a visit, introduced himself through an interpreter as a native of Norwich, England, named Benjamin Foxen, and begged the comandante not to cannibalize such a fine craft as *La Joven Angustias*.

"I can repair the hull for you," Foxen promised De la Guerra, "and I guarantee to make her seaworthy again or I get no pay."

Don José, who had written off his *goleta* as a total loss, replied, "Repair that vessel, Señor Foxen, and she is yours."

Foxen set to work. He felled tall pine trees then growing on the ridge of the Santa Ynez Mountains, and had Indians carry them down to the Goleta Slough to use as masts and spars. He not only refloated *La Joven Angustias* on a providential high tide and kedged her into the estuary to complete repairs, but talked De la Guerra into taking him into business as a full partner. This association lasted until 1829, to their mutual profit.

When the Republic of Mexico was established by the overthrow of Spanish rule in 1822, the fertile land in the vicinity of Goleta Slough was sectioned into small parcels called *suertes* ("chances") which were drawn by lot by families of presidial soldiers. Here they raised corn, peppers, onions, beans and fruits for private use, and even built *fincas*, or summer homes. The first known *suerte* in the Good Land was drawn in a lottery by Don Mariano Pico, a nephew of Governor Pio Pico and Gen. Andres Pico, both noted personages in California history. His *suerte* was located north of Hollister Avenue and east of Fairview Avenue, near Mandarin Drive. A grandson of Don Mariano's, John B. Pico, was a blacksmith and early-day constable in Goleta. Title to the Pico *suerte* remained with the family for more than 130 years.

Pablo Sola was the Governor of California when Mexico overthrew the tyranny of Spain. His successor in office was Luis Arguëllo, California's first Mexican governor. Don Luis was an astute businessman, and he resented seeing Yankee, Russian and Aleut otter hunters stealing pelts in California waters for the rich China trade. By the 1820s, excessive hunting had made the otter almost extinct, and pelts were drawing the equivalent of $2,500 each on the Canton waterfront. Governor Arguëllo was determined to put the Mexican government into the otter skin business, by purchasing a ship and hiring a crew to operate it. In making this decision, Arguëllo was indirectly shaping the future of the Goleta Valley.

The American ship which Governor Arguëllo bought, paying $9,000 worth of seal skins, was the *Rover*, 83 tons burden, engaged in the Sandwich (Hawaiian) Island trade. Her owners were Captain John Rogers Cooper, and two Boston merchants, Nathanial Dorr and William Blanchard. Arguëllo closed the deal on December 29, 1822.

On the seventh day of February, 1823, the *Rover* changed from American to Mexican registry and set sail for Honolulu. Her last port of call in California would be Refugio Bay, where all trade restrictions had been recently lifted by the new Mexican regime. Here Capt. Cooper hoped to complete his cargo.

When Cooper went ashore at Refugio by whaleboat, he was accompanied by his first mate, a stocky, wide-nosed, bushy-haired seaman named Daniel Antonio Hill, from South Billerica, a Boston suburb. Hill had run away from his ancestral farm at an early age to follow the sea. He was now in his twenty-sixth year.

Waiting on the beach to welcome visitors, as was his gracious custom, stood the current owner of Refugio Rancho, Don José Vicente Ortega. With him that morning was his lovely fourteen-year-old daughter, Rafaela Sabrina Luisa Ortega.

Daniel Hill took one look into Rafaela's limpid brown eyes and lost his heart to the voluptuous young *damosela*. Later in the day he met Ortega's wife, Maria Estefana, and their other children, Luis, José and Pedro, but he only had eyes for Rafaela.

Cooper borrowed a mule from their host and dispatched Dan Hill to Santa Barbara to see if there was any cargo worth sailing there to pick up. The round trip through the Goleta Valley altered the destiny of both the man and the valley.

The Good Land was at its best that spring of 1823. Golden poppies made flame-colored patches on the rounded foothills; between them and the mountain chaparral line, in the mile-wide frost-free belt, wild flowers were blooming in riotous profusion. Lupin, verbena and Castilian roses made a rainbow-hued blanket on the overflow lands closer to the Slough. Daniel Hill, reveling in the clouds of ducks and geese, the herds of antelope and deer glimpsed through the liveoaks, was convinced he had stumbled onto the Garden of Eden—with an Eve to go with it.

Riding back toward Refugio next day, with the Santa Ynez Mountains turning rose-gold in the alpenglow of late afternoon, Daniel Hill made up his mind then and there to quit the sea forever.

He had acquired two new mistresses: Goleta, the Good Land, and Rafaela of Refugio Rancho.

Before too long the sailor from Boston would possess both.

CHAPTER III

Yankee Don from Boston: Daniel A. Hill

By the time the *Rover* was hull-down on the horizon off Point Concepción, China-bound under the red, white and green ensign of Mexico, her erstwhile first mate, Daniel A. Hill, was on his way to Santa Barbara in an ox-drawn *carreta*. Loaded thereon was Hill's sea-chest and a cargo of assorted drygoods, iron tools, spices, boots and shoes—Yankee trade goods which Hill had shrewdly requisitioned from the *Rover*'s manifest in lieu of the sea pay due him.

Hill had been offered a vaquero's job on the Ortega Ranch, which was tempting in that it would keep him close to Señorita Rafaela. In spite of the language barrier between them, the Boston seaman and the *ranchero*'s daughter had established an amorous rapport. But Hill was a practical man. Breaking horses and branding steers was not for him. He had other resources, including a cart load of Yankee merchandise, which he knew would give him a foothold in this alien land despite the fact that he spoke no Spanish and, being a hardshell Presbyterian, was a heretic in a Catholic world.

According to the eminent historian of the 1880s, Jesse Mason, upon arriving in Santa Barbara Daniel Hill leased an adobe somewhere in the vicinity of the Mission, stocked it with the trade goods he had brought ashore at Refugio, and opened Santa Barbara's first American trading post.

The success of Hill's first business enterprise was so overwhelming that before the week was out his shelves were completely empty of stock—which he could not replace until another Boston ship touched at Santa Barbara, and then he would have to pay tribute to a middleman. A bag in his sea chest was filled with gold and silver, in a land where there was nothing money could buy. The prices Hill had set on his merchandise were so exorbitant that they made even a barnacle-encrusted seafaring man blush, but he afterwards realized he could have doubled his prices and left his customers begging for more. Santa Bárbara in 1823 was a hide and tallow town, without clocks, calendars, locks or coins. The male population was starved for tools, boots, tobacco and cloth loomed in New England; the females craved dressgoods, soap, spices and other unattainable niceties of a civilized world.

Having sold himself out of the mercantile business, Daniel Hill had a look around the town which was his new home. Santa Bárbara at the outset of the Mexican period was an unlovely place. It had no streets, only winding paths. El Camino Real was a *carreta* track leading northwestward toward the Goleta Valley, and in the opposite direction to the East Valley, or El Montecito. Another well-beaten trail linked the presidio with the Mission.

The adobe houses of the town, as an early traveler reported, looked as if they had been fired out of a blunderbuss to land at random in the vicinity of the presidio. Of flowers and ornamental trees there were none. The first palms, transplanted from their desert habitat in a canyon near Palm Springs, were curiosities growing in the Mission garden. Pepper trees, native to Peru, were growing no closer than San Luis Rey, from whence seedlings would be brought to Santa Bárbara for shade tree planting by the padres some two years in the future.

Santa Bárbara's yards and alleyways were littered with garbage which made a stench on warm days. The only scavenging was done at night by rats, coons and skunks, and in daytime by dogs, gulls and buzzards. One early writer described Santa Bárbara as follows:

Her streets, or rather byways between the houses, were strewn with refuse, horns and hoofs from domestic beef slaughter, each family slaughtering its own animals, and were unpaved and wound up in cul de sacs and courts.

Windblown dust made breathing extremely difficult at times. The mission edifice, at the time of Daniel Hill's arrival, was only three years old, and had only one bell tower.

The presidio still showed the battering it had taken in the 1812 earthquake. De la Guerra's soldiers were an apathetic lot, not having received a *peseta* in pay for several years. Their footgear and clothing were unfit for a scarecrow, and their weapons were a farce. No wonder, Hill mused, these Californians seem so slothful: they had no incentive to work, living by a philosophy that one should never do today what could be put off to *mañana*.

One of the first customers to visit Daniel Hill's trading post was an American, the only fellow Yankee in the whole town. His name was Daniel Call; he was a 24-year-old Bostonian who had been a carpenter aboard the ship *Atala* when it put in at Santa Bárbara for emergency repairs (permitted by the old Laws of the Indies) in 1816. Call had had doubts the leaky old tub would hold together for the voyage to China, so had jumped ship and thereby won the distinction of becoming Santa Barbara's first permanent American settler. (The *Atala*, incidentally, was scrapped as unseaworthy after she limped into a Chinese port a few months later.)

The two Yankee Daniels, Hill and Call, naturally developed a quick friendship. Daniel Hill was astonished to see how a fellow Bostonian had "gone native" so completely in the short span of seven years. Call now spoke English with a marked Iberian accent; he wore the sombrero and serape of a *paisano*; he had learned to enjoy such cruel Mexican sports as bull and bear fighting and rooster pulls. He would not deign to walk across the plaza if there was a horse handy.

Daniel Call introduced Hill to another customer the day his store opened for business—gray-robed Padre Antonio Ripoll, the saintly Franciscan who was in charge of Santa Bárbara's spiritual affairs and the management of the Mission. By 1823 the Mission was on the decline, and new Secularization legislation was being formulated in Mexico which would abolish the mission system in California forever.

The Indian population was also in its terminal decline. When Daniel Call arrived in 1816 there were 1,259 neophytes at Santa Bárbara Mission, the majority of whom were from the Goleta Slough and Dos Pueblos districts. Now only 962 Indians remained at the Mission village, from a peak of 1,792 twenty years previously.

When Daniel Hill confided to Daniel Call that his main reason for staying in California was because he had fallen in love with the daughter of Don Vicente Ortega, Call gave him some valuable advice on how to reach the altar with a California señorita.

"First off," marriage counsellor Call said, "you got to git used to the idea that your wife will never be able to read or write, either Spanish or English. That's how it is out here with women. Only the rich folks, like the De la Guerras, or the priesthood, git any book l'arnin'. Then this business of you bein' a Presbyterian—that's *muy malo*, very bad. You got to turn Catholic pronto, son, or the Ortegas will never let you marry Rafaela."

Daniel Hill shrugged. "Turnin' Catholic won't make no never-mind to me. What else have I got to do to git her?"

"Give up yore American citizenship, for one thing. Only way a Yankee can marry a California girl is to get naturalized a Mexican citizen, become what they call a *hijo del pais*."

The idea of renouncing his allegiance to the United States jolted Daniel Hill, a descendant of Revolutionary patriots, but if that was the price he had to pay to win his lady love, so be it.

His mercantile business halted for want of trading stock, Daniel Hill turned to other ways of making a living. He was a skilled carpenter, soap maker and stone mason, and these skills were much in demand in Santa Barbara. He dug wells and privy pits; he chiseled sandstone boulders into building blocks to make aqueducts to conduct water from Mission Creek to fields and gardens. He built wooden flumes to sluice irrigation water to the Mission gardens; he erected adobe houses and roofed them with baked tile of his own manufacture.

Such git-up-and-go dumfounded the easy-going Barbareños; they had never seen such industry and ambition in one man.

At regular intervals, Daniel Hill mounted his faithful mule and rode westward across the Goleta Valley, bound for Refugio Ranch and his lady love. His courtship of Rafaela was severely circumscribed by old Spanish customs, which demanded that the girl be chaperoned by a *dueña* at all times.

By long-established custom, Hill could not propose marriage to Rafaela directly; that romantic overture had to be relayed through the girl's father. Assuming Don Vicente was agreeable,

Rafaela was then free to accept or reject Hill's proposal, but the initial selection of a mate was out of her control. In Daniel Hill's case, there had never been any doubt about the outcome of their romance. Theirs was a case of mutual love at first sight.

Hill applied himself diligently to learning Spanish. In April, 1825, he and Rafaela attended the wedding of Don José de la Guerra's daughter Teresa to a prominent Monterey merchant, Englishman William E. P. Hartnell, agent for a hide and tallow exporting firm. The sound of wedding bells rekindled the ardent fires in Daniel Hill's blood and made him impatient for the day when he could lead sloe-eyed Rafaela to the altar.

Hill had a series of conferences with his good friend, Padre Ripoll, which paved the way for the Yankee ex-sailor to abjure what the priest termed his "Presbyterian errors." With José de la Guerra acting as his *patron* or sponsor, Daniel was baptized into the Catholic faith in 1825. Removal of the only other obstacle on his path to the altar, becoming a Mexican citizen, was already being arranged with the proper authorities.

During his first years in Santa Bárbara, Hill had more house-building contracts than he could handle. Unfortunately for posterity, the majority of Hill-built adobes wound up in the middle of streets when the Haley Survey of the city was made in 1851, resulting in their ultimate demolition. For his own home, however, Daniel Hill built the one-story "Carrillo Adobe" which still stands at 11 East Carrillo Street. This *casa*, according to local folklore, had the first wooden floor in Santa Bárbara, although there is no documentary evidence to prove what is likely a charming fragment of apocrypha. Most adobes of the time were floored with rammed earth, some of them hardened with asphaltum from Carpinteria or Goleta beaches, or admixed with steers' blood. The floors of the De la Guerra mansion were laid with fire-glazed tiles.

For Daniel and Rafaela, the wedding bells at the Mission chimed on September 16, 1826. The groom was 26, his bride 17. Father Ripoll performed the nuptial mass, despite the fact Daniel Hill's naturalization papers had not yet arrived—red tape would delay them for another three years. The fact that Hill had the recommendation of Padre Ripoll and Don José de la Guerra made his change of citizenship a mere technicality.

By now the hide and tallow trade had replaced the otter and seal skin industry in California. Santa Bárbara was second in export volume only to Monterey, the capital where all trading ships had to clear Mexican customs.

In December 1827, Spaniards born in the old country were declared ineligible to hold government offices in Mexico. This removed Don José de la Guerra as comandante of the Santa Bárbara Presidio. He went into the trading business, and in 1828 purchased another *goleta* or coastal schooner, the *Dorotea*. She began her maiden voyage from San Blas, with Don José aboard. One of her passengers was Abel Stearns, destined to become Los Angeles' leading American Don.

As the *Dorotea* was tacking across the Channel toward her home port in Goleta Slough, a southeaster caught her and drove her aground on the east end of the Sandspit at almost the identical place where Don Jose's first *goleta*, the *Joven Angustias*, had been stranded. Everyone on board reached land safely, but the *Dorotea*'s hull was stove in and she was ruined beyond salvage.

Some historians claim it was the bones of the *Dorotea* which gave the Valley the name of Goleta. *Quien sabe?*

By 1828, several Americanos had discovered Santa Bárbara and settled there. Among them was Captain William Goodwin Dana, proprietor of a thriving business with the Sandwich Islands. Needing another trading vessel for his fleet and finding none available for purchase on the West Coast, Dana (a cousin of Richard Henry Dana who wrote *Two Years Before the Mast*) decided to build one. His shipbuilder would be Benjamin Foxen; the shipyard is believed to have been on the banks of a deep inlet which once existed 400 yards north of the present KTMS transmitter on More Mesa. Because local oak and sycamore lumber was unsuitable for shipbuilding, Dana imported hardwoods around the Horn and rafted them ashore at Goleta Beach.

Benjamin Foxen was by now a prominent Santa Bárbara merchant in his own right, thanks to his early partnership with De la Guerra. Daniel Hill had coached Foxen in the mysteries of the Catholic faith, becoming Foxen's *patron* so he could marry Dona Eduarda Osuña, of San Ysidro Rancho in El Montecito.

Setting to work to build Dana's schooner—the first ship ever launched by an American in Pacific waters*—Benjamin Foxen did not hesitate to cannibalize the wreckage of the *Dorotea* to obtain expensive brasswork and teakwood.

When the time came to launch the Dana schooner, Foxen circulated word that he would need every yoke of oxen he could muster to drag the hull to deep water. On the day the ship was christened *La Fama*, the owner of every ox team from neighboring *suertes* in the Goleta Valley was on hand to assist Foxen.

But Foxen was a practical joker. He had constructed *La Fama* in a regulation cradle, and when he knocked out the shoring timbers with a sledge, the hull slid down the greased ways into the estuary, the prow tossing up a great rooster-tail of white water and leaving her floating as gracefully as a swan.

Don Thomas Robbins, who had been second mate on the *Rover* under Daniel Hill, became *La Fama*'s first skipper. He later was the grantee of Santa Catalina Island and also the Rancho Las Positas y Calera (Hope Ranch).

Eventually Goleta's first locally-built schooner was sold and renamed the *Santa Bárbara*. Eighteen years after her launching, Daniel Hill bought her and, with an utter lack of originality, re-christened her *La Goleta*. She was eventually sold to a shipper in Acapulco, and disappeared from maritime records.

Foxen's shipbuilding project of 1828 was not the last to be carried on at the Goleta Slough, but lack of local lumber sources precluded the Good Land from ever becoming an important shipbuilding center.

As years went on, Daniel Hill became more and more a part of the woof and warp of Santa Bárbara life. Alfred Robinson, author of the classic *Life in California*, described Hill as "a sort of factotum for the whole town, carpenter or mason by turns, as his services were needed."

His wife, Rafaela, bore him fifteen children, all but one of whom she raised to maturity—a remarkable record in an era of high infant mortality. The first five children were born at the 11 East Carrillo

---

* Joseph Chapman is sometimes credited with building and launching the first American vessel on the West Coast, a schooner belonging to Yankee Don Abel Stearns. However, Chapman's craft was launched at San Pedro in 1831, by which time Dana's vessel had been plying coastal waters for nearly three years.

Street adobe. Their first born, Rosa, arrived on October 4, 1827. She was destined to become the "first lady "of the Goleta Valley.

Henry Allen Smith, a Goleta Valley resident at the turn of the century, was an assiduous dilettante in the field of local history. In voluminous notes inherited by his daughter, Virginia Rose Smith, of Montecito, there appears an interesting but undocumented theory that Daniel Hill built his historic adobe on La Patera Lane in the Goleta Valley sometime in the early 1830s.

According to Smith's account, Hill had qualified for one of the *suertes* or small land grants parceled out to descendants of the presidial garrison. Since Hill's wife was a granddaughter of Captain Ortega, the first comandante, such a grant was legally possible. Smith believes that Daniel Hill built his *finca*, or "temporary summer home in the country," at 35 La Patera Lane, about 1832. In any event it is the oldest residence extant on the Good Land.*

Daniel Hill played an intimate part in some of the most dramatic history connected with Santa Barbara. A year after he arrived, the famous 1824 revolt of the Channel Mission Indians against the tyranny of the whites took place, climaxed by the wanton murder of four Dos Pueblos oldsters by Spanish soldiers in front of the Old Mission at Santa Barbara.

There is every reason to believe that Daniel Hill's talents as a carpenter and stone mason were utilized by Padre Antonio Ripoll when the second tower was added to the Mission in 1833. Catholic authorities disagree as to which tower came first, the left or the right.

Also in 1833, Daniel Hill became the *padrino*, or sponsor, of the first baby born in California of American parents. On January 31, 1833, a girl, Ysabel, was born to Mrs. Rachel Holmes of Boston, who was staying in the Daniel Hill adobe during her confinement. The birth register lists Thomas O. Larkin of Monterey as the father. The baby died July 8, 1833, and was buried at the Mission cemetery. Her death record lists a Guillermo Cuper (William Cooper) as the father. However, Mrs. Holmes married Larkin, who went on to fame as California's first and only U.S. Consul at the time of the American Conquest.

---

* Daniel Hill, in a homestead application dated April 1864, testified that he had been living in the adobe only 14 years, or since 1850. Hill obtained title to the La Patera homesite, by purchase, in September 1851.

The year 1836, which saw the fall of the Alamo and the independence of Texas from Mexican rule, was a fateful year in the life of Daniel Hill and the future of the Goleta Valley.

It was Hill's habit to ride his mule down to the beach whenever a trading vessel was in port. Hill did this one December day in 1836, when the brig *Kent* of Boston splashed her mudhook in the Santa Bárbara roadstead. Her master, John Hinkley, came ashore with a short, stocky Irishman of 24 who was his supercargo.

After conducting his business with the mission fathers and local rancheros who had hides, tallow and wine for sale, the *Kent*'s supercargo sought out Daniel Hill to relay Thomas Larkin's greetings from Monterey. This was a tryst with destiny, for the supercargo with the fleecy blond hair and ice-blue eyes was the future owner of much of the Good Land. His name was Nicholas Augustus Henry Den.

CHAPTER IV

Nicolás A. Den, Don of Dos Pueblos

When the *Kent* sailed for Boston, Nicholas Den remained behind at Santa Barbara, much as Daniel Hill had left the *Rover* at Refugio 13 years before.

Within a few moments after introducing himself to Hill on the beach at the mouth of Mission Creek, young Den accepted an invitation to dine with the Hills that evening. From that moment to the end of their lives the two were steadfast friends. The Hills' eldest child, Rosa, was a black-haired, dark-eyed girl of ten that evening when she brought Nicholas Den his brandy and cigar, all unaware she was waiting on her future husband.

Den told his host and hostess that he had been born in 1812 at Garandara in County Kilkenny, Ireland, the scion of a wealthy family whose antecedents had crossed the Channel with William the Conquerer, and members of which had married British royalty.*

Financial reverses had struck the Dens in 1834, forcing Nicholas to leave Trinity College, Dublin, a few months short of graduating with a doctor's degree in medicine. Sailing to Newfoundland to seek employment with a cousin in St. Johns, he wound up in Boston awaiting passage home to Ireland.

Fascinated by the hide and tallow droghers at Boston's Long Wharf, Den eavesdropped on Yankee tars singing the praises of

---

* In the interests of objectivity it should be pointed out that Den's claims are not verified by *Burke's Peerage* and therefore must be considered as without foundation in fact. Den, known to have been a man of unimpeachable integrity, was probably quoting family folklore in the mistaken belief that he had royal blood in his veins.

California, a golden land on the far rim of the continent. Den was intrigued to learn that the Mexican government, as an inducement to colonize its California provinces, was giving away 48,000-acre cattle ranchos to qualified Catholic citizens.

Den told Hill that he had always had a yen to be a farmer and livestock raiser, rather than a doctor. In order to reach this Circean land of California, Den had signed on with the *Kent* as a green forecastle hand before the mast, sailing from Boston on April 12, 1836. Thanks to his schooling, he soon graduated to the post of supercargo and a less strenuous life rounding the Horn.

Daniel Hill understood what motivated Nicholas Den to remain in California. He explained how the recent Decree of Secularization (he called it Decree of Confiscation) had stripped the Franciscan missions of their stewardship over millions of acres of choice grazing land in California. Hill described in glowing terms the beauties of the Goleta Valley, and the choicest of the local mission's five Royal Ranchos, Los Dos Pueblos. He added that he had plans to acquire that portion of the Good Land lying between the Goleta Slough eastward to the Cieniguitas swamps. Everything else from the Slough westward to the Ortega's Refugio Rancho was available to private ownership; the only reason it hadn't been snapped up before was because it measured only three and a half leagues, one-tenth of the maximum 48,000 acres which Governor Alvarado was empowered to grant an individual.

The following day, Nicholas Den accompanied Daniel Hill on a muleback journey to Tajiguas Arroyo, west of Refugio Bay, where Hill was remodeling an 1807 Ortega adobe for his own use. His Santa Barbara *casa* was getting too cramped to accommodate his growing family, so he had sold it to a sea captain from Scotland, John Wilson, whose wife was Dona Ramona Pacheco. (Her son, Romualdo, became the State of California's first and only Mexican-born governor in 1875).

Den's passage of the Goleta Valley thrilled him as much as it had thrilled Daniel Hill 13 years before. When they arrived at Refugio Canyon, Hill introduced his Irish companion to his father-in-law, Don Jose Vicente Ortega. That courtly old grandee promptly invited Den to make the Ortega *hacienda* his home while he picked up the rudiments of how to operate a California cattle ranch—"*Mi casa es suya*," my house is yours. So graciously was the invitation extended that Den accepted it on the spot, thereby casting the die of his own future.

In following months, Den worked hard at becoming a Californian. He stopped speaking English, even with Daniel Hill, and concentrated on mastering Spanish. He even dropped the Irish spelling of Nicholas, and became Nicolás the rest of his life. His acceptance by the Californians was evidenced immediately by their calling him "Don Nicolás," a title not lightly bestowed upon a foreigner.

During his trips back and forth across the Goleta Valley to help Daniel Hill move his family possessions to Tajiguas Arroyo, Nicolás Den became obsessed with a desire to someday own Dos Pueblos Rancho, which reminded him of the green acres of his ancestral domain in Ireland.

Nicolás Den became the object of secret adoration by the eligible señoritas of Santa Barbara, including the aristocratic daughters of Don José de la Guerra and Carlos Carrillo; but quite unknown to Den, Rosa Hill had laid claim to his affections.

Nicolás was known as "Doctor Den" to the Barbareños. Not possessing a medical diploma, he did not hang out a professional shingle; but whenever his skills were needed he gave them without stint or charge. Phlebotomy, or blood-letting, was his specialty, and in the 1830s had the status of a cure-all. In his time, Den set many a fractured bone, delivered many a baby, and nursed many a Californian through a severe illness.

The era of the Mexican land grants in California, which began with the Secularization of the missions, was already under way before Den's arrival in 1836. The Ortega family had received the first local land grant, Nuestra Señora del Refugio, in 1834. During the year 1837, when Den was busy learning how to rope and ride and wield a branding iron, enormous blocks of land aggregating more than 157,000 acres were deeded to the Carrillos, Arrellaneses and De la Guerras by Governor Juan B. Alvarado. Some of these huge grants were near Santa Barbara, such as the San Julian and Los Alamos and Guadalupe Ranchos. Den began to worry for fear some presidio veteran, who had priority with the governor over an Irish immigrant, might claim his coveted Dos Pueblos ahead of him.

According to Daniel Hill, the best way to establish a priority to a given piece of ex-mission land was to run cattle on it, thereby enriching the provincial coffers with tax money. A Santa Barbaran, Alpheus B. Thompson, had 500 head of longhorn Spanish cattle to sell at a ridiculously low price, but Den was penniless.

When word of his ambition to buy Thompson's cattle reached the ears of Fr. Narciso Durán at the Mission, that prelate loaned Den the money. Durán knew that if private ownership of his mission's royal ranchos was inevitable, it would be best for a devout Catholic layman such as Den to become that owner.

After his first *matanza*, or round-up, Den had enough money left over after paying back his debt to Fr. Durán to buy himself a homesite, at what is now the corner of State and East Figueroa Streets in Santa Barbara. But when he applied to the *ayuntimiento*, or town council, for permission to build an adobe house on his quarter-block, he was rejected because he was a "foreigner."

Nicolás A. Den had been so preoccupied with learning how to become a Spanish-speaking *ranchero* that he had neglected to apply for Mexican citizenship! He remedied this oversight immediately, and in 1841 formally renounced his former allegiance and became an adopted *hijo del pais*, or citizen of Mexico.

Being a naturalized citizen of Mexico made Den eligible to apply to Governor Alvarado for a land grant. By now, his desire to own the entire Goleta Valley had been curtailed somewhat on both the east and the west. Daniel Hill had advised him that he intended to apply for the land between the Goleta Slough and Las Positas, while his host and mentor, Ortega, had applied for the 8,875 acre Cañada del Corral rancho, which extended from the eastern edge of the Refugio grant to Las Llagas Canyon.

Even so, some 15,534 acres of the Good Land remained unclaimed. Early in 1842, as prescribed by Mexican law, Nicolás A. Den drew a sketch of his proposed Los Dos Pueblos Rancho on a sheet of parchment. He dispatched this map, or *diseño*, to the governor in Monterey, together with his prayer for a gift of land, starting at Mescaltán Island on the east and running to Las Llagas Canyon on the west, between the foothills and the beach.

While waiting for Governor Alvarado to act on his petition, Nicolás Den joined other prominent Santa Barbara citizens in welcoming to California the Rev. Francisco Garcia Diego y Morena, the first Bishop of the Californias, who arrived by ship on January 11, 1842, and later established his Episcopal See at the Mission.

On April 18, 1842, Governor Alvarado approved Den's application for a grant of public land in the Goleta Valley. The *expediente* or deed described the new grant as follows:

> Los Dos Pueblos [Rancho is] located in the neighborhood of the Mission of Santa Bárbara, and is bounded as follows: by the beach of the Channel of the same name; by the high hills in the direction of the sierra; by Cañada del Corral, a boundary of the rancho of Antonio Maria Ortega; and by the place called La Cochera, in the direction of the Presidio.

(La Cochera is a 2,000-acre parcel of Goleta Valley between Los Carneros Creek and Fairview Avenue, from the lower foothills to Hollister Avenue. The name, Spanish for coach house or wagon shed, refers to a *suerte's* adobe barn built near La Patera Lane in the early Nineteenth Century.)

Fume and fidget as he might, the frustrated Nicolás Den had to mark time until December 21, 1842, before Judge Joaquin Carrillo and two witnesses, José M. Covarrubias and Esteban Ortega, accompanied him out to the Cañada de Los Dos Pueblos for the formal ceremony of "taking possession" as required by Mexican law, and to confirm the official measurement of the grant's boundaries.

The rancho, measured by the rawhide lariat method of the times, was 3,110 varas long by 1,350 varas wide, and contained three and one-half Spanish leagues. Judge Carrillo's confirmation of the grant indicates that as originally surveyed, Dos Pueblos Ranch included the entire Goleta Slough area now covered by part of the Santa Barbara Airport. (When a U.S. Patent was issued to the property in February 1877, however, the Slough area was excluded for some unknown reason. In the 1930s this became the crux of a litigation between the federal government and the T. B. Bishop Company over ownership of the potentially oil-rich Goleta Sandspit, with the U.S. Supreme Court finding in favor of the original *expediente*.)

When the laborious job of measuring the ranch lines had been completed by two Indian assistants, Nicolás Den was next required to "enter and walk over the lands" after which, in symbolic token

Nicolás A. Den, Don of Dos Pueblos

of accepting the government's gift, he knelt and pulled up two fistfuls of wild rye grass, forded the creek to break twigs off an *aliso* (sycamore) and a willow tree, and finally, in full view of Judge Carrillo and the other witnesses, tossed the twigs and the tufts of grassroots to the four winds.

The judge then solemnly recorded on parchment, for transmission to His Excellency the Governor, the following validation of the Dos Pueblos grant:

Don Nicolás A. Den made these demonstrations and acts of possession as a sign of that which he saw and as he took of said lands, I, the said Judge, ordered that from that moment, Don Nicolás Augustus Den should be taken and considered as the true and lawful possessor of El Rancho de Los Dos Pueblos.

Den's elation of the moment was marred somewhat when a rider galloped up from the direction of Santa Barbara, identifying himself as one Leandro Gonzales, majordomo of Santa Barbara Mission. He had come to protest, on behalf of Padre Durán, the granting of mission trust property to a private citizen, however worthy.

Judge Carrillo brushed off the protest as an idle formality on Fr. Durán's part. However, the following March, when a new governor, Manuel Micheltorena, arrived to replace Alvarado, his first official act was to repeal the Secularization laws and restore the missions to Franciscan control. Padre Durán promptly petitioned Governor Micheltorena to return Dos Pueblos Ranch to the Mission.

This was dismaying news for Nicolás Den, who had just become bethrothed to marry Daniel Hill's sixteen-year-old daughter, Rosa, with the wedding date set for the coming first of June. An official hearing of the case before Governor Micheltorena, held in Los Angeles on March 21, 1843, resulted in a compromise whereby the church got back "exclusive and perpetual domain to all that land lying east of El Arroyo de La Cañada de las Armas" (now known as Ellwood Canyon), while Nicolás Den could keep the rest of the rancho.

In effect this reduced Nicolás Den's grant by half, including the La Patera, or La Cochera, tract north of the Goleta Slough. The loss proved to be only temporary, however, for Micheltorena was soon ousted from power and the Franciscans permanently lost control of California's mission lands, which restored Alvarado's grant to Den *in toto*.

The wedding of Don Nicolás to Doña Rosa took place on June 1, 1843, at Santa Inés Mission. This location for the nuptial mass, rather than the more fashionable Santa Barbara Mission, was dictated by the fact that the bride's residence, Tajiguas Arroyo, lay inside the parish of Santa Inés.

Overlooked by the flustered father of the bride, Daniel Hill, was Governor Micheltorena's granting of Las Positas y Calera Rancho (now Hope Ranch Park) to a presidio lieutenant, Narciso Fabrigat. This was land Daniel Hill had intended to claim, but he had procrastinated too long.

The newlywedded Dens had two homes in construction simultaneously, one on their town lot at State and Figueroa Streets, the other out at Dos Pueblos on the west rim of the canyon, half a mile inland from the beach.

Their first house guest in Santa Barbara, the following September, was Nicolás' younger brother, Richard, destined to play a vital rôle in the future development of the Goleta Valley. Richard, a graduate physician, was surgeon aboard the brig *Glenswilly*, on its homeward voyage from Australia to London. While his ship was in a southland port, Dr. Richard S. Den was taking advantage of a chance to visit an older brother he had not seen for nine years.

The upshot of Richard Den's visit was that he became so enchanted with California he elected to remain for the rest of his days. He became one of Los Angeles' foremost pioneer doctors. Before leaving for Los Angeles in November, 1843, he confirmed the happy news that Rosa Hill de Den was expecting a baby.

The Den's first child was Catarina, born July 22, 1844. By her married name of Kate Den Bell, she would write her signature large in Goleta Valley affairs up to the moment of her passing, at a ripe old age, in 1926.

Meanwhile, history was accelerating at a bewildering pace in California. Because of their intimate relationship with Monterey's most important American resident, Thomas O. Larkin, both Daniel Hill and Nicolás Den were among the first to know that the United States had its eye on annexing California to the Union, by force of arms if necessary. The polite euphemism for these territorial am-

Archaeologist Phil C. Orr excavating 5000 B.C. Indian burial on Mescalitán Island, Goleta Slough, in 1940

Daniel A. Hill of Boston, married Rafaela Ortega of Refugio Rancho; grantee of La Goleta Rancho in 1846

Fifteenth Century anchor, 8' long, found in Slough mud flats near UCSB mesa in 1891—origin unknown

Irish-born Nicolás A. Den married Hill's daughter Rosa, became owner of the Los Dos Pueblos grant

Rosa Hill de Den, wife of Don Nicolás, as she appeared in middle life. From an oil portrait dated 1875

T. Wallace More married Hill's daughter Susana; murdered by squatters at Rancho Sespe in 1877

Nicolás A. Den built his adobe home at Dos Pueblos Ranch in 1843. This picture was taken in 1924. The adobe was razed in 1931 by owner H. G. Wylie—an irreplaceable historical landmark

Daniel A. Hill built his adobe in 1850 (?) at 35 La Patera Lane. It was re-roofed and sheathed in redwood siding in 1902. This picture was taken in 1966, when the Hill Adobe had the distinction of being the oldest house in the Goleta Valley. It belongs to the five heirs of James Williams

First homesteaders in Goleta foothills were Mr. and Mrs. F. D. Havens of Maria Ygnacia Canyon

James McCaffery, first outside settler in Goleta Valley, farmed San Jose Vineyard from 1854

A familiar sight in the Seventies and Eighties was Irish immigrant Patrick Farren and his one-horse cart. He and his sons Mike, Ed and Bill lived on a lonely homestead in the hills above Eagle Canyon

Ida Catlett poses beside parental homestead shack built in 1868, where she was born. Ida was the second nurse to graduate from Cottage Hospital, Class of '95. Still residing in Santa Barbara, she was 93 in 1966

Discharged Confederate soldier Ezra Catlett bought ranch in Goleta foothills in 1868

Tom Lillard was Catlett's partner, from Missouri. He owned the famous Slippery Rock landmark in foothills

Champion b'ar hunter and raconteur "Uncle Ben" Owen found Ezra Catlett a wife but never one for himself

Joseph Sexton's Nursery, founded in 1869, brought nation-wide fame to the verdant Goleta Valley

bitions was "Manifest Destiny"—i.e., the United States were divinely intended to stretch from the Atlantic to the Pacific, and any foreigners would be trespassers.

Many signs pointed to the truth of Larkin's warning. In March 1844, a young American army engineer, Lt. John C. Frémont, marched into interior California from beyond the Sierra Nevadas with an armed force which he called a "scientific expedition." One month later, Thomas O. Larkin was suddenly appointed United States Consul to California, to assist in espionage work.

In Santa Barbara, the Californians looked to the Goleta Valley for political leadership in these tense times, when they elected Don Nicolás Den of Dos Pueblos Rancho as their *alcalde* or mayor. But the destiny of California now hinged on events transpiring in far-off Washington, D. C.

On March 5, 1845, a new American president took office: James K. Polk, a statesman frankly dedicated to the annexation of California from Mexico, by purchase if possible, by war if necessary. Less than a week later, Governor Manuel Micheltorena abdicated his office under pressure from powerful *paisano* chiefs and sailed for Mexico. His successor was a political opportunist and anti-mission extremist named Pio Pico, an uncle of Don Mariano Pico of the Goleta Valley.

Pio Pico began granting thousands of acres of real estate to worthy Mexicans, either in the form of grants or by sales. He began accepting bids for the sale or rental of the various California missions, sales which were later declared null and void by the American courts.

This news was received in Santa Barbara with dismay by Fr. Durán. In desperation he turned to Nicolás Den and Daniel Hill to rescue the Queen of the Missions by leasing it or buying it outright.

Den and Hill were devout Catholics, the one by birth, the other by conversion, so they had a pious motive for wanting to save Santa Barbara Mission from possible desecration by a private owner. They were also shrewd business men, who recognized a bargain when one dropped in their laps. Accordingly, on July 21, 1845, Den and Hill offered to lease Mission Santa Barbara and its lands for nine years at an annual rental of $1,200 in gold, a bid which Fr. Durán hastily forwarded to Governor Pico for action.

Not until December 4, 1845, did Pio Pico get around to approving the lease.

By now Daniel Hill was beginning to get panicky for fear he had put off too long petitioning the Mexican government for a free grant of the remaining acres of the Goleta Valley which he desired for his future rancho. He was realist enough to know that if the Americans took over California, hordes of land-hungry Yankees would swarm into the territory to grab every acre of available land in sight.

Disgusted with himself for his own procrastination, Daniel Hill hastily sketched a *diseño* of the land he wanted, even including such a landmark as the wreck of an unidentified *goleta* on the eastern end of the Sandspit. His description of the rancho was typically vague:

> ... bounded on the south by the seashore; on the north by the foot of the ledge of mountains about one league distant from said shore; on the east by the lands known as the Mission Lands of Santa Barbara; and on the west by the lands of Don Nicolás Den, called "Dos Pueblos."

Daniel Hill dispatched the necessary application papers to Pio Pico, well knowing that that harried official might be engulfed by the rising American tide before he found time to study, let alone validate the tardy petition.

Every Mexican grant had to carry a label. The name Daniel Hill bestowed upon his proposed land grant was the one it bears today, Rancho La Goleta, the Ranch of the Schooner.

What schooner was Daniel Hill referring to?

Nobody knows.

CHAPTER V

When Frémont Came Over the Mountain

Ailing Father Durán conveyed 1,000 head of Mission cattle to Nicolás Den and Daniel Hill on the second day of January, 1846, which proved to be the most momentous year in California history. Indian vaqueros from Dos Pueblos rebranded the cattle with Den's iron and transferred most of them from the transalpine rancho, San Marcos, to the Goleta Valley, hoping to cut down the heavy losses from grizzly bears and other predators. This transformed the Goleta Valley into a working cattle ranch, and it remained in that category for the next twenty years.

Den's term as the unsalaried *alcalde* of Santa Barbara expired in February. He declined to continue in office, and in such troubled times no successor was elected to head the *ayuntimiento*.

The pueblo was saddened on April 30 by the death of Bishop Garcia Diego, and, two months later, that of Fr. Durán. The passing of these two dedicated men of God marked the end of the Franciscan period in pastoral California.

On June 10, 1846, Den and Hill quit-claimed their nine-year lease on Santa Barbara Mission so that Den's brother, Richard, of Los Angeles, could buy the property outright. He paid $7,500, but shared a half-interest with Nicolás in the 35,573-acre San Marcos Ranch north of the mountains. With Dos Pueblos constricted by mountain and ocean, Don Nicolás knew he would soon have need for added grazing range to accommodate his increasing cattle herds.

The tenth of June was also a red-letter day in the annals of the Goleta Valley, for on that date Governor Pio Pico affixed his signature and *rubrica* to a deed which granted possession of La Goleta

Rancho to Daniel A. Hill. For the first time in history, the entire Goleta Valley had fallen into private ownership.

Daniel Hill was vastly relieved to consummate the deal. As finally drawn up, the grant comprised 4,426 acres—only one-tenth as large as many Mexican land grants of the period. Beginning at a point which today is the intersection of North Fairview Avenue and Via Lemora, at the northwest corner of the John Pagliotti ranch, the north line angled slightly north of due east for a distance of about three and a half miles, to a point in the east fork of Maria Ygnacia Creek near the intersection of modern La Espada Drive and La Riata Lane. There the line ran due south to the ocean, a short distance east of such modern landmarks as Tucker's Grove and San Marcos High School, and west of Puente Drive, to become the boundary of Hope Ranch Park. The south boundary of La Goleta Rancho was the beach as far as the end of More Mesa, where the line angled northwestward to join the Dos Pueblos Ranch boundary at Placencia Street and South Fairview Avenue. The overall area enclosed one Spanish league.

Hill was not aware of how lucky he was to get the grant at all. Only four days after Governor Pico signed the deed for La Goleta —one of his last official acts—the Bear Flag Revolt occurred at Sonoma, which was the forerunner of the American annexation of California. (Actually the United States and Mexico had been at war since May 15, but this intelligence did not reach California until mid-summer.)

Meanwhile, military events were transpiring which would alter the destiny of the Goleta Valley. On July 7, Commodore John Drake Sloat of the U.S. Navy hoisted the Stars and Stripes over the custom house at Monterey. When word of this outright act of international aggression reached Governor Pio Pico (who was unaware a state of war existed between the two countries), he retreated to Santa Barbara to establish his capital, and issued an impassioned proclamation calling upon all male Mexicans between fifteen and sixty to rally to the defense of California. This draft included such naturalized citizens as William G. Dana, Isaac Sparks, George Nidever, Benjamin Foxen, Alfred Robinson, Nicolás A. Den, and Daniel Hill.

Ailing Commodore Sloat turned over his command to a martinet,

Capt. Robert F. Stockton of the frigate *Congress*, who anchored off Santa Barbara during the first week of August and came ashore with Midshipman William Mitchell and a platoon of ten U.S. Marines. The American flag was raised at the presidio, and Stockton notified the startled Barbareños that the sleepy pueblo was now under American military occupation, and a strict curfew would be enforced. He then sailed for San Pedro to attend to the subjugation of Los Angeles.

By now, Governor Pico had fled into exile. The Mexican defenses were so weak that Stockton left only a 50-man occupation force, under Capt. Archibald Gillespie, to secure the entire Los Angeles area.

On September 7, the *Congress* reappeared at Santa Barbara, en route to Monterey. Stockton picked up his ten Marines and sailed away, feeling that Santa Barbara would be no problem. Hardly had the warship disappeared around Castle Rock than the hot-blooded young patriots of Santa Barbara, led by Don José de la Guerra's Yankee-hating son, Pablo, ripped down Old Glory, ran up the Mexican colors, and vowed to kill every Yankee in the pueblo.

Providentially, Captain John Charles Frémont rode into Santa Barbara next day with a company of mounted riflemen, heading overland to Monterey to join Stockton. Daniel Hill sought out Frémont and begged him to protect the American colony in Santa Barbara from Mexican reprisals. Frémont complied by assigning ten men, under Lt. Theodore Talbott, of Kentucky, to secure Santa Barbara for the duration of the war.

On September 13, Frémont and his men resumed their northward journey along El Camino Real, camping that night beside the *estero* at the mouth of Dos Pueblos Canyon. While the Americans were making bivouac, Don Nicolás Den appeared from his nearby *casa grande*, welcoming them to his rancho. Den, who as an Irishman had always feared the British might someday seize California from Mexico, openly supported the American conquest.

Den's orchard of peaches, pears, apricots, lemons, oranges, pomegranates, olives, and limes, on the mesa west of the canyon, was just coming into bearing. Frémont was profoundly impressed by the fecundity of the Goleta Valley, and Den's gifts of fresh fruit, and a fat steer for the men to barbecue, won Frémont's warm regard. In fact, their visit that September evening in 1846 was the beginning of a lifelong friendship between the two men.

Next day, Frémont and his cavalrymen resumed their way north, supremely confident that California had been conquered for the Stars and Stripes. But this was far from the case. Down in Los Angeles, an army under the command of General José Maria Flores laid seige to Captain Gillespie's troops in their barrack on Fort Hill. Gillespie dispatched a courier named Juan Flaco (Slim John) Brown to ride to Monterey and summon help from Stockton. In so doing he instigated the California version of Paul Revere's classic ride, only more so.

Flaco left Los Angeles at dusk on September 24. Four days later he arrived in San Francisco, having covered 630 miles—a horseback record which has never been equalled. In Santa Barbara, Juan Flaco had received a fresh horse from Lt. Talbott at the presidio; Tom Robbins gave him another when he reached Las Positas (Hope Ranch); crossing the Goleta Valley by moonlight, Flaco stole a mount from Nicolás Den's corral at Dos Pueblos. In this fashion he carried out his entire incredible ride, for which the government paid Brown the munificent sum of fifty dollars.

Before Stockton had time to send any reinforcements south, Capt. Gillespie surrendered to the Mexicans, after giving his pledge that he would march to San Pedro and leave California on the first available transport.

Now that the American flag no longer flew in Los Angeles, General Flores turned his attention to the liberation of Santa Barbara. Although Lt. Talbott had only ten men to hold the town, Flores sent Don Manuel Garfias with 200 men to take Santa Barbara. Talbott and his force wisely elected to retreat up Mission Canyon. Garfias impressed Daniel Hill into serving as a hostage to go up the canyon and attempt to persuade the American soldiers to surrender. Instead, they slipped over La Cumbre Peak and, several weeks later, made their way overland to join Frémont in Monterey. The Mexicans had set fire to the brush in Mission Canyon, and were of the belief that Talbott and his men had perished in the flames.

Garfias, well aware that Stockton and Frémont would be back to get revenge, began picking up American-born citizens to serve as hostages. Santa Barbara prisoners included Daniel Hill, Tom

Robbins, Alpheus B. Thompson, William A. Streeter and Isaac J. Sparks. This group of prisoners was taken to Los Angeles, held a brief period, and then paroled home.

Daniel Hill, now almost 50, felt he was too old for such strenuous adventures. Accordingly, when he got back to Santa Barbara he kept going, across his newly-acquired La Goleta Rancho and on to Dos Pueblos Ranch, where his daughter, Rosa Den, provided him a hot meal and a night's lodging. From there Hill hurried as fast as his trusty mule could carry him to Tajiguas Arroyo, where his wife, Rafaela, and their thirteen children awaited his return. The babe at Rafaela's breast had arrived on July 7, the day California went under the American flag, and was therefore born a Yankee.

On the night of November 24, Nicolás Den was roused from bed at his home in Santa Barbara by the news that an old friend was a prisoner of war, captured near Monterey and now en route to jail in Los Angeles. Den hurried over to the presidio, where he found the prisoner to be none other than U.S. Consul Thomas O. Larkin. He had not been back to Santa Barbara since his honeymoon in the Daniel Hill home thirteen years before.

Larkin was ill with a chest cold, so Nicolás Den prevailed upon the Mexican authorities to permit him to keep the sick man under house arrest, rather than in a drafty cell in the *cuartel*. This permission was granted, and Larkin afterward credited "Dr. Den" with saving him from developing pneumonia.

On December 15, 1846, news reached Santa Barbara of the bloody Battle of San Pascual, which had taken place December 6. Gen. Andres Pico's California Lancers had won a smashing victory over a column of U.S. Infantry led out of New Mexico by Gen. Stephen W. Kearney, who might have been annihilated had it not been for reinforcements rushed from San Diego by Commodore Stockton.

There was great joy over the Mexican victory in Santa Barbara, but the joy was soon replaced by terror. On December 20, Augustine Janssens, the *alcalde* of the military district of Santa Ynez, sent a courier over San Marcos Pass with alarming news: a force of nearly 500 heavily-armed Americanos, led by Lt.-Col. John C. Frémont, was approaching on El Camino Real from Monterey, to join forces with Kearney and Stockton in the south.

Frémont's California Battalion was the strongest military unit in the entire province. It included a company of artillery, with wheel-mounted cannon capable of pounding the Santa Barbara Presidio to dust. According to Janssens' communique, Frémont had already reached Foxen Canyon, and on the morrow would be in sight of the campanile and colonnades of Mission Santa Inés.

At the speed they were travelling, Frémont's Battalion would be marching into Santa Barbara before her menfolk could be summoned back from Los Angeles, where every able-bodied male had gone to join Flores' army. Santa Barbara was defenseless!

While Santa Barbara seethed with alarm on the evening of December 20, Frémont was making bivouac beside Alamo Pintado Creek, at a point four miles south of what is now Los Olivos. Among the 428 men in his battalion was Lt. Theodore Talbott, now Frémont's adjutant, and the other erstwhile occupation force which had fled Santa Barbara in September and were presumed dead.

At an historic officers' call staged in front of battalion headquarters at the Alamo Pintado encampment, Lt.-Col. Frémont broke the news of a "brilliant military maneuver" which was to throw the spotlight of history, for a brief while, squarely on the Goleta Valley. Instead of continuing along El Camino Real and crossing the Santa Ynez Mountains at Refugio Pass, Fremont was going to take what he called a "short cut"—the old Indian trail over San Marcos Pass, linking Los Prietos and Mescaltitlán in ancient times—and thus capture Santa Barbara "by surprise."*

What, Frémont asked his staff, did they think of this coup?

Frémont's officers dared not disparage a superior officer's "brilliant" idea by calling it poppycock, but they wrote what they really thought in journals which are available to historians today. These accounts show that Frémont's officers were unanimous, in private, in their disgust for the Pathfinder's ridiculous scheme. The troop-

---

* The most indestructible bit of apocrypha in Santa Barbara County history has it that Santa Barbara's defenders had gathered at Gaviota Pass narrows, 30 miles to the West, intending to roll boulders down on Frémont's Battalion when they were trapped in the narrow defile. They are supposed to have been warned of such an ambush trap by Benjamin Foxen, who is supposed to have guided Frémont (the Pathfinder who never found a path in his life) over San Marcos Pass. The truth is that Gaviota Pass was not open to wheeled vehicles until 1859 at the earliest, and that Frémont conceived the abortive shortcut idea himself and announced it to his officers at Alamo Pintado on December 20, as related above.

ers were tired, hungry, clad in rags or buckskin, and sorely in need of fresh mounts. San Marcos Pass was known to be a steep, rocky defile, whereas Refugio Pass had a well-traveled ox-cart road linking Santa Inés Mission with the Ortega rancho, at the seaward end of Refugio Canyon.

The caustic comments on their leader's strategy, as revealed by existing diaries, make interesting reading today. Captain Louis McLane, commander of the artillery company, wrote:

We are now 13 leagues from Santa Barbara by the main road, [via Refugio Pass] but Frémont intends taking one of his damned short cuts, which will be fagging to the men and death to our animals.

An infantryman named Pat McChristian confided to his diary that the enlisted men "freely applied the terms of coward and old woman to Frémont, who seemed to feel that the coastward approach to Santa Barbara [i.e., via the Goleta Valley] would be a death trap."

A professional newspaperman accompanying the march, E. C. Kemble, had this to say about Frémont's "short cut" over San Marcos:

Frémont's theory was so absurd that it dropped below criticism at our campfires. . . . The foe's well-mounted spies knew all about our movements, and where we encamped every night. However, the "surprise maggot" in our leader's brain was about to hatch again . . .

The march resumed, turning eastward toward San Marcos Pass when they reached the Santa Ynez River. On Christmas Eve, the advance scouts under Lt. Edward Bryant reached the summit of the mountains and camped in an oak grove which still stands below West El Camino Cielo, due north of Goleta's Patterson Avenue of today.

Bryant was subsequently the author of a book *What I Saw in California*, in which he gives this vivid word picture of what the Good Land of the Goleta Valley looked like to a stranger on that fateful night before Christmas in 1846:

With the spyglass we could see in [the Goleta Valley] far below us, herds of cattle quietly grazing upon the green herbiage that carpets its gentle undulations. The plain is dotted with oak groves, surrounding the springs and belting the small watercourses, of which there are many flowing from this range of mountains. Ranchos are scattered up and down the plain [Bryant could see Las Positas y Calera, La Goleta, Los Dos Pueblos and Cañada del Corral ranchos from his vantage point on the ridge] but not one human being could be seen stirring. A more lovely and picturesque landscape I never beheld.

Around daylight on Christmas morning, a terrible storm blew up, with rain in cloudburst proportions. Frémont's bedraggled troops took the full brunt of this tempest, spending all of Christmas Day slipping and sliding along the brushy slope, the column strung out in disorder for miles on end. Before the ordeal was over, Frémont had lost an estimated 150 horses and mules that slid over precipices in the driving rain. By some miracle, not one human life was lost on the storm-pounded mountainside.

Around sundown of Christmas Day, Bryant and his advance detachment reached the timber at the foot of the mountains, in what is now known as upper Catlett Canyon. The rest of the battalion, far in the rear, had to spend another night exposed on the open slope, with the storm redoubling its fury.

At what he described as "the first level piece of ground," Bryant found a huge oak tree to serve as partial shelter. This tree was positively identified for the writer in 1962 by Mrs. Ida Catlett Chamberlain, then in her 90th year, who remembered how one of Frémont's soldiers had shown her father the oak tree. It stands today in a greenbelt area above Rancho del Ciervo Estates.

The Frémont Trail has been obliterated by time and the elements. It followed the southwesterly trend of that ridge which lies immediately to the east of the "Slippery Rock" ridge which stagecoaches were to traverse in a later period.

All through Christmas night, waterlogged remnants of Frémont's wretched force dragged their way painfully down to the oak tree camp. All packs, cannon, hand weapons and supplies had long since been abandoned along the mountainside above them.

The storm finally blew over. December 26 dawned overcast. The battalion was far too exhausted to have even defended themselves, let alone mount an attack on Santa Barbara. Frémont sent the hardier of his men out into the Valley for beef steers.

By noon of December 27, the troops had returned to the mountain wall to recover their cannon and other material. Captain McLane's diary is specific in reporting that all ordnance was recovered, but this has not hindered generations of relic-hunters from swallowing tall tales about "Frémont's cannon" being hidden back in the brush. This writer has spent many a gruelling weekend probing the throats of thicket-choked arroyos in search of Frémont's legendary cannon.

The afternoon of December 27, three Barbareños rode up to greet Frémont. They were Don Nicolás Den, already a friend of the Pathfinder's; and American otter-hunters Lewis T. Burton and Isaac J. Sparks. They relayed the welcome intelligence that Santa Barbara's menfolk were absent in Los Angeles, so no force would be necessary to capture Santa Barbara.

After the passage of nearly one and a quarter centuries, without benefit of detailed charts and documents, we cannot guarantee any exact route Frémont took across the eastern corner of the Goleta Valley on December 28, 1846, in reaching Santa Barbara. We can, however, make some educated guesses, based on contemporary maps of existing trails of the period. In terms of landmarks in existence in 1966, then, Frémont's route was probably as follows:

Emerging from Catlett Canyon where the ornamental stone portals of a subdivision stand at 1134 North Patterson Avenue; thence southeasterly to avoid the knoll occupied in 1966 by the Joseph Sexton III and Alma Sexton residences; continuing southeasterly to cross San Jose Creek, then in flood, at Cathedral Oaks Road; on past the Turnpike Road overpass at the freeway; veering easterly between the Goleta Cemetery and San Marcos High School, to intersect Hollister Avenue in the vicinity of the east end of Auhay Drive; thence along the line now followed by Modoc Road to La Cumbre Junior High School; and thence southeasterly to where West Anapamu Street crosses over Mission Creek.

There is documented evidence that the Frémont Battalion pitched its tents along both banks of Mission Creek from West Anapamu to West Canon Perdido Streets, with field headquarters behind what is now the Knights of Columbus building (the old St. Vincent's Orphanage). Frémont commandeered quarters for himself and staff in the San Carlos Hotel at State and De la Guerra Streets, owned by Captain Alpheus B. Thompson.

Daniel Hill and Nicolás Den served as liaison between Frémont and the Barbareños during the week the Americans spent in Santa Barbara resting up from their ordeal, sighting in their guns and repairing their equipment. Frémont requisitioned horses and cattle from Dos Pueblos Rancho, for which the U.S. Government later paid Nicolás A. Den the sum of $1,962 in a California Claims action.

Captain McLane's diary contains this interesting comment about the grantees who between them owned the Goleta Valley:

> Daniel Hill and his son-in-law, a little Irish doctor [Nicolas A. Den] were both very kind to us. The women are beautiful. Den's wife [Dona Rosa] has few equals for beauty at home.

Frémont resumed his march southward on January 3, 1847. Ten days later, on the Cahuenga Plain, General Andres Pico capitulated to Frémont, rather than suffer the ignominy of surrendering to Stockton or Kearney.

The Mexican War in California was over.

CHAPTER VI

Goleta Beef Feeds the 'Forty-Niners

Although the war was over in California, the pueblo of Santa Barbara had to endure military occupation from April, 1847, until September, 1848. Civil authorities were accountable to the military forces of the United States as represented by Col. J. D. Stevenson's New York Volunteer Regiment, Company F, Captain Francis J. Lippett commanding.

It was a hectic time for Barbareños, but such stresses and strains as curfews, baseball games on State Street, the Lost Cannon or Canon Perdido fiasco, and the hoodlumism of soldiers fresh from the Bowery and Hell's Kitchen had little or no effect on the placid back-eddy of the Goleta Valley. Grass kept growing, cattle kept multiplying —what else could happen around the Good Land?

But two epochal events were soon to shatter this halcyon torpor of the Valley: the Gold Rush of 1848-'49, and California's admission to the Union in 1850.

Jim Marshall's discovery of gold on the American River brought hundreds of thousands of Argonauts to California from every corner of the globe. They came by covered wagon across the plains and mountains, around Cape Horn or via Panama and Nicaragua by steam and sail. A vast influx of Mexican gold-seekers from Sonora and Sinaloa provinces flooded into California along the old mission route. This caused the Goleta Valley to experience a swelling current of traffic on El Camino Real from the fall of 1848 until well into the Fifties.

Many of these Mexicans were wealthy *haciendados* who traveled in caravans with impressive retinues of Indian servants. They found the verdant Goleta Valley a welcome oasis after their waterless passage of Los Angeles Basin. Many camped for weeks on end around the perimeter of Goleta Slough, or in the cool arroyos to the west.

Nicolás A. Den visited the diggings early in 1849, not to pan for gold, but to visit his brother, Dr. Richard S. Den, who with a party of Angeleños was working a placer claim at Sullivan's Diggings near Angels Camp. When Don Nicolás saw miners paying an ounce of gold dust worth $19 for a tough beefsteak, he realized he possessed a gold mine of his own back in the Goleta Valley, where sleek fat cattle were just waiting to be driven northward to feed the beef-hungry 'Forty-Niners.

Hurrying home, Den had his vaqueros round up 822 head of Goleta beef steers and put them on the trail north, one of the earliest large-scale cattle drives in California history. At San Juan Bautista, eager stock buyers paid Den $50 a head, or $41,000 for longhorns which up to now had been worth $2 each for their hides. In the next two or three years cattle bearing the Dos Pueblos brand were a common sight in northern stockyards, and Nicolás Den became a virtual millionaire as a result.

Other southern California rancheros were quick to follow Den's lead, notably the Arrellanes family of Rancho Guadalupe, and the De la Guerras and Oreñas who ran cattle on such big spreads as the San Julian, Cuyama and Los Alamos ranchos.

Doña Rosa took quick advantage of her new standard of living. She began entertaining the important visitors who passed her way, with gourmet dining for which string quartets provided background music. Exotic foods were kept refrigerated in a root cellar stocked with glacial ice shipped from Alaska. Doña Rosa was fitted for Paris gowns by *couturiers* straight from the Rue de la Paix. Don Nicolás paid a visit to Ireland for the first time since he had left home, and returned with extravagant gifts of silver, china, crystal, oriental rugs and antique furnishings for his wife and family.

Among the enterprising Yankees who were drawn to California by the Gold Rush and made their fortunes by driving cattle from Southern to Northern California, and in so doing altered the course of history in the Goleta Valley, were the More Brothers of Medina County, Ohio.

The *pater familias*, Peter Alexander More, was born in Scotland in 1797, and emigrated to central Ohio in 1816. All six of his sons eventually settled in California. In 1849, two of the More brothers, Thomas Wallace and Andrew, came separately to the Sierra Nevada gold fields, and met there accidentally. Later they were joined by a younger brother, Henry. The three formed the More Brothers Company, borrowed money from Abel Stearns of Los Angeles to buy cheap cattle in the south, drove them over the Tehachapis to sell them at fabulous profits in the north, and invested their money in real estate. Their holdings in the Santa Barbara area included Santa Rosa Island, the Lompoc and Santa Clara River valleys, and land in the Goleta Valley itself.

When California became the thirty-first state in September, 1850, the owners of Mexican grants had to prove ownership in order to hold their lands under the terms of the Treaty of Guadalupe Hidalgo. Thousands of newly-arrived squatters were settling on land previously granted to Mexicans, and were demanding that all deeds issued prior to the American conquest be nullified and the land thrown open to homesteaders. Congress, in order to cope with this chaotic situation, passed a special Land Act in 1851, with a Board of Land Commissioners to adjudicate title disputes and rule on the validity of all Mexican and Spanish grants in California.

Naturally much concerned over the future were Nicolás A. Den and Daniel Hill. Both the Dos Pueblos and La Goleta grants had been authorized by Mexico prior to July 7, 1846, the date Commodore Sloat seized Monterey to mark the official beginning of American control in California. However, the entire Goleta Valley had originally been under the guardianship of Santa Barbara Mission, which was a complicating factor. One of the first acts of the new American regime was to cancel Pio Pico's sales of missions to private individuals. Thus Santa Barbara mission and its contiguous cemetery, which had been part of the package deal for which Dr. Richard Den had paid $7,500 on June 10, 1846, was returned to the Church, together with certain outlying parcels including the San Jose Vineyard in the Goleta Valley foothills. The Den Brothers, however, remained the legal owners of ex-mission Rancho San Marcos.

Approximately 800 California Land Claims were ultimately reviewed by the Land Commissioners, and of these 275 were found invalid. Nicolás Den and Daniel Hill had their Goleta Valley titles confirmed on December 26, 1854, after having been carried by appeal to the District Court of the United States for the Southern District of California.

Final confirmation did not come from the U.S. Supreme Court until May 15, 1861, and an even longer wait was in store before the issuance of a U.S. patent. Daniel Hill's patent, authorized by President Abraham Lincoln, was dated March 10, 1865; Nicolás Den's patent to Los Dos Pueblos, authorized by President U. S. Grant, was dated February 23, 1877. Neither Hill nor Den lived to see their ranches receive a U.S. patent.

When California became a state, Santa Barbara County was created. Its first Grand Jury was headed by Nicolás A. Den; its first County Attorney was Daniel Hill. The latter's job was to collect delinquent taxes, but Hill resigned his office within a few months.

By this time Hill's wife, Rafaela, had borne him fifteen children. Only one, Daniel Jr., died in infancy. At this time Hill was 53, and had been living for some time at Tajiguas Arroyo, identified a century later as the Stewart Abercrombie ranch.

Daniel Hill had always coveted the Cochera, or La Patera district at the eastern end of the Dos Pueblos grant, bounded by Carneros Creek on the west, the foothills on the north, La Goleta grant line (now Fairview Avenue) on the east, and what is now Hollister Avenue, then El Camino Real, on the south.

On September 15, 1851, Nicolás A. Den deeded the Cochera tract to his father-in-law, who paid him 50 cents an acre for 2,000 of the most fertile acres in the Goleta Valley. (In 1965 portions of the same tract were selling for as high as $120,000 an acre!) Only one string was attached to this, the first major real estate transaction in Santa Barbara County history—Den's cattle were to have perpetual use of the pond called *la patera*, now Los Carneros Lake.

An unsolved riddle in Goleta Valley annals is when Daniel Hill built his historic adobe at 35 La Patera Lane. Various historians have cited dates ranging from 1832 to 1854. The most reliable evidence found by this writer indicates that Hill built the adobe in 1850, a year previous to purchasing the Patera from Den.

As originally constructed, the *casa* was a one-story structure 30 by 60 feet in size, with a unique adobe partition running down the center lengthwise. A porch flanked the east elevation, and an asphalt roof, with rafters supported by a ridgepole improvised from the mast or spar of an unidentified shipwreck, completed the house.

The first outside settler besides Den and Hill to build a home on the Good Land was James McCaffery of County Monaghan, Ireland. Born in 1811, he joined the California Gold Rush and opened a general merchandise store in one of the rooms in the deserted San Jose Mission. Here he met Nicolás A. Den, while the latter was on a beef-selling junket in 1852.

Den's high praise of the Goleta Valley as a place to live sold McCaffery on the idea of buying a wagon and team, loading his family thereon and heading south via El Camino Real. The journey from San Jose to the Goleta Valley took him two months. With Den's assistance, McCaffery rented the historic San Jose Vineyard and winery from Bishop Thaddeus Amat, and adjacent acreage from Richard S. Den in the disputed mission lands which the latter had purchased from Pio Pico in the sunset hours of Mexican sovereignty. Ruins of the mission winery, where McCaffery produced up to 8,000 gallons of wine per year, still stand at San Jose Ranch, at 1106 North Patterson Avenue, now owned by Joe Cavaletto.

On June 1, 1853, one of Daniel Hill's daughters, Susana, married one of the More Brothers, Thomas Wallace More. Because another prominent Yankee in the area was named Thomas W. Moore, Susana's husband became known as T. Wallace More for the rest of his life.

More took his bride to live on the Sespe Ranch in the Santa Clara River Valley of what is now Ventura County, but he had fallen in love with the Goleta Valley and would shortly return to make his permanent headquarters.

In January, 1854, a fateful event transpired which went all but unnoticed at the time: the arrival in the Goleta Valley of a sheepherder and his band of sheep. But the tall, bearded man of 35 was no ordinary shepherd, nor were his sore-footed Merino sheep an ordinary flock. Together they were to make history.

The sheepherder was Colonel William Welles Hollister of Hanover, Ohio—the title came from a brief stint with the neighborhood militia. He had driven his flock of sheep some 2,500 miles over desert and mountain from Licking County in central Ohio, one of the most remarkable feats in frontier annals. Of the 6,000 head of sheep he had started with the previous spring, only 1,000 survived to reach Goleta's Good Land, at which point Hollister saw they could be driven no further.

Hollister's destination was the San Benito Valley, in what was then Monterey County. He had recognized the sheep-raising potential of that area in 1852, when he had paid a brief visit to California. Returning to Ohio by way of Panama and New York, Hollister had borrowed $10,000 from a widowed sister, Lucy A. "Auntie" Brown, and had assembled the flock of 6,000 sheep. On the trail drive west, Auntie Brown had accompanied him in a covered wagon. Fifteen drovers and a younger brother, Hubbard Hollister, also made the trek.

The sheep drive had followed the Oregon Trail as far as Utah, where Hollister had angled southwestward through hostile Mormon country and entered California by way of the Mojave Desert. By this time he had lost 4,000 sheep to the hazards of prairie fires, bad water, lack of feed, heat exhaustion, and, in the vicinity of Las Vegas, Nevada, an attack by Piute Indians. On the 100-mile waterless stretch in the Mojave, Hollister lost another 1,000 head.

At the California line, Hollister's flock joined up with a band of sheep driven by Thomas Flint and Llewelyn Bixby of Maine. The combined flocks crossed Cajon Pass on New Year's Eve, 1853. Flint & Bixby wintered their sheep in the San Gabriel Valley, before pushing on to Monterey County in the spring. Hollister continued as far up the coast as the Goleta Valley before his crippled animals gave out on him.

Colonel Hollister negotiated with Nicolás Den for grazing privileges in beautiful Tecolotito Arroyo (now known as Glen Annie Canyon). During the weeks Hollister spent resting his sheep, the size of his flock was doubled by the lambing of his ewes.

The fertility, beauty and sublime climate of the Goleta Valley enchanted Hollister. When he resumed his sheep drive north in the early spring of 1854, he told Nicolás Den that he would return after making his stake in Monterey County, and buy Tecolotito Arroyo as a country estate for his retirement years. Told that the land was not for sale, Hollister retorted, "I will offer you such a high price you cannot refuse me."

In order to get through Gaviota Pass, Hollister was obliged to dismantle his sister's wagon and transport it through the gorge on mule back.

The decade of the 1850s was marked by a statewide collapse of law and order, especially in Santa Barbara, which, because it lay between San Francisco and Los Angeles, seemed to attract the riffraff from both places.

This was the era of the notorious outlaws of California song and story, such as Joaquin Murrietta (who probably never existed, but was a composite of several Mexican *bandidos* named Joaquin); Salomon Pico, whose lair was in Los Alamos Valley, immortalized in fiction under the name of Zorro; Tiburcio Vasquez; and the worst outlaw of them all, Irishman Jack Powers, a former sergeant of Company F, Stevenson's Regiment. He made Santa Barbara his bailiwick, and organized a gang of robbers who preyed on gold-laden miners and cattle buyers traveling the lonely reaches of El Camino Real.

Jack Powers leased a pasture in the Arroyo Burro from Nicolás Den. When Den learned that Powers was the ringleader behind the wave of murders and highway robberies then plaguing Santa Barbara County, he refused to renew Powers' lease. This precipitated the famous Arroyo Burro Battle between Powers' gang, forted up in the canyon on North Ontare Road, and a sheriff's posse numbering 200 men.

In the early Fifties, Powers and his henchmen made numerous attempts to ambush Den as he rode across the Goleta Valley to and from his ranch. Every oak tree and clump of willows became a potential death trap. Den's ranch foreman, Tom Meehan, was bushwhacked at the summit of Refugio Pass by three of Powers' lieutenants, who brazenly confessed the murder but were never punished for it.* Outraged public opinion finally banished Powers and Salomon Pico to Mexico, where both came to violent ends as the Fifties ran their course.

The most sensational statewide manhunt in the history of the San Francisco Vigilante Committees had its climax in the Goleta Valley in 1856, when Judge Ned McGowan was hiding out from Vigilante justice. He was believed to have been an accessory to the murder of

---

* For details of the Powers-Den feud, refer to *Santa Barbara's Royal Rancho*, by Walker A. Tompkins, Howell North Books, 1960.

James King of William, the crusading editor of the San Francisco *Bulletin*, which was attempting to clean up the Barbary Coast. The Vigilantes posted a $20,000 reward for McGowan, dead or alive. The Judge fled southward with the intention of booking passage on a Panama steamer to return to his native Pennsylvania, where he had also had a criminal career.

Using a variety of disguises, including the gray cassock of a Franciscan friar, the grossly overweight Judge McGowan finally made it to Santa Barbara. There he was recognized by a Vigilanteman, who hurried to find Sheriff Russel Heath. Jack Powers hid McGowan, and threw Heath's posse off the scent long enough for McGowan to escape into the foothills behind Santa Barbara.

McGowan hid out in Mission Canyon the first night. Next day, keeping to the chaparral, he worked his way as far west as Maria Ygnacia Canyon. The second day he made it to Bartlett Canyon, northeast of Goleta Slough, where he narrowly escaped being killed by a giant grizzly bear. Two weeks later, McGowan showed up at daylight in front of the Den adobe on Dos Pueblos. He was unkempt and half starved. Don Nicolás was absent on a business trip, but Doña Rosa and her 12-year-old daughter, Kate, took pity on the porcine fugitive and let him spread a blanket in the concealment of a corn patch, which is now the site of the conservatory of the Dos Pueblos Orchid Company.

McGowan hid for more than six months on the Den rancho. Later he was allowed to move from the corn patch to the *casa grande*. Heavily-armed posses on horseback combed the Goleta Valley for months searching for McGowan, but it was not until the rewards posted for his capture had been removed, in February 1857, that McGowan surrendered to the law.

He was taken to Napa County for trial and was acquitted by a drunken jury in what was widely deplored as a miscarriage of justice. Nicolás Den was censured by his neighbors for the part he had played in concealing Judge McGowan while the Vigilantemen were hunting him, but Den defended his action by saying that lynch law was immoral and that McGowan deserved a fair trial.

It was during the summer of McGowan's travail that Daniel Hill's wealthy son-in-law, T. Wallace More, moved back to the Goleta

Valley so that his wife, Susana, who bore him four children, could be closer to her mother.

More was a tall, handsome, black-bearded man of 30 at this time. He had set his mind on acquiring the level bottomland between Atascadero Creek and the Santa Barbara trail (Hollister Avenue), but Hill was determined not to sell any of his La Goleta grant.

More offered Hill a dollar an acre, which was the going price for choice level farmland in Santa Barbara County at the time, and kept increasing it until Hill succumbed to temptation at an offer of $5 an acre. Five years before, Hill had acquired the La Patera tract from Nicolás Den at 50 cents an acre for 2,000 acres; now More was paying him $2,000 for only 400 acres! Hill and his spouse Rafaela, who had to sign legal documents with an "X," deeded the 400-acre tract to T. Wallace More on April 21, 1856, which became the nucleus of the famous More Ranch. The original 400 acres were bounded on the north by Hollister Avenue, on the east by Maria Ygnacia Creek, on the south by Atascadero Creek and on the west by San Jose Creek.

A year later, Nicolás Den was elected County Assessor. He placed a valuation of $29,770 on the 33,000 acres of his Dos Pueblos and half of the San Marcos ranch. Daniel Hill's total of 6,000 acres in La Goleta grant and the Cochera tract were appraised for tax purposes at $18,400. Tax rates for 1857 were $1.625 per $100 assessed valuation.

During this period, T. Wallace More did some asphalt mining on a small scale from outcroppings of tar on the beach east of Goleta Slough. He sold the natural tar for $2 a ton in San Francisco, where it found a ready market for roofing and street paving.

Although the Goleta Valley is famous for its mild year-round climate, in 1859 the Good Land was scorched by the hottest day ever recorded at any place on the continent, a record which stood for more than half a century.

The Channel's freak one-day heat wave occurred on Friday, June 17, 1859. It was caused by the first and only simoon ever recorded in North America. During the morning of that day, the temperature hovered between 75 and 80 degrees. Then, around 1:00 p.m., a blast of superheated air from the direction of Santa Ynez Peak suddenly hit the Goleta Valley, filling the inhabitants with terror; they thought the end of the world had come.

By two o'clock the heat had soared to an incredible 133 degrees, the burning wind from the northwest bringing with it great clouds of impalpable dust.

"*No human being could withstand such heat*," reported the U.S. Coast Survey in 1869. "*All betook themselves to their dwellings and closed every door and window, the thick adobe walls giving admirable protection.*"

In the Goleta Valley, people took refuge behind the three-foot-thick walls of the Daniel Hill adobe, and the *casa grande* at Dos Pueblos Ranch. McCaffery's adobe winery at San Jose Vineyard offered similar sanctuary, as did Maria Ygnacia's cabin at the Indian Orchard ranch and Martinez' tannery on upper San Jose creek.

"*Calves, rabbits and cattle died on their feet*," the government report said. "*Fruit fell from trees to the ground, scorched on the windward side; all vegetable gardens were ruined.*"

At five o'clock that afternoon the hot wind died, and the thermometer "cooled off" to 122 degrees. By seven o'clock it was a comfortable 77 degrees, and the Goleta Valley's half-smothered inhabitants ventured out of doors to survey their dry-baked world. Birds had plummeted dead from the sky; others had flown into wells seeking cooler air, and had drowned. A fisherman in a rowboat made it to the Goleta Sandspit with his face and arms blistered as if he had been exposed to a blast furnace.

Nothing like the Simoon of 1859 has ever struck the Good Land again, *laus Deo*. Goleta's heat record remained on U.S. Weather Bureau books until 1934, when a thermometer in Death Valley, 200 feet below sea level, registered 134 degrees, the existing record.

The year following the freak simoon, Daniel Hill made a trip back to his birthplace, Billerica, Massachusetts, his first in nearly forty years. For some reason he did not look up his living kinfolk, nor did he claim inheritances which could have been his, had he agreed to live in Massachusetts.

Daniel Hill returned to his beloved Goleta Valley, mercifully unaware that the Sixties were to be fraught with disaster for both the Valley and his own fortunes. Indeed, he would be in his grave before the decade had half run its course.

CHAPTER VII

Deluge and Death, Drought and Death

Grizzled old Daniel Hill had been living in California so long, almost forty years, that he had assimilated the Mexican acceptance of the live-for-*mañana* philosophy. But California was American now, and where American settlers went, schools and churches and roads were not far behind.

Hill's son-in-law, Nicolás Den, should have done something about improving the road to Dos Pueblos Ranch a long time ago, but had not. A gift to Doña Rosa of a brougham from England had to be kept in the barn because there were no bridges across the numerous streams between Dos Pueblos and Santa Barbara.

But Hill's other son-in-law, T. Wallace More, was more aggressive and progressive in his thinking. It galled him to waste most of a day hauling a load of hay seven miles to town from his Goleta Valley ranch. He made a vow to get a decent road built, and soon.

In 1859, the State Legislature passed an Enabling Act whereby the State appropriated funds to build a public road up the coast between Los Angeles and San Francisco, roughly following El Camino Real. Santa Barbara County was allocated $15,000 from this road fund, providing the voters bonded the county—which at that time also included Ventura County, making it almost as large as the State of Connecticut— for a matching sum of money. The supervisors called an election for May 21, 1859. Only 105 taxpayers took the trouble to show up at the polls, but the road bond issue passed by a count of 86 to 19.

T. Wallace More decided to capitalize on this opportunity by submitting a bid to construct a county road from the San Luis Obispo County line to Los Angeles County for $15,000 in bonds.

Pablo de la Guerra, John F. Maguire, Russel Heath, James L. Ord and Francisco Arrellanes were appointed Road Commissioners to confer with the Overland Stagecoach Company in regard to the best route for a county road. In due time T. Wallace More's bid was accepted by the County Supervisors, who were Maria Antonio de la Guerra, Felipe Puig and Jose Arnaz.

More began assembling men, teams and material for the job in the summer of 1860. He got off to a bad start; labor was hard to come by. On October 8, More petitioned the Supervisors to pay him the $15,000 in advance. They compromised by paying More $10,000, but required his wealthy brothers, Henry and Alexander, to post bond to guarantee More's completion of the contract.

Things went from bad to worse for More during the autumn months. He quarreled incessantly with his chief engineer, George Black. When he attempted to substitute brush and earth fills for bridges, an unexpected heavy rain washed his shoddy work away. On December 4, More petitioned the Supervisors for an extension of time on his contract, which was granted reluctantly. The situation continued to deteriorate, so that on February 12, 1861, the County Supervisors spread a resolution on the minute book condemning More's general management of the road project.

Finally, on March 5, T. Wallace More gave up. He notified the Supervisors he could not complete his contract, and offered to deliver to the Road Commissioners all his teams, tools, lumber and equipment. The Supervisors angrily filed suit against T. Wallace More and his sureties to recover the $10,000 they had paid out, with little or nothing to show for it. After months of tedious litigation, a judgment of $950 was awarded against More.

Engineers and crews who had made excellent progress with road building in Los Angeles County, were called in to repair T. Wallace More's bungling. During the spring of 1861, 12 days before the Confederate attack on Fort Sumter triggered the Civil War, the coast road through Santa Barbara County was opened to traffic for the first time. Sturdy wooden bridges spanned the larger creeks—Maria Ygnacia, Eagle Canyon, and Dos Pueblos—while lesser streams such as the Atascadero, San Jose, Carneros and Tecolotito were forded for years to come.

On Monday, April 1, 1861, a six-horse team pulled the first Concord stagecoach through the Goleta Valley, bound for Los Angeles from San Francisco. In Santa Barbara, this historic event was greeted by the firing of cannon and a Spanish-style fiesta.

What was known for generations as "the Gaviota stage road" left Santa Barbara at Mission and De la Vina Streets, meandering westward past the adobe orphanage (St. Vincent's) built in 1856 by the Sisters of Charity; past the present General Hospital and Goleta Cemetery; across the San Marcos High School campus; and extended westward to the future intersection of Fairview Avenue and Hollister Avenue along a right of way located approximately midway between the modern Hollister Avenue and the railroad. West of Fairview the stage road ran north of the present railroad. At Ellwood Canyon it turned north at right angles for one mile, and thence wound over the steep hill at Tecolote Canyon. In September, 1891, Dos Pueblos homesteader W. E. Nichols was killed under his overturned wagon at the sharp curve at the base of this grade, resulting in the road being straightened out.

Prof. William H. Brewer of Yale University was making a geological survey of Southern California in 1861. Under date of April 7, Brewer wrote this description of how the Good Land appeared more than a century ago:

> Until now, Santa Barbara County has been nearly isolated from the country around by rugged mountains. During the last few months, $30,000 to $40,000 have been expended by the County on getting a good wagon road through from San Luis Obispo . . . to Los Angeles. . . . This road we are following—sometimes it is a mere obscure trail across [the Goleta Valley], scarcely visible yet for want of travel, at others well engineered, built over and along high hills, and through deep canyons at great expense and labor.
>
> Fine bridges of wood span the streams and gulches, the first bridges we have seen in the southern country. Our mules are shy of these, to them, strange structures. . . .
>
> We camped on the seashore where a fine stream emerges from a canyon on the ranch of Dos Pueblos. During the day's ride [across the Goleta Valley] we saw immense herds and flocks of cattle, horses and sheep feeding. We passed one herd of over 2,000 head, kept in a close body by a large body of bucaros (herdsmen on horseback), while the owners were separating the cattle for some drover to take north.
>
> This fertile, level strip is well watered by frequent streams that come

down from the mountains, and is all occupied, either by rancheros under old Spanish* grants, or by the recent wandering, worthless American "squatters."

In mid-November of 1861, rains started to fall in the Goleta Valley, as elsewhere in California. They never seemed to stop. In one forty-hour period there was a precipitation of seven inches, almost half the annual average rainfall. Day followed day without letup in the downpour.

By the end of the first week of continuous deluge, the Goleta Slough had become a vast, shallow bay from the Devereux Ranch lagoon to the vicinity of General Hospital. The lowlands flanking the bluffs of More Mesa bordering Atascadero Creek were part of the inundation.

Incalculable amounts of detritus, uprooted trees and chaparral were being spewed out of the foothill canyons by the coffee-colored run-off from San Jose, San Pedro, Los Carneros and Tecolotito Creeks. Maria Ygnacia Creek ran bank-full for miles, overspilling onto T. Wallace More's place. The Goleta Slough became the catchment, or settling basin, for all this silt, since the free outflow of fresh water from the mountains was periodically impeded by incoming tidewater from the ocean. Sediment quickly filled tidal estuaries and lagoons which had been navigable to ships for centuries.

What little communication the Goleta Valley had with the outside world—since road washouts and destroyed bridges abruptly ended the daily mail stage service—told of even worse punishment being meted out to other portions of California. It was truly the rainstorm of the century.

Los Angeles reported twenty-eight days and nights of rain without let-up. Sonora, up in the gold country, had 102 inches of rain— eight and a half feet!—between November 11, 1861 and January 31, 1862. Up in Sacramento, the tops of telegraph poles were submerged by floodwaters and the legislators had to move out of the inundated capital city. Steamers were evacuating marooned livestock from

---

* Prof. Brewer's reference to "Spanish grants" in Santa Barbara County is a common error. All land grants involving title to private owners came from Mexico, not Spain. His comment about squatters had to do with transients, rather than with the legitimate homesteaders who would be moving into the Goleta foothills following passage of the National Homestead Act a year later.

Deluge and Death, Drought and Death 63

ranches as far as fourteen miles from normal river channels. In the San Joaquin Valley a lake formed which was twenty miles wide by over 300 miles long.

Daniel Hill and Nicolás Den had no way of estimating how many of their Goleta Valley cattle perished by drowning. When at last, in February, the rains ceased and the sun showed its face on a half-drowned land, the topography of the Goleta Valley had been altered beyond recognition.

Gone forever were the deep-water inlets of the Goleta Slough. Ancient boat channels were now lost under ten to fourteen feet of silt scoured off the mountain wall. The Valley's upper canyons in many places had trebled in width. Giant sycamores and oaks, centuries old, had been uprooted like carrots, to form massive log jams which had impounded flood water and, breaking, created catastrophic onrushes of water. Many historic adobe houses literally dissolved under the weeks of pelting rain, like sugar cubes under a faucet.

T. Wallace More's bean and hay crops were buried under hip-deep mud, although he considered the siltation as just that much more fertile topsoil.

California, and the Goleta Valley, would experience periodic floods in the following century, but none to compare with the deluge of 1861-'62. Forever afterward that rainy season would be the standard by which other wet years would be compared.

The adobe homes of Nicolás Den and Daniel Hill survived. So did McCaffery's mission winery and Maria Ygnacia's hovel at Indian Orchard. At Dos Pueblos Ranch, however, Nicolás Den lost all his bottomland vegetable crops, his hayfields, barns, corrals and gardens, everything on the canyon floor, which had been raised six to eight feet by siltation.

Don Nicolás celebrated his fiftieth birthday in January, 1862. At the time, he was at the peak of his affluence and influence in Goleta Valley and state affairs. Doña Rosa, his spouse, was only 35. She had borne him eleven children since their marriage in 1843, all but one of whom were still living. They were Kate, 18; Manuel, 16; Nicolas, 14; William, 11; Alfredo, 10; Alfonso, 8; Maria, 6; Augusto, 5; Rosita, 3; and Susana, 10 months.

But time was running out for the Irish Don of Dos Pueblos. He contracted a severe chest cold, due to overworking during the wet weather, when he and his vaqueros had toiled around the clock saving bogged-down cattle from the flood and getting them to the safety of higher range.

On February 27, 1862, Den was visited by his personal physician, James L. Ord, and his priest, Fr. Comapla. They signed as witnesses to a codicil which Den attached to a will he had originally made in San Francisco in July, 1859. Whether or not Den had a premonition that his life was nearing its end will never be known, but he chose that February day to make two important changes in his will. His brother-in-law, Juan Hill, who had gone insane, was replaced as executor by another of Daniel Hill's sons, Jose Maria; while Den's San Francisco attorney, the celebrated Eugene Casserly, who had recently moved to New York, was replaced by a Santa Barbara lawyer named Charles E. Huse. Alfred Robinson of Santa Barbara remained on as the third executor.

When Nicolás Den made Huse an executor of his will, he committed the gravest error of his life, an error which was to affect the shape of many lives in the Goleta Valley in years to come.

Four days after drawing up the codicil, on March 3, 1862, Den got up from his sick bed at midnight to assist an Indian woman giving birth at her hut near El Capitan Beach. He returned home, took to his bed, and lapsed into a coma immediately. Dr. Ord and Fr. Comapla were summoned from town. Double pneumonia developed, and death came at seven o'clock that evening. A century later Den's biographer evaluated the Valley's loss:

The death of Nicolás A. Den was like the crash of a sequoia in a grove of saplings. His untimely passing left a vacuum in the daily life of his community, and a great gap in the familiar horizon of the times.

Den's body was entombed with highest honors by the Church he had served so zealously as a layman. His surface tomb can be seen today beside the east wall of the Friars' Vaults at Mission Santa Barbara.

When Den's last will and testament was filed for probate on March 20, it was revealed that he had bequeathed his personal property and the half of Dos Pueblos Rancho lying west of Tecolote Canyon to his widow, Rosa Hill de Den. The remaining half of the

Deluge and Death, Drought and Death

ranch, extending into the Goleta Valley as far east as Los Carneros Creek (the remaining 2,000 acres having been sold to Daniel Hill ten years before) was to be held in trust for Den's minor heirs, each to receive a one-tenth portion of the estate as he or she came of age. Trustees were his widow, Rosa; his brother, Richard; and Alfred Robinson.

Less than a month after Den's funeral, a tall, bearded stranger, bearing a striking resemblance to President Abraham Lincoln, knocked on the door of the Den residence in Santa Barbara.

"You do not remember me," he said, "but I am Colonel W. W. Hollister, of Monterey County. I wintered my sheep in Tecolotito Canyon in '54, at which time I told Don Nicolás I would be back to purchase that canyon from him when I had made my stake. That is why I am here—to buy the Tecolotito."

Doña Rosa could speak no English, but her eldest daughter, Kate, who had been educated at a convent in San Jose, interpreted Colonel Hollister's statement for her mother. With deep shock Hollister learned of Don Nicolás' recent death—and that all business deals would have to be discussed with C. E. Huse in Santa Barbara.

Hollister conferred with Huse, and returned to Monterey County with very bad news indeed: Tecolotito Canyon lay inside that portion of the Den Estate which was tied up in a trust agreement until the last minor heir came of age. That would be in 1882, at which time Hollister would be seventy years old. His fond dream of owning the Tecolotito portion of the Good Land, therefore, would have to be put aside forever.

If 1861 and 1862 had been the years of the Big Deluge, 1863 and 1864 were destined to go down in history as the years of the Big Drought. The Goleta Valley, green as emeralds from the foothills to the sea and with wild flowers blooming in profusion, began to turn sear and brown as the spring of 1863 merged into summer without a drop of redeeming rainfall.

As the grass began to wither, the cattle worked their way deeper and deeper into the foothills and the upper canyons, in search of feed.

Slowly at first, then perceptibly from day to day, streams were subsiding. Eventually their flow soaked underground into blotter-dry subsoil. Former rushing creeks became chains of disconnected mud puddles in which dying fish gasped and dead fish rotted. Overnight the puddles evaporated and gaunt-ribbed cattle began crowding the sun-checkered rims of the waterholes, the only way to quench their thirst being to lick dew off the rocks at night.

Old time Goleta residents who lived through the Big Drought related their memories of the ordeal to C. A. Storke, later a prominent figure in Goleta Valley and Santa Barbara life. The following is taken from Storke's unpublished memoirs, written in 1928:

> The carcasses of dead horses, cattle and sheep lined Goleta's roads and dotted the open valley. There was no pasture left and no railroad with which to bring in feed in quantity. A few milch cows were kept alive by the ranchers who cut for them the branches of the liveoaks.
>
> Vultures fattened and grew bold. It was a melancholy sight to see cattle in the last stages of thirst and hunger standing motionless, heads hanging low, unable to take another step. It was pitiful to see their legs finally give way under them, until they sank slowly to the earth, never to rise again.
>
> Day after day the sun came up in a dull heat and traveled laggingly across a brassy sky. It was the same always, as though the drought was timeless. There was no other topic of discussion among the people but the awful desolation; none could think except for brief moments of anything else.
>
> Some held the theory that rain was more likely to come with darkness, and rose frequently during the night hours to scan the cloudless sky, but "the dern stars kept on a-shinin'." Prayers for rain went up fervently; the superstitious secretly invoked charms, but to no avail.
>
> There was a curious stillness over [the Goleta Valley]. The small rodents of the fields, with their undernotes of squealing, rustling noises, were gone. Insects withered away. The birds had long since flown to farther climes. The listless people became submerged in a deep apathy. They came to believe that rain would never fall again; that the burning sun would reduce to powder this fair valley of theirs; that its day was done. . . .

Daniel Hill had no one to turn to for counsel, now that Nicolás Den was gone. The Dos Pueblos mayordomo suggested driving their moribund herds to green grass in Kern County, or beyond the Sierra Nevadas where melting snows irrigated the range; but the stock were by now too emaciated to be driven anywhere.

Lawyer Huse authorized the sale of 100 head of Den cattle,

formerly worth $40 a head, for $3.50 each at a "Big Matanza" or public slaughter staged at Miramar Beach beyond Santa Barbara. By the end of 1864 there were only 40 cattle left alive in the Goleta Valley, with 50 horses, mares and colts, and 250 half-starved sheep, according to a livestock census submitted to the court by C. E. Huse.

Gaspar Oreña, stopping for siesta with the Hills one day, told of shifting 1,500 head of longhorns from the barren Cuyama Valley to the San Julian, but at last count only 36 survived. Oreña had already come to realize what most rancheros refused to face: that the cattle industry, which had been the backbone of the economy of California's southern counties since the hide and tallow days, was irrevocably ruined by drought losses. The era of the big ranchos, which had begun in 1834 with the Secularization of the mission lands, was drawing to a close thirty years later.

On April 6, 1863, before the drought had really made itself felt, Daniel Hill parted with 300 acres of his La Goleta grant to buyers outside the family—Abel C. Scull and Samuel Shoup of Ohio. They paid him $8 an acre for flat land in the vicinity of San Marcos High School and the base of the hills of Hope Ranch, and as far west as the bed of dry gravel which had once been Maria Ygnacia Creek.

Very little is known about Samuel Shoup (also spelled "Sharp" in some of the early deeds). He conveyed title to his holdings to Scull on March 21, 1865, and moved to Santa Barbara to operate a restaurant. The Goleta Valley's first school teacher, a Mrs. Steele, taught the Three Rs in a barn on Shoup's place in the late Sixties.

During 1864 a devastating plague of *chapules*, a variety of voracious grasshopper, swarmed into the Goleta Valley from the direction of the Ojai and destroyed every blade of grass and green leaf left in sight. Cattle bones whitened along the banks of the dust-dry streams from the Cieniguitas to Refugio Bay. Former artesian springs lay buried under many feet of dirt left from the recent Deluge of '61.

By now Daniel Hill was beginning to feel older than his 67 years. The drought had reduced his only tangible asset, cattle, almost to zero. He found himself land poor. He faced the very real threat of having creditors attach his house and his lands. So, on April 11 he took advantage of a legal means of protecting his home from foreclosure: he filed a non-attachable homestead claim on a quarter-section which he already owned by purchase (La Patera tract) and Mexican grant (La Goleta). The southeastern corner of this homestead was marked by two blazed sycamore trees, one of which still grows on the south side of Hollister Avenue, just west of the San Jose Creek bridge on the Bottiani property.

The homestead at least put the Daniel Hill adobe and 160 acres of land out of the reach of foreclosure for non-payment of debts.

The longer the dry spell lasted, the more critical became Daniel Hill's circumstances. He could not even raise garden vegetables for want of water. His daughter, Rosa, was in the same predicament out at Dos Pueblos Ranch; she could only stand by and watch the value of her husband's fine estate diminish by the minute. She crossed herself piously and breathed her thanks to God and the Virgin that Don Nicolás had not lived to see the ruination of his proud rancho because of an adverse weather cycle.

The county cattle census going into 1864 stood at 250,000 head, which most rancheros believed was too conservative. Of that number, only 5,000 head remained alive in December. Range land dropped in assessed value to ten cents an acre in the Goleta Valley. Cattle were assessed at a dollar a head for tax purposes.

Worry was fast eroding Daniel Hill's health. Personal tragedy had struck in 1862, when their 24-year-old son, Tomás, died. Son Juan had been declared hopelessly insane, and was committed to a state mental asylum in Stockton, where he was to die in 1866. To provide for Juan's spouse, Maria de los Angeles Burke de Hill, and her two children, Daniel Hill on April 9, 1864, deeded 35 acres in Juan's name, located on the north line of La Goleta Rancho opposite McCaffery's San Jose Vineyard.

Ten days later, Hill deeded a section which he had obtained from the School Lands, including historic Mescalitán Island, to his son, Ramon. On May 31, Hill sold an additional 233 acres to Abel Scull and his son, Charles, receiving from $5 to $8.50 per acre depending on the quality and lay of the land.

The continuing drought brought Daniel Hill to the brink of bankruptcy. He had overextended his credit, hoping rains would come and his cattle would increase. By the fall of 1864, the Good Land itself was virtually worthless. On September 10, Hill took the drastic step of mortgaging La Goleta Rancho north of the county

Col. W. W. Hollister, Goleta Valley's leading citizen from 1868 to 1886

Annie J. Hollister, the Colonel's lady, for whom Glen Annie Canyon was named

Lucy "Auntie" Brown, whose money was behind Hollister's lifelong success

The far-famed Carriage House at Hollister's Lower Ranch was more than that: Annie used to give grand balls there, with Jose Lobero and his orchestra providing the music. Fire caused by spontaneous combustion in the hayloft destroyed this landmark in 1929

In 1872, to keep the peace between wife Annie and sister Auntie Brown, Col. Hollister built his second manorhouse (left) at upper end of Glen Annie Canyon. This was the house which Annie was accused of setting afire in 1890 to prevent the Den family from living there. The Hollister children had a private schoolhouse (right) which in 1966 was used as the foreman's cottage

Ellwood Cooper, one of California's great horticulturists. His Ellwood Canyon home (right) burned down in the 1920s

Sturges Brothers' ranch house in Tecolote Canyon, 1885

Major Shelton Sturges purchased Tecolote Ranch for his sons

Dr. R. F. Winchester, who gave his name to Winchester Canyon

Goleta Valley's pioneer Rafaela School (left) built in 1875 near present Community Hospital; "Two-Story School" (right) built 1883 on South Patterson above Hollister Ave.

Second La Patera Schoolhouse after addition of belfry (left). Right: Original Cathedral Oaks Schoolhouse, now a residence

"Goleta School," built in 1911 to replace Two-Story School. Moved 1928 to Goleta Union School grounds; demolished 1957

I. G. Foster home at 5360 Hollister Avenue, built 1868, was Goleta's first house

Philander Kellogg's house at 170 S. Kellogg Ave. was built in 1872

Harry Langman home, built in 1875, still stood in 1966 at 5486 Calle Real, Goleta

Humane Society now owns David Beck home, built 1887, at 5399 Overpass Road

Largest building in La Patera for many years was the old Birabent House, built in 1870 on north side of Hollister Avenue between Magnolia and Nectarine; razed 1928 and lumber used to build the Ellwood Hotel on rear of Birabent lot

road to Juan Camarillo, of San Buenaventura, a notorious usurer and loan shark, in the amount of $8,000. Hill promised to repay this astronomical sum, plus interest, within one year.

Camarillo had refused to make the loan until Daniel and Rafaela Hill filed an Abandonment of Homestead notice with the County Clerk. This nullified the protection against foreclosure which the homestead filing had accomplished a few short months earlier, and with that Hill lost all semblance of peace of mind.

Having paid off his more pressing personal obligations, Hill now faced the nightmare of repaying Camarillo. At this juncture Hill's wily son-in-law, T. Wallace More, a man of shrewd business instincts, came forward with an offer to buy 1,000 acres of land extending from Mescalitán Island to Hope Ranch, including the seashore tableland now known as More Mesa, and extending northward to the county road and eastward to the Scull ranch. More offered to pay $5 an acre for this land, some of the finest in the valley. In his extremity, Daniel Hill had little choice but to accept the $5,000. This gave T. Wallace More a total of 1,400 acres of bottomland and mesa, plus title to the asphaltum deposits on the beach.

Hill still needed another $3,000 if he was to satisfy Juan Camarillo's mortgage loan. He turned to a unique source of raising capital, unique at least as early as 1864. He leased the oil and gas rights under La Goleta Rancho to Carpinteria's leading citizen, ex-sheriff Russel Heath, withholding a one-fifteenth royalty on any oil, petroleum, naphtha or similar products found under Rancho La Goleta. On December 6, 1864, Heath paid $6,000 for his oil rights—and Daniel Hill was off the hook at last.

He paid off his $8,000 to Juan Camarillo on January 17, 1865. By that act he had set his worldly affairs in order.

An overwhelming lassitude seemed to come over the old ex-mariner from Massachusetts. The sight of his drought-ravaged valley filled him with a deep melancholy. He took to his bed on January 18. Next day his faithful spouse, Rafaela, gathered their anxious family about his bedside to receive his paternal blessing—in Spanish. The following day, January 20, the old man died quietly in his sleep. He was only 68. Rafaela would always believe that a broken heart killed Daniel Hill.

CHAPTER VIII

1868: Goleta Valley Subdividing Begins

Daniel Hill, the Presbyterian from Massachusetts who forsook the sea to wed the daughter of a California Don, was given a Catholic burial. He lies beside his son, Tomás, in the consecrated earth of the Old Mission's *campo santo*. The two graves are located inside a fenced enclosure near the cemetery gate, a scant hundred paces from the vault where Nicolás A. Den was laid to rest.

After Hill's funeral, his grieving widow, Rafaela, turned to her recently-widowed daughter, Rosa Den, for comfort. The stunning realization touched both women that the responsibility for managing the entire Goleta Valley cattle range now rested on their inexperienced shoulders. While both had married English-speaking husbands, neither could speak or write that language.

Rafaela had borne fifteen children, thirteen of whom survived their father. Those who had attained their majority by 1865 were Rosa Den, Jose Vicente, Josepha, Susana More, Juan Jose, Ramon, Elena, and Maria Antonio. The minor children, ranging in age from 17 to 13, included Lucretia, Enrico, Florentin Daniel, Jose Maria and Adelaide. Juan was hospitalized in Stockton. Daniel Jr. had died in 1837 at fourteen months, Tomás in 1862 at age 24.

Daniel Hill's last will and testament, dated November 3, 1864, was an elementary two-page document containing none of the complex trust arrangements which were so confounding to the administrators of the Den Estate. The terms of Hill's will, like the man himself, were uncomplicated. One half his worldly goods he bestowed on his spouse Rafaela. The other half was to be divided

1868: Goleta Valley Subdividing Begins

equally among the thirteen surviving children. His sons Ramon and Jose Maria, as executors, filed the will for probate on February 18, 1865. The Hon. Francis J. Maguire, presiding judge of the Probate Court, appointed Augustín Janssens and Henry Carnes to appraise the estate, which they valued at $5,000 for the real property and $6,275 for personal property.

Rafaela hired one of the Den executors, Charles Enoch Huse, to handle her legal affairs. Huse was a native of Massachusetts who had come to California in 1852 and passed his bar examination in San Francisco. He had resided in Santa Barbara since 1853. He was destined to become a highly controversial participant in several fraudulent land schemes. Many believed he had been mentally ill most of his adult life, and he, in fact, died hopelessly insane in 1898. At the time Rafaela Hill retained him, however, Charles E. Huse was regarded as a brilliant and resourceful young lawyer.

It was agreed that Rafaela's half-share of Hill's real estate should be the Patera, or Cochera, tract on which the Hill Adobe was located—the 2,000 acres between Carneros Creek and the future line of Fairview Avenue, which Hill had bought from Den in 1851. Rancho La Goleta would be divided equally among the thirteen children, less approximately forty-five per cent of its area under the ownership of T. Wallace More and Abel C. Scull, and a small acreage deeded to son Juan prior to Hill's death.

Edmund Pew, a civil engineer, was engaged to handle the complicated task of subdividing the grant for distribution among the heirs. Commissioners appointed by the court to pass on Pew's judgment of equal shares were M. H. Biggs, a Santa Barbara business man; Abel C. Scull, of the Goleta Valley; and Charles Fernald, an ex-sheriff, county judge and now a busy attorney.

Less than two months after Hill's death, on March 10, 1865, the U.S. General Land Office issued the long-awaited final patent covering Rancho La Goleta; it had been authorized by President Lincoln a scant five weeks before he was assassinated. Rafaela had to wait another twelve years before her La Patera tract received a patent, inasmuch as it had been part of the Dos Pueblos grant which was not finally cleared until 1877.

The Civil War ended at Appomattox without attracting any more notice in the Goleta Valley than a cloud shadow flitting across the tideflats. A few Goleta Valley vaqueros had enlisted in Company C, First California Native Cavalry, a unique outfit in that it was the only one in the Union Army which spoke no English. Company C had seen no combat.

The termination of the struggle between the States would indirectly affect the Goleta Valley's future, however, for discharged soldiers in both blue and gray would be immigrating West and some of them—Pat Kinevan, Shelton Sturges, Salathiel Fast, Jacob Pensinger, C. A. Storke, John Pickett, and Ezra Catlett, to name but a few—would be settling on the Good Land.

Surveyor Pew toiled for months on the first subdivision map of the Goleta Valley. Meanwhile the widowed daughter of Daniel Hill, Rosa Den, was having money problems. During the three depressed years, 1862 through 1864, her total income from Dos Pueblos Ranch had been $2,844 from the sale of wool, sheep and hides; during the fiscal year from July 1864 to July 1865 her income dropped to a mere $551.

C. E. Huse, who had taken over the execution of Nicolás Den's will, arranged for the sale of the western half of the Cañada del Corral Rancho (which Den had purchased from the Ortegas) in 1866 to Orella & Hazard for $7,000 in gold, which temporarily eased the critical financial situation for the Den family. The hard times brought the eldest son, Manuel, back from the English university where he had matriculated in palmier days.

Rosa Den desperately needed someone to lean upon. On February 10, 1867, she startled the community by marrying her 41-year-old coachman, Greenlief C. Welch, of Vermont, who had been in the employ of the Dens since 1859. The nuptial mass took place at Santa Barbara Mission, with Fr. Jaime Villa officiating.

Doña Rosa, now plain Mrs. Welch, had gained a companion for her sunset years and a competent stepfather for her children, but whether Welch could save his wife's estate from going on the sheriff's auction block for unpaid taxes was extremely doubtful.

By year's end, engineer Edmund Pew had completed the subdivision map of Rancho La Goleta. It was approved by the commissioners and the various Hill heirs, and on February 1, 1868, was accepted by Probate Judge Maguire for use in the final distribution of the Hill Estate. This first subdivision map of Rancho La Goleta was relatively simple compared to the bewildering mosaic of home-

1868: Goleta Valley Subdividing Begins

site lots shown on maps of the same area today. The modern alignment of Hollister Avenue follows ranch lines laid out by Edmund Pew.

Pew had carefully jigsawed the Hill grant into 38 farmsteads ranging in size from 31 to 258 acres, all but one of which lay north of Hollister Avenue. The value of the farms varied on the quality of soil and lay of the land rather than on acreage, taking into account that level lowlands with deep, well-watered soil were worth more than rolling hills where the topsoil was thin and often non-arable, and fit for grazing purposes alone.

Later in February, Daniel Hill's children assembled in the adobe on La Patera Lane to choose their inheritances by drawing lots. When the drawing was over, each heir had land equal in value to his brothers and sisters. They were now on their own, insofar as disposing of their heritage; the minor heirs, of course, being under the protection of the court, just as the Den minors were.

Early in the spring of 1868, advertisements were placed in San Francisco and Los Angeles newspapers, announcing that small farm parcels were now available for $22 per acre in the Rancho La Goleta in Santa Barbara County. The reaction to these advertisements was immediate. Although many of the old Mexican land grants in California had changed to Yankee ownership as a result of the ruinous Drought of 1864, they were being held more or less intact for future speculation. Now, for the first time, an original Mexican grant was being split up into small farms.

Prospective buyers converged on the Goleta Valley from all directions, by stagecoach, steamship and on horseback. Many of the newcomers had been in California for a decade or longer; the time was yet early for an influx of discharged war veterans.

Among the earliest purchasers of farm lands from the Den heirs were Ira A. Martin, of New York; Edward Orr, of North Carolina, who located opposite today's Fairview School; J. O. Williams, who had come to California from Maine in 1853, and who bought eighteen acres a block north of Hollister on the Patterson Avenue-to-be; John Edwards, father of the noted banker, George S. Edwards; B. A. Hicks; and Randolph Baber.

(Not all of Goleta's 1868 pioneer settlers bought land from the Hill Estate, of course. Those who filed on foothill homesteads will be recounted in Chapter X.)

One of the most important newcomers was a prosperous Sonoma County nurseryman and capitalist named Richard K. Sexton. He had brought his wife and five children, one a babe in arms, by steamer from New York, across the malaria-infested Nicaraguan Isthmus by muleback, and by slow boat to San Francisco. This family from Cincinnati, Ohio, had first settled in San Francisco, later moving to Amador County, where the Drought of 1864 destroyed Sexton's entire nursery stock. He had recently relocated in Petaluma, when he read of La Goleta land sale in Santa Barbara County and decided to investigate.

Leaving his nursery in charge of two older sons, William and Joe, the elder Sexton journeyed to Santa Barbara by steamer. Within the hour of being rowed ashore in a surf boat he had been captivated by the Mediterranean charms of the somnolent tile-and-adobe ex-mission town, where Spanish was still the mother tongue of half its 3,000 inhabitants.

Richard Sexton bought three contiguous city blocks in the southwestern corner of Santa Barbara, the area bounded by West Montecito Street, Castillo Street, West Beach and the Mesa bluffs. Electing to make Santa Barbara his permanent residence, Sexton began construction of a two-story redwood house, which in 1966 still stood in excellent preservation at 229 Castillo Street.

While this was going on, Sexton took several horse and buggy trips on the Gaviota stage road to reconnoiter the Goleta Valley and Daniel Hill's ranch. Recognizing a fine opportunity to pick up prime agricultural land at a low figure, Sexton bought 100 level acres east of San Jose Creek, bounded on the south by the stage road and extending inland to where the railroad is today. He paid $2,200 to three Hill heirs, Ramon, Henry and Lucretia. A few months afterward, Lucretia Hill died at the age of 23. She was the twelfth of Rafaela's babies, and the fourth to die.

The largest block of land to be sold to a newcomer was a number of parcels totaling nearly 1,000 acres, the new owner being a land speculator from Geneva, New York, named J. D. Patterson. He secured title to land bounded on the west by San Jose Creek, running as far north as McCaffery's San Jose Vineyard, and extending eastward in places as far as Turnpike Road. He farmed much of his land until well into the 1880s, before selling off the parcels. An

1868: Goleta Valley Subdividing Begins

Englishman, Harry Langman, managed the farm for Patterson, and later purchased the 1875 ranch house which still stands at 5486 Calle Real, the home of Langman's daughter, Nellie, who was born under its roof in 1877.

The narrow, sandy lane which led to Patterson's ranch became known as Patterson Avenue as early as 1870, the name it bears today. Later the road was extended nearly two miles northward to La Goleta grant line, where it turned westward almost as far as Fairview Avenue, which came into existence in the year 1874, along the Dos Pueblos-La Goleta grant boundary.

Another outstanding personage among the 1868 pioneers lured to the Hill ranch by newspaper advertising was Isaac Giles Foster, a native of Plainfield, Illinois. Foster was a 'Forty-Niner who had ridden horseback to California in company with his father, I. G. Foster Sr., and brother, Vincent. The elder Foster remained in San Jose, where he eventually became a judge. Isaac Jr. returned to Illinois in 1853 to get his family, moving them West by covered wagon. In 1861 he settled at Half Moon Bay, where he was residing when he first read the announcement of the subdivision of Daniel Hill's rancho in the Goleta Valley.

The fame of the Good Land had already spread throughout the State, despite its relative isolation and transportation difficulties. I. G. Foster decided to pay Goleta a visit, doing so near the end of May, 1868. While sizing up various sites in the Valley, Foster heard where he could pick up a bargain. In February, a man named Andrew Anderson had purchased a choice 12-acre tract at what is now the northwest corner of Patterson and Hollister Avenues, paying Ramon Hill $500. Anderson was short of money, and would sacrifice the acreage now for $300, or $25 per acre.

Foster made a temporary financial arrangement with another newcomer, William Dewlaney, and on June 2 the two received a joint deed to Anderson's farm. Within five years it had become the nucleus of Goleta village. Six months later Foster bought Dewlaney's half interest for $200, Dewlaney moving westward to buy a 31-acre tract fronting on Fairview Avenue between Encina Road and Calle Real (these place names are modern, of course).

Foster returned to Half Moon Bay and sold out to a neighbor. In late July of 1868, he and his three sons, Eugene, Fred (who had been born in a covered wagon while crossing the Mormon territory of Deseret in '54) and Frank, loaded their household belongings into a Conestoga wagon and started south. Driving five milch cows and a team of work horses ahead of them, they took all of August and into September to reach the Goleta Valley by way of Gaviota Pass.

Waiting for them in Santa Barbara, at Dr. James Shaw's old American Hotel on lower State Street, were mother Roxanna Foster and 15-year-old daughter, Lucy, who had arrived ten days earlier by steamer.

Foster and his sons pitched tents under the spreading oaks where the University Medical Building now stands at 5370 Hollister Avenue. The whole Goleta Valley north of More's Ranch appeared to be a vast ocean of yellow mustard, the stalks higher than a man's head. Obviously it had never known the bite of a plowshare since the dawn of creation.

Next day the Fosters received a visitor—the Santa Barbaran who owned the 100 acres immediately to the west, Richard K. Sexton. Before the hour was out the Sextons and the Fosters had begun a lifelong friendship, soon to be cemented by intermarriage.

When Sexton learned that Foster intended to have Redwood City lumber shipped by schooner from San Francisco to build a house, he suggested that they go in together and buy an entire shipload, since every new arrival in the valley needed lumber for his own home. Foster agreed, with the result that a lumber schooner began discharging its entire cargo of siding, shingles and dimension timbers for the incoming tide to deposit on Goleta Beach. Waiting there to stack up the lumber before the surf could ruin it were ten Goleta Valley settlers with houses to build. The identities of these settlers have been lost, but it is known that ten homes were going up simultaneously in Goleta's first housing tract, that autumn of 1868. All were roofed in before the rains came.

Foster built a two-story, box-shaped, elaborately gingerbreaded frame house at what is now 5360 Hollister Avenue, facing south. Instead of adopting the simple design of California mission colonial architecture, with adobe walls and red tile roofs to blend with the Hispanic heritage of the Good Land, Foster fashioned his home along the austere lines of any midwestern rural house. The roof was

1868: Goleta Valley Subdividing Begins

pitched to shed snow (which never fell in this semiarid land); the eaves were wide to keep moisture from rotting the siding (where 17 inches of rainfall per year was the average).

The primitive method of floating lumber ashore on incoming tides would continue until John P. Stearns built his wharf in Santa Barbara in 1872, and T. Wallace More completed a landing at Goleta two years later. In the late 1860s, Captain Samuel Burtis, of the trading schooner *Restless*, employed a "chute landing" to get cargoes from shore to ship. This consisted of a chute anchored by cables to Shark Point, on the bluffs at the southeastern edge of what is now the UCSB campus. The chute extended seaward to an anchored barge. Grain, wine and other Valley products were skidded down this chute to the barge, which was then towed out to Burtis' schooner for transhipment below decks.

In retrospect, the Goleta Valley has been singularly free of major crimes, but two murders occurred that fall of 1868 in the vicinity of Patterson and Hollister Avenues. They were not listed in the haphazard records which the coroner kept in those days, but Lucy Foster Sexton makes a vague reference to the matter in her book *The Foster Family, California Pioneers of 1849*:

Shortly after coming to Goleta [the Fosters] were startled by a near neighbor being found killed, probably for money he was known to have had with him. Another miner with his gold, unknown to his new neighbors, was also killed. There was no evidence, and nothing was known of the murderers, but their suspicions [remained] unvoiced. The Fosters had been getting their water from the murdered man's well while their own well was being dug.

Unfortunately Mrs. Foster did not give the names of the Goleta Valley's first two murder victims, nor the dates of the tragedies.

Every settler dug a well, the depth ranging from ten to fifty feet, depending on the elevation of the ground. The Fosters struck water at a depth of thirty-two feet without hitting bedrock, testifying to the depth of Valley topsoil at that location. The well was lined with brick below the water line, and fieldstone above, with wooden curb and lid. The water was lifted by means of a primitive rope and bucket, windmills being still in the future.

Roxanna Foster early learned something which generations of

Goleta housewives were to learn after her: that the water in the Valley is exceedingly hard, defying the best of home-made soaps to lather, precipitating mineral sediments on pots and pans, and presumably in the inner tubes of human consumers.

In November, 1868, Richard Sexton was joined in Santa Barbara by his son, Joseph, who was destined to become one of the Goleta Valley's foremost citizens. He was a husky six-footer, 26 years old. Joe Sexton brought with him from Petaluma a load of nursery stock, including a 120-pound sack of assorted Persian walnuts imported from Chile. That sack of nuts held the key to the Goleta Valley's future walnut industry, a major activity until the mid-1950s.

Joe Sexton built himself a small board-and-batten shack at the corner of Montecito and Castillo streets, to live in while he established a nursery below the Mesa bluffs where Pershing Park is now located. His major task, that first winter in Santa Barbara, was setting out 1,000 walnut seedlings. Joe Sexton's green thumb made rival nurserymen's thumbs seem gangrenous by comparison, as he was soon to demonstrate, before Dan Cupid helped him move his nursery to the Goleta Valley.

Daniel Hill's heirs continued to prosper from the sale of their inheritance. But what of their cousins, the Dens of Dos Pueblos, whose birthright was hopelessly tied up by their late father's red tape? For Rosa Welch and her new husband, financial disaster was looming ever-nearer.

Only three of the Den children were old enough to receive their tenth share of Dos Pueblos land—Manuel, Kate, and Nicolás. Manuel owned 1,000 acres in Las Armitos (Winchester) Canyon. Between his south line and the beach lay the choice 519 acres of Bell Canyon, which sister Kate received. She did not live to see the discovery of the fabulous Ellwood Oil Field on this site in 1928. Nicolás C. Den received 655 acres in upper Tecolotito (Glen Annie) Canyon. The other brothers and sisters had to wait until each became twenty one, as dictated by their father's will.

The Dens looked with frustration and envy on the way their Hill cousins were subdividing La Goleta Rancho. The Dens by now were too impoverished to afford the cost of surveying their broad acres, even if the land had been available for sale.

As the shadow of the sheriff's auction gavel came closer and closer

1868: Goleta Valley Subdividing Begins

to the Den Estate, the administrator, Charles E. Huse, suddenly came up with a plan which electrified the family.

"You remember how eager Colonel W. W. Hollister was to buy Tecolotito Canyon at any price?" Huse said. "The Colonel is a millionaire now. I believe we could arrange to sell him Tecolotito Canyon, probably at an exorbitant figure. Hollister wanted that land so badly he could taste it."

The Dens had heard how Hollister had become a wealthy man, thanks to his sister's financial assistance, raising sheep on the San Justo grant in the San Benito Valley. Only a few months before, Hollister had sold his sheep ranch for nearly half a million dollars to a Homesteaders' Association which founded the town of Hollister on the Colonel's old home place.

In partnership with Albert and Thomas Dibblee, Hollister had been buying vast acreages in western Santa Barbara County from such empire builders as the More Brothers, who had gone broke as a result of the Drought of 1864. Hollister & Dibblee now owned the former Ortega rancho, Nuestra Señora del Refugio; the presidio's historic "kitchen ranch," San Julian; the Lompoc and Mission Viejo ranches; Las Cruces in Gaviota Canyon, and the Salsipuedes on the lower Santa Ynez River.

"Why do you tantalize me this way, Señor Huse?" Rosa Welch asked her attorney. "You know we aren't allowed to sell any of the Den Estate's trust property."

"If all the heirs agree to sell the Tecolotito, and all the trustees concur in the sale, then *why* couldn't we sell?" Huse argued. "Your late husband would certainly have agreed to such a sale, had he foreseen the Big Drought forcing his family to the verge of destitution. Mrs. Welch, may I have your permission to write Colonel Hollister and ask him to make an offer on the Tecolotito Canyon property? There could be no harm in at least soliciting such an offer."

When Rosa Welch gave her consent for Huse to write Hollister, she unwittingly set in motion a chain of events which are still having repercussions in Goleta Valley affairs nearly a century later.

CHAPTER IX

W. W. Hollister, Squire of Glen Annie

Huse's letter, with its startling offer to sell a portion of the Den Estate's trust property, reached Col. Hollister at the headquarters of his Lompoc Ranch. Within 24 hours an excited Col. Hollister presented himself at Huse's adobe home, a relic of the presidio days which blocked State Street from curb to curb between Canon Perdido and Carrillo Streets.

"You told me I could not buy Tecolotito Canyon until 1882, when the youngest Den heir came of age," Hollister said. "How can you ask me to make an offer now, thirteen years ahead of schedule?"

C. E. Huse had a pat answer well rehearsed.

"The Den Estate is about to be lost due to debt and delinquent taxes," Huse explained. "Mr. and Mrs. Welch are desperate for funds to feed, clothe and educate the children. The three heirs who are of legal age—Kate, Manuel and Nicolas—are willing to sell. The four trustees representing the minor heirs—Alfredo Robinson, Rosa Welch, Dr. Richard Den and myself—will also approve the sale, providing you make a satisfactory cash offer. Therefore, nothing stands in the way of all parties concerned getting what they want."

Hollister could hardly believe his ears. Shutting his mind to the fact that he would be buying his earthly Paradise with a slight cloud on the title, he made Huse and the Den Estate an offer so extravagant he knew it could not be rejected. Instead of the $1.30 an acre he had paid for hilly land elsewhere in the county, he offered the Dens $10 an acre for 5,000 acres bisected by Tecolotito Creek, between the east ridge of Ellwood Canyon and Carneros Creek. For depression times, this was an astronomical amount of money for canyon and foothill land.

Huse was flabbergasted; he had in his wildest dreams anticipated not more than $5 an acre for canyon property. Only cleared, level land on the floor of the valley was considered saleable.

Hollister went on eagerly, "This is the tenth of February. I would like to take immediate possession, before we even draw up the legal papers, so I can start my building program and set out nursery stock. You see, I intend to make a real showplace out of Glen Annie Ranch."

"Glen Annie?" echoed Huse.

"I plan to name my estate Glen Annie," Hollister said, "in honor of my wife, Annie James Hollister."

Thus was created one of the Good Land's proudest place names.

Huse set to work at once canvassing the other trustees. Alfred Robinson and Rosa Den were the first to approve the sale. From Los Angeles Dr. Richard Den wrote on February 24, 1869:

The sooner we close the deal, the better for all parties concerned. I consider a sale of a part of the Dos Pueblos, even though technically contrary to the expressed wishes of my late brother's will, to be indispensably requisite for paying the debts of the estate, and educating my nephews and nieces. . . . I prefer Colonel Hollister as a purchaser, feeling his presence in the Goleta Valley will greatly enhance the economy of that region.

Col. Hollister, taking for granted that the transaction was as good as closed, purchased a large adobe house at 110 West Carrillo Street in Santa Barbara for the temporary use of his family. In 1869, the family consisted of his wife and three children, Jennie, William, and Harry. He bought the house from Jose Lobero, a talented Italian musician who operated a tavern at State and Canon Perdido Streets.

During the month of March, 1869, Hollister placed orders for the immediate delivery of $80,000 worth of redwood lumber from Santa Cruz mills, farming machinery for large-scale operation from San Francisco, Los Angeles and Sacramento dealers, and nursery stock from as far away as the British West Indies. As Hollister had told Huse, he had every intention of converting Glen Annie Ranch into a horticulturist's showplace.

Surveyor W. H. Norway was hired to lay out the metes and bounds of the ranch (known since 1890 as the Bishop Ranch).

Hollister had two shiploads of lumber already at sea when, on April 2, a hitch developed. A pony express rider from Los Angeles, carrying special delivery mail to Santa Barbara, brought a letter from trustee Richard S. Den saying he could not sign the deed Huse had sent him until it bore the approval of the Santa Barbara County Probate Court.

Hollister was not perturbed. He had dabbled in politics enough to know that judges could be swayed, and Judge Francis Maguire was a personal friend of his. But Maguire rocked Col. Hollister back on his heels with a flat refusal to approve the Den Estate sale of Glen Annie. "If you make this purchase, you will do so in violation of the express conditions of the trust set up by Nicolás Den's will," Maguire warned Hollister. "My court cannot approve such a sale. If you buy, your title will be faulty. So proceed with caution."

Hollister's passionate desire to own Glen Annie blinded him to all possibility of future disaster. At the time there seemed to be no reason to worry. He had paid a fantastic price for foothill land, which was assessed at only ten cents an acre. The sellers were the only persons who conceivably could challenge his title to the ranch, and they were unanimously on his side. Indeed, the $50,000 Hollister would pay them would restore the Dens' standard of living from penury to the luxury they had grown accustomed to in the boom days before the Big Drought so drastically reduced their assets.

On April 7, a patient Colonel Hollister wrote to Dr. Richard Den, asking for a temporary agreement to tide him over until the technicalities could be ironed out. He continued:

> My great object is to get physical possession of the ranch as soon as possible, so as to facilitate my business for the planting season. I want the Glen Annie very much on account of my three little ones, who already feel the advantages of the Goleta Valley climate. I want to make it for my family . . . a general headquarters forever. I do not want one acre for speculation.
>
> So, my dear friend Dr. Den, just put me in a position to go ahead without fear of consequences—send me a "provisional deed" or bond for a deed—and I will consider the matter settled.

The prudent and conscientious Dr. Richard Den wrote back apologizing for being so cautious, explaining he was only doing his duty as a trustee for his nieces and nephews. He went on:

There is some divergence of opinion as to the *manner* in which this sale is to be consummated, but as all are in agreement on the main points, feel free to take physical possession of the ranch at once. Go to the expense and trouble necessary to carry out your plans for this first summer. Pay over the monies so the debts of the Den family can be settled, and their children educated. Whatever becomes necessary to complete the transfer according to law can be done later. I don't wish you to lose one moment on my account. . . . Begin to fence in your land as you wish.

Thus reassured, Col. Hollister ordered the lumber schooners to discharge their cargo into the ocean off Las Armas (Ellwood) beach, where his teamsters were waiting with heavy wagons to haul the building materials to the site Annie Hollister had chosen for her baronial mansion overlooking the Goleta Valley.

The Hollister ranch headquarters were located on a level terrace at the base of a rounded foothill midway between Carneros and Tecolotito Creeks, half a mile north of the county road. (The site is now called Corona del Mar, meaning "crown of the sea," and is located immediately east of El Encanto Heights subdivision.)

Hollister was California's leading proponent of Trespass Laws which would oblige a big rancher to fence his land so as to prevent his livestock from destroying a neighbor's crops. Without such legislation, he knew California would never be a farming state. Putting into practice what he preached, Hollister proceeded to fence his 5,000 acres, the first fencing to be seen in the Goleta Valley.

Hollister's fences were five boards high, with four by six redwood posts set eight feet apart around the six-mile perimeter of the Glen Annie estate.

Nursery stock began arriving by ship and was lightered ashore to the new short wharf at the foot of Chapala Street. Former State Governor John G. Downey of Los Angeles supplied 3,000 English walnut trees between three and four years old for 23 cents each, enabling Col. Hollister to establish the Goleta Valley's first large walnut grove. A factory in San Leandro shipped a fleet of gang plows, symbol of a new technology in farming the Glen Annie, where the virgin sod had never been broken by a plowshare.

The Colonel's father-in-law, Samuel Levis James, a former Vigilanteman in San Francisco, was a carpenter by trade. To James went the assignment of planning and building the Hollister manorhouse, two stories, sixty by 100 feet in size, with twenty-nine rooms.

Before he got the foundations ready, Sam James was having trouble finding labor, just as T. Wallace More had found in 1860 when he contracted to build a county road. Local *paisanos* were utterly incompetent, and the available Yankees in Santa Barbara were what Hollister termed "bummers," many of them veterans of Stevenson's New York Regiment, who were even more slothful than the laziest Indian.

Finally, in utter disgust, Col. Hollister boarded the coastal sidewheeler *Orizaba* for San Francisco, where the manpower pool was swarming with coolies fresh from China, lured by the railroad which the Big Four of Huntington, Stanford, Crocker and Hopkins was building over the Sierra Nevadas. Hollister, who for the rest of his life would be a vigorous exponent of Chinese labor, returned to Santa Barbara with 30 pigtailed coolies whom he installed on the Glen Annie to do everything from housework to field work, at a fraction of the wages an American would demand.

Colonel Hollister was sharply criticized for his espousal of cheap Chinese labor in California. A coolie would work for practically nothing so long as Hollister catered to their Oriental palates and kept them supplied with sweet rice crackers, bamboo sprouts, cuttlefish, dried oysters, abalone, tea, rice, salted cabbage, vermicelli and poultry.

Hollister's influence in high places extended to the White House in Washington. He and President Rutherford B. Hayes had been classmates at Kenyon College in Gambier, Ohio, and Hollister appealed to old school loyalties to persuade Hayes to veto anti-Chinese legislation when it reached his desk.

Sam James and his carpenters finally began to show some progress on the new Hollister home. The roof was finished on May 10, 1869, which was a red-letter day elsewhere in American history: the driving of the Golden Spike at Promontory, Utah, to span the continent with its first railroad. This opened the gates to Westward immigration, and would have a bearing on the future settlement of the Goleta Valley.

Sam James made no attempt to design the Hollister mansion to fit its California setting. Just as I. G. Foster had done a few months previously, he copied the midwestern American style of rural architecture, with steep roofs and wide eaves.

Outwardly unpretentious, the interior of the Hollister home was considered palatial for the times. Annie went to "the City," as San Francisco was universally called, and bought a whole housefull of drapes, carpets, furniture, iron stoves, bedding, linens, chinaware, a grand piano, garden ornaments and other status symbols of the era.

Hollister, the gentleman farmer, busied himself with his ranching. Forty- and eighty-acre squares of the flat bottomland in upper Glen Annie Canyon began to take on a chocolate-brown tone as the new gang plows cultivated the virgin soil. Here Hollister planted 10,000 Languedoc almond trees, one year old, obtained from a nursery in San Jose. This gave the Goleta Valley the distinction of having the largest almond orchard in America, if not the world. Unhappily this experiment ended in failure within a few years.

Elaborate ornamental landscaping began to give the Hollister home grounds the look of the showplace it was destined to be. A serpentine avenue bordered by cypress and pines was laid out to the county road, later named Hollister Avenue in the Colonel's honor. At the ranch entrance an ornate white archway was built. It was equipped with trundle gates, powered by an ingenious counterweight which was raised or lowered in a 30-foot dry well, so that the driver of a vehicle could open or close the gates without getting down from his seat. The white archway stood until 1962, when it was moved to the Howard Goldman ranch, at 570 Glen Annie Road.* Its original redwood had been restored several times.

On his seventh wedding anniversary, June 1, 1869, Hollister moved his family from Lobero's adobe in Santa Barbara to what he was to call the "Lower Ranch." Moving in with Annie and the Colonel were Sam and Jane James, Annie's parents; a large staff of Chinese house servants; and the Colonel's aggressive, ultra-competent sister and business associate, Auntie Brown. Her august pres-

---

* Around the turn of the century Hollister's avenue of cypress and pines was replaced with palm trees which a developer would transplant, out of season and with dubious success, along the north side of Hollister Avenue bordering his industrial park. This was the Avenue of Palms which author Stewart Edward White featured in *The Rose Dawn*, a fictional account of Col. Hollister's life on the Glen Annie Ranch.

ence in Annie's household caused frictions which grew steadily worse as Auntie Brown took almost complete command.

Before the summer of 1869 had waned, the landscaping in front of the mansion, some of it still in existence nearly a century later, began to take form. Sparing no expense, Hollister imported all manner of exotic flora—weeping acacias, arborvitae and gingko from China, Moreton Bay figs from Australia, now grown to huge proportions; Abyssinian bananas and rare fernleaf beeches. He planted buckeyes to remind him of his Ohio boyhood, a bird of paradise tree, Korean cinnamon, deodar cedars from the Tibetan Himalayas, cork oaks, Eugenia hedges, California redwoods, Oregon myrtle and Washington firs. Anything from coffee to conifers, it seemed, thrived on the Good Land of the Goleta Valley.

Some 4,000 assorted grapevines were set out on the side hills, along with 500 limes and 1,000 Sicilian olive trees. The vaunted almond orchard was finally taken out in favor of lemon trees, the aromatic almondwood being touted as fuel for the 90 fireplaces of the Hotel Arlington in Santa Barbara, which was a Hollister project of later years.

The first élite social event of many to follow on Glen Annie Ranch was the wedding, on Valentine's Day, 1870, of the Colonel's niece, Mary Hollister, to Gen. Phineas Banning of Maine. He was noted as the developer of the great Port of Wilmington and was considered to be the "railroad king" of Los Angeles.

While the Colonel lavished a great deal of money on his new ranch home, one of the most spectacular sights at the Lower Ranch was the huge Octagonal Carriage House with archways facing the cardinal points of the compass. This building was so big Annie later gave grand balls inside it; it remained a Valley landmark until destroyed by fire in 1929.

Hollister was also responsible for the Americanization of Santa Barbara to a major degree. His first big project was the establishment of Santa Barbara College, incorporated for $100,000 in 1869. Other directors included T. Wallace More; lumberman John P. Stearns, who would build Stearns Wharf with Hollister money in another couple of years; lawyer Charles E. Huse; and newspaperman George P. Tebbetts.

Although known as a "college," the institution was actually a boarding school from kindergarten through twelfth grade. It was located in an impressive $40,000, three-story, mansard-roofed brick building at State and Anapamu Streets, now the site of the San Marcos Building.

Later that spring of 1870, the Colonel and Auntie Brown were visited by their older brother, Albert G. Hollister, who had owned a prosperous flour-milling business on the Nodaway River in Holt County, northwestern Missouri. Because he supplied flour to the Union forces during the Civil War, Hollister's mill was twice burned down by guerrilla raiders from Kansas and Nebraska.

Discouraged and in failing health, Albert came west on the newly-opened overland railway to see for himself the fabulous Goleta Valley, which his younger brother had described as a veritable Garden of Eden. Also influencing Albert to come west was the fact that the new college was opening in Santa Barbara, and his 19-year-old son, Edgar Hollister, was in need of completing his education.

Albert was enchanted with the Good Land the first moment he laid eyes upon it. He eventually purchased 480 acres of choice land which became the famous Fairview Ranch, as will be described later.

When Col. Hollister was living on the San Justo sheep ranch in Monterey County, he had employed a private family doctor in his early twenties, Robert Fulton Winchester. In 1870, the Colonel prevailed upon Dr. Winchester to join him as a neighbor, helping him buy 1,040 acres from Manuel Den in the second canyon west of Glen Annie. The doctor paid $8,250 for the lovely sylvan glade known today, in his memory, as Winchester Canyon. The even larger defile between Winchester and Glen Annie Canyons, then called Las Armitas Arroyo, but now known as Ellwood Canyon, was named for Ellwood Cooper, another friend whom Hollister brought to the Goleta Valley in 1870, as will be detailed in a later chapter.

Outwardly, things were going well for Col. Hollister's ego as well as his pocketbook. But behind the scenes, the domestic situation was far from tranquil. Annie, the Colonel's lady, was a spoiled, headstrong and hot-tempered young woman. She had been at dagger's points with her autocratic sister-in-law, Auntie Brown, from the day she and the Colonel had been joined in holy matrimony by the Rev. Thomas Starr King in 1862. Back in Ohio, the Hollisters had considered themselves of the aristocracy. The James family was bourgeois even by the rude standards of San Francisco's post-Gold Rush society, or so Auntie Brown expressed herself on occasion. In other words, Auntie Brown felt the Colonel had married beneath himself, and Annie sensed this.

In the closing weeks of the summer of 1870, therefore, Annie gave her husband an ultimatum: he had to choose immediately between his sister and his wife. Large as it was, Glen Annie's castle was not roomy enough to hold a pair of queens.

Colonel Hollister was taken aback. He tried to reason with Annie, reminding her that it was impossible to send Auntie Brown away when it had been her money which had set him up in the sheep business in Ohio back in 1853. It had been Auntie Brown's $12,000 which had enabled Hollister to buy half of the San Justo land grant in Monterey County in partnership with Flint & Bixby. In all the intervening years, not one penny of those loans had been repaid; Auntie Brown's share of the profits of their sheep business had been plowed back into the partnership, including the vast acreage of land acquired with the Dibblee Brothers in Santa Barbara County.

"In other words, dear," Colonel Hollister told his tight-lipped spouse, "Auntie Brown is as much owner of this house as I am."

Annie, pregnant for the fourth time, was adamant. "Either she goes or I go!" Annie proclaimed angrily.

In desperation, Colonel Hollister set about to effect a compromise whereby both his rock-willed sister and his headstrong wife would be mollified. The solution he finally came up with was an expensive one, costing him over $100,000. It involved the duplication of the Lower Ranch complex at the head of Glen Annie Canyon, for his and Annie's personal use, while Auntie Brown would continue to to rule the roost at the Lower Ranch.

Once again, hastily-summoned coastal schooners anchored off Las Armas beach and discharged cargoes of redwood lumber into the sea. The dusty Glen Annie Canyon road was churned by the wheels of Hollister's heavy draft wagons, hauling lumber to Annie's new manorhouse. Grandpa James and his carpenters toiled from dawn to dusk on a seven-day-a-week schedule, hoping to have the new mansion ready to move into before the birth of Annie's fourth baby, due in December.

While she was still able to travel, Annie Hollister took ship for the City and spent $30,000 in three hectic shopping days on furnishings for her new home, including such frills as stained glass windows, imported statuary, a pipe organ, and a silver service for entertaining up to 50 persons on a royal scale.

But no matter how many carpenters and stone masons Grandpa James put on the job, he could not finish the new Glen Annie mansion before Dr. Winchester delivered his fourth grandchild. This event took place on December 7, 1870. The infant was christened John James Hollister. Ahead stretched a long and fruitful life which would see Jim Hollister elected to the State Senate, become one of the county's most prominent cattlemen, founder of the local Farm Bureau, and *pater familias* of the Colonel's numerous descendants before he died in 1962 at the age of 92.

Colonel Hollister's experiments in horticulture, which were to make his Goleta Valley ranch renowned throughout the country, included such exotic tropical crops as bananas, coffee, tea, and dates. His date palm grove, located at the extreme northern end of Glen Annie Canyon road, was a commercial success. Fifty thousand tea plants, imported from Japan along with two Japanese tea gardeners, flourished until a sudden frost killed them overnight, ending that experiment. The bananas and coffee beans did well as ornamentals, but produced inferior crops. The Colonel had to admit that even Goleta, the Good Land, *did* have a few limitations in what it could produce.

As soon as Annie moved into the new mansion in upper Glen Annie Canyon, the domestic atmosphere cleared. Auntie Brown was happy bossing things at the Lower Ranch. Annie was free to give extravagant parties for Santa Barbara's social élite on the barbered lawns of her rural estate, or grand balls in the Octagonal Carriage House at the Lower Ranch.

Grandpa Sam James was promoted to general superintendent of the ranch. His shrewish wife, Jane, a religious fanatic, decided to leave Sam, which she did to the relief of everyone concerned. George Coffin, later a mayor of Santa Barbara, became business secretary to the Colonel. A private tutor joined the governess at Glen Annie to educate the Hollister children, in a 14 by 14 foot schoolhouse which is in use as a foreman's cottage today.

Hollister had many irons in the fire outside the Goleta Valley. He was the prime promoter of the 90-room Arlington Hotel in Santa Barbara in 1875, a $100,000 property which became his, as majority stockholder, when it went into receivership. The same fate befell the Santa Barbara College at State and Anapamu; Hollister converted it into a commercial hotel named the Ellwood, after his friend Ellwood Cooper of the Goleta Valley.

The Colonel took the lead for many years in promoting a railroad for Santa Barbara. His money subsidized Jose Lobero in building Southern California's first opera house at Canon Perdido and Anacapa Streets, which also reverted to Hollister's ownership when the Italian impresario failed to keep up his mortgage payments.

Hollister loaned Stearns $40,000 to build his wharf in 1872, one asset he failed to foreclose in the long run. It was Hollister who owned the Santa Barbara *Morning Press*, and imported the great Harrison Gray Otis from Ohio to edit it; Otis went on to publish the Los Angeles *Times*.

In association with his partners, Albert and Tom Dibblee, Hollister also launched the temperance colony and homesteader's association at Lompoc, and built the important wharf at Gaviota.

While all these activities kept the Colonel busy, he also had time to charm the fair sex. As popular as he was with rank and file Barbareños, the Colonel could not escape being tarred by the black brush of gossip. Snide jokes were made about the curvaceous female "managers" he imported to run his various business enterprises in town. One lady in particular, Mrs. Josephine Walcott, a poetess, amateur spiritualist medium, singer and actress, was linked romantically with the Colonel by many scandalmongers. Her husband, John Walcott, was a highly-respected Santa Barbara grocer.

Finally gossip about *la belle* Josephine became so prevalent it reached the ears of the Colonel's father-in-law, Sam James, who ventured to suggest that Hollister might forego Mrs. Walcott's company in future, because the gossip was making wife Annie seek solace in alcohol at an alarmingly accelerated rate.

Hollister took offense at this well-meant paternal advice. He fired Sam James as his ranch superintendent, warning him never to set foot on Glen Annie as long as the Colonel lived—an order James obeyed to the letter.

Shortly after this crisis, Mrs. Walcott decamped to Berkeley. A few months later, Santa Barbara buzzed to the news that she had given birth to a daughter whom she christened "Queenie."

The fact that Mr. Walcott remained behind in Santa Barbara, and that Josephine was never seen there again, elevated many a Victorian eyebrow. Before 10 years had passed, the name of Queenie Walcott would titillate the gossipers again, as we will shortly see.

... On January 15, 1876, the Den Estate deeded 1,000 acres in Tecolote Canyon, immediately west of Winchester Canyon, to Major Shelton Sturges of Zanesville, Ohio. Sturges was distantly related to Col. Hollister, and had come to the Goleta Valley to purchase land at the Colonel's recommendation.

Within a year Tecolote Canyon, then as now one of the most beautiful sylvan properties in California, became a full-scale cattle-ranching operation under the management of Major Sturges' three sons, William, Harold and Shelton Jr.

The Sturges Brothers' enterprise in Tecolote Canyon was fated to have a tragic *denouement*—a tragedy in which W. W. Hollister would also be intimately involved. But in January, 1876, there was no hint that the shadow of disaster would shortly becloud the tranquil reaches of the Good Land.

CHAPTER X

Homesteading in the Goleta Foothills

In 1862, Congress enacted the National Homestead Act, which opened the Western Territories to settlement on free land.

In 1865, the Civil War ended, to release thousands of combat veterans eager to start their lives anew on a fresh frontier.

In 1869, the overland railway was completed, ending the era of the covered wagon trains and bringing New York within ten days of San Francisco.

These three distant and related historical events helped shape the future development of the Goleta Valley.

Millions of acres of public land were available for homesteading in California alone, but it was land left over after the *rancheros* of the Mexican era had taken their pick of the best areas. In Santa Barbara County, the only free space left outside the forty-odd land grants was the sandy desert of the Santa Maria Valley, the rugged mountain hinterland, and the Santa Barbara Pueblo Lands.

In the Goleta Valley, two relatively small Mexican grants, Los Dos Pueblos and La Goleta, had taken the choicest open agricultural land into private ownership, a generation before the National Homestead Act had been conceived. However, Goleta's sprawling, rounded foothills, and the steeper slopes above them, contained hundreds of acres of arable soil in a frost-free zone where berries, vegetables and oranges grew even more prolifically than on the floor of the Valley proper.

History has almost forgotten the name of the first homesteader to file on 160 acres of free land in the Goleta foothills. It was Francis D. Havens; he was born in 1831 in Weedsport, New York, and came

West in the early Fifties to engage in gold mining near Coloma. His health being too frail for such labor, he moved to San Francisco, where he took part in the Vigilante movement. He brought his wife and four children, Adelaide, Alice, Mary Emily and Francis Jr. to the Goleta Valley in 1867, and picked out his homestead in about the most inaccessible spot imaginable—the dead end of Maria Ygnacia Canyon's east fork. His 160 acres were not in the form of the usual quarter section, but a rectangle extending westward over the ridge to embrace Maria Ygnacia Creek, a stream originating in springs below Painted Cave, behind the eastern rampart of San Marcos Pass. This gave Havens riparian rights upstream from his neighbors on the Indian Orchard ranch, and was to involve him in many water disputes with the Ygnacia family.

Havens built the cabin required by homestead regulations, in the shelter of giant oaks which are still growing on the George W. Smith property, 1743 San Marcos Pass Road. Nearby was a sheer sandstone cliff down which a lacy waterfall sluiced in early days. Havens, a romantic man, named his hideaway "Ceanothus Hills."

Noting how well the mission padres' orange trees, planted in the 1830s, had flourished on the sunset side of the ridge to the west— the famous Indian Orchard, portions of which still exist—Havens set out oranges on his own. They thrived. He also planted the Goleta Valley's first commercial berry patch.

Not being overly fond of toil, Havens turned the farm over to his wife and children while he engaged in a most unusual occupation in Santa Barbara—running a detective agency, of all things, known as the Bureau of Intelligence.

Life on the Havens homestead was certainly rustic, and ofter arduous. A more isolated homesite could scarcely be imagined. Steep mountainsides towered on all sides, shutting out the sky. The arroyo was subject to scorching heat in summer and frosty nights in winter, extremes unknown on the floor of the Valley where gentle sea breezes tempered the climate all year round. Havens' homestead was also vulnerable to the recurring hazards of fire and flood. He had to rebuild his frame shack three times due to brush fires gutting the canyon during his lifetime. (The place missed destruction by the narrowest of margins in both the Refugio Fire of 1955 and the Coyote Fire of 1964.) At the opposite extreme, cloudbursts often sent gully-washing avalanches of water down the canyon, tumbling giant boulders through their front yard and uprooting orchards.

There were other frontier hazards. One night when Havens was returning home on horseback with a sack of groceries tied to his saddle, a pack of ravenous coyotes caught his scent and forced him to jettison a side of bacon to keep them at bay. In after years, when Adelaide Havens rode her pony to Goleta to attend church, she sat in her pew with a Colt revolver strapped to her waist, for protection from varmints encountered on her ride down the gulch.

A true tale of buried treasure has its setting on the Havens homestead. Addie, the oldest daughter, was subject to sleep-walking. One night she dreamed that bandits were going to steal the family's savings, which were kept in a buckskin poke under a loose brick in the hearth. Addie got out of bed, took the bag of gold and silver from its hiding place, and in her somnambulistic state, groped her way out into the night.

When Addie awakened she was a considerable distance up the canyon, carrying a treasure pouch which was empty. Had she hidden the contents in some hollow tree, in a crack of a boulder, or at the bottom of a trout pool? No one ever solved the riddle, although members of the Havens family, including Addie herself, tried for years to retrace her nocturnal wanderings. This practice was given up one winter afternoon when Mrs. Havens, out looking for Addie's cache, saw her dog torn to pieces before her eyes by a mountain lion. According to Havens' granddaughter, Mrs. Oliver Wilson of Santa Barbara, her aunt's lost treasure may still be there.

. . . The two most prominent names associated with Goleta's homestead era in the fringe of foothills between Fairview Avenue and San Jose Creek are those of two friends from Missouri, Ezra Catlett and William Thomas Lillard, Sr.

Tom Lillard was born in 1839 in Williamsburg, Missouri, and first came west by ox-drawn prairie schooner in 1859, taking the Oregon Trail to the Pacific Northwest. After dabbling unsuccessfully in mining for a few years, Lillard turned to packing supplies to the miners, and made a comfortable stake for himself. Ten years later he returned to his native Missouri, with the hope of talking an old boyhood friend, Ezra Catlett, into moving West with him.

Catlett, born in Texas in 1843, fought with the Confederate Army throughout the war. After Lee's surrender, Catlett returned home

Homesteading in the Goleta Foothills

to run the Missouri plantation for his widowed mother and help rehabilitate their freed slaves. This filial obligation took four years to fulfill, leaving Catlett free for other adventures when, early in the spring of 1869, young Tom Lillard returned from the wild West with his glowing tales of frontier opportunity.

Lillard convinced Catlett that the Pacific Coast was the place to make a fortune. Since the overland railroad was not quite completed, the two Missourians went to New York, caught a steamer for Aspinwall, walked across the Isthmus of Panama, and boarded another steamer for San Francisco.

Being from the Show-Me State, Lillard and Catlett decided to tour California and settle wherever they found the best location. The fame of the Santa Barbara Channel coast had reached Missouri, prompting the two bachelors to sail for Santa Barbara on the packet *Orizaba*.

They first explored the lush Carpinteria Valley, then the bosques of El Montecito. They probed into the Mission Canyon and San Marcos Pass areas, and finally emerged onto the verdant Goleta Valley. Like so many others before and after them, Lillard and Catlett knew immediately they wanted to spend the rest of their lives on the Good Land.

Neither of them could afford the high prices which the heirs of Daniel Hill were getting for their La Goleta subdivision; so Lillard and Catlett went outside the Mexican grant line into the foothills and bought cheap, but fertile land, in a broad, unnamed canyon between San Pedro and San Jose creeks. They also filed on contiguous homesteads higher up the mountain, giving them a total of around 1,000 acres. The ranch area now embraces the Rancho del Ciervo ("Ranch of the Stag"), and the arroyo, which Catlett used to call Los Alisos or Sycamore Canyon, has been known since 1900 as Catlett Canyon. Frémont's Battalion used it as an exit from the mountains in December, 1846, as did stagecoaches from 1869 to 1892.

The two Missourians built separate shacks to validate their respective homestead claims. Lillard's was at what is now the corner of Camino Meleno and North Patterson Avenue, and serves as a tract sales office. Catlett's cabin was half a mile farther up the canyon.

Both men earned money that first winter by chopping down oak trees, paying Indians and Mexicans to buck the wood into stove lengths for $2.50 a cord, and hauling it to Santa Barbara for sale at $8 a cord. Catlett, on his return trips to the Valley, often had a payload of supplies for the Chinese workmen at the old whaling camp which was operating at the west end of the Goleta Sandspit.

Further to the west, at the upper end of Fairview Avenue where Holiday Hill is now situated, a Virginian named B. A. Hicks owned a small ranch. He had a comely 15-year-old daughter named Eliza, whose charms caught Lillard's attention. When she turned eighteen in 1872, he married her.

The Lillards' first child was a son, Jeremiah, who was to graduate from Stanford University and become president of the Sacramento Junior College. Jeremiah was followed at approximately yearly intervals by a succession of sisters: Mary, who married a future Santa Barbara postmaster, George "Ed" Sawyers, who later bought the northern quarter-section of the Lillard ranch where Slippery Rock is located; Ella, who became a teacher and later married Irving Cole; Hattie, who married Henry Shepard, a leading citizen of Carpinteria; Rebecca, now Mrs. Otto Hilmer, of Sunland; and Lena, the widow of William Blair of Ventura.

This tendency toward female offspring was frustrating to Lillard, who needed strong sons to plow and plant and herd cattle. In 1884 he said to his wife, Eliza, "By grannies, we'll keep tryin' till we ketch us another boy, and then we'll call 'er quits."

Some nine months later a bouncing heir male, William Jr., answered Lillard's prayers. The family *menage* stopped right there. Billy Lillard was destined to make some history himself as Goleta's colorful country judge from 1932 to 1956. He was born on the old Lillard place at 1134 North Patterson Avenue, the aforementioned tract sales office.

Although his partner had "got hisself hitched in double harness," Ezra Catlett went on enjoying the celibate life of a bachelor at his canyon home. His favorite source of fresh meat was a "quail tree" near his shack, the selfsame oak where Frémont had camped the stormy Christmas night of 1846. All Catlett had to do was fire a shotgun into the tree at random, and then gather up enough quail to feed himself, with plenty left over for the growing Lillard family down the road a piece. (The tree is still a favorite roosting place for wildfowl.)

Homesteading in the Goleta Foothills

In the spring of 1872, the good folk of the Goleta Valley, still rather sparse in number, decided to stage a community picnic on the Sandspit so that neighbors could get better acquainted. A passle of people turned out—the Fosters and Sextons and McCafferys, the Sculls and Hicks and Mores, the Turners and Tuckers and Hills, the Williamses and Dens and Smiths. Everyone, in fact, except bachelor Ezra Catlett, who was so busy grubbing out brush in the back hills he hadn't heard about the lowlanders' clambake and fish fry.

Among the picnickers present was a colorful character known as "Uncle Ben" Owen, who had come to the Goleta Valley in 1863 with Abel C. Scull. Owen, by his own admission, was a mighty hunter and a champion raconteur. He regaled three generations of Goletans with his tall tales about his prowess as a deerstalker, b'ar wrassler and duck hunter.

One example from his repertoire must suffice: Uncle Ben was hunting wild ducks on La Patera pond, northwest of today's lemon packing house. "Reckon my gunsights was a mite faulty," Uncle Ben recounted, "because a big flock of geese flew over and I blasted 'em with both bar'ls, an' be dogged ifn the buckshot didn't fly so low all I got home with was a gunnysack full of goose feet."

Anyway, at the big beach picnic of '72, Uncle Ben made the acquaintance of a newly-arrived family of homesteaders, Myron and Elizabeth Parks Smith, of Iowa. Their place was in a remote gulch forking off San Pedro Creek, still called Smith's Canyon, above the Stow Ranch. The Smiths had a lovely daughter named Annette.

Uncle Ben Owen wasn't interested for himself, you understand, but he forked his saddle bronc and lit a shuck for the mountings to fetch back the lonesomest bachelor in them thar hills, Ezra Catlett. This account of what happened is vouched for by Catlett's daughter, Ida, who celebrated her ninety-second birthday in 1965:

"Ezry," Uncle Ben greeted the Confederate veteran, "the Good Book allows that man warn't meant to live alone. You had ort to pick yoreself a wife, same as yore pardner Tom Lillard went an' done. How about it?"

Catlett grinned through his brindle whiskers. "Single women ain't exactly as thick as ticks on a bull's tail in these parts, Uncle Ben," he allowed, "but tell you what. You find me a woman, an' I might try sparkin' her for a spell."

"Already picked her out," said the Goleta matchmaker. "Filly name of Annette Smith. Lives 'tother side of the ridge yander, west of you. Good looker. Past her gigglin' days, I reckon. She'd make you a mighty fine wife, Ezry. Think it over."

A few days later Catlett accidentally strayed into the neighborhood of Smith Canyon—at mealtime. Annette, who more than lived up to Uncle Ben's glowing description, invited Catlett to come in and set a spell, have a sasser of coffee and some vittles.

Ezra Catlett and Annette Smith were married inside the year.

Their first-born was the aforementioned daughter, Ida, who is the widow of Clarence L. Chamberlain. Other Catlett children were Otis E., Jessie E. (Mrs. Elmer Kellogg), Leonora C. (Mrs. Jerome B. Roberts), Earl L., and Nina M., who married a cousin from the East, E. M. Catlett.

The Lillard-Catlett partnership was amicably dissolved in 1889, when Catlett bought out most of Lillard's holdings. The Lillards moved a short distance west, and built a new home in the middle of what is now the intersection of Camino Mandero and Camino Galatea. The Catletts, having outgrown Ezra's humble shanty up the canyon, moved into the Lillard's roomy two-story house.

Ezra and Annette died in 1921, each aged 78, and were laid to rest in the Goleta cemetery.

Tom Lillard lost his wife in June 1890. He was a lonesome man, and after four years sold his remaining Goleta land to an Italian emigrant, Antonio Pagliotti, and moved to Los Angeles. Later he returned to Goleta to live with his son, Billy, who was farming the Pinkham ranch on North Patterson Avenue. Tom Lillard passed away in 1932, at the age of 93, at the Lillard home on Chapel Street, next door to the Federated Church.

Courthouse records list innumerable expired timber and mineral claims in the Goleta foothill area, including coal claims. F. E. Bartlett in 1873 homesteaded the beautiful glade now called Bartlett Canyon, northeast of the Bishop Ranch; it became a beekeeping center.

Several important pioneer families were clustered in the Maria Ygnacia district. Philip C. Marble owned a walnut orchard in the northeastern corner of Daniel Hill's La Goleta grant. In 1897 he married Mrs. Mary Hails, the widow of a nearby farmer, who had come to Goleta in 1873 from Iowa.

Neighboring Marble on the north was homesteader Jacob Pensinger, a Union Army veteran from Pennsylvania. He married a neighbor girl, Hattie Glass, in 1877. Their children were George, Jennie (Mrs. Robert Rowe), and Christina (Mrs. Ed McCaffery). John Glass, who homesteaded in the canyon below the Havens ranch, came from Missouri in 1852. Glass sold a large acreage on San Antonio Creek, in the hills north of the General Hospital, to John Pickett.

Patrick Farren and his sons Mike, Ed and Bill were among the most widely-known and beloved homesteaders of early days. They settled above Eagle Canyon, along with J. N. Hiller. Above Winchester canyon were the homesteads of Carsten Wade and Luther Ackerman.

James McCaffery who had grown up on his father's San Jose Vineyard, filed on a quarter section nearer the mountains, and raised walnuts for many years. He married Bridgit Finneran, who had been carried through the surf at Gaviota to be a nursemaid for Tom Dibblee's children on the San Julian Rancho. Their sons, Ed, Bill and Hugh, were born in San Jose Canyon. Bridgit's father, Mike Finneran, was an *opera bouffe* character who enlivened life on San Marcos Pass with his long-running vendetta against fellow Irishman Pat Kinevan, a feud which included burning each other's haystacks and cutting fence wires.

During the summer of 1886, the Havens homestead was the locale of the first manhunt in Goleta Valley's history. The fugitive was a halfbreed named Antone Martinez, who had worked for Ezra Catlett for years. He lived in a tumble-down adobe tannery across San Jose Creek from McCaffery, the Martinez Adobe.

Antone's brother was murdered under circumstances lost to the record. To drown his grief, the usually temperate *mestizo* got drunk. On the dirt road which the Catlett children used in getting to Cathedral Oaks School, Antone encountered Leonora Catlett, aged 12, and started chasing her. The timely appearance of Mrs. Catlett saved the child from molestation, although Mrs. Catlett always insisted the kindly Antone would never have harmed her daughter.

Antone showed up next at the Havens homestead. He was toting his hunting rifle, as he often did. He found the Havens children shooting at a tin can target near the house. Perhaps Antone Martinez' alcohol-befuddled brain conceived the idea that young Francis Havens was the slayer of his brother. At any rate, he knelt and drew a shaky bead on the boy. Before he could fire, Francis' sister, Alice, flung herself in front of the rifle, the bullet creasing her neck. Antone, overcome with horror, fled into the brush in the direction of San Marcos Pass.

Alice's wound was superficial, but it stirred up a frenzied manhunt. For three days and nights every able-bodied man in the Goleta Valley joined a sheriff's posse in combing the wilderness between Havens' Ranch and the Pass. They found no trace of the fugitive Indian.

Finally, on a hunch, Antone's stepfather went back to the adobe in San Jose Canyon where Antone lived. There he found his stepson lying dead on his cot, a suicide. It was Antone's way of purging his soul of the guilt of a murder he thought he had committed while under the influence of alcohol.

Alice lived to a ripe old age, but for the rest of her days she wore choker collars to hide the ugly red track of Antone's rifle slug across her neck—her memento of wild west adventure during the homestead era in the Goleta foothills.

More's Landing, built in 1874, made a seaport out of Goleta for 30 years

"Slippery Rock," showing ruts worn by stagecoach wheels, as it appears today

Gaviota-Goleta stagecoach on Hollister Avenue

Classic photo of Concord "mudwagon" of 1890 toiling up slope of Slippery Rock

Philander Kellogg

Florentine Kellogg

Frank E. Kellogg

Capt. R. P. Tucker

German Senter

Sherman P. Stow

Harry Langman

George W. Hill

Martin Hemmenway

PIONEER CHURCHES IN GOLETA VALLEY: Top left, Methodist, on Chapel Street, still standing; Center, Baptist Church, 1884, 5257 Hollister Avenue, destroyed by fire 1955; Below, St. Raphael's Catholic Church, corner Hollister and Fairview from 1890 until 1930

Hiram Hill's pioneer blacksmith shop, Fairview Ave. Left to right: Fred Maiers, Joe Lane, John B. Pico

Pettis & Simpson, "the two Franks," operated this blacksmith shop on Hollister Avenue east of Patterson Avenue. Vintage automobile dates picture after 1905; heyday of the shop was in 1890s

Joe Sexton's calla lilies growing in 1890 on what is known today as Kellogg Park tract. First irrigation in Goleta Valley was here

Kellogg Dairy, a landmark from 1882 until 1907, stood on south side of Hollister Ave. where Ward Drive now intersects. Note Sexton's rose bush hedge, lower left

CHAPTER XI

The Twin Villages: Goleta and La Patera

While young Joe Sexton was getting his nursery started in Santa Barbara, he became aware of a pretty 15-year-old girl who was boarding with his parents on Castillo Street. Her name was Lucy Ann Foster; weekdays she attended Santa Barbara College, weekends she spent in the Goleta Valley with her parents, Isaac and Roxanna Foster.

Love hit Joe Sexton like a lightning bolt. Within a few weeks he brashly proposed marriage. Lucy coyly put him off, saying her mother disapproved of the 11-year gap in their ages. Sexton shrugged this off as "a mere bag of shells," and began making plans for a future which Lucy would share.

He rented a saddlehorse and rode out to the Goleta Valley to have a look at the 100 acres his father had purchased, west of the Foster farm. It did not take Joe long to decide that Goleta's soil and climate were superior to Santa Barbara's, so far as a nursery was concerned, so he bought the entire acreage from his father for $2,200, the price the Hill Estate had received. Joe then turned around and sold all but forty acres, fronting on Hollister Avenue, to J. D. Patterson for $2,200, thereby getting his own forty acres for nothing. The Sexton ranch was bounded on the west by San Jose Creek, on the south by Hollister Avenue, on the east by the Foster farm (which didn't exactly make Joe Sexton unhappy) and on the north by Patterson's ranch, the line being 1,200 feet inland from Hollister Avenue.

It had been exactly 100 years since Fr. Juan Crespí of the Portolá Expedition had described this Valley as "the Good Land." But what changes had occurred in the vegetation during that century! In 1769, not one sprig of wild mustard was to be seen; now the sloping plain between Hollister Avenue and the near foothills was a solid sea of the golden weed, with stalks as thick as a man's arm, and so tall that six-footer Joseph Sexton had to stand in his saddle stirrups to see over the blooms. Before he could cultivate his land, he had to get rid of this mustard jungle—a considerable task in an age before the omnipotent bulldozer began its unilateral feud with Nature.

Sexton conferred with neighbor T. Wallace More across the road and was advised to hitch a two-horse team to either end of a big sycamore log and drag the mustard flat, rake it into piles, let it dry a few days, and then burn it.

The system worked. When his level 40 acres had been cleared and was ready for its first plowing, Sexton bought building supplies from neighbor I. G. Foster, who had stockpiled lumber on his premises, and built himself a house. It was a plain, box-shaped, two-story dwelling located about 150 feet northwest of the Sexton home at 5494 Hollister Avenue, which has been a valley landmark since 1880.

When friends remarked that the house seemed unduly large for a bachelor, Sexton replied enigmatically that he didn't figure to live there alone.

That spring of 1869, Sexton moved 250 of his 1,000 Peruvian walnut seedlings from Santa Barbara to the Goleta Valley, planting them alongside San Jose Creek on a site now buried by Ward Memorial Boulevard. He sold the remaining 750 seedlings to Bern Franklin and Col. Russel Heath, of Carpinteria. The latter's walnut grove became known as the largest in the world.

While this work was occupying Sexton's attention, an embryo village which historians designate as "Old Goleta" was taking form at the intersection of Patterson and Hollister Avenues. A mile further west on Hollister, at what was to become Fairview Avenue, was the site of a second small village. It was called La Patera, or, since it boasted a saloon, "Whiskey Flats." Goleta, by contrast, was populated by total abstainers.

On May 14, 1869, T. Wallace More donated an acre of ground for public school use, on the south side of Hollister Avenue opposite the present Chapel Street. The Rafaela School District, named in honor of Daniel Hill's widow, was organized in June, 1869. It

The Twin Villages: Goleta and La Patera

extended from the Daniel Hill Adobe in La Patera to the western city limits of Santa Barbara (De la Vina Street and the future Alamar Avenue), and included all the territory from the foothill homestead belt to the sea.

Where the Medical Center of the Goleta Valley Community Hospital now stands, a one-story "little red schoolhouse", 16 by 20 feet in size, was erected by public subscription and donated labor. Two "conveniences" were discreetly hidden behind the spreading oaks at the rear corners of the schoolyard. The first term, with all eight grades in the one room, convened that fall under a teacher named Mrs. Briggs.

The Rafaela School had twelve teachers during its first eight terms. This high pedagogic turnover was occasioned partly by the propensity of pretty schoolmarms to marry local swains, and partly by disciplinary problems which were inherent in rural schools the country over.

The teachers who followed Mrs. Briggs, according to historian Horace A. Sexton, included Phoebe Wood and Nellie Williams in 1871; Phoebe Owen, Mrs. White and Mrs. Stone, 1872; Mrs. Ford and Charles Drake, 1873; C. M. Woods, 1874; Rose Everett and C. A. Menefee, 1875; and Frank E. Kellogg, who took over in 1877 and taught for ten consecutive years, by which time Rafaela School had been replaced.

The second public building to rise in Goleta village was Isaac Giles Foster's two-story, false-front general store. Upstairs was given over to a meeting hall for the Odd Fellows lodge, public dances, election boards, amateur theatricals and similar functions of a georgic society. This was at 5300 Hollister Avenue.

The central figure of most Nineteenth Century rural American communities was the blacksmith. The Goleta Valley's first monarch of forge and anvil was Hiram Hill, no relation to Daniel Hill, who built his pioneer blacksmith shop on the northwest corner of Fairview Avenue and Hollister Avenue, in La Patera.

Competition arrived in 1872 in the leather-aproned person of Benjamin F. Pettis, recently of the Nevada mines. He located his shop at the north-east corner of Patterson and Hollister Avenues, across from Foster's general store. One of his helpers was Joe Lane, who later bought out Hiram Hill.

Miles H. Lane and his wife Elizabeth came overland from Illinois to Anaheim in the 1850s, moving to Goleta in the early Seventies and buying a ranch in the Hope District for $1 per acre, later donating one acre as the site of Hope School. Their children were Serena; Jasper, who married Mary Foster; Joseph, the blacksmith; Dallas, who married Abbie Johnson; Dorothy, Mrs. Newton Johnson; Napoleon, who married Annie McCaleb; Miles Jr.; Mary, Mrs. George Mills of Lompoc; and Rose, Mrs. Billy Hicks.

When Miles H. Lane died late in 1899, his family employed a novel way to divide up his estate. They numbered the shares of farmland, put the numbers on slips of paper which were placed inside hollow walnut shells, and glued the shells back together. On January 16, 1900, the Lane family met in solemn assembly and cracked nutshells drawn by lot. In this way ten heirs, aged 37 through 61, selected their inheritances!

The largest building in the Goleta Valley was erected in 1869, at La Patera, by a Frenchman from Bordeaux, Jean Marie Birabent. Used as a hotel, store and saloon, it stood fifty feet north of Hollister, between the future Magnolia and Nectarine Avenues. Birabent's wife was the former Maria Ortega of Refugio Ranch. Their son, Frank, born in 1864, attended the first session of Rafaela School in 1869, and was a well-known Santa Barbara pioneer when he died in 1947.

Contrary to published reports, the Birabent house was never used as a stage station, although drivers used to water their horses at Birabent's public trough. He moved to Santa Barbara and died there in April, 1909. His two-story Inn, built in the Monterey style with upper and lower railed galleries, was dismantled in 1928 and the lumber was used to build the Ellwood Hotel apartment house at 170 Magnolia Avenue.

Getting back to Joe Sexton: His ardent courtship of Lucy Ann Foster caused her to become a school "dropout" that fall, over her parents' mild but ineffectual objections. Fearing the young couple might elope, they consented to their daughter marrying Joe Sexton at the age of sweet sixteen. Their wedding was the first ever performed in the Goleta Valley proper, and came on Thanksgiving Day, November 18, 1869.

The ceremony took place under the primeval oaks in the Foster's side yard. Santa Barbara's Presbyterian minister, Rev. Y. T. Cool, officiated. Valley neighbors, 35 in number, were guests.

The Sexton-Foster nuptials, uniting two early families, were an unforgettable affair. A parlor organ provided suitable music; toasts were drunk "in bubbly cider resembling champagne" from Dos Pueblos Ranch. The Good Land itself supplied the ingredients of the wedding feast, reflecting the bounty of this verdant, as yet thinly-settled Eden.

Turkeys, eggs and chickens came from the More Ranch across the road. Green tomatoes and tender suckling pigs were from A. C. Scull's ranch. Don Nicholás Den's thirty-year-old fruit orchard at Dos Pueblos, which had so impressed John C. Frémont in 1846, furnished apples, plums, pears, apricots, figs and pomegranates.

The oranges, and pumpkins for pies, came from the historic Indian Orchard up in Maria Ygnacia Canyon. The long rustic table was dressed with snowy linen which the Fosters had brought by covered wagon across the plains from Illinois in the Fifties. The Sextons and the Fosters pooled their heirloom silver and chinaware for the gala occasion.

A year later, civilization laid its mark across the Goleta Valley in the form of a single strand of iron wire looped between peeled pine poles—the first telegraph line from San Francisco to Santa Barbara. The first message service started in September 1870, and was eventually extended to Los Angeles. Goleta was never to have a telegraph station of its own; messages were handled in Santa Barbara.

The rapid changes occurring in the Goleta Valley, as a result of the subdivision of Daniel Hill's grant, were bewildering to his widow, Rafaela. She continued to live in the old adobe on La Patera Lane, but she was lonely, and envied the comfort of her daughter Rosa, who, after five years of widowhood, had married G. C. Welch.

And then a suitor appeared for the hand of Rafaela. He was German Senter, a New Englander from Belfast, Maine, then in his 58th year. Rafaela was now past sixty, and had been a widow for six years.

German Senter had moved to New York early in life, married a Dutch girl, and finally wound up in Galena, Illinois, as co-owner of a plow factory. When his wife died of cholera in 1857, Senter married his sister-in-law, who also died soon after. Senter finally sold out his interest in the plow factory, and headed for California, by way of Panama, in 1859.

After nine years working on a farm belonging to his brother, Isaac, of Santa Clara, Senter moved to Santa Barbara, where he soon met the widow Hill. After a three-year courtship the two were married, on April 21, 1871, in a ceremony performed by Rev. Jaime Villa, at the same mission altar where Rafaela had married Daniel Hill 45 years before.

Up to then, Rafaela had refused to sell any part of her inheritance, the La Patera or Cochera tract. Her new husband persuaded her that now was the time to do so, while it was a seller's market. As a result, a flurry of real estate transactions altered the map of the Goleta Valley between Carneros Creek and the La Goleta Ranch boundary. The first sale, in 1871, was the largest—nearly 1,000 acres, which became the historic Stow Ranch, as will be described in Chapter XIII.

Colonel Hollister's older brother, Albert G., had made Rafaela several offers for the northeastern quarter of the Cochera tract, without success. Three years after Senter's marriage to Rafaela, they deeded Hollister 480 acres lying west of Fairview Avenue and north of Stow Canyon Road. They were paid $125 an acre for land which Daniel Hill had purchased from Nicolás A. Den 23 years previously for only fifty cents an acre.

Albert Hollister built a two-story frame house which was still standing in 1966 on a knoll at the base of the foothill, a quarter-mile northeast of the Goleta Valley Junior High School. Albert sent back to Missouri for his family. When his wife gazed out her kitchen window at a vista of emerald valley, azure sea and magenta islands on the horizon, she exclaimed "What a fair view!"—or so the folk tale goes—which gave Fairview Ranch its name. The narrow dirt road leading to the farm, originally bordered by olive trees, straddled the Dos Pueblos-La Goleta grant line. It is known today as "Fairview Avenue", one of the Valley's most important lateral highways.

To close out the record on Rafaela Ortega de Hill y Senter: On March 14, 1879, after eight years of happy marriage to her second husband, the Goleta Valley's Spanish-American matriarch passed away at her adobe residence on La Patera Lane, at the age of 70. She was buried in the original Catholic Cemetery, which ranchero Tom Hope had deeded to the Church, on the north side of Hollister Avenue opposite Arboleda Road.

Within a week after his wife's funeral, German Senter virtually

The Twin Villages: Goleta and La Patera

completed the dismemberment of Rafaela's La Patera tract by selling to a land promoter named Titus Phillips the 490 acres remaining between Stow Canyon Road south to Hollister Avenue. Phillips paid $8,773 for the property, a figure he increased many times over through subsequent resale. Included in the deal was the historic Daniel Hill Adobe.

In 1873, the County Supervisors appointed Santa Barbara city surveyor James L. Barker as a "viewer" to locate an alternate public road to Goleta, to bypass the Cieniguitas marshes. The new Goleta Road, as it was called at first, was to follow the north line of the Las Positas y Calera land grant, then owned by a contentious Irishman named Thomas Hope.

Hope had vigorously opposed past efforts to dedicate the existing road to the public, claiming the original survey of the Mexican grant was in error and had left a 100-yard-wide strip of no-man's-land between his ranch and the Pueblo Lands. Hope claimed ownership of this disputed strip, but later accepted $1,000 to quit-claim the area to the county.

Barker went out in the field with district road manager Ed Martin and Goleta rancher T. Wallace More. The latter was the principal backer of the new Goleta Road, since it would enhance the value of his holdings in the Valley.

Hardly had Barker set up his transit than Tom Hope arrived, sided by two dangerous-looking Indian employees. Hope was very truculent. Although Barker and his companions were well outside Hope's fence, Hope grabbed a club and ordered them to leave.

The order had been addressed to black-bearded T. Wallace More, but suddenly Hope turned on the surveyor and clouted Barker over the head, knocking him flat. Dazed, but not seriously injured, Barker decided to knock off work for the rest of the day.

On his way back to town, with a lump growing on his pate, James L. Barker decided to swear out a complaint before the Justice of the Peace, charging Hope with assault and battery.

When Barker reached the J.P.'s office he was chagrined to learn that Hope had beaten him there, pleaded guilty, and had paid a $25 fine. The more Barker pondered the matter, the more he believed his headache was underpriced at $25. Accordingly he filed suit in

Superior Court, charging Thomas Hope with interfering with a public officer in the discharge of his lawful duties, and demanding damages. While this suit was pending, Barker returned to the scene of the crime and resumed surveying the new Goleta Road. This time he kept a loaded rifle handy, a precaution duly respected by Hope and his Indian henchmen.

The Superior Court found in favor of Barker, and fined Hope $1,000 exemplary damages. The judgment was rendered at a time when U.S. paper money was being discounted 10 per cent under gold, the Panic of 1873 being under way. It was not considered ethical for a debtor to pay off a creditor with greenbacks, since in effect this cheated the creditor out of a dime on every dollar. However, in the case of "involuntary debts", such as court fines, it was considered legitimate to pay off in currency. Thomas Hope gleefully took advantage of this loophole, so that James L. Barker received only $900 gold value for the $1,000 worth of greenbacks Hope paid him.

Hope continued to harass travelers on the New Goleta Road from time to time. On one occasion he had a giant Indian named Justo tie a lariat across the road and turn back wagons and riders. The U.S. Army happened to be waging war on the renegade Modoc tribe in the Oregon border lavabeds at the time, which resulted in the New Goleta Road receiving a nickname which became official —Modoc Road.

The name of pioneer George M. Williams first appeared on the tax rolls in 1873, when he bought 150 acres on Modoc Road, now known as the Bueneman property, scene of a 1965 zoning controversy of major proportions. He eventually became one of the principal land owners in the Goleta Valley, with parcels adding up to 3,000 acres, including large farms in Smith Canyon, San Pedro Canyon and La Patera. He was noted as an early-day walnut grower, and for his vegetable, watermelon and berry crops, which were hauled by Studebaker wagon before daylight to the public market in Santa Barbara.

Williams was born in Baltimore in 1847. Left fatherless in his middle teens, he worked his way to San Francisco in 1866. While strolling along the *embarcadero* he offered to help a man carry some heavy luggage. This kindness altered his life. The man was the cook aboard a ship leaving for San Diego. Williams worked his passage to the southern port by peeling potatoes in the galley. In San Diego he got a job driving a herd of cattle to Santa Barbara.

Arriving there, he went to work for a farmer named Elliot Cofer, at West Micheltorena and Gillespie Streets. He fell in love with one of Cofer's nieces, Eliza Towne, eldest daughter of Goleta rancher Edward Towne. The two were married in February, 1872. "Uncle George", as Williams was known to everyone, fathered five children: Mary (Bueneman); James G.; Edith (Lefevre); Charles, and Dorothy. Since his death on March 11, 1935, Williams' original home place has been occupied by his daughter, Mary Bueneman.

The aforementioned Edward Towne, a native of St. Louis, arrived in Santa Barbara from Petaluma in 1870 with his wife, Fannie Cofer Towne, and children Eliza (Mrs. George M. Williams), Martha, John, Smith, Fannie, and Edward. Daughter Ida, still living in 1966, was born in Santa Barbara shortly before the Townes moved out to the Stow Ranch in Goleta. There two more children, Lilly and Frank, were born. Towne had first come West as an outrider and trail scout for a covered wagon train in 1847. He returned East, then came back to California in 1849 in the Gold Rush.

In 1878, the Townes moved to a house on Fairview Avenue, where a lumber yard now stands. There a tenth child, Marina, was born. Seven Towne children had died in infancy, making a total of seventeen.

Edward Towne died in 1910, surviving his wife by ten years.

Due to the nation-wide Panic of 1873, there was no significant amount of immigration to the Goleta area during that year. In 1874, a year which saw the death of venerable Benjamin Foxen on Tinaquaic Ranch due to a spider bite, William Rife Coffey arrived from Missouri. A year later, H. H. Koster came from Illinois and opened a cobbler's shop in Goleta Village. Harry Langman arrived from England in 1875 to become superintendent of the Patterson Ranch.

Probably the most widely-known Goleta pioneer to settle in the early Seventies was Captain Reasin Penelope Tucker, one of the rescuers of the Donner Party in 1846. Losing his home in Napa County due to a bad title, in 1872 Tucker came to Goleta and bought 18 acres on the east bank of Maria Ygnacia Creek, fronting on Hollister Avenue.

Tucker's son, Charlie, was a Valley "character," weighing 300 pounds, who could twist horseshoes into pretzels and tie knots in iron bars with his bare hands. A portion of Tucker's estate on San Antonio Creek Road, in the northeastern part of La Goleta Rancho, became Tucker's Grove County Park in 1912.

Daniel Boone Turner, of Indiana, was another early settler. His home, quite possibly one of the first ten built in 1868, was still standing in 1966 at 1500 North Patterson Avenue, a Lemon Association property.

Goletans of the Baptist faith held services in various private homes in the early years, but in February, 1873, formally organized the "Oakdale Baptist Church" with Rev. J. T. Huff as pastor.*

The nucleus of the Baptist congregation included letters of transfer from William and Mary Mitchell, Tom and Fannie Hicks, Beverly Hicks, Orson and Lydia Peck, Lester Peck, and Eliza Lillard. New members taken in at the first meeting were Tom Lillard, C. Clark and Thomas Lankstern.

The Baptists did not build a church edifice until 1884.

The year 1872 saw the arrival of Florentine Erwin Kellogg, founder of one of the Valley's most important early families, for whom the Kellogg Tract and Kellogg Avenue are named. He was a dynamic little man who stood five feet seven. He could lift a half-ton weight; he held Goleta's standing broad jump record of 11 feet 6 inches, quite an accomplishment in a community of athletic farm boys. He could clear 18 feet in the running broad jump. Kellogg attributed his athletic prowess to the fact that he never touched liquor or tobacco.

Born on New Year's Day, 1816, in Batavia, New York, Florentine Kellogg came west at the age of 30, prior to the Gold Rush. His wagon train missed by a matter of hours being trapped in the same blizzard which caused the Donner Party tragedy. Kellogg first settled in Napa County, where he planted Northern California's first grape vineyard and walnut orchard.

Arriving in the Goleta Valley, Kellogg bought twenty acres

---

* The name "Oakdale" was considered more euphonious and appropriate for the Valley than the Spanish "Goleta" by early settlers.

across San Jose Creek west of Joe Sexton's new nursery. There he built a large frame house, no longer in existence, at 170 South Kellogg Avenue. His tankhouse was equipped with a unique vertical-louvred windmill, the first to be seen in the Goleta Valley.

An ardent Methodist, Kellogg set to work to build a church on a lot donated by I. G. Foster. On October 11, 1875, a board of five trustees was chosen, with Kellogg as chairman of the Building Committee. Within sixty days Goleta had its first church—and half the $1,500 roughing-in costs of the redwood edifice came out of the pockets of Kellogg and his stepdaughter-in-law, Mrs. Margaret Ellison.

Another family which became prominent in Goleta Valley life in the early Seventies was that of George Washington Hill and his wife, Rhoda. No relation to Daniel Hill or Hiram Hill, they arrived in Goleta from Iowa on July 4, 1874, and bought sixty acres where the New Horizons subdivision is now located. Their children were Lewis, Margaret (Mrs. Salathiel Fast), Orilla, Achilles (who married Captain Tucker's daughter, Nettie), Lelia, Delenno, and Minnie (Mrs. Martin Hemmenway).

The afore-mentioned Salathiel Fast deserves special mention. A Union war veteran from Ohio, he immigrated to the Goleta Valley the same time as the George Washington Hills. Fast was a remarkably enterprising young man who, during the long and bloody Mississippi Campaign, bought pies from Southern housewives for a nickel each and sold them to fellow soldiers at a big profit. He emerged from his military service with a nest egg of $10,000. One of his sisters was the wife of Gen. Harrison Gray Otis of the Los Angeles *Times*.

The Fasts settled on a farm where the General Hospital now stands, later selling it at a profit. Fast became a notorious professional "loan shark". Their son, Justus, worked in the Goleta asphalt mines to make his stake, and in 1901 married Angeline Kellogg, daughter of Philander Kellogg. They acquired the original Florentine Kellogg home place, which is now the site of the residence of their daughter, Marion (Mrs. H. A. Sepulveda). Their son, Norval, teaches in San Francisco.

Salathial Fast would lend money on anything from a garden hoe to a 10,000-acre ranch—and would foreclose on the hoe as quickly as the ranch, if his usurious interest payments were not met on time. On one occasion, when he applied for an investment loan from the Commercial Bank, George S. Edwards angrily informed him that Fast had more money than did the bank.

Any doubts that Goleta had sunk permanent roots as a settlement were dispelled in 1874, with the incorporation of that ultimate in real estate subdivisions, a communal burying ground.

The non-denominational Rafaela Cemetery Association was formed, embracing the same area as the Rafaela School District. William C. Marcy donated 5.83 acres for perpetual cemetery use, east of the La Goleta Rancho and north of Hollister Avenue. It now comprises the pioneer section of the present 12-acre Goleta Cemetery.

Until Highway 101 was moved north of the railroad in 1947, the only way to reach the county General Hospital was through the Goleta Cemetery via San Antonio Road. This incongruity was gleefully noted by Robert L. Ripley in his *Believe It Or Not* cartoon in 1939—the only hospital in America where you went to the cemetery first, instead of afterwards!

CHAPTER XII

Ellwood Cooper, the Olive-Oil King

Because two strangers with an interest in horticulture chanced to meet in a stagecoach station in San Juan Bautista one late spring day in 1868, a life-long friendship was kindled between two of the most important pioneer personages in Goleta Valley history. They were Col. W. W. Hollister and Ellwood Cooper.

"Ellwood" is a ubiquitous place-name in the Good Land. It identifies a large ranch, a scenic canyon, a major oil field, a vanished railroad terminal, and a Union School District. Yet few Ellwood residents are aware that Cooper was named for Thomas Ellwood (1639-1713), an English author who read for the blind poet Milton.

Ellwood Cooper was born of colonial Quaker stock in Lancaster, Pennsylvania, in 1829. He became a horticulturist. In 1853 he "self-married" (i.e., a Quaker ceremony without a minister) Miss Sarah P. Moore, of Philadelphia, a foremost authority on ferns. The newly-weds moved to Port-au-Prince, Haiti, where Cooper was an agent for an exporting firm in partnership with Capt. Oliver Cutts.

Ever-recurring earthquakes finally drove the Coopers out of the West Indies after eight years. They returned to New York in 1864, at the height of the Civil War. Four years later, aged 39, Ellwood took a solo pleasure trip to the West Coast by way of Panama.

As a tourist in Santa Barbara in April, 1868, Cooper became intensely interested in the mission padres' gnarled old olive trees which gave Los Olivos Street its name. Cooper was convinced Santa Barbara olive oil could compete commercially with Italian oil.

While en route to Portland, Oregon, by Flint & Bixby stage, Cooper ran into Col. W. W. Hollister, of San Justo, the sheep baron.

113

After Cooper returned home he corresponded with Hollister, enjoying vicariously the Colonel's move to Glen Annie in 1869. As a direct result of Hollister's extravagant paeans of praise for Goleta, the Good Land, Ellwood Cooper was persuaded to move there himself. With Hollister acting as his agent, and with Hannah Cutts, the wealthy wife of his business partner in Haiti, assisting him financially, Ellwood Cooper bought 2,000 acres from the Den Estate for $22 an acre. The land was a strip seven-eighths of a mile wide, running "from the sierra to the sea", and adjoined Hollister property on two sides, sandwiched between Glen Annie and Winchester Canyons.

Cooper's beach frontage extended from Kate Den Bell's Las Armas Ranch (site of the future Ellwood oil strike) to Alfonso Den's ranch at Coal Oil Point (now the Devereux Ranch School campus) on the east. Las Armitas Creek forks at the north end of the Bell Ranch, to form Winchester Canyon on the west and Ellwood Canyon on the east.

In 1870, Cooper brought his wife and family, which consisted of a son, Henry, and daughters Ellen and Fanny, across the continent to San Francisco on the recently-opened railroad. They disembarked from a steamer at Santa Barbara on August 30. Finding no suitable hotel accommodations, they purchased a frame house and a quarter of a city block of land cornering at Chapala and West Anapamu Streets, in the rear of the Santa Barbara College—an institution which was to become a major avocation of the Coopers.

The house and lot cost $1,100, and provided the family with a home for a year. The original plan was for the Coopers to live in town, but the twelve mile commuting trip by horseback to the Goleta Valley ranch became irksome, so Cooper built himself a homestead-type board and batten shack for overnight use. Soon Sarah moved in with him, and additions were made as needed. As a result, the big formal residence which Ellwood Cooper had planned for a hilltop view site was never built.

The Good Land, when Ellwood Cooper arrived in 1870, was only just beginning to become Americanized. The rustic scenery in his private canyon was as pristine as it had been 100 years before, when Padre Serra and Gaspar de Portolá admired its beauty. Upper portions of Ellwood Canyon still offer spectacular cliffs, ancient trees of vast size, oak parks and a beautiful meandering creek, little changed from prehistoric times.

In a letter written to a relative in the East, now in the possession of his granddaughter, Mrs. Carl G. Erickson, of Santa Barbara, Cooper gives this earthy description of his first impressions of the ranch:

> The appearance [of the Goleta Valley] is perfectly lovely, the prospect grand and sublime, mountains on the one side, the great ocean on the other. The building sites on our ranch cannot be surpassed anywhere. I can have wild ravine views, rugged mountains, the ocean and look all over the country between me and Santa Barbara 12 miles distant, the west view being of equal beauty.
>
> The people who have come here are rather above the average, and most have means. There are very few squatters. In fact, that class cannot get on here. This is no place for poor people, and I would discourage all such from coming. Those who have about $10,000, so as to purchase a small place and all the implements necessary to work it, and sufficient means to live upon for a couple of years, could build themselves a nice home and live like princes.
>
> When we look over [the Goleta Valley] where no cultivation is going on, and see the brown burned appearance, we would not believe anything could grow; yet side by side exists the most luxuriant vegetation. It is incomprehensible, and yet not at all surprising, that Spanish people who have lived here for 50 years have always assumed nothing would grow without irrigation, and hence never made the trial. Not only Spaniards, but the early American settlers were of the same mistaken opinion.
>
> The Goleta Valley is in reality only two years old, and hence one has to live a pioneer life without those advantages which are so necessary to a high state of civilization. It will however be only a few years until we are in advance of any country section on this continent. Land that sold a few years ago for $2.50 an acre will be worth $1,000 an acre some day.... This is the Italy of America, the Paradise of the Western World, the climatic perfection of this Globe!

As a prophet on land value appreciation, Cooper erred on the side of conservatism; in 1966, parts of his ranch were worth $10,000 an acre.

Cooper's unpretentious redwood house, intended to be temporary only, instead became the focal point of a complex of barns, machine shops, an olive mill and other buildings, most of which have been removed by later owners.

Cooper planted 400 of his level acres in the canyon bottom to assorted fruit trees. His main interest, olive culture, produced an orchard of 7,000 trees in 1872. He also set out 12,500 walnut trees, making him California's largest grower of that crop for several years.

Mrs. Maud P. Meyers of Lompoc, daughter of Sarah Cooper's brother Ellis, who at one time managed the Cooper Ranch, supplies her memories of pioneer days in the walnut industry:

In September and October the schools would close so the children could help harvest the walnut crop. This meant picking up the walnuts as they fell from the trees, and removing the green hull, which was already cracked and slightly dried. The nuts were placed in a gunnysack which weighed from 70 to 80 pounds when full. Each sack was given a number and the picker got a ticket bearing that number. The sacks were gathered at the end of the day and taken to the weighing yard, where each picker was given credit for his day's labor. The walnuts were washed and dried in the sun and fresh air. After 1882, the final bleaching and grading was done by Mr. Frank E. Kellogg who owned the big creamery in Goleta. In those days each child had to buy his own schoolbooks and clothes, which was where we spent our wages from picking walnuts.

Olives were harvested in the winter time, mostly by crews of Italians or Mexicans. After passing through a fan room, where leaves, twigs, and dust were blown away, the ripe black olives were placed in flat drawers in a two-story "dry house", where they were dehydrated of most of the water, which is what gives raw olives their bitter taste. The dehydrator was heated by means of slow-burning oak logs in a brick-lined furnace in the basement.

The extraction of the olive oil followed. Ellwood Cooper's olive mill was the largest in the United States. It attracted droves of wealthy winter tourists from Santa Barbara, bringing nation-wide publicity to the Cooper Ranch.

Cooper's olive mill had iron cogwheels eight feet in diameter which drove heavy millstones, mounted vertically on their axles. These crushed the dried olives, pits and all, into a mushy mass. Power to drive the millstones was supplied by mules walking in a circular pit and yoked to a beam, similar to the Mexican *arastras* used for crushing ore at the gold mines in the days of '49.

The crushed olive pulp was placed into wooden forms called "cheeses", three feet square by six inches deep. These were lined with a special loosely-woven linen crash, which Cooper imported from France (he had sent a man to the Continent to find out how olives were processed, and patterned his Ellwood Canyon mill after those in Europe). When one "cheese" was filled and covered with the linen crash, another was placed on top of it, and another, until the stack of cheeses was five feet high.

Then a heavy wooden beam, weighted on one end by a ton of rocks suspended in a well in the floor of the mill, was used to press the stacks of pulp-filled cheeses, squeezing the pure olive oil through the linen fabric into vats. Grooves in the wooden floors of the vats conveyed the olive oil into settling tanks to get rid of any water. The nutritious olive pulp remaining in the cheeses was fed to Cooper's hogs in an odoriferous wallow, located well up-canyon and up-wind from inhabited areas of the ranch.

When the olive oil was drawn off by a spigot from the settling tank, it was filtered twice through a special coarse-fibered paper, which Cooper also imported from abroad. Then it was stored for several months until the bottling season came along the following summer. Cooper charged $1 per twelve-ounce bottle. Collectors of antique bottles treasure those marked ELLWOOD COOPER - PURE OLIVE OIL - SANTA BARBARA, CAL.

Among the thousands of tourists who made the tallyho excursion out to the Cooper olive ranch during the next thirty years were Kalakahua, the last King of Hawaii; and Queen Victoria's son-in-law, the Marquis of Lorne, governor-general of Canada.

The Marquis, who was consort to the Princess Louise, wrote the following about Ellwood Cooper's ranch following a Christmas week visit in 1882, as published in a leading American weekly of the day, the *Youth's Companion*:

[Ellwood Cooper] is a gentleman who owns a magnificent farm on the Pacific, and has shown that California can produce better olive oil than France, Spain or Italy; grapes as good as any man could desire; English walnuts and European almonds, in crops whereof the old countries hardly ever dream; oranges, lemons and Japanese persimmons, with other fruit and crops too numerous to mention; and all hedged from the gentle sea winds by belts and bands of Australian eucalypti, which grow in ten years to be 100 feet tall. But such a paradise is not for the beginner, who must make his money before he indulges in as many broad acres as Ellwood Cooper's.

Oddly enough, although Ellwood Cooper was widely hailed as America's "olive oil king", the enterprise was a financial failure, due to the competition of inferior olive oil being imported from Sicily at a fraction of the cost of Cooper's product. As a matter of fact, the most lucrative crop on Cooper's ranch came from his Japanese persimmon orchard, two miles farther up the canyon.

Many historians credit Ellwood Cooper with introducing the ubiquitous eucalyptus windbreak to the California landscape. This is not entirely true, since many varieties of eucalyptus arrived from Australia by clipper ship during Gold Rush days. However, Cooper does deserve recognition as being the first American nurseryman to propagate and distribute eucalyptus seedlings on a commercial scale in California, and his trees now grow from the Mexican border to the upper Sacramento Valley.

Of the more than 600 species of eucalyptus or gum trees identified by botanists, Ellwood Cooper imported only fifty varieties from Baron Ferdinand Van Müeller of Australia. Eucalyptus thrived in California's soil and climate, and one of Cooper's first improvements on his canyon ranch was setting out blue gum windbreaks along the boundaries between his property and Winchester Canyon adjoining on the west. His tree planters were mostly Scotsmen.

Cooper's main eucalyptus nursery was south of the Gaviota stage road, on a plot near today's Ellwood Union School. The jungle-thick stand of eucalyptus is still growing there. Cooper's reason for planting the seedlings as close as hairs on a brush was to make them grow tall and slim as lodgepole pines, so he could market them for wharf pilings.

The word had spread that the only wooden pilings on the San Francisco *embarcadero* which had withstood the teredo and other marine borers were eucalyptus. It was later determined that the reason they were impervious to marine worms was because they happened to be near sewer outfalls; the acids in the effluent kept the teredos at bay, not the oils in the eucalyptus wood.

Although several of the wharves along the Santa Barbara Channel coast used eucalyptus pilings, workmen found them hard to handle because they would not float when green. Eventually, eucalyptus gave way to fir and creosoted pine.

Commercially, eucalyptus wood was valuable, bringing up to $22 a cord in stove lengths; but when dry it was impossible to saw or split. It rotted quickly underground, making it useless for telephone poles or fence posts. It could not be milled into lumber, due to its coarse and curly grain. Its primary usefulness, then as now, was for quick-growing windbreaks.

Except for the Santa Maria Valley, where most of the existing eucalyptus trees were grown from seedlings sold by Joseph Sexton's Goleta nursery, most of the county's familiar eucalyptus trees originated with Ellwood Cooper. One historic specimen, a lemon-scented gum tree (*Eucalyptus citriodora*), still grows in lonely splendor in a pasture near the site of the long-vanished Cooper olive mill. It has been known since the turn of the century as "The Ellwood Queen", and at 130-plus feet is reputed to be the tallest tree in the county. According to botanist Maunsell van Rensselaer, the Ellwood Queen grows atop a fault line, and was thrown off balance by the 1925 Santa Barbara earthquake.

In the early Eighties, Ellwood Cooper's almond trees became infested with cottony cushion scale. If unchecked, this pest could destroy the almond industry in Southern California. Later, black scale invaded the Good Land, threatening Cooper's walnut groves. Cooper made an intensive scientific study of the problem, traced the origins of the trees, and learned that a natural parasite existed which fed on the scale—the ladybug, or, as Cooper more correctly called them (shades of LBJ!), "ladybirds".

Cooper sent to China for a supply of the little red insects. The first batch arrived dead of freezing. A second shipment reached Cooper in a viable condition. With his entire fortune riding on the results, Cooper turned loose thousands of the bugs in Ellwood Canyon. Within a matter of weeks, the scale had been stripped clean!

Farmers throughout the State were electrified by the news from Ellwood Canyon. Ladybirds were imported from the Orient in vast quantities, resulting in the black scale menace being eradicated in time to save California's walnut industry—the chief crop of the Goleta Valley at the time—from extinction.

To honor Ellwood Cooper for this great achievement, he was

elected president of the California State Board of Horticulture in 1883, which important post he held for several successive terms.

Cooper was a highly educated and articulate man. He was the author of numerous magazine, encyclopedia and newspaper articles, on subjects ranging from local politics to horticulture. Two of his abstruse technical books, *Fruit Culture and Eucalyptus Trees* and *Olive Culture*, are considered authorities in their fields.

Despite his austere Quaker upbringing, Ellwood Cooper was a mischievous, fun-loving man. His neatly-trimmed blond Van Dyke, sparkling blue eyes and pink complexion made him easily recognized in his travels around the Goleta Valley. He was a frequent visitor at Colonel Hollister's ranch in Glen Annie Canyon.

Cooper's private beach frontage was a favorite place for family picnics, as were the rocky defiles at the upper end of the canyon (in the mid-1960s being considered for a county park). Santa Barbara beachcombers considered Cooper's stretch of seashore to be the best shell beach in Southern California.

In July, 1894, Cooper hired his wife's nephew, Ellis Moore, from Newport, Minnesota, to oversee the operation of the ranch. After a short time, Moore moved over the ridge to manage the Winchester Canyon ranch for the Hollister Estate.

An excellent rider, Cooper did most of his traveling in a pony cart, always wearing a linen duster and carrying a whip. He and Sarah did little formal entertaining. Inside the home, the Coopers spoke in the Biblical patois of their Quaker ancestors. Once when chiding Sarah for failing to notice something underfoot he remarked, "Well, Sarah, I guess thee did not have thy specks on!"

Ellwood Cooper was the only person alive whom Col. Hollister accepted as a social equal and intimate friend. In 1878, when the Santa Barbara College closed its doors due to financial difficulties and the buildings reverted to Hollister as majority stockholder, Hollister converted the college into a commercial class hotel and named it Ellwood Hotel in honor of his friend.

The failure of Santa Barbara College was a bitter disappointment in the lives of Ellwood and Sarah Cooper. They had been closely associated with the institution almost from the day of their arrival in 1870, Cooper as chairman of the board of directors, Sarah as a director and counsellor. In 1872, Sarah Cooper made a trip back East to assemble a cadre of qualified professors to serve on the faculty of Santa Barbara College. Among them was a brash young Civil War veteran, Charles Albert Storke, then 25 years of age. He was engaged to teach Latin and mathematics. During his first and only term in the schoolroom, Storke fell in love with one of his pupils, Mattie More, born in the Daniel Hill Adobe in 1854 to Mr. and Mrs. T. Wallace More.

Storke married Mattie More in September, 1873. With the financial backing of T. Wallace More, young Storke founded the Los Angeles *Herald*, but lost it a year later due to the economic depression following the Panic of 1873. He returned to Santa Barbara to become a noted lawyer, politician, rancher and newspaperman. He purchased a 291-acre ranch in the Goleta Valley, south of Hollister Avenue and east of Storke Road, which had belonged to Mary Tyler, one of Nicolás Den's heirs.

Storke's son, Thomas, born in November, 1876, started his own newspaper career at the turn of the century, and rose to become one of Santa Barbara's most influential citizens, with extensive Goleta Valley holdings purchased or inherited from his father.

Ellwood Cooper's reluctant involvement with his neighbor, Colonel W. W. Hollister, in the prolonged Den Estate litigation will be recounted in Chapter XVII. The mental strain of the long trial lessened Cooper's interest in Ellwood Ranch and resulted in his putting it on the market about 1890. An English syndicate opened negotiations to purchase, and their representatives, Dr. and Mrs. Harold Sidebotham of Santa Barbara, actually lived for one year on the ranch at that time, but the sale never materialized.

Cooper was interested in many other phases of community life. On March 1, 1910, he circulated a petition to change the old Rafaela Cemetery District to the present Goleta Public Cemetery District, and presented it, with 152 signatures of Goleta Valley citizens, to the County Supervisors. The new enlarged area ran from Cooper's ranch on the west to San Roque Creek on the east. This cemetery district was approved on April 4, 1910, with Edgar A. Hollister, A. M. Hoel and Frank Simpson as the first trustees.

The three Cooper children grew up on the ranch. Henry married a distant cousin, Anna Cooper, of Philadelphia, and for years was chief electrician for the Pennsylvania Railroad, inventing many devices which are still in use. In 1894, he returned to Goleta to help his father run the ranch, persimmons then being more profitable than olives, which were gradually phased out. Henry Cooper died in Santa Barbara at the age of 87, in 1941. His daughter, Helen Erickson, resides on West Quinto Street.

Ellen Cooper, a talented water colorist and musician, married Isaac R. Baxley. She died in November, 1949, at the age of 89. Her sister, Fanny, married James C. Heron, of Marin County. She died in 1936 at the age of 71.

Ellwood's beloved mate, Sarah, passed away in 1909 of asthma. Life soon became intolerably lonely for the old man, so he offered Ellwood Ranch for sale for a quarter million dollars. On December 1, 1912, a syndicate headed by a Scottish nobleman, Charles Julian Maitland McGill-Crichton, bought the ranch for $225,000. One of the major stockholders, Clarence P. Day, of Pasadena, took over the management of the ranch, and converted it to lemons and walnuts. Ellwood Cooper moved to the Arlington Hotel in Santa Barbara.

McGill-Crichton was killed in action with the British Expeditionary Forces in World War I, and the Cooper Ranch became the property of a railroad magnate, Frank H. Green. He retained possession until his death in 1921, at which time the ranch was sold at auction to Joseph Archambault and the Doty Brothers of Las Varas Canyon.

Ellwood Cooper's long and distinguished life ended on a note of senility and anticlimax. On a trip east to visit relatives in 1913, he stopped off in Chicago long enough to impulsively marry Mrs. Addie Fleming, of Denver, whom he had met at the Arlington Hotel and had known less than a week. The new Mrs. Cooper, unfortunately, did not care for California; but she made no objections to the three Cooper children receiving their mother's share of the community property.

Ellwood Cooper died at the Arlington on December 28, 1918. His son, Henry, saw to it that he was laid to rest in Goleta Cemetery alongside Sarah, his first love. The funeral occurred on the last day of the old year. The newly-widowed Mrs. Cooper departed for Denver. She made no attempt to keep in touch with her step-children in following years.

CHAPTER XIII

Sherman P. Stow Pioneers Irrigation

In the summer of 1871, the Goleta Valley was visited by perhaps the most controversial political figure on the contemporary California scene—William Whitney Stow of San Francisco. A former speaker of the house in the State Legislature, lawyer Stow was the head of the "political department" of the corporation which ruled California politics with a ruthless hand, the Southern Pacific Railroad.

Stow was looking for some kind of farm property on which to ensconce his twenty-year-old son, Sherman Patterson Stow, recently driven out of Europe by the outbreak of the Franco-Prussian war. "Shermy" had been studying sugar beet culture in France and Germany, and was set on making a career in agriculture.

The only Goleta Valley resident Stow knew was Col. W. W. Hollister, who had rubbed shoulders with him in the halls of the statehouse in Sacramento during Hollister's long years of advocacy of statewide Trespass Laws—which would soon break the domination of the cattle kings and open California to the small-acreage farmer.

Hollister entertained Stow at his ranch, listened to the great lobbyist's plans for his son, Sherman, and immediately suggested that Stow look into the possibility of acquiring La Patera ranch adjoining Hollister on the east side of Carneros Creek. This fine property only recently had become available for sale, thanks to Rafaela Hill's marriage to German Senter.

Stow, as shrewd and canny an investor as they came, took a hike up San Pedro Creek to look over the water supply situation. In Smith

Canyon he located waterfalls and everlasting springs which, if he could obtain water rights thereto, would supply water for irrigation and transform pasture land into an Eden of orchards and gardens.

Learning that no one had yet filed on the water rights to the San Pedro's overflow, Stow opened negotiations with German Senter. On July 17, 1871, Senter, with Rafaela putting her "X" on the deed, conveyed title to 1,043 acres of La Patera tract to W. W. Stow for a consideration of $28,677. The land lay between Carneros and San Pedro Creeks, from the foothills to the north boundary of George Williams' ranch, a line now marked by the railroad. One of the important landmarks included in the sale was the original *patera*, or duck pond, which henceforth was called Stow Lake or Stow Pond (since 1963, Los Carneros Lake).

Surveyor W. H. Norway was hired to run the boundary lines of the new Stow Ranch. W. W. ordered 1,000 redwood fence posts and 30,000 board feet of fencing to match Col. Hollister's five-board fence, the lumber being floated ashore at Goleta Beach. Wells dug on the ranch showed an average topsoil depth of 33 feet.

Stow also shopped around for eucalyptus seedlings, and found he could beat the prices Joe Sexton's nursery was asking. By steamer *Kalorama* Stow shipped in from San Jose 2,000 eucalyptus plants six inches high, paying at the rate of two for a nickel, and had them planted ten feet apart across the front of the ranch and along the west bank of San Pedro Creek. Many Italian and Scottish emigrants whose descendants are now active in Goleta Valley affairs found employment on the Stow ranch, setting out eucalyptus plants which are now 100 feet tall and six feet through the bole.

Sherman P. Stow, who turned 21 in the fall of 1872, began the construction of the main ranch house on a knoll on the west side of Stow Lake, a mile north of Hollister Avenue. The house, still standing in 1966, was built of fir instead of redwood, because W. W. Stow owned a sawmill on Puget Sound. Instead of the 1 x 12 boards 18 feet long which W. W. ordered, the ship discharged random-width boards from six to twenty inches in size and only sixteen feet long, which in W. W.'s opinion gave the Stow home a "squatty look." Although Stearns Wharf had been completed a few months before, Sherman P. Stow had his lumber delivered in the pioneer fashion by floating it ashore from the steamer, loading it on wagons and hauling it to the ranch.

Sherman P. Stow Pioneers Irrigation

All of the tools and ranch implements ordered by W. W. Stow were purchased in San Francisco and unloaded at the wharf in Santa Barbara. The draft teams were also purchased in "the City" and ridden out to the ranch by their teamsters.

Colonel Hollister's brother, Hubbard, a veteran of the 1853 overland sheep drive, died in San Luis Obispo in January, 1873. His bereaved daughters, Ida and Nellie, accepted an invitation to visit Colonel and Mrs. Hollister at Glen Annie. Through some misunderstanding, there was no one on hand to meet the two girls when the stage driver let them off at the Birabent House in La Patera at 5:45 one cold morning, stranding them five miles from the Hollister Ranch.

At this juncture a handsome, bearded young Lochinvar came out of the west—not on a white charger, to be sure, but with a handy horse and buggy. He was Sherman P. Stow—and for him and Ida Hollister, it was a case of love at first sight.

That summer, while courting Ida, Sherman bought enough walnuts and almonds from the Sexton nursery to make a 100-acre orchard, planting at a ratio of five almonds to four walnuts, with a scattering of pecans purchased from Russel Heath of Carpinteria. The trees were planted at a rate of 24 walnuts per acre, 30 almonds per acre. W. W. Stow later purchased 1,500 four-year-old walnuts from Governor Downey of Los Angeles for 23 cents apiece.

On September 10, 1873, Ida Hollister became the bride of Sherman P. Stow, in a garden ceremony beside their new home overlooking Stow Lake and the valley. Although W. W. Hollister and W. W. Stow approved of the marriage which made them in-laws, no love was lost between these two self-centered, domineering men. Friction developed over common boundary lines and water rights, and when Stow received his 1874 tax bill and found it double the previous year, he wrote his son, "Shermy," in great anger:

This big increase in tax rate is directly due to Col. Hollister's meddlesome disposition and propensity to brag. He has done our neighborhood more harm than we can repair in some time.

On December 22, 1873, W. W. Stow filed a claim to divert water from San Pedro Creek in Smith Canyon by means of a small dam at a sylvan nook popularly called the "Picnic Spot," running a 300-foot wooden flume along the east bank of the creek and tying into a metal pipeline 4½ inches in diameter, made of riveted tin dipped in hot tar from T. Wallace More's asphalt mine.

Securing rights to the water entailed considerable use of Stow's talents for making undercover arrangements, influencing the proper politicians, and the other details of a good lobbying job. At least two squatters, Myron Smith and a homesteader named Feliz, had to be placated and easements acquired across their claims. As early as May 18, 1873, W. W. Stow had sent a highly confidential memorandum to Sherman in Goleta:

My plans for securing title to San Pedro Creek water have progressed with entire satisfaction and secrecy. When I am master of the situation I will deal liberally with the squatters downstream. In 90 days I probably will be boss.

Having successfully secured perpetual water rights from an acre of land encompassing cold water springs in upper Smith Canyon (still owned by the Stow Ranch), W. W. ran his pipelines to a reservoir near his ranch dairy and the main cottage, as well as a half-inch line all the way to the Daniel Hill Adobe. Water from a small earthen reservoir on a hill near Stow Lake flowed by gravity to the flats below, for watering livestock and irrigating trees—an historic event, inasmuch as it marked the first time that irrigation had ever been practiced in the Goleta region. Stow laid nearly a mile of pipeline at a cost of over $30,000.

One of the first crops planted on the Stow Ranch was tobacco. W. W. had seen a tobacco plantation near Gilroy, which had netted the owner a profit of $600,000 from 400 acres. William C. Ralston, probably the most famous banker in early California history, advised Stow that a man could make more money raising tobacco than he could from banking or mining. Stow convinced himself that he could clear $120,000 from a 400-acre plantation.

The tobacco experiment on the Stow Ranch ended in failure. Grasshoppers were a scourge, and the Goleta Valley climate was too mellow to produce a good leaf. A similar failure was suffered by a tobacco planter named B. C. Langdon south of Hollister Avenue, although in one favorable season his crop amounted to a ton of tobacco per acre.

The crop which was to make the Stow Ranch famous was lemons. W. W. Stow objected to California lemons, because their skin was bitter and their pulp contained little juice; but on the Hales Farm near Alameda Station, "The Encinal," he had seen a 20-year-old Lisbon lemon tree whose owner thought nothing of picking twelve dozen lemons at a time for several crops annually.

From this remarkable tree in Alameda, W. W. Stow obtained a number of scions, or grafting shoots, which were cut the week of February 15, 1874, and shipped to Geary's Nursery in Los Angeles for grafting to sweet orange rootstock.

Crews of Italian woodchoppers were kept busy clearing oak trees off the rolling acres of the Stow Ranch. One of the best-known Italian workmen, Frank Manzetti, raised five sons and three daughters while living on the Stow Ranch.

In the spring of 1874, Sherman P. Stow set out 3,000 trees, a mixture of walnuts, oranges and lemons. The latter pioneer lemon grove of 30 acres, from which the Goleta Valley's $3,000,000-per-year lemon industry was to evolve, was located on land now known as the Crestview Oaks subdivision, east of modern La Patera School and Stow Grove County Park. These trees bore bountifully until their removal in 1938.

Ferdinand Morrell was responsible for much of the ornamental landscaping on the Stow Ranch, as well as the Hollister Ranch.

Much of Stow's fruit-tree planting was supervised by Christian Larson, a native of Denmark, who entered Stow's employ in 1871 and, with his wife Minnie, lived on the ranch for 16 years. Stow rewarded him for his faithful service by selling him 40 acres between San Pedro Creek and Fairview Avenue. Larson worked this farm until his death on May 29, 1916. The Larson children were a son, Louis C., and a daughter, Inga, who married A. W. Conover of Goleta, who became a County Supervisor.

Lemons became such an important crop on the Stow Ranch that the packing and marketing was turned over to Harleigh Johnston, of the San Ysidro Ranch in Montecito. Finally Johnston's independent packing house could not handle the growing volume of lemons, so growers from Goleta to Carpinteria banded together on February 16, 1897, to incorporate the "Johnston Fruit Company."

Sherman P. Stow was president, James Birss manager, and other charter directors were J. A. Fithian, J. R. Fithian, W. W. Burton, I. G. Waterman, and Harleigh Johnston.

Between 1889 and 1892, Johnston packed lemons on the Stow

Ranch itself, using the famous "Mission Brand" label. When a rival packing house near Corona began shipping lemons under the Mission brand, a lawsuit followed and the courts found in favor of Goleta growers, who had used the trademark first.

In the 1920s, the Johnston Fruit Company became a farmers' non-profit co-operative, and operated as such until declining lemon acreage brought about its disbandment in 1962.

When Sherman was 25, in 1876, his father deeded him a portion of La Patera Ranch. On June 19, 1883, W. W. mortgaged the entire ranch to his son for $40,000, to be paid off in ten years at 7% interest. Sherman actually discharged the debt by 1890.

On February 11, 1895, W. W. Stow died of a stroke at his desk in San Francisco. He is best remembered today as the park commissioner who did the most to develop beautiful Golden Gate Park, where Stow Lake is named in his memory.

All the older shops, red barns and outbuildings on the Stow Ranch dated from Sherman P.'s era, including the original earth fill dam at the south end of Stow Lake, which doubled the pond's water storage capacity.

Sherman Patterson Stow died in 1907, leaving three daughters and three sons to mourn their loss. They were Anne, who married Barrett Fithian and bore Dorothy (Heaney). She died in 1949. The second child, Sherman Hollister Stow, never married and succeeded his father as ranch manager. Samuel M. Stow, the third child, was a celebrated U. C. football star around the turn of the century. He died in 1922. Katherine, who married Charles Ealand and bore him a daughter, Maria, became a widow and later married Loren D. Van Horne, who fathered Garrett and Peggy (Seligman). Edgar, the fifth child born to Sherman and Ida Stow, was also a noted athlete on the Berkeley campus of the University. Peggy, the youngest of the Stow children, married Edward Bruce and lives in Washington, D. C.

Shortly after Sherman Hollister Stow took over the management of his father's ranch, on July 12, 1907, the Sherman P. Stow Company was incorporated for $100,000 capital stock at $100 per share. The charter directors included Sherman, Ida, Katherine Ealand and Margaret.

Sherman H. Stow spent his life as a bachelor. He served as a director of the Johnston Fruit Company, the County National Bank of fond memory, the S. B. County Walnut Growers' Association, and the Goleta Valley Bean Growers' Association. He had the misfortune to be bucked off a horse in 1915, rupturing his appendix and dying from his injuries shortly thereafter.

The next manager of the ranch was Edgar Whitney Stow, Sherman's younger brother. His wife was Mrs. Arthur Alexander, the former Sally Taylor of the De la Guerra family of Santa Barbara. They had no issue.

The Stow Ranch enjoyed its golden heyday under the management of Edgar Stow. He removed all the old walnut trees, and leveled the undulating land with the use of the first tractors to be seen in the Goleta Valley, around 1912, making it possible to lay pipelines and irrigate areas which only rain had reached before. He raised the dam on Stow Lake twice to impound over 500 acre feet of water, and built three permanent reservoirs. The place was now known as "La Patera Ranch."

Edgar purchased laboratory equipment from the government when it closed its kelp processing plant at Summerland, and built his own scientific experimental laboratory near the Stow house. His contributions to the lemon industry are recognized by citriculturists all over the world.

Throughout the Good Land, lemon trees were being threatened by oak root fungus, a legacy of the prehistoric oak groves which by now had disappeared. Edgar Stow made numerous trips to Florida to study fungus and its control, and came back with the news that he had seen a grapefruit tree growing in healthy condition in a jungle of other trees infested with fungus. As a result of Stow's experiments, both on his own ranch and on neighboring Glen Annie, he determined that by budding Lisbon or Eureka lemons to grapefruit rootstock, the resulting trees were impervious to the dreaded oak root fungus.

Stow's laboratory work was directed toward four main problems of the lemon grower: the results of excessive irrigation, resistance to disease, the best rootstocks, and the effects of high budding. Although Stow never made a major scientific break-through with his test tubes and retorts, news of his experiments helped spur other scientists at the state university and in the big oil companies to greater endeavors, out of which has developed the field insecticide industry, which is a multi-million-dollar operation today.

During his management of La Patera Ranch, Edgar increased his lemon acreage to 300. He also planted the beautiful redwood grove on upper La Patera Lane and Cathedral Oaks Road, Stow Grove, which since 1920 has been a public picnic ground second in popularity only to Tucker's Grove. In 1964, the Sherman P. Stow Company deeded Stow Grove to the county as a public park.

During his busy lifetime, Edgar Stow served with distinction as both a State Assemblyman and as a State Senator. His last bid for re-election saw him defeated by a cousin, Jim Hollister.

Edgar Stow died in 1949. His successor as manager of La Patera Ranch was a nephew, Garrett Van Horne, the son of his sister, Katherine. Van Horne had served as a gunnery officer with the navy during World War II, and was awarded a Bronze Star for heroism under kamakazi attacks on his minesweeper during the bloody Iwo Jima and Okinawa campaigns in the Pacific.

During Van Horne's administration the Stow Ranch was partially rezoned from agricultural to residential, a phase of history which will be dealt with in a later chapter.

CHAPTER XIV

Stagecoach Days in the Goleta Valley

A significant milestone in the development of the Good Land was reached in the summer of 1874, when T. Wallace More completed a wharf off More Mesa, half a mile east of the inlet to the Goleta Slough. This gave Goleta the status of a coastal port of call. It was undoubtedly the most important single event in the Valley's economic history prior to the coming of the railroad in 1887.

The location of More's Landing was dictated by an artesian spring midway down the seacliff at 1170 South More Ranch Road. This was the main source of water for the More Ranch, and was convenient for stockmen who would be using the wharf. The proximity of large outcroppings of asphalt at the base of the palisades below 1148 South More Ranch Road was also a factor in locating the wharf.

More's Landing was 900 feet long and 35 feet wide, with a warehouse at the seaward end. Ships had two fathoms of water at low tide when they reached the pierhead. Access roads were dug out of the shale cliffs to form ramps, both east and west of the wharf. Traces of these ramps are still visible on the Jacob Dekker place, but time and tide have long since obliterated the barnacled stubs of pilings marking the site of the historic landing.

On September 10, 1874, the County Supervisors awarded T. Wallace More a 20-year franchise for the wharf, and set up a scale of fees he could charge his customers, identical to the wharfage rates charged by John P. Stearns in Santa Barbara. They were as follows:

Vessels to 100 tons, $25 annually; over 100 tons, $50.
Vessels tied up to wharf, $3.50 per day.
Assorted merchandise, $1 per ton.
Lumber, $1 per thousand board feet.
Shingles, 12½c per square.
Sheep, 5c; hogs, 10c; cattle, 25c.
Horses and mules, 25c per head.
Dried cowhides, 2c each.
Fence posts, 1c; firewood, $1 per cord.

Asphaltum was More's most lucrative source of income. Tar still extrudes copiously from the cliffs at several places along the beach between 1148 South More Ranch Road and the 5200 block of Austin Road. Dynamite was used by More to fragmentize the asphaltum, which was washed clean by wave action and then loaded on carts which were hauled up the ramps to the wharf by ox teams— the only use of oxen by Americans in Valley history. The first paving materials for the streets of San Francisco came from More's outcrop at the foot of Anderson Lane. More, who wore a black spade beard, used to say to his men, "When it's time to trim my whiskers, it's time to mine some more ashfelt."

By 1890, more than 32,000 tons of asphaltum had been shipped from More's landing, at prices ranging from $12 to $20 per ton.

Valley farmers used More Ranch Road from Hollister Avenue to haul their lima beans, honey, walnuts, barley and other products to More's Landing for loading aboard coastal steamers.

Early in 1875, Isaac G. Foster applied for a U.S. postmaster's appointment. Mail stages had passed his front door for many years on the way to Gaviota. A population of fifty families in the Valley seemed to justify Goleta having its own post office.

President U. S. Grant concurred by appointing Foster postmaster on May 17, 1875. The name "Goleta" was officially applied to the germinal hamlet taking form at Hollister and Patterson Avenues. This was the first time the Spanish article "La" had been dropped from the original La Goleta which Daniel A. Hill had titled his Mexican grant in 1846. Although many settlers were disappointed in the name Goleta (they thought "Oakdale" was more fitting to the

Stagecoach Days in the Goleta Valley 133

locale), the Americanized version of the original Spanish nomenclature had come to stay.

The mid-Seventies saw the heyday of the stagecoach in Goleta life. The ubiquitous Concord, which played such an important part in the winning of the West—what thud-and-blunder movie or TV script could do without it?—filled a vital place in the daily life of rural Goleta for over forty years. The first stagecoach traversed the new county road through the Valley on April 1, 1860; the last made the run to Lompoc on March 31, 1901.

For the first eight years of its existence, the Flint & Bixby Stage Line coaches forded the Santa Maria River at Suey Crossing, on the outskirts of modern Santa Maria, followed the south bank of the river to Foxen Canyon, thence southward to Santa Inés Mission and Alisal Canyon to Gaviota Pass, and down the Channel Coast through the Goleta Valley to Santa Barbara and points south. This meant the stages were traveling two sides of a triangle. The shortcut hypotenuse, by way of San Marcos Pass, was not yet open to wheeled traffic, any more than it had been in Frémont's time.

In 1868, when Daniel Hill's estate was being broken up by subdivision, a group of Santa Barbara business men headed by the town's first permanent resident doctor, Samuel B. Brinkerhoff, incorporated the Santa Ynez Turnpike Road Company and began construction of a private toll route over the Santa Ynez Range at San Marcos Pass, to serve as a link in the San Francisco-Los Angeles stage line. Coolie labor gangs from "China Camp" assaulted the pass from both sides with picks, shovels, wheelbarrows and black powder, following stakes set out along the historic Frémont Trail by Benjamin Foxen, whom legend credits with being the Pathfinder's pathfinder in 1846.

Relay stations were located at the north foot of the grade, on what is now Rancho San Fernando Rey, with a rest stop (but no change of teams) at Cold Spring, midway to the summit, and a second relay station at Patrick Kinevan's homestead south of the summit.

The toll gate was located at the San Jose Creek bridge in front of Kinevan's "Summit House," the noon dinner station, which was still standing in 1966. Kinevan charged a tariff to use the road as follows: wagons, $1 to $2.50 depending on size of team; horses, cattle and riders, 25 cents each; sheep, goats and pedestrians, 5 cents each.

From Summit House, the stage road followed Kinevan Canyon westerly to the summit, where the stages dipped onto the south slope at what is now known as Yogi Rishi Grewal's place on West Camino Cielo. The Turnpike Road then slanted down the backbone of a rocky declivity in a southwesterly direction toward Goleta Slough. On the Lillard homestead, at the 1,200-foot elevation, an impassable expanse of naked sandstone was encountered on the ridge between San Pedro and Catlett Canyons. Here the grade was so steep it was necessary to chisel six-inch-deep ruts in the bedrock for the stage wheels, and crosswise corrugations for the horses' hooves. This 100-yard stretch was called "Slippery Rock," and two sets of ruts ranging as deep as 14 inches were eventually worn into the sandstone. Slippery Rock was a favorite spot for highway robbers to lie in wait for the slow-crawling stagecoaches.*

From Slippery Rock, the stage road was staked out to follow the ridge onto the Ezra Catlett ranch, and emerge into the Valley at Patterson Avenue. But the road gangs, spying the level bottoms at the foot of the ridge, decided to change the route to flatter terrain, and moved their stakes accordingly.

At sunrise next morning, the Chinese workmen were confronted by an angry Ezra Catlett, his trusty Rebel rifle cradled across an elbow. In typical Wild West fashion, the homesteader delivered his ultimatum to the road graders: "Fust man I ketch rammin' a pick or shovel into my pasture gits a musket ball through the noggin. This is private property, so git!"

The road gangs took one look at Catlett's eyes and the muzzle of his Confederate rifle and beat a hasty retreat back to the crest of the ridge. The road they graded down to the Valley floor is plainly visible almost a century later, on the slopes flanking the Rancho del Ciervo Estates on the west.

---

* Slippery Rock in 1966 was still a spectacular sight to see. Unfortunately, because a minority of vandals and litterbugs have begun to despoil Slippery Rock, the private owner of the property is forced to forbid trespassing. Another source of damage to the soft sandstone has been the steel-cleated bulldozers of the U. S. Forest Service, which have taken the Slippery Rock short cut even when no fire emergency existed.

Stagecoach Days in the Goleta Valley

The original stage road emerged from the foothills at what is now the corner of Camino Meleno and North Patterson Avenue, and followed the latter route southward to its junction with Hollister Avenue, where Goleta village was located. It continued to use that route from 1869 to 1892.

Judge W. T. Lillard is fond of telling how as a barefoot kid he used to get the stage drivers to toss him a nickel to open and close the gate below Slippery Rock. But young Billy was not always available, and by 1892 his father, Tom Lillard, became fed up with careless stage drivers leaving gates open so livestock could stray into the brush. He closed off the road above Slippery Rock, thus forcing the Turnpike Company to build an alternate route further to the east. It is known today as San Marcos Road.

Instead of turning west up the canyon from Kinevan's toll gate, the new "trotting grade" followed the shady canyon of San Jose Creek downstream to the vicinity of the intersection of West Camino Cielo and modern Highway 154 over the pass. The stages continued on to the Ruiz Ranch in the heart of San Marcos Pass (later known as Sweetwater Ranch, now the Hidden Valley Guest Ranch) where traces of the old stage road are still visible in the neighborhood of Hobo Rock, a monolithic landmark which was blasted to bits to make way for the new four-lane freeway over the Pass.

Near the present junction of the Painted Cave and Trout Club roads, the new stage route dropped into the Goleta Valley by a very crooked grade which included a series of torturous hairpin switchbacks known to this day as the "Ws."

San Marcos Road crossed Maria Ygnacia Creek on a stone bridge at Philip C. Marble's ranch. A short distance beyond stands the tallest bay tree in the world, known for generations as "the Laurel of San Marcos," remarked upon in the journals of the earliest settlers. In 1966 it was reported to be dying, thanks to a subdivider putting a blacktop seal over its root system. *Sic transit gloria.*

South of the big laurel tree, the stages intersected Cathedral Oaks Road approximately a third of a mile west of the entrance to Tucker's Grove, followed Cathedral Oaks Road easterly for a quarter of a mile, and then turned south on a series of farm lanes which are now known collectively as "Turnpike Road." This road joined Hollister Avenue between the Pickett and Phillips ranches, at a spot now identified as the southwest corner of the San Marcos High School campus—a full mile closer to Santa Barbara than the old Slippery Rock-Patterson Avenue route had been.

The classic Concord stagecoach, familiar to all *aficionados* of Wild West fiction as the prototype of the Fisher Body trademark, was too light to stand up under mountain duty. This model was used locally only for the level runs to Lompoc Valley, behind four-horse teams.

In order to negotiate the rugged San Marcos Pass run, a yellow, Concord-built "mudwagon," mounted on laminated bullhide springs called thoroughbraces, was used behind a six-horse hitch. These sturdy vehicles could hold twenty-one passengers, twelve inside and nine topside. In cost and weight they approximated a used Volkswagen—$1,500 and 1,250 pounds, f.o.b. the Abbott & Downing Factory in Concord, New Hampshire. One of the old San Marcos mudwagons is preserved in the corridor of the county courthouse near the sheriff's office.

Paul Manchester, who recalls the stagecoaches of old Goleta, writes:

The Concord coaches and wagons had a peculiar rattle coming from the axle and boxing, which you could hear for miles. You could always identify a Concord stage by this distinctive rattle.

Several bad accidents overtook the stages on the steep mountain grade above Goleta, although the only human fatality reported was in 1893, when rookie driver Selin Carrillo attempted to ford Dos Pueblos Creek during a spring freshet. One of his roof passengers was lost overboard when the coach careened. He was swept out to sea and the body was never recovered.

There were never any relay stations or stage barns in Goleta or La Patera. The first relay station between Santa Barbara and Gaviota was at Naples, in the pit of Dos Pueblos Canyon below the Nicolás Den Adobe. Here a small, Western-style town blossomed during the Eighties and Nineties, complete with a hotel, saloon, dance hall, Wells-Fargo barn and its own United States post office. When the railroad put the stagecoaches out of business in 1901, Naples quickly withered into a ghost town, and disappeared entirely soon after

May 31, 1923, when its U.S. post office was deactivated and Naples mail was handled through Goleta.

A whole anthology of Goleta stagecoach tales could be compiled. T. Wallace More once had a hungry wildcat pounce through the open window of the stage he was riding and land on his lap; More carried the scars of fang and claw to his grave, but he killed the varmint.

This yarn is topped by one about "Whispering George" Cooper, a stage driver who was so named because his bellow could be heard from Slippery Rock to La Patera when the wind was right. George once made emergency repairs on a cracked singletree by a novel use of Yankee ingenuity. No baling wire or rope being handy, he shot the head off a five-foot rattlesnake and knotted the reptile around the singletree as a temporary expedient until he reached Goleta.

Stagecoach robberies were not uncommon, although most of them took place on the north side of the mountains, which offered more convenient places for a bandit to make his getaway.

A school housing problem developed very early in the Goleta Valley (and continues to the present). Children living on the foothill homesteads could not walk all the way to Rafaela School, so as early as 1874 classes were held in a barn rented from Charles Hails in Maria Ygnacia Canyon.

In March, 1876, the settlers organized the Cathedral Oaks School District, and in August, 1877, bought an acre of ground at the northeast corner of San Marcos and Cathedral Oaks Roads, where the daily stagecoaches passed. They paid Captain R. P. Tucker $50 for the land, and a one-room country school was built by neighborhood volunteer labor. This schoolhouse, remodeled into an attractive private residence, is located at 4974 Cathedral Oaks Road.

The first teacher at Cathedral Oaks School was Rose Everett, in 1877. According to an alumnus of the school, Horace A. Sexton, other teachers included May Hamilton, 1877; Henry F. Cook, 1881 and 1888; Ada Ferris, 1887; H. G. Mosher, 1887 and 1895; Louis Hibbard, 1896; Abbie Johnson and Emma Edmondson, 1897; Mary Sutton, 1902; Dora Garrison, 1907; Clydia Adamson, 1910; and Nettie Hall, 1911.

Cathedral Oaks School was fortunate in that it had its own recreation center, a vacant house on "Uphill Road" across from the school grounds, from which the partitions had been removed and a small stage built for amateur theatricals. The Uphill Club, as it was called, soon became the center of entertainment for the young people of the Cathedral Oaks district.

The Goleta Valley's third school district was La Patera. It came into being in 1877, to accommodate children living too far west to attend Rafaela School. Its first schoolhouse was a two-story frame structure located 150 yards west of Fairview on the road which used to lead from Hiram Hill's blacksmith shop, north of today's drive-in theater, toward the lemon packing plant. This house had been remodeled for school purposes by removing the partitions from the downstairs floor. The weight of the teacher's living quarters upstairs caused the foundations to settle and made the floor convex, which led to the school being dubbed "The Hump-Floored School."

This building was replaced in 1881 by a new schoolhouse situated on an acre of ground purchased for $100 from Edward Orr, on the east side of Fairview Avenue opposite Fairview School. Two tall palm trees mark the site today; the school yard is the property of the Christian Science Church of Goleta.

Only five teachers served at the Hump-Floored School between 1877 and 1881: James Stugfield, Lucy Cramer, Ida Holmes, O. H. Cramer and Molly Owen. At the new location, teachers included Clara Harrison, 1881; Ella Fury, 1882; May Owen, 1883; Annie Elliott and Abbie M. Holden, 1885; M. A. Colly and Grace Ross, 1887; Gertrude Leland, 1888; Daisy Campbell, 1891; Annie Baber, 1892; and Effie Baber, 1893.

In 1895, the La Patera School was moved to a new location on property jointly deeded by the Stow Ranch and Billy Hamilton on La Patera Lane, north of the present railroad. The house-moving job involved driving an anchor post in the road, attaching block and tackle between it and the schoolhouse mounted on rollers, and using several teams of horses as motive power.

At its new location, La Patera School was remodeled with a large belfry, which also housed a library.

Pioneer teachers at this location included George Callis, 1895;

Carrie McCausland, 1898; B. L. Evans, 1899; Laura D. Tanner, 1900; J. W. Marbut, 1902; Nellie Buck, 1904; Mabel Pierce, 1907; Imogene Pierce, 1908; and A. A. McDonald, 1910. Miss Nellie Langman, one of the Valley's oldest living pioneers in 1966, served as a substitute at La Patera School from 1912 to 1917. The original La Patera school bell was mounted atop a pylon in the yard of the modern La Patera School in the spring of 1965.

To take care of educating the ranchers' children residing in the far western end of the Valley, the Dos Pueblos School District was organized in 1878, with a gingerbreaded one-room schoolhouse located north of the county road near the Nicolás Den adobe. It was later moved down into the canyon. In 1889 the "Naples School" changed its name to the Den School District.

Another one-room schoolhouse stood on a hilltop beside the county road at the mouth of Tecolote Canyon, when the Tecolote School District was formed in 1891. (These outlying districts consolidated into the Ellwood Union School District in 1929, which annexed to the Goleta Union School District July 1, 1966.)

A friendly rivalry quickly developed among the farm children attending the three Valley schools. Those from Cathedral Oaks were called "Punkin-Rollers"; the Rafaela School children were "Clodhoppers"; while those attending La Patera, because of its proximity to the swamps and saltflats of Goleta Slough, were nicknamed "Webfoots".

The Goleta Valley came to the attention of various worldrenowned archaeologists during the middle Seventies, because of its abundance of prehistoric Indian sites. Skeletal remains of mammoths and mastedons were found at El Capitan and in the Hope District, proof that milleniums ago the Good Land had been "elephant country" with jungle vegetation and a very rainy climate.

H. C. Yarrow, acting assistant surgeon with the U. S. Geological Survey, on June 4, 1875, made the first governmental reports on *rancheria* sites in La Patera neighborhood. Dr. Yarrow's guide to the various known burial mounds and midden heaps was rancher T. Wallace More.

Paul Schumacher of the Smithsonian Institution in Washington, D. C., conducted extensive archaeological surveys on Dos Pueblos

Ranch during June of 1875. He shipped 50 huge crates of artifacts and human bones back to his museum. The richest treasure house of all was Mescalitán Island, and it remained so, especially for amateur pot-hunters, until the outbreak of World War II, which saw the island virtually leveled by bulldozers to obtain fill dirt for the airport runways.

During the summer of 1877, the noted French scientist Leon de Cessac excavated scores of Indian burial sites in the Good Land. Schumacher made vigorous efforts to prevent Cessac from exporting 10 tons of bones, mortars, pestles, wampum, Stone Age tools and other Indian specimens to France, but failed. Today, countless items of Goleta Valley origin are on display in Continental museums, their identity forever lost under the vague label of "North American Indian."

The most notorious despoiler of Canaliño burial grounds during the 1870s was a country preacher from Ventura, the Rev. Stephen Bowers. This controversial pot-hunter looted countless graves on Mescalitán Island, in Glen Annie Canyon, on More Mesa and Dos Pueblos Ranch, in Tecolote and Winchester Canyons, and on the Devereux Ranch. He sold his relics to the highest bidder. Among the prehistoric treasure houses stripped by Rev. Bowers was Painted Cave, located east of San Marcos Pass above the headwaters of Maria Ygnacia Creek. Basketry, weapons and other priceless Canaliño artifacts from Painted Cave were shipped to Boston.

In the modern era, Goleta Valley archaeological work has been carried out by the late David Banks Rogers under the auspices of the Santa Barbara Museum of Natural History, from 1922 through 1926, and by Curator Phil C. Orr of the same institution. Orr made many important discoveries on Mescalitán Island in 1940-41, working just ahead of the invading bulldozer blades of the U.S. Army Corps of Engineers.

Students of the archaeological department at the University of California at Santa Barbara did considerable work in the mid-1950s on Dos Pueblos Ranch through a grant-in-aid from the Samuel B. Mosher Foundation. Mosher, chairman of the board and majority stockholder of the oil company which owns Dos Pueblos Ranch, is also a member of the Board of Regents of the University of California.

Goleta, the Good Land, continues to be a rich source of Indian relics—providing one knows where to dig. Some of the prehistoric cemeteries and Indian village sites are now lost forever under the asphalt, wood and stucco of Twentieth Century "rancherias." The finest private collection of Goleta Indian artifacts is that of former movie cameraman Robert Phelan, who exhibits them in the historic Rochin adobe in Santa Barbara. Phelan enjoyed special excavating privileges on Mescalitán Island in the early 1920s. Clifford Hill of Goleta, who grew up on the Island, also has a fine private collection of artifacts.

CHAPTER XV

Trouble Ahead--A Sinking Water Table

In the true pioneer period of the Goleta Valley, before the virgin soil had been leached of its primeval fertility by repeated harvests, vegetables and fruits often grew to fantastic sizes. A twelve-pound turnip was grown on the Hollister Ranch; a ten-pound onion on the Cooper Ranch. But the vegetables which assumed preposterous, world-record dimensions were pumpkins—or "punkins", as they were universally called by dwellers on the Good Land.

In 1880 Samuel Rowe, an employee of foreman Harry Langman of the Patterson Ranch, exhibited seven pumpkins at the Santa Barbara Fair which weighed over 200 pounds each. The largest, 280 pounds, was shipped to San Francisco for use in the county display at the State Chamber of Commerce exhibit.

Pumpkins were extensively used for cattle and hog feed by Valley ranchers, and the large ones had to be chopped to pieces before a single workman could load one onto a wagon bed.

The all-time champion giant pumpkin was raised on the Philander E. Kellogg place in November, 1881. It weighed over 300 pounds, and was so huge Kellogg hollowed it out and had his petite eighteen-year-old daughter Jennie, later Mrs. David M. Culver, get inside the pumpkin shell and stick her head out for the benefit of an itinerant photographer.

This picture was published from coast to coast, and resulted in a spate of mail from bachelors who waggishly ordered "Goleta pumpkin seed of the variety that comes with a pretty girl inside; if there is a choice of color, would prefer blonde."

But the Good Land's bountiful cornucopia was not inexhaustible.

Trouble Ahead—A Sinking Water Table

By 1890, in fact, there were depressing signs of trouble ahead in the rapid lowering of the water table, in the area from San Marcos Pass to Dos Pueblos Canyon. Some farmers feared the day might not be far off when the underground water supply would be insufficient to tide the Valley over a drought cycle.

The falling water table, of course, was due to the population increase and the advent of irrigation. In a semi-arid area which averaged only eighteen inches of rainfall annually, the running streams had a flow sufficient to support approximately the number of Indians who had lived there when the Spaniards came—and the Indians had never practiced irrigation.

The first irrigation on the floor of the valley proper took place at Joe Sexton's "West Place", a twenty-one-acre plot identifiable today as a portion of the Kellogg Tract lying between Kinman Avenue and Mallard Drive, north of the Goleta School. This flat ground was planted to calla lilies. Water for irrigation was lifted from a ten-foot-deep well, located near the corner of Cardinal and Armitos Avenues. A "Chinese pump," powered by a horse, and consisting of an endless chain of wooden blocks running through an enclosed trough, was used to lift the water to where gravity could carry it down the irrigation furrows toward Hollister Avenue. Archie Phillips, a bachelor who lived in a shack nearby, kept a gourd dipper handy, where passersby could dip themselves a cold, refreshing drink.

A lowering water table meant digging deeper wells as time went on. In 1868, pioneers often struck water ten feet below the surface; hand-dug wells were usually four feet square, with 4 x 4 redwood posts supporting 1 x 12 redwood shoring planks. Further inland, wells had to be dug to 30 or 40 feet before striking water.

Every Goleta farm had its own windmill and tankhouse; a typical pioneer tankhouse still stood in 1966 on the old Henry Hill place on Patterson Avenue east of the freeway overpass, and another behind the Daniel Hill Adobe on La Patera Lane, just to mention two examples of this rapidly-disappearing bit of rural Americana.

In the 1890s, wells were drilled by means of hydraulic rigs owned by Charley Sexton, who lined his wells with six- or eight-inch metal casing. Later came gravel-packing for wells from 100 to 200 feet deep.

Horse-powered pumps were used in the Goleta Valley until the introduction of gasoline engines around 1900. Albert Stevens owned the first gasoline engine in the Valley, using it to irrigate a strawberry field from a surface well near San Jose Creek, three blocks north of the present freeway bridge. The well was fed by the creek, and provided neighborhood kids with a swimmin' hole of fond memories. Gasoline engines were replaced by electric motors about 1914 on all farms reached by power lines.

The largest artesian wells in La Patera area, which also spouted like fountains to a height of several feet, were located on Fairview Avenue north of Hollister, at the Miguel Pico and El Plimier homes (in the rear of 58 and 50 South Fairview Avenue respectively). They flowed from 40 to 100 gallons an hour year in and year out, finally tapering off to surface seeps about 1910.

Historian Isaac A. Bonilla recalls an artesian well with its casing head eight feet above the ground, which flowed until 1916, the latest date known for an artesian spring in the Goleta Valley. It was located alongside the railroad between Hollister Avenue and the San Marcos grade crossing, and was a sight which train conductors always pointed out to passengers.

Pioneer George Washington Hill was killed in 1896 in a freak accident resulting from the valley's lowering water table. When he first arrived to farm the land cornering on Fairview Avenue and Encina Road, he had only to drive an iron pipe in the ground to get a bountiful supply of water. By 1896 it became necessary to deepen his well to 100 feet or more—a dramatic demonstration of how drastically-increased water use had depleted the subterranean supply. Hill was engaged in thus deepening his well when a windlass broke. A flying chain struck him in the chest and killed him.

Charley Sexton was killed in March, 1898, by a dynamite explosion in Carpinteria, while working on a well-drilling rig he intended to use to explore for oil near Goleta Point. His funeral is often referred to by old-timers as the saddest event in Valley annals. He was only twenty-seven.

To return to earlier times, before the threat of a water shortage overshadowed the Good Land:

While Goleta and La Patera were slowly taking on more substance than mere wide spots on the stage road to Gaviota, Joseph Sexton was developing his Goleta Nursery into an important part of the economy not only of the Valley, but of Santa Barbara and Montecito.

The original 250 walnut seedlings he had transplanted in 1869 produced sixty trees which bore a soft-shelled walnut, of a variety Sexton hoped to develop for commercial use. He moved the sixty soft-shell trees to a special experimental grove on the east end of his ranch, now the Sumida property. Of these sixty trees, only one produced a soft-shelled walnut which satisfied horticulturist Sexton. He budded other trees from this individual, and thus created a new variety of walnut known as the Sexton or Santa Barbara Soft Shell. From this parent tree evolved Goleta's walnut industry, which flourished for half a century in the Valley, later extending to other parts of California as well.

In the early Seventies, every settler on the Good Land had a fruit orchard in bearing—apples, plums, apricots, and peaches predominating. Most of these were marketed in dried form at first, but the fresh fruit business came into being later, with rancher George M. Williams dominating the field.

Joe Sexton had the largest fruit-drying and sulphur-treating house in the Goleta Valley, even larger than those on Col. Hollister's ranch. Goleta began tapering off its fresh fruit production in the 1880s as walnuts took over more and more acreage.

Sexton's Nursery, in addition to stocking fruit and walnut seedlings, also maintained the most extensive selection of exotics and ornamentals in California. It was Sexton who introduced the beautiful Norfolk Island or star pine to Santa Barbara in 1874, after obtaining a single burlap-wrapped specimen which a sea captain had brought all the way from Norfolk Island, a speck in the South Seas, and sold to an unidentified associate of Sexton's in San Francisco. This associate met incoming clipper ships and sent rare seeds and plants directly to Sexton in Goleta. Sexton always planted one sample of each rare new tree or shrub in his front yard at 5490 Hollister Avenue, which accounts for the jungle-like arboretum existing there in 1966.*

---

* This arboretum, which interested citizens have been trying to get the County to acquire in the public interest for many years without success, is a botanist's paradise. For the benefit of readers interested in the rare flora to be found there today, a census was taken for this book by professional botanist Don Kenyon Sexton in the summer of 1965. The following rare specimens are still alive: silk tree, *Albizzia*

The best-known of Joseph Sexton's star pines is Santa Barbara's "Tree of Light", or municipal Christmas tree, at the corner of West Carrillo and Chapala Streets.

Sexton achieved his widest recognition as a horticulturist outside the United States through his marketing of Argentinian pampas grass plumes, an industry which will be described in detail in Chapter XXII.

Sexton's most important crop, however, was babies. Lucy Foster Sexton bore him twelve children at approximately annual intervals, beginning in 1871. All became prominent in Valley affairs, seven sons and five daughters.

The first eight children were born in the original Sexton farmhouse: Charles, 1871; Harry Eugene, 1872; Lottie, 1873; Mariette, 1874; Howard, 1875; Evalina Rose, 1876; Edna Lora, 1878; and Joseph Jr., 1879.

"If we don't get more room," Sexton told Philander Kellogg in 1880, "we'll have to swarm." Since his nursery was thriving (the horticultural as well as the domestic nursery, no pun intended), Joseph and Lucy Sexton decided they could afford the luxury of a home which would be the grandest in the Valley, although smaller than the Hollister and Stow residences in the foothills.

Sexton commissioned Santa Barbara's leading architect and builder, Peter J. Barber, to create the Victorian landmark at 5490 Hollister Avenue. Barber had designed the first Arlington Hotel in 1875. Several sturdy examples of his work still exist in Santa Barbara in 1966—the homes of Mortimer Cook (J. W. Cooper), C. C. Tinker, Lord William Broome, Thomas Hope, and Dr. Henry Stambach, among others; and Santa Barbara's oldest hotel, the Lincoln House of 1872, still doing business as the Upham.

The Sexton "mansion," as it was called by awe-struck neighbors, carries Barber's two trademarks, elaborately scrollsawed eaves

---

julibrissin, now dying; Tikoti, *Alectryon excelsum*; the tallest Norfolk Island Pine in California; *Araucaria heterophylla*; Queensland pyramid tree, *Lagunaria patersonii*; cajeput tree, with bark resembling layers of tissue paper, *Melaleuca leucadendron*; white silk oak, very rare, *Grevillea hilliana*; cork oak, *Quercus suber*, the bark of which was stripped off by the government during World War II; *Hymenosporum flavum*; the so-called "Sexton Flame Tree," a hybrid between *Sterculia diversifolia* and *Sterculia acerifolia*; Bird of Paradise tree, *Strelitzia nicolae*; Bunya-bunya, *Araucaria bidwillii*, mistakenly called the Monkey Puzzle tree; *Escallonia grahamiana*; and a rare Red box eucalyptus.

brackets and a square observatory cupola or "widow's walk" on the roof. The Sexton home boasted the Goleta Valley's first indoor bathtub, of soldered zinc, and the first metal roof, of the same material—which in 1966, after the passage of over 85 years, had yet to leak a drop.

There were eleven spacious, high-ceiled rooms, and according to Mrs. Sexton, the first walk-in closets ever built in a Valley home, doing away with old-fashioned wardrobes or curtained-off corners. There was even cold running water piped in from the tankhouse to the kitchen and an upstairs room, at a time when housewives took it for granted that water had to be carried from a well in buckets.

Sexton's first windmill was a duplicate of Florentine Kellogg's vertical louvre model on the west side of San Jose Creek. The wind blew through the louvres to strike vertical vanes and rotate the cogwheels attached to the pump. Both Sexton and Kellogg soon abandoned the vertical windmill in favor of the conventional fan type, which proved more efficient under Goleta's prevailing winds.

The Sextons moved into their commodius new quarters late in the autumn of 1880. The old residence was moved across Hollister Avenue by John F. More, and served for many years as a bunkhouse for employees of the Kellogg Creamery. It was torn down in 1907.

The Sextons' remaining children were born in the downstairs bedroom of the new home. They were Ernest, in 1881, who became a well known nurseryman in his father's footsteps, responsible for planting the palm trees along Modoc Road, in the Mission patio and along West Beach boulevard. In 1883, son Walter came along, followed in 1885 by Horace, whose historical recollections have contributed substantially to this book. The last of the dozen Sexton babies, Lucy, was born in 1888.*

Another family prominent in Goleta Valley annals arrived in 1878 from Indiana, a 33-year-old Civil War cavalry veteran named John Pickett, and his wife Euphemia. Pickett's cousin, General George Pickett, was the famous Confederate leader in the Battle of Gettysburg. The Pickett children, born in Nebraska between 1866 and 1871, were Edward, Catherine and Kenneth.

---

* For a definitive history of the Sexton family, read *Fourteen at the Table* by Walker A. Tompkins and Horace A. Sexton, privately printed but available at either the Goleta or Santa Barbara public library.

The Picketts purchased a farm at the corner of Turnpike Road and Hollister Avenue, extending north to Cathedral Oaks Road. They built their home on the spot now occupied by the auditorium of San Marcos High School; their springhouse for the cooling of milk was under a huge oak where the school's outdoor amphitheater is located. The north end of the Pickett ranch is now occupied by the grounds of the Cathedral Oaks School. The Picketts also bought a large foothill acreage on upper San Antonio Creek from John Glass in 1882.

John and Euphemia Pickett died in 1916 and 1933, respectively. They are buried in Goleta Cemetery.

Their son, Edward, bought and farmed a walnut ranch adjacent to Maria Ygnacia Creek, at what is now called Walnut Park. Daughter Emma married Eugene Shirrell Kellogg, a Goletan who was county agricultural commissioner for 26 years. Eight years after his death, Emma married Henry Simpson, of the prominent Scottish pioneer family. They now reside on upper San Antonio Creek Road, on the grazing land purchased from John Glass.

The Picketts' daughter, Catherine, married George Rowe, of Goleta, in 1889.

Son Kenneth married Mima Lane, daughter of Dallas Lane. Aged 93 in 1965, Mima Pickett was an invaluable source of fugitive history for this volume. She and her husband operated a mobile hay-baling outfit with a five-man crew, which would range up and down the Goleta Valley during the summer months baling hay for farmers. At times they went as far afield as the Santa Ynez Valley, making the return circuit in the fall and baling bean straw until about November.

Pickett's baling rig was accompanied by a cook house on wagon wheels, where Mima prepared meals for the crew on a primitive coal oil range. In spite of working away from home a great deal, Mima Pickett raised four fine daughters, two of whom still reside in Goleta—Mae, the wife of Judge W. T. Lillard, and Edith, now Mrs. William Hummell.

T. Wallace More had stubbornly refused to part with a square inch of his Goleta Valley land south of Hollister Avenue, despite many lucrative offers. But in the year 1877, More found himself in trouble. Hordes of squatters were trying to settle on his Sespe Ranch in Ventura County (separated from Santa Barbara County in 1873). More had become a very unpopular figure there when he set fire to squatters' shacks. A libel suit for $100,000 against the San Francisco *Bulletin* resulted from the newspaper's accusing T. Wallace More of attempting to poison some of the squatters—he had intended the poison for gophers. Although More won the libel suit, he was awarded only $100, which made him a laughingstock.

Finally More reached a point where he had to raise some cash to prosecute the Sespe landgrabbers. To raise funds, he very reluctantly sold a choice sixty acres, located south of Hollister Avenue and east of Ward Drive, to Florentine E. Kellogg. More received $150 an acre, a handsome profit on land for which he had paid his father-in-law Daniel Hill only $5 an acre, 20 years before.

Kellogg's son, Frank, arrived in February, 1877, to be the principal of Rafaela School. He remained to become one of Goleta's outstanding civic leaders for many years. Florentine gave him the More acreage as a gift, which Frank planted to walnuts. In 1882 he founded the famous Goleta Dairy, largest in the Valley, and turned it into a full-scale creamery operation in 1889.

T. Wallace More pocketed Kellogg's draft for $9,000 and climbed aboard a Flint & Bixby stagecoach, bound for his Sespe Ranch and a showdown battle with the squatters.

It was the last time his wife Susanna ever saw More alive.

Two weeks later, just after midnight on March 23, 1877, a gang of masked raiders set fire to a haystack alongside More's horse barn, near the site of modern Bardsdale.

T. Wallace More rushed outside in his nightshirt to rescue his horses from the burning barn. He was met by a hail of ambush lead. Next day the coroner of Ventura County found fourteen bullets in More's corpse.

CHAPTER XVI

"King John", the Monarch of More Mesa

The cold-blooded murder of T. Wallace More shocked Californians everywhere. The ringleader of the Sespe bushwhackers was known to be a squatter named F. A. Sprague. C. A. Storke, More's son-in-law, vowed to send Sprague and his henchmen to the gallows. "In my opinion", Storke declared, "the three greatest men who ever lived were Jesus Christ, Abraham Lincoln and T. Wallace More. I will bring the killers to justice if it takes all my life!"

But Storke failed. Hung juries over a period of years turned all of the conspirators free except Sprague, who got off with a ten-year penitentiary sentence.

Meanwhile, More's widow could not run the Goleta ranch by herself. Susanna Hill de More had little education and even less business experience. In her extremity, she turned to brother-in-law John, at 38 the youngest of the six More Brothers. He assumed the management of More Ranch in the late spring of 1877. Storke took over the beleaguered Sespe Ranch, which his wife Mattie had inherited.

John Finley More became a legend the day he arrived in the GoletaValley. A native of Akron, Ohio, he was married to the former Miriam Hickox. Many of his neighbors disliked him; to them he had a disposition as sweet as a raw olive and a tongue as barbed as a fish hook. Goleta Valley children adored him, however, for he was always good for a lift in his Petaluma cart, or a penny for candy.

A local wag dubbed him "King John, the Monarch of More Mesa," because of his irascibility and intolerance of trespassers. While Joe Sexton and Sam Manchester acclaimed More a prince among men, Frank Kellogg considered him a villain, for John More quickly made it clear he resented Kellogg farming a sixty-acre parcel inside the feudal domain of his martyred brother's ranch.

During John's first year on the ranch, he and his brother Alex, who had plastered Santa Rosa Island with "No Trespass" and "Keep Out" signs, built a schooner for transporting sheep and cattle from the island to the mainland. The *Santa Rosa* was a familiar sight around Goleta waters until she was wrecked on San Miguel Island in 1899.

On the second of January, 1879, John F. More bought his murdered brother's Goleta ranch from the heirs. Local gossip had it that John obtained the ranch through some kind of extrajudicial chicanery to crowd out other kinfolk. If so, the public records give no hint of how he managed it.

A man whose hunger for land amounted to an obsession, John added Mescalitán Island to his domain, buying it from the Daniel Hill heirs, and also the 471 acres of slough, marsh and submerged lands now occupied by part of the Santa Barbara Municipal Airport.

At the time More took over the ranch, one of his brother's workmen was a young Canadian, David M. Culver, then 26 years old. Culver was quickly promoted to the superintendency of the ranch, and served in that capacity for a quarter of a century. He was also wharfinger at More's Landing. Incoming steamers such as the *Coos Bay*, *Santa Cruz* or *Bonita* would give three toots of their whistle when they were a mile from the wharf. No matter what the weather or the time of day or night, Dave Culver would harness a mare to a breaking cart and hurry down to the wharf. On foggy days he would operate a hand-cranked air siren to assist boat skippers in groping their way to the pierhead. In the late 1890s, Culver turned over the wharfinger duties to Owen H. O'Neill, a kin of the Hill and Ortega families, who later became county surveyor and editor of a county history published in 1939.

It was Culver who located the site for the main More ranch house, built in 1880 by Peter J. Barber after he had completed the Joseph Sexton home. The More house stood 400 yards south of the Atascadero Creek bridge, on the high ground of More Mesa, commanding beautiful vistas of mountain, valley and sea. It became the center of a complex of huge barns, machine sheds, shops, workmen's bunkhouses, cookhouses and other out buildings. The ding-dong of the

More Ranch dinner bell became a time signal for residents of the Good Land to set their watches by for years.

The More house was thirty feet square in floor plan, two-storied, and contained sixteen huge rooms. Landscaping included native oaks, olives, oranges and lemons, with a windbreak of eucalyptus trees, now grown to gigantic height, along the west side of More Ranch Road which led to the wharf. The house remained a landmark of the valley until it was damaged in the 1925 earthquake and remodeled to a story and a half, with considerably less floor space. The modernized house in 1966 was the residence of J. A. Anderson.

It was inevitable that legends should grow up around the colorful, cantankerous personality of John Finley More. His name occupies many columns in the court records of the county; lawsuits seemed to be his hobby. He feared neither God, the Devil, nor the County Board of Supervisors.

Hollister Avenue, in front of the More Ranch, was lined with Lombardy poplars, cypress, black walnut and cork bark elms. The latter two trees were unsuitable for farming country; the walnuts cross-pollinated with More's softshell variety, while the elms sent sucker roots in all directions which, if left untrimmed, could quickly create a jungle-thick growth to sap the soil of its vitality.

More appealed to the County Supervisors for permission to remove the objectionable elms and walnuts at his own expense. The supervisors rejected his request, pointing out that tree-bordered Hollister Avenue was one of the county's most scenic country lanes, recently widened to a full 100 feet through the largesse of Colonel Hollister, and therefore an aesthetic asset to be preserved.

More said nothing, but with characteristic independence of spirit, took matters into his own hands. One weekend he had his crew chop down every black walnut and cork bark elm along his ranch frontage. "Now sue me, if you dare!" he growled at the Board of Supervisors—and that ended the matter.

The Valley's handyman, Billy Hoover, heard that John More was building some new corn cribs on the mesa, and decided to apply for a carpentering job. On his way along More Ranch Road through broad fields of vegetables, he came across a brindle-whiskered, poorly-dressed man pulling turnips from one of More's vegetable patches.

This was at a time when the Southern Pacific Railroad crossed the More Ranch, and hoboes were quite a nuisance. The unwashed gentry were wont to hop off the rods on the More Ranch, where so many unguarded chicken coops, unfenced vegetable gardens and fruit orchards practically begged a hobo to rustle up a free menu at mealtime.

Hoover paused to pass the time of day with the unkempt knight of the road, asking him if he was looking for work; if so, More was hiring now. "They tell me this new Mr. More is a tough old S.O.B. (meaning Surly Old Buzzard)", Hoover added, "and when you ask for a job he never tells you what your wages will be, but they say he pays generously."

The tramp agreed that John F. More had a reputation for being a cranky old S.O.B., but left Hoover with the distinct impression that finding a job was the last thing on his mind, other than assembling the ingredients for a mulligan stew.

Hoover scaled the road to the top of More Mesa and braced foreman Dave Culver for a job. He got one on the corncrib-building project. Leaving for home that evening, Hoover caught sight of the turnip-stealing hobo emerging from one of More's poultry houses with a plump pullet under his arm. This theft offended Hoover's sense of propriety. He collared the man and marched him over to the blacksmith shop to confront Culver.

"I just caught this hobo stealing a chicken out of Mr. More's coop, boss," Hoover said heatedly. "Shall I take him in to the constable on my way home?"

Culver looked aghast. "He's not a hobo!" Culver expostulated. "He's your boss, John More!"

... The corn cribs on which carpenter Billy Hoover worked were in two rows of ten each with a driveway between, and were located west of the main house and north of the KTMS radio towers of today. Each corn crib rested on a foundation of stone dressed to the shape of a cube, stones not indigenous to the Goleta Valley, where all available rock was soft sandstone. The square-cut blocks had been obtained from a heap of ballast stones discarded by ships from the seven seas, which in the remote past had taken on cargo in an ancient arm of the Goleta Slough, near today's Pacific Lighting Gas Supply Company's injection plant.

The floods of 1861 had filled the inlet with silt, ending its navigability for ocean-going vessels. In comparatively recent times, the ballast stones were bulldozed into the tules, sinking out of sight during winter floods. This same inlet is believed to have been where Benjamin Foxen launched California's first locally-made schooner in 1828.

The More Ranch had a dairy which was operated by an Italian emigrant named James Giordano, the spelling later changed to Jordano. The Jordanos lived in a humble shack near the edge of the cliffs where More Ranch Road slanted down the ramp to the wharf. Here were born three sons, John, Dominic and Peter, who in partnership with a younger brother, Frank, created the string of modern Jordano supermarkets from a humble beginning in a grocery store in Santa Barbara in 1915. Jordano later owned a ranch near 500 North Turnpike Road, now the Racquet Club Estates.

Among the milkers employed by James Jordano on the More Ranch dairy was a Sonoran youth, Frank Romo, whose parents lived on a homestead in the foothills north of Holiday Hill, between the Albert G. Hollister and Tom Lillard ranches. Young Frank figured in a John More episode which he was reticent to discuss, even after he had grown to manhood. It is printed here for the first time.

It was Frank Romo's task every evening to round up More's milch cows from the pasture at the foot of the More Mesa bluffs, bordering Atascadero Creek near its confluence with Maria Ygnacia Creek. On one warm summer evening, while searching for a stray calf in the thick willowbrake, Romo stumbled over a pair of blood-stained, tooled-leather *alforjas*, or saddlebags, lying in the salt grass. The bags were full of shiny gold coins!

Further investigation turned up a dead saddle horse deeper in the willows, with two bullet holes in its brisket. Near the horse, Romo made another gruesome discovery: a dead man with a bullet hole in his back. Romo figured afterward that he must have been a bandit who had been shot while robbing a stage or a bank, and had fled into the concealment of the willow jungle on More's Ranch, where he and his mount had bled to death.

"I was scared stiff", Frank Romo confessed long afterwards. "I ran up to the big house on the mesa and told Mr. More what I had found. He told me to forget about the stray calf and take the rest of the day off, so I went home. Next day, in bright sunlight, I screwed up enough courage to go into that willow thicket again. The dead horse and the dead man weren't there. The bags of gold were gone, too. I never did find out what became of them."

John More, with Dave Culver's capable assistance, converted his Goleta Valley ranch into one of the most profitable operations in the area, rivaling the Hollister (Bishop), Cooper and Stow ranches. He was the first Goleta rancher to import Shorthorn cattle from Kentucky, in May of 1888.

The elevated ground of More Mesa, extending eastward to the Hope Ranch boundary, became high-yielding lima bean and wheat fields. The beaches by More's Landing were open to the public on week days, but More always locked his big gate on Hollister Avenue on Sundays. This created a source of friction with the public, who felt the beach was their property, also.

Threshing outfits, as many as four at once, were going full blast on More Mesa during harvest time. More's lemon and walnut groves on the bottomlands were among the finest in the Valley, the ordered rows of trees resembling the tufts of a candlewick bedspread, when viewed from the foothills. More also planted olives and oranges in the vicinity of his home.

More built a two-story frame house on Mescalitán Island for the use of a Mrs. Rowe, his sister, and clamped down rigid restrictions against digging on the island for Indian relics. A favored few families, headed by the Sextons and Manchesters, were allowed to maintain vacation camps on the shores of the Estuary, known as Camp Lupine, where they spent several weeks every summer boating, clamming and fishing.

Always hungry for more wealth, John F. More leased Santa Rosa Island from his brother, Alexander, for $20,000 a year, raising sheep for the wool. More started with 60,000 sheep and worked up to around 125,000 head. His brother had made $80,000 profit from the sale of 300,000 pounds of wool in 1875, but in 1876 the wool market collapsed and a *matanza* was held at which 1,200 sheep per day were slaughtered.

John wanted to buy Santa Rosa Island, but Alex was asking $1,000,000 for its 62,696 acres of gullied chaparral wilderness, and once turned down a cash offer of $750,000.

Brother Alex was one of the more eccentric members of the More Brothers combine of Gold Rush days. His chief claim to notoriety came in 1886, when he caught one of his Chinese cooks attempting to stow away on a cattleboat to escape what amounted to involuntary servitude on the island. In a fit of blind rage, Alexander More shot and killed the Celestial. Haled into court at Santa Barbara on a manslaughter charge, More was convicted; but an appellate judge reversed the decision on the grounds that since the victim had been on a wharf over channel waters at the time he was shot, and the sovereignty of said waters was in dispute among County, State and Federal governments, the Santa Barbara court had no jurisdiction over the matter—so Alex P. More went free.

Alex died in Chicago in October, 1893, leaving no will. His estate at that time was worth over $800,000, including Santa Rosa Island and the sheep thereon, leased to brother John. Left to fight over the distribution of this bonanza were four sisters, Eliza M. Miller, Eleanor H. More, Martha Jane Orcutt and Cornelia Baldwin; one brother, John F. More, of Goleta; the late T. Wallace More's three children, Mattie Law (recently divorced from C. A. Storke), Wallace H. and Thomas R. More; the late Andrew More's children, Helen K. Rowe, Albert W. and John C.; and the late Lawrence More's children, H. Clifford of Tajiguas Rancho, Winfield R. and M. Rose More.

John F. More promptly filed a petition for letters of administration of his deceased brother's estate. The court appointed him special administrator on an *ex-parte* application, but his application for general letters was opposed by his sister, Eliza Miller. She had her attorney, C. A. Storke, file a petition asking that she be named administratrix, alleging that John F. More should be disqualified because he had been Alex's business partner as leasor of Santa Rosa Island. This put John in a position of making reports on his cash income to himself as the administrator. John countered by saying Mrs. Miller was ineligible to administer the estate in California, because she lived in Chicago.

Goleta residents noticed that marine traffic at More's Landing picked up at a dizzy rate as John began transferring thousands of head of cattle and sheep from Santa Rosa Island to the mainland. Stock buyers were waiting to buy them and drive them to rail. John

F. More, who was functioning as administrator under $500,000 bond, was closely watched by attorney Storke, who advised the other heirs that John was not accounting for or properly sharing his profits with the other heirs.

This *intrafamilia* feud was enlivened in January of 1895 by the claim of a Santa Barbara blacksmith, J. B. Quintero, that he was Alexander P. More's illegitimate son and therefore sole heir to the $800,000 estate. A firm of Los Angeles shysters had agreed to handle his case on a contingent fee basis, but nothing ever came of it.

For two years, John F. More continued to strip livestock from the brushy canyons of Santa Rosa Island. Finally, on May 21, 1896, C. A. Storke filed a petition to have John removed from the administrative job he had enjoyed to his own profit since February 12, 1894. A San Francisco judge agreed that John More had made too good a thing out of the arrangement, and suspended him as administrator while his business transactions were audited.

On June 10, 1896, the Santa Barbara *Herald* broke the sensational story that John F. More had swindled the other heirs out of $80,000, which the court ordered him to pay back to the estate.

More did not have $80,000; he had been losing heavily in Nevada mining stock promotions, a weakness which almost bankrupted him. In order to salvage what he could, More surrendered his eighth interest in Santa Rosa Island to the estate. His sister, Martha, promptly sold her share to George Edwards, the banker; Thomas R. More sold his share to Jarrett T. Richards, founder of the law firm of Price, Postel & Parma. Sister Eleanor died and willed her share back to John. In 1901, Alexander's remaining five heirs sold their interest in Santa Rosa Island to Vail & Vickers, of Los Angeles, for $200,000. They later bought John F. More's share, which had been Eleanor's, ending his complicated interlude on Santa Rosa Island.

More's ranch superintendent, Dave Culver, married Jennie Kellogg, famous as the "girl in the pumpkin," in 1884. She bore him a son, Edgar, before her death of tuberculosis on July 4, 1889. In 1894, Culver married Martha Tucker, daughter of George and Angeline Kellogg Tucker. They resided in the main ranch house when John F. More retired to his town house, a stately, shingle-sided Edwardian structure which in 1966 still stood at 131 East Arrellaga Street. To the Culvers were born daughters Mildred, now Mrs. Harold

Love, and Ruth, Mrs. Harvey Hammond, both well-known Goleta residents.

Culver's salary was only $30 a month, but to make up for this More promised to deed Culver ten acres where the Community Hospital now stands at Hollister and Patterson Avenues. When Culver went to take title to this land, More was so deep in debt that he could not live up to his promise, the land being mortgaged to others because a mining bonanza near Searchlight, Nevada, in which More had invested heavily, proved to be a fraud.

Culver had accumulated enough money to buy a small acreage on the east side of South Patterson Avenue in 1887. When he left More's employ in 1898 he built the house which in 1966 still stood at 92 South Patterson Avenue. Here he and Martha spent the remaining years of their lives. Culver died in 1938, his widow in 1964.

Shortly before leaving the More Ranch, Culver played a trick on a crew of Chinese wood choppers who were camped in tents on the west end of More Mesa overlooking Goleta Slough. On the mudflats between the mesa and Mescalitán Island, on what is now Sanitary District property, natural gas bubbled to the surface. A favorite stunt used by Goletans to impress strangers was to touch a match to these gas pockets, causing them to burn like torches until extinguished by the next incoming tide.

David Culver, thinking to have some fun with the Orientals, set fire to a dozen or so gas springs, and then summoned the Chinamen to have a look. "There's a Chinese dragon trapped under those tideflats," Culver joked, "and he's snortin' fire trying to climb out into the fresh air. He'll make it, too."

To Culver's astonishment, the Chinese took him literally and raced back to their camp with black queues flying. Wadding up their tents without bothering to pull the pegs, they started hotfooting it for Santa Barbara, where they could find refuge from fire-breathing dragons in the Chinatown joss house on Canon Perdido Street next to Lobero's Opera House.

"When I saw they were serious, I offered to drive them into town in a wagon," Culver recalled, "but they wouldn't wait. They never came back, either."

The bane of John F. More's existence was the sixty-acre farm on Hollister Avenue which T. Wallace More had sold to Florentine

E. Kellogg for $9,000 a fortnight before his murder in 1877.

For years, John F. More pestered Kellogg to sell. Kellogg stubbornly refused. Finally, in April 1907, in an effort to rid himself of More's offers, Kellogg said jokingly, "If you want it for $1,000 an acre, the ranch is yours." At the time, Goleta farms in the vicinity were worth about $300 an acre.

Next day, to Kellogg's chagrin, John More showed up with a bank draft for $60,000 and a deed for Kellogg to sign. Kellogg, being a man of his word, had no choice but to sell the farm he had worked for thirty years, and had no real desire to give up.

It was characteristic of More's contentious nature that as soon as the sale was recorded, he leveled the creamery buildings, obliterating to the last splinter and brick all traces of an alien ownership inside the More domain.

The Mores had three children: Isabel, who married Charles Perry Austin; John Faxon, and Miriam. Isabel attained prominence as an artist and writer before her death in 1941.

Salty old John F. More died in Cottage Hospital, Santa Barbara, on April 27, 1919, just short of his 80th birthday. He was the last survivor of the six empire-building brothers who had made so much history in California in the post-Gold Rush years.

John Faxon More married Mary E. Rouse, of Oakland, in March, 1901. Their only child, John More III, died in 1921 of scarlet fever at the age of fifteen. John Faxon More died of cirrhosis of the liver in 1933 at the age of fifty-four. During his widow's lifetime, the ranch was managed by Peter Irvine. By the time she died in 1955, the More Ranch had been sold off piece by piece.

Since no males are left to carry on the More name in the Goleta Valley, *finis* must be written to a saga which began with T. Wallace More's courtship of a daughter of Daniel Hill, more than a century before.

CHAPTER XVII

The Den Estate Sues Colonel Hollister

By the time 1876 rolled around, administrator C. E. Huse had been directing the affairs of the Nicolás Den Estate for fourteen years. The consensus of Goleta Valley settlers was that Huse had not only mismanaged the Dens' affairs, but had robbed them blind. As an example, they cited the Rincon Ranch scandal.

Rincon Ranch stretched along the coastal mesa between Pelican (Goleta) Point and Coal Oil Point, the area now occupied by UCSB, Isla Vista and the Devereux Ranch. The name Rincon (not to be confused with the promontory near Ventura of the same name) means "corner" in Spanish, and refers to the right-angled bend in the early ranch road which is now the place where Storke and El Colegio Roads meet, near Isla Vista School.

This portion of the Den Estate had gone to two of Nicolás' heirs, son August getting the eastern half, son Alfonso the western. August Den had been mentally retarded since birth, and his 407-acre inheritance, covered with an oak grove, had little value either as farming land or for grazing. Later a lucrative asphaltum mining operation was developed there, and Gus Den wound up a rich man.

Alfonso Den had just come of age, but the interests of 19-year-old Gus Den still rested in the hands of C. E. Huse. Huse leased Gus' ranch to Henry H. and Alexander P. More, who paid Huse $2,500 in cash. Huse pocketed the money without accounting for it, concealing the transaction by juggling his books of the Den Estate. But something he could not conceal from the sharp eyes of Goleta Valley neighbors was the fact that the More Brothers were chopping down the luxuriant growth of liveoaks and selling the wood to a nearby whaling camp as fuel for their blubber pots. The trees did not belong to the Mores under the terms of their lease. When the oaks had been thinned out, high ocean winds quickly stripped away the shallow topsoil, reducing the future Isla Vista and UCSB campus to a treeless waste of blow-sand. Worse yet, at one time more than 1,000 cords of valuable oak wood lay rotting on the ground unsold. Attorney Charles Fernald of Santa Barbara protested this wanton waste later on during court testimony:

> C. E. Huse wrongfully permitted the More Bros. to cut and sell for firewood, valuable liveoak timber growing on the Rincon lease, the unauthorized cutting of which was a loss and a detriment to the trust property. Though notified by the Den heirs of this spoilage, and that the wood was still lying on the ground unused, Huse made no effort to secure the wood for the Estate, but allowed the More Bros. to convert same to their own use.

All of the Den heirs were spendthrifts, and none were good managers. They had stood by for fourteen years, watching Huse dissipate their patrimony either through non-payment of taxes or through downright fraudulent acts. But there was one exception to this lethargic acceptance of Huse's misdeeds: Nicolás Den's oldest child, Kate, who had married John Stewart Bell, of Los Alamos, in 1872. The Bells lived on a fine ranch furnished them by John's father, Tom Bell, a controversial San Francisco capitalist.

In October, 1876, Kate Bell learned that Charles E. Huse had petitioned the Santa Barbara District Court to wind up the Den trust and put its seal of approval on Huse's past administration. Kate knew if this approval were forthcoming, there would be no way to bring Huse to account for his sins. She decided to discuss the possibility of filing a countersuit against Huse. That meant consulting a lawyer outside of Santa Barbara. She was advised to see Thomas B. Bishop, of Bishop & Evans, Montgomery Street, San Francisco, a law firm specializing in checking out loopholes and minor flaws in land titles based on Mexican land grants in California.

Obtaining an appointment with Tom Bishop, Kate and her husband journeyed to San Francisco. They outlined as best they could the alleged skulduggery practiced by Huse, but their allegations were based on hearsay and were of little interest to Bishop. However, when Kate Bell injected such well-known Goleta Valley personages as Colonel W. W. Hollister and Ellwood Cooper into her narrative, she detected an immediate quickening of interest on Bishop's part.

When she had finished, Bishop riffled through her copy of Nicolás A. Den's will, paying particular attention to the trust agreement clauses therein. What he found made his pulses race.

"Now let me see if I have this straight in my mind, Mrs. Bell," Bishop said. "Your father set aside the eastern portion of Los Dos Pueblos grant in trust for his children. Do I understand correctly that the Hollister Ranch, the Sturges Brothers' Tecolote Ranch, Winchester Canyon Ranch and Ellwood Cooper's Ranch all lie inside that portion of the estate covered by the trust?"

"That is correct, Mr. Bishop."

"And these sales were not approved by the Probate Judge?"

"No, the probate court was ignored entirely," Kate Bell explained. "However, this was done with the knowledge and consent of all the heirs, including myself, and by my mother and the trustees representing the minor children. Our family was destitute at the time, and the money received from the ranches was desperately needed."

Bishop waggled his head in utter disbelief.

"It makes no difference if everyone concerned approved the sales —Huse forfeited his case when he failed to get the approval of the probate court. Mrs. Bell, I am going to recommend that you file suit against Huse, Hollister, Cooper, and the Sturges Brothers, to recover the trust property sold by Huse. I will stake my reputation that the courts will not only restore these properties to the Den Estate, but all improvements that have been made from 1869 to the present!"

Kate Bell was stunned. The possibility of recovering any portion of her late father's estate had never occurred to her; she was only after damages from Charles E. Huse.

Kate well knew how land values had skyrocketed in the Good Land during the first half of the Seventies. Her brother, Manuel, had received $8,250 for 1,000 acres in Winchester Canyon in 1870; Colonel Hollister had only recently bought that property back from Dr. R. F. Winchester for $33,937. Isadore Dreyfus had paid

$30,000 for 1,000 acres in Eagle Canyon, the arroyo adjoining Dos Pueblos Canyon on the east. Since 1869, more than half a million dollars had been poured into improvements on the Tecolote, Ellwood Cooper and Glen Annie ranchos.

"There is one thing you should know, Mr. Bishop," Kate Bell said. "Your fees, I am sure, come high. I am afraid I cannot—"

T. B. Bishop waved her into silence. "Bishop & Evans will take this case on a contingent fee basis, Mrs. Bell. If we recover any land for you, we will take our fee in land—say on a 50-50 basis? If we lose—and I must warn you that a case of this magnitude could easily take years to prosecute—you and your family would not owe us a penny in legal fees or court costs. Is it a deal?"

It was a deal, one that would shatter the peace and quiet of the Goleta Valley as not even an earthquake could have done.

Santa Barbara's newspapers first broke the story that the Den Estate, through Bishop & Evans of San Francisco, had filed suit to recover all trust properties in the Goleta Valley which had been sold without court sanction by administrator C. E. Huse.

At his baronial mansion in upper Glen Annie Canyon, Colonel Hollister felt a twinge of alarm. Ever since that day in 1869, when Judge Maguire had warned him not to purchase the Glen Annie on Huse's terms, Hollister had lived with a gnawing maggot of anxiety in his brain that some day his act might return to haunt him. Now it would appear that after fourteen years, Nemesis had come in the person of Tom Bishop, one of the toughest, shrewdest, most capable legal minds in California.

Hollister saddled his fastest horse and raced to Santa Barbara to confer with his local attorney, Charles Fernald. Fernald reassured his client there was nothing to worry about. In this poker game called the law, Bishop was bluffing, Fernald opined, hoping to squeeze some kind of out-of-court settlement from the defendants. He advised the Colonel to go home and forget all about it.

Ellwood Cooper, another Goleta Valley rancher who with his financial partner, Mrs. Hannah Cutts, was named as a defendant in the suit against Huse, received a less encouraging report from his attorney, Robert B. Canfield.

Canfield said, "I will have to agree with Bishop that the Dens have a valid case, and could win in the event of a lengthy litigation.

My advice would be to avoid the expenses of such a litigation by agreeing to any reasonable compromise which Bishop may offer you, Ellwood."

Bishop did offer a compromise, only a week before the case was docketed for Judge Ygnacia Sepulveda's 17th Judicial Court in Santa Barbara, early in 1877. T. B. Bishop booked a suite at the Hotel Arlington and posted identical memoranda to the principal defendants in the forthcoming action—Hollister, Cooper and Cutts, the Sturges Brothers—inviting them to meet with him and attempt to settle the case out of court.

"Bishop can go to hell!" W. W. Hollister's defiance echoed off the Goleta Valley foothills. "I will never yield an inch of land to that shyster."

Ellwood Cooper, swayed by his friend Hollister against his better judgment, elected to stand by the colonel and fight the Dens. The Sturges Brothers Company, William, Harold and Shelton Jr., also cast their lot with Hollister, their father having purchased the Tecolote Canyon Ranch in 1876 on Hollister's recommendation.

The day the trial opened—a trial destined to rank as the most important land case of the century in Southern California—every resident of the Goleta Valley who could manage to do so found a seat in the jam-packed courtroom.

T. B. Bishop, a dynamic, suave, eloquent man whose neatly barbered Van Dyke beard and steelpen fustian coat gave him an impressive appearance, was opposed by Charles Fernald, a rather mousy-appearing small-town lawyer, as chief counsel for the defendants. It became obvious, from the moment Bishop started his case by enumerating eighteen specific charges he intended to prove against C. E. Huse, that Fernald was a badly mismatched lightweight in this legal arena.

With fiery oratory, Bishop hammered home point after point, winding up by damning Huse's general attitude and conduct as "proof that he has not only been grossly careless and incompetent, but actually antagonistic to the interests of the Nicolás Den heirs entitled to his protection and guardianship."

Colonel Hollister, after sweating through his first hour of listening to Charles Fernald's bumbling attempts at rebuttal, hurried out to the telegraph office and dispatched an SOS to his business partner

John Pickett farmhouse stood on site of San Marcos H. S. auditorium

Pioneers James and Elizabeth Anderson in front yard now occupied by Highway 101 and Fairview Avenue overpass

Sherman P. Stow's home, built in 1872, was still a Stow Ranch landmark going into 1966

Joseph Sexton home at 5494 Hollister Avenue was built by P. J. Barber in 1880, the finest on Valley floor. Still standing in 1966

A familiar landmark of the Goleta Valley from 1873 to 1962 was W. W. Hollister's ranch gateway and Avenue of Palms at what is now Coromar Drive. It has been moved to 570 Glen Annie Road by Howard M. Goldman

Stamp collectors know of only 15 existing specimens of famous Goleta "Kicking Mule" cancellation, featured by Goleta post office from 1880 to 1885. This rare copy courtesy of Lee H. Cornell, noted philatelic author

Summer vacation encampment on Goleta Estuary was popular before the turn of the century. Mescalitán Island (right) was then completely surrounded by tidewater. Goleta Mesa on left was Gus Den ranch, now UCSB. Tents and boats of the Sexton, Manchester and Stevens families. Sandspit owned by John More

Pampas grass plumes drying on Sexton Nursery field now occupied by playground of St. Raphael parochial school, St. Joseph Road. Pampas plumes were a booming industry in Valley, principal markets being England and Germany

Sexton family, Christmas Day 1893. Standing l. to r.: Marriette, Joseph Sr., Lucy Foster Sexton, Charles, Rose, Harry, Howard, Horace. Seated, l. to r.: Ernest, Edna, Lottie, Joseph Jr., (kneeling), Walter, Lucy. One of Valley's most prominent families.

Samuel Manchester

Miles D. Lane

August Linquest

John Pickett

John Troup Sr.

George M. Williams

Russell Rowe

Peter Irvine Sr.

Stephen Rutherford

in San Francisco, Albert Dibblee, requesting him to hire the "best available lawyer as Fernald's assistant in this case." Within the hour Dibblee wired back that he had engaged the services of S. M. Wilson, one of California's legal aces, for a retainer of $1,000.

Hollister was outraged at such a fee and angrily telegraphed Dibblee that he wanted "a lawyer, not a pirate." Dibblee, knowing that the hot-tempered Colonel could not pinch pennies in the legal market as he did for Chinese coolies in the labor market, paid the $1,000 retainer out of his own pocket and sent Wilson south on the next steamer to help Fernald counter Bishop's heavy artillery.

Wilson evened the match against Bishop during the following weeks of the case, which saw the Goleta Valley become the focus of attention of newspapers from San Francisco to Boston. Colonel Hollister, Ellwood Cooper and the other defendants were on the witness stand for days on end; Santa Barbara could discuss nothing else.

Courtroom spectators, violently partisan, broke out with hoots and catcalls when the man they regarded as the villain in the drama, Tom Bishop, began his final summation. The defense attorney, Wilson, drew cheers and whistles of approval when he castigated Bishop for his "arbitrary application of trivial technicalities in seeking minute flaws in substantial titles." He cited as examples of Bishop's nit-picking, the great issue he had built up over the final decree of distribution having been published three times instead of the four required by law, an oversight of the newspaper involved; or a minute typographical error in an obscure legal document, which set 10 a.m. instead of 11 a.m. as the time of a hearing.

When the trial ended, Judge Sepulveda took it under advisement, giving the citizens of the Goleta Valley some time to chew their nails in suspense. Everyone was aware that the future of three of the Good Land's most important ranches hung in the balance.

The tension ended on March 29, 1878, when Judge Sepulveda ruled in favor of Hollister and his co-defendants.

Tom Bishop seemed almost jaunty in defeat. As he boarded the steamer *Orizaba* to return to San Francisco, he told reporters gathered on Stearns Wharf that while he had lost a minor skirmish, the war was only just beginning.

As expected, Bishop took an appeal to a higher court, which reviewed the complexities of the Den Estate case for an interminable year and a half before handing down a ruling. During this interval, the defendants' legal staff remained on payroll. An angry Ellwood Cooper wrote to Albert Dibblee shortly after he and Hollister had paid out $9,000 in legal fees:

> I see but little hope for California—too many lawyers. The public welfare is imperiled. In Santa Barbara a greater set of asses never existed. Those who are alive 50 years from now [1928] will form Vigilance Committees and hang half the lawyers.

The appellate court on November 13, 1879, plunged the Hollister camp into deep despair by reversing the decision rendered by Judge Sepulveda in the lower court, and remanded the case for a new trial.

The first thing Colonel Hollister did after recovering from this shock was to dictate a sarcastic telegram to his high-priced counsel, S. M. Wilson, advising him that his services were no longer required. This threw Charles Fernald into a panic, for while he was the acknowledged civic leader of Santa Barbara and a man of great courage and integrity, he recognized his own small-town professional limitations and knew he stood little chance against a titan of Thomas B. Bishop's stature in the legal world.

The court reversal demoralized Ellwood Cooper. He drove his pony cart over to Glen Annie and told Colonel Hollister he was going to compromise with Bishop & Evans; that he could not endure the nervous stresses and torments of another long, drawn-out litigation. Better half a loaf than none at all, Cooper opined.

Hollister told Cooper he was a fool to compromise but that their mutual friendship would not be impaired in any way if Cooper decided to defect to the enemy. If need be, Hollister said, he would stand and fight Bishop alone to the bitter end.

Bishop proved to be magnanimous in his treatment of Ellwood Cooper. He told him he had only to turn back to the Den Estate that portion of his ranch lying between the county road and the ocean, excluding Cooper's 160 acres of eucalyptus seedlings. In return, Cooper would receive a quit claim deed to the remaining two-thirds of the ranch in Ellwood Canyon, which included Cooper's extensive persimmon, olive and walnut orchards, his olive mill, home, and other improvements. Bishop would also grant Cooper a perpetual right-of-way easement to the "sea shell beach" where the family loved to picnic.

Cooper and his wife, Sarah, accepted the compromise gratefully.

The new trial against Hollister and the Sturges brothers was scheduled for Judge Fawcett's court in Santa Barbara, but the latter, having been associated with Colonel Hollister in the formation of the Lompoc temperance colony five years previously, disqualified himself. A change of venue shifted the second trial to Santa Clara County Superior Court in San Jose, Judge Francis E. Spencer presiding. (The new Superior Court system had just replaced the former District Court system which had been used in California since 1850.)

With Round Two coming up before an out-of-town judge, W. W. Hollister faced the problem of replacing Wilson, the defense counsel he had fired. This time, not trusting his partner, Albert Dibblee, to make the selection, Hollister went to San Francisco himself and signed up the highest-ranking lawyer in the State, Henry E. Highton. The latter's fees made Wilson's retainer seem like petty cash, but by now Hollister realized there was an outside chance of losing his beloved Glen Annie to the perfidious Den family, and he had to hire the best brains available to counteract Tom Bishop.

Highton decided on a radical shift in tactics for the defense in the second trial. The defendants, Hollister and Sturges, would concede that their 1869 purchases in the Goleta Valley had been irregular, due to the bypassing of the probate court by C. E. Huse. However, the defendants felt they were entitled to recover the vast sums of money they had expended in improving the two ranches.

"By employing this strategy, we will pull Bishop's fangs," Highton explained. "I am confident we can win our case on these terms, as in order to get back the property, the Den Estate would have to repay the enormous sums of money you have invested in improving the land. This they would find impossible to do. You would wind up retaining your ranches by default."

On this happy note the litigation went into temporary adjournment—a hiatus which stretched on for three weary years, until the second trial was finally opened in San Jose in October, 1884.

By then, Highton had persuaded Hollister to hire him an assistant in the person of P. G. Galpin, a San Francisco attorney of similar standing to himself. Hollister, paying his legal fees without protest now that he was genuinely frightened about the outcome of the case, tried to convince himself that this array of legal talent would out-match heavyweight challenger Tom Bishop. Charles Fernald had long since been discarded.

In a brilliant summation to the court, Henry Highton pointed out that Hollister had transformed the Good Land of the Goleta Valley from an undeveloped virgin wilderness to an Elysium which was famous to millions of people in the United States, through newspaper publicity, if not actual visits.

In his impassioned plea to the court, Highton said:

> The Glen Annie in the Nicolás Den era was devoted to pastoral purposes, the lowest use to which land can be put. Under Colonel Hollister's administration, it has been converted to diversified horticulture, the last and highest step in the economic development of soil short of conversion to cities.
>
> The heirs of Nicolás A. Den heartily approved every step of the sale to Col. Hollister. The case for the defense summarizes, therefore, as follows:
>
> (1) Colonel Hollister paid in full and over value for the land he bought in the Goleta Valley.
>
> (2) The Den Estate used this money to pay its debts and feed, clothe and educate the children.
>
> (3) The improvements made by Hollister were appropriate, permanent, and valuable, and not only definitely increased the value of the ranch itself, but the surrounding Goleta Valley countryside as well.

On that lofty note, Highton and Galpin rested their case for the defense. The hearing ended in San Jose, and there would be another frustrating delay while Judge Spencer pondered the lengthy transcript of the case.

For Colonel Hollister, the interlude had one diversion, not a pleasant one for him. His oldest child and only daughter, Jennie, lame because of a congenital deformity and then aged 22, announced her engagement to a multi-millionaire widower from Cleveland, Robert L. Chamberlain, aged forty-eight.

Hollister vigorously opposed the union, pointing out that Chamberlain was a semi-invalid whose three children, Joseph Jr., Selah, and Ellen, were nearly as old as the intended stepmother.

Annie Hollister and her daughter brushed aside the Colonel's angry protests and went on planning for a formal garden wedding at Glen Annie which would be the most glamorous social event in the history of the Goleta Valley. Anti-climactically, when Jennie's wedding day arrived on August 26, 1885, it found the bride ill, so she had to repeat her nuptial vows from a sickbed.*

Colonel Hollister had not yet had time to recover his spleen over Jennie's marriage—which caused a permanent estrangement between father and daughter—when Judge Spencer announced his ruling in the Den Estate case. It spelled calamity for the Hollisters and Sturgeses.

The court ruled the Den Estate was entitled to recover all Dos Pueblos trust property illegally sold by administrator C. E. Huse, and that the defendants were not entitled to compensation for what they had spent in improvements over the years, the court holding that they had received enough income off the ranches during that time to offset this amount.

Harold Sturges, who had been sole owner of Tecolote Ranch since his two brothers left California in 1883, bowed to the inevitable and vacated the Tecolote Ranch. After ten years' residence there, he took a 100 percent loss of time and money. On October 17, 1887, a T. B. Bishop subsidiary, the Tecolote Ranch Company, took over the property from the Den Estate in partial payment of legal fees and money loaned to the Den family over a period of several years.

Hollister's title to Winchester Canyon was confirmed by the court, having been purchased from Den heirs who were of age, and in a manner which did not violate the terms of Nicolás Den's will. Winchester Canyon remained in the Hollister Estate until 1965.

---

*Chamberlain died of a spinal ailment on August 11, 1888, two weeks before their third wedding anniversary, leaving his 25-year-old widow with three stepchildren and a $5,000,000 estate. In 1894 Jennie married Clinton Bennett Hale of Chicago. Their stately home at Laguna and Pedregosa streets in Santa Barbara was a social center for the élite for many years. Hale died in 1925, Jennie in 1940. Her will specified that their home be razed following her death.

Unlike Sturges, Hollister did not surrender. His legal staff, which stood to gain financially by keeping a hopeless case alive year after year, took advantage of the Colonel's almost psychopathic stubbornness and announced they would appeal the fight to the State Supreme Court and, if necessary, to the U.S. Supreme Court.

Judges McFarland, Thornton and Sharpstein of the State Supreme Court took the case to study in bank. Their verdict was not expected for two or three years at the earliest.

Faced by this delay, life in the Goleta Valley returned to something like normal again.

CHAPTER XVIII

Glasgow to Goleta: The Scottish Exodus

In the year 1872, Ellwood Cooper wrote a letter to a horticulturist friend in Scotland, in which he described his new ranch in California, and casually mentioned he was looking for reliable men to plant eucalyptus and walnut trees.

A few months later a group of six brawny young Scotsmen from Aberdeenshire arrived at the Cooper Ranch, looking for work. These men—James Smith, William N. Hendry, John Rutherford, William Begg, Jim Milne and John McClaren—were the vanguard of an influx of Scotsmen who were to establish a flourishing Caledonian colony in the Goleta Valley.

Later in 1872, Stephen Rutherford of Edinburgh followed his brother John on the Glasgow-to-Goleta voyage. Disembarking at Stearns Wharf in Santa Barbara, he walked down the beach as far as the Carpinteria Valley, hunting for work. Finding none, he headed back along the green foothills until he arrived at Glen Annie, where Colonel W. W. Hollister put him on the payroll.

Shortly thereafter, Hollister began negotiations with a Santa Cruz emigrants' association, which led to the founding of the Lompoc temperance colony. The secretary of the Lompoc Valley Homesteaders' Association, George Long, of La Patera, was a friend of Hollister's. He took a strong liking to young Rutherford.

When Long moved to Lompoc in 1874, he offered Steve Rutherford first option to buy a choice 100-acre tract on the south side of Hollister Avenue from San Jose Creek to Fairview Avenue. Rutherford bought the property, and built a two-story frame house on what is now Rutherford Avenue, at the northwest corner of the

Duke & Duchess apartment building. In 1875, he sent to Glasgow for his childhood sweetheart, Miss Agnes Lawrie. They were married immediately upon her arrival in California, and six of their children were born in the La Patera farmhouse: William, Agnes, Jessie, Alice, Steve and Mary.

After working for Ellwood Cooper planting eucalyptus trees, the original Scottish sextette went their separate ways. Jim Smith returned to Aberdeen to get married, and never came back, although he persuaded his brother, Charles, to trade the craigs and braes of Bonnie Scotland for the Good Land of Goleta. William Hendry bought a farm in Veronica Springs Canyon or the Arroyo Burro, the mouth of which was known as Hendry's Beach for two generations.

Jim Milne farmed on the Alphonso Den ranch, which is now the Isla Vista district, later moving to Santa Barbara. William Begg moved out to the San Julian Ranch and made his home in Lompoc. John Rutherford farmed on the Kate Bell ranch near Ellwood, later worked on the Dos Pueblos Ranch, and finally moved to Shasta County. John McClaren is best remembered as the man who helped W. W. Stow develop Golden Gate Park in San Francisco.

In 1884, Stephen Rutherford bought five sections of land lying athwart Dos Pueblos Canyon from G. C. Welch, and began raising potatoes, corn and hay on a large scale. In 1888, he built the commodious redwood home which now belongs to Mrs. Margaret Mosher on her Dos Pueblos Orchid Company property.

Two more children were born to the Rutherfords at Dos Pueblos, George and Lawrie. George grew up to farm the historic Ortega *hacienda* in Refugio Canyon; his tractor knocked down the adobe walls in 1922 which Bouchard's raid had spared in 1818. In 1965, he sold out to Stewart Abercrombie, the laird of Tajiguas Rancho. Lawrie Rutherford was killed in action with the A.E.F. at Argonne Forest, the Goleta Valley's first casualty of World War 1.

Stephen Rutherford operated the Dos Pueblos Ranch until 1917, when he sold out to oilman Herbert G. Wylie. Moving to Santa Barbara, he developed the Rutherford Park subdivision around Argonne Circle, named in honor of the battlefield where his youngest son perished. He died at his home at 201 Calle Palo Colorado in 1939, at the age of 91.

The Simpson clan of Scotland left an indelible mark on Goleta Valley affairs. Francis R. Simpson, of Aberdeen, married Jessie Milne in 1870, and moved to Goleta in 1873 with their baby son, Frank, who became a Valley blacksmith of note. The elder Simpson went to work as foreman of Ellwood Cooper's ranch, and was also employed by the Stow Ranch, where he set out some of the historic early orchards, which years later were removed by his son. It was Francis Simpson who cleared the dense oak grove off the E. P. Ripley ranch at Hollister Avenue and Old San Marcos Road, raising a bumper crop of wheat there the following season.

George Simpson, the second child, was born in Goleta in 1875, and was the only Simpson of his generation to become a farmer. William took up locomotive engineering; Annette moved away; Thomas became a machinist; Reginald a telegraph operator, learning his trade from Harry Brown at the Goleta depot; Jessie died in early childhood; while Henry, the youngest, became a machinist and auto mechanic in the Sexton & Simpson shop in Santa Barbara, in partnership with Horace A. Sexton. Henry presently resides at 1100 San Antonio Creek Road, originally a part of the ranch inherited by his wife, Emma Kellogg Simpson, from the estates of her grandfather and father, John and Edward Pickett.

The early Eighties saw an acceleration in Scottish immigration to the Goleta Valley, as word-of-mouth advertising began to draw friends and relatives from the old country. Charles Smith, 31, and his nephew, Jim Anderson, both of Aberdeenshire, arrived in 1884 and went to work mining asphaltum on the More Ranch beach. They saved their wages with proverbial Caledonian frugality, and in 1888 were able to send back to the land of heather and haggis for their bonnie wee brides-to-be.

On July 11, 1888, a messenger galloped out to the More Ranch to inform Smith and Anderson that their sweethearts had just arrived by train from New York by way of El Paso. The two Scots dropped their mining tools and hurried to Santa Barbara to an adobe house on Canon Perdido Street, where lived another recent arrival from Scotland, Robert Main. There, in a double ceremony performed by Presbyterian minister Elar A. Farrow, Miss Barbara Dawson, 26 (for whom Dawson Street in Goleta is named) became Mrs. Charles A. Smith, while Miss Elizabeth Rae, 22, became the wife of James Anderson. Both couples lived to celebrate their joint golden wedding anniversary in 1938.

Smith went into partnership with William Hendry on the Arroyo Burro ranch, and after two years moved out to Kate Bell's ranch, on Hollister Avenue at Storke Road. Later he moved his growing family over to Gus Den's Rincon Ranch, where his house and barns were located near the present UCSB Arts Building.

The Smiths had eight children. The eldest, named Jim after his uncle in Aberdeen, became Goleta's popular village blacksmith, an artist in wrought iron work, and the Valley's most authoritative historian. For fifteen years he manned the "Old Blacksmith Shop" float in Santa Barbara's Fiesta parades.

Jim was followed by George, a carpenter; Charles, a farmer; Frank, a lumberman; Jeannie (Mrs. D. B. Pitts); Sydney, also a carpenter; Barbara (Mrs. Frank Soundy); and Stanley, a horticulturist.

Jim Anderson bought a 12-acre ranch on Fairview Avenue, now split in two by the freeway and the railroad, and went into the vegetable business. He also leased land near Ellwood Union School and raised hay. The Andersons had seven children: Elizabeth; Albert, drowned off Goleta Point's fishing rocks at age 19; Emma (Mrs. George Smith); Annetta (Mrs. Thomas B. Jamison); William and Walter, both deceased; and James Jr., who recently retired after serving 26 years as custodian of Ellwood Union School. Elizabeth Rae Anderson died in 1946, Jim Anderson surviving her by ten years. Both are buried in Goleta Cemetery.

Robert Main, shortly after the Smith and Anderson double wedding in his home, moved out to the Goleta Valley to work for Frank Kellogg. He had immigrated to California with his wife, Jane Sangster Main, and sons, Alex and William, in 1887. In 1890, Main was hired by Thomas B. Bishop to superintend the operations of the Corona del Mar Ranch. He held that responsibility for 39 years, and on his retirement was succeeded by his son, William, who carried on until 1937, when he was followed by Ben Hartman.

Born to the Mains while living at Corona del Mar Ranch were Jeannie Annie, who married John Troup Jr., a Goleta farmer; Carrie May, who married David Begg; Margaret, and James B. Main.

Peter J. Begg and his wife, Jessie, were natives of Edinburgh, who followed pioneer William Begg of Lompoc to the Goleta Valley in 1885. Engaging in farming and stock raising, they founded one of the most prominent Scottish clans in the Valley. Their six children were Mary (Mrs. Peter Irvine), John, of Goleta, who married Minnie Poole; George, who managed the historic Sisquoc Ranch for many years; David, who married Carrie Main; Jessie (Mrs. John Gilstrap) and Rosie (Mrs. Fred Irvine).

David Begg's marriage to Carrie Main took place on June 28, 1911. Their issue included Robert, an engineer; James, an electrician; Dorothy (Mrs. Frank Silva); Carrie (the late Mrs. William Bonazzala); Charles ("Chuck"), a commercial fisherman; George, a D.A.'s investigator; Carden, a contractor; and Thelma (Mrs. George Daut). David Begg for several years was the Goleta constable, succeeding John B. Pico in that office.

John Begg married Minnie Poole and moved into a small frame home which in 1966 was still standing on the west bank of San Jose Creek, in the trailer park next to the Goleta Union School. Here were born Margaret (Mrs. Leroy Thomas), Evelyn (Mrs. James Durham), Johnnie, Christine (Mrs. Delbert Davis) and William.

John Troup, *pater familias* of another well-known Goleta Valley Scottish clan, was born in Aberdeenshire in 1864. Before leaving Scotland for Canada in 1888, he married Elizabeth Logan Milne.

In Canada, Troup managed horse ranches and wheat farms for various banks and railroading interests who were seeking to encourage colonization of the western and central provinces. In 1890, Troup sent for his wife, and they moved immediately to the Goleta Valley. There Troup was hired to run banker George S. Edwards' two ranches, one near Doty Canyon west of Dos Pueblos, the other at the corner of Hollister Avenue and Old San Marcos road, the corner now marked by the General Telephone Company building.

The Troups had six children: Margaret, John, Walter, William, Mary, and George. This family bore more than its fair share of personal tragedy. William was burned to death on April 6, 1902, when a kerosene stove exploded. His father was seriously burned while attempting to rescue his six-year-old son. Walter died in infancy, John Jr. of appendicitis in his early thirties.

Present survivors of their generation include Margaret, the wife of Robert Seaton, who owns the Joseph Sexton home place; and Mary, whose late husband, William Smith, was manager of the Tecolote Ranch for twenty years under the ownership of Silsby Spalding.

After leaving the employ of George Edwards when the latter sold his ranch to E. P. Ripley, president of the Atchison, Topeka and Santa Fe Railroad, Troup ran the San Julian ranch west of Gaviota for several years. While there, he imported thoroughbred cattle from his native Aberdeenshire, along with Clydesdale horses from Scotland, which won Troup many awards at state and county fairs.

Upon the death of his son, John, in 1927, Troup went back to managing the Ripley ranch. He died in 1957, and is buried in Goleta Cemetery.

Scotsman John Stronach and wife, Anne Skinner Stronach, did not arrive in the Goleta Valley until 1885, but several of their offspring had sunk roots in the Good Land ahead of them. Daughter Anne married William Hendry, of Arroyo Burro, in 1882. Her sister, Mary, married James Milne in Scotland that same year, before coming to Goleta to live on the Rincon Ranch. Brothers William and George, who married Helen Craig Keith and Agnes Sangster, respectively, did not show up from Scotland until 1893. The elder Stronachs settled on a farm on Cathedral Oaks Road.

George Sangster, another native of Aberdeenshire, reached the Goleta Valley in 1887, and went to work on the Hollister Ranch in the last years before Bishop took ownership. He was then 23 years of age. In the summer of 1893, he married Mary Grant of Aberdeen, whose parents, David and Christine Grant, had settled in Goleta the year before. The youngest of their six children, George, served overseas in World War I. He died shortly after the Armistice was signed, his body being returned to Goleta Cemetery for burial. George Sangster was a partner in the Main & Sangster blacksmith shop which stood close to Fairview Avenue on Hollister Avenue.

One of Goleta's most colorful and beloved Scottish citizens was Alexander "Sandy" Shewan, who arrived in 1888. He was a jolly, handlebar-mustached bachelor, whose resonant baritone voice made him very popular at parties. Many fantastic tales were recounted of

Sandy's drinking prowess, a favorite being his Saturday night habit of imbibing himself into happy oblivion at McCaffery's Bar in Santa Barbara. Loving hands would load him aboard his breaking cart, and point his faithful mare in the direction of Goleta. When dawn broke on Sunday, Sandy invariably awoke bright-eyed and bushy-tailed, inside his cozy barn on the flatlands west of the airport.

James Ross, perhaps the best-known sheriff of recent memory, came from Aberdeen to Goleta in 1895 by way of Canada, and hired out as a day laborer on the two George S. Edwards ranches. Later he went to work for Stephen Rutherford on Dos Pueblos Ranch. In 1902, while employed by Rutherford, Ross was appointed Chief of Police of Santa Barbara by the then mayor, who was his former boss, George S. Edwards. From that office Jim Ross was elected county sheriff in 1918, an office he filled with conspicuous merit until he retired in 1946 and was succeeded by his son, John.

Another Scottish name of great import in the Goleta story for nearly three quarters of a century is that of Irvine.

Peter Irvine, who passed away in February, 1965, at the age of 90, was born in Aberdeenshire and came to Goleta at the age of 17. He spent his first year working for George S. Edwards and then worked for five years on the Charles Smith ranch. After managing sundry ranches in Saticoy and Santa Barbara, Irvine purchased his own lemon and walnut ranch at 5001 Hollister Avenue, on the old A. C. Scull estate, where his widow, Mary Begg Irvine, currently resides. They were married in 1902. Their daughter Gladys (Mrs. Franklin Churchill) resides in Santa Barbara.

The head of the clan Irvine, Peter Sr., did not join his son in Goleta until 1908. He served as custodian of the Goleta Cemetery for ten years, until his death in 1918. His widow, Elizabeth Duguid Irvine, passed away in 1921.

Brother Fred Irvine, born in Aberdeenshire in 1895, reached the Goleta Valley in 1909 and got his first job from Sandy Shewan. Later he and his brother David leased the Goleta county farm and worked it in partnership. After combat Army duty in France in World War I, Fred Irvine returned to Goleta to work briefly on the John More and Pomatto Brothers ranches. In 1924 he moved to the old Gus Den ranch, where he raised hay and beans on the acres which now comprise the UCSB campus. Another brother, Alex, resides in Santa Barbara.

Goleta's Scottish immigrants tended to marry Scottish girls, and this was true with Fred Irvine. On December 30, 1921, he married Rose Begg, daughter of Peter and Jessie Begg. Their sons, now prominent Goleta citizens, are Albert and Peter.

An interesting characteristic of Goleta's Scottish immigrants is the rapidity with which they adapted themselves to American ways. None of them ever donned kilt, sporran, tamoshanter and tartan; no Goleta Scotsman can skirl and drone the bagpipes. Some of them joined the now defunct Caledonian Club of Santa Barbara, and celebrated Bobby Burns Day and other Scottish fête days; but the social function for which they are best remembered was the Fourth of July celebration known far and wide as Goleta's "Scottish-American Picnic."

No one seems to know how or where these picnics began. Some say they originated in the early Eighties with two-day fishing parties at Goleta Point. The picnics have been held under the grand old oaks of Tecolote Canyon and under the redwoods at Stow Grove, but mostly at Tucker's Grove. Occasionally the bill of fare included a steer to barbeque—a gift from the Bishop or Stow ranches. The dance floor at Tucker's Grove rocked to quadrilles, Highland Flings, Schottisches and Yankee square dances. The men engaged in foot races, horseshoe pitching, putting the shot, and other athletic competitions.

The annual Scottish-American Picnic at Tucker's Grove was a thing to remember. They continued until the outbreak of World War II. After the war, no one could generate any interest in reviving them. Times had changed. There were dissentions in the ranks of the Goleta Scottish-American Association, the sponsoring body in days of yore, and the kids, who had been victimized by the anti-fireworks ordinances which emasculated Fourth of July fun, couldn't be bothered anymore. Thus ended a Goleta custom of long standing, a regrettable sacrifice on the altar of a more sophisticated age.

CHAPTER XIX

How Glen Annie Became the Bishop Ranch

Something was wrong up at the Glen Annie mansion.

Colonel Hollister's neighbors down on the valley floor, and next door at the Stow Ranch, began to sense this around early autumn of 1885. They suddenly realized that the familiar sightseeing tallyho tours from the Hotel Arlington to the Glen Annie Ranch had ceased, after ten years of popularity. Wealthy tourists from the East now contented themselves with a visit across the Good Land to Ellwood Cooper's olive mill, stopping on their return trip to gape at "California's largest oak tree" on the David Beck place (at what is now the Humane Society, 5399 Overpass Road. The present oak in front of the old Beck residence grew from an acorn when the Big Oak was destroyed by its own weight and old age in the Nineties.)

Loose-tongued servants in the Hollister household dropped tantalizing crumbs of gossip for Goleta housewives to nibble on. The Colonel, they said, was getting more quarrelsome with Annie, who was drinking heavily of late. She discontinued her fabulous garden parties, with Jose Lobero's orchestra in attendance; she seldom drove to town in her fringe-topped surrey any more.

The Colonel, ordinarily an extrovert of considerable vanity, no longer acted as the Arlington's official greeter when steamers unloaded well-heeled passengers at Stearns' Wharf. He had even lost interest in his Goleta Valley horticultural experiments, formerly his prime passion.

The Colonel's personal physician, Dr. R. F. Winchester, admitted to friends that his patient's health was deteriorating, augmented by a narrow escape from strychnine poisoning intended for gopher bait, but mostly due to nervous strain resulting from the protracted Den Estate litigation. The suspense of waiting for the State Supreme Court to rule regarding his title to the Glen Annie was eroding Hollister's strength as surely as would a cancer.

On April 10, 1886, Hollister's financial adviser, cashier A. L. Lincoln of the First National Gold Bank (of which Hollister was president), persuaded the Colonel to make minor changes in his will, to allow for a possible loss of his Goleta Valley holdings. On May 17, 1886, the Colonel made his first admission that T. B. Bishop might win his case, when he headed a codicil to his will as follows:

If upon my death the Den Estate litigation shall not have terminated, or shall have resulted in depriving me of my Dos Pueblos properties, all the interest in my remaining lands shall be distributed equally among my surviving sons. . . .

For many years Annie and the Colonel had made plans to spend their silver wedding anniversary at Lake Tahoe, the glittering emerald waters of which Hollister had first glimpsed on his trip to California with a covered wagon train in 1852. When that anniversary neared, June 1, 1886, Hollister was in such poor health he had to make the ninety-mile trip to the nearest railroad junction, Newhall, by ambulance. He had to be carried aboard the private car he had chartered for the sentimental journey into the Sierra Nevadas.

Two weeks later, Annie wired Dr. Winchester in Santa Barbara to express alarm over her husband's mental depression. Dr. Winchester hurried to Lake Tahoe, where he told the Colonel that the 6,000-foot elevation was affecting his heart, and ordered him to return to Santa Barbara immediately. Privately, Dr. Winchester told the Colonel's lady that W. W. was in his terminal illness, suffering from metabolic ailments of liver, heart and kidneys.

The squire of the Goleta Valley got back to Santa Barbara on July 10, after a layover in San Francisco where the doctor almost despaired of saving his patient's life. Despite Col. Hollister's expressed desire to be driven the extra dozen miles to his beloved Glen Annie, Dr. Winchester put the patient to bed in a private suite on the second floor of the Ellwood Hotel at State and Anapamu Streets, the former Santa Barbara College building.

How Glen Annie Became the Bishop Ranch

Health bulletins on the Colonel's condition were published daily in the Santa Barbara newspapers, and sent by wire to San Francisco and eastern dailies. These bulletins resembled those issued for ailing heads of state:

> July 17—Col. Hollister is considered to be dangerously ill.
> July 24—Col. Hollister took an airing in his phaeton.
> July 28—Col. Hollister swooned again today in his hotel room.
> August 2—Col. Hollister has taken a turn for the worse.

The entire second floor of the Ellwood Hotel was reserved for the use of the family. Annie Hollister, who had reconciled her marital differences with her husband during their anniversary trip to Lake Tahoe, occupied the room adjoining the Colonel's. Ellwood Cooper drove his cart in from his ranch twice a week to shave his old friend, who would permit no one else to attend him.

Hollister's tall, handsome sons—Will, Harry, Jim and Stanley, ranging in age from sixteen to twenty—came to their father's bedside occasionally. But they came stiffly, virtually as strangers, prompted by duty rather than filial devotion. By his own belated admission, the Colonel had been a failure as a father, spending more time working for his community or his pet causes, such as Chinese labor laws, a transcontinental railroad terminal for Santa Barbara, or the Trespass Laws, than he did being a companion to his family.

Death came to Colonel Hollister at 4:10 in the morning of August 8, 1886. Ironically, that was the day his wastrel son, Will, reached his 21st birthday. The Colonel was only 68.

The Goleta Valley, and Santa Barbara as well, had lost its most distinguished citizen. The news of Hollister's passing had its echo of grief as far away as the Atlantic coast, where editors had their printers invert column rules to put black borders on editorial eulogies to a man they saluted as one of California's outstanding pioneer citizens. Typical of these editorials in the nation's press is this excerpt from a lengthy eulogy in the Columbus (Ohio) *Journal*:

> We do not exaggerate when we say Col. W. W. Hollister was one of the foremost men in California. He did more to develop and enrich that state than any other man in it. His Trespass Laws alone are enough to entitle him to the everlasting thanks and gratitude of all the people of California.

Practically every man, woman and child in the Goleta Valley joined the throng of mourners passing the Colonel's catafalque in the black-draped lobby of the Hotel Arlington. The funeral services, scheduled for 2 p.m. on August 10, were delayed an hour pending the arrival of the steamer *Santa Rosa*, bringing back many of the Colonel's friends who had been attending a G.A.R. convention in San Francisco, which had adjourned upon receipt of the news of the great man's death.

Hollister, while by no means an atheist, had never expressed a religious preference. His funeral was conducted by Annie's Trinity Episcopal minister, Rev. John S. Bakewell. Two of the six pallbearers were from the Good Land—Ellwood Cooper and John F. More.

The procession to the cemetery, led by Jose Lobero's brass band playing a dirge, was the longest in Santa Barbara history. When the horse-drawn hearse reached the graveside in Santa Barbara Cemetery, the last carriage in the cortege was just leaving the Arlington grounds, three miles away.

There was some disappointment among his Goleta Valley neighbors that the Colonel had not secured a family burial plot in the Goleta Cemetery. Annie had vetoed this idea years before; she did not consider Goleta's version of God's Acre to be prestigious enough to receive the remains of a Hollister. On the other hand, Santa Barbara Cemetery tombstones carried the names of many great and important people, lending a dignity and status which Annie felt the Colonel's station in life deserved.

Hollister's grave is marked by two Mexican fan palms, *Washingtonia robusta*, planted by his own hand in 1880. They now stand 90 feet tall, their slim trunks soaring skyward like vapor trails, each ending in a rocket-burst of green fronds against the blue. Those twin palms are far more symbolic of the man they memorialize than the Pharaonic slab of polished granite which his daughter, Mrs. Clinton B. Hale, placed on the grave in the late 1930s.

... One discreet week after the funeral, the contents of Hollister's will were published. Certain provisos therein created as much excitement in Santa Barbara as they did in Goleta Valley circles. The biggest shock was that the Colonel's sister, Lucy A. "Auntie" Brown, whom everyone assumed would receive at least a half-interest in the estate her money had helped create, was cut off with a token bequest, a town lot on Gutierrez Street worth $50. Goleta Valley folk buzzed with indignation over this injustice, blaming the imperious Annie for disinheriting Auntie Brown.

The most talked-about item in Hollister's will, however, was a clause appearing in a codicil dated February 27, 1886, probably inserted in sentimental remembrance of an old friendship:

I give and bequeath unto Queenie Walcott, youngest daughter of Josephine Walcott of Berkeley, Alameda County, California, the sum of $1,000; and I direct that in no event shall the said Queenie Walcott become entitled to any part of or share or interest in my estate other than the aforesaid $1,000...

Judge R. B. Canfield appointed a local attorney to represent "the minors holding an interest in the Hollister Estate," naming these minors as Harold, James and Stanley Hollister, and Queenie Walcott of Berkeley. Queenie, then a moppet of nine years, takes leave of the Hollister saga at this point in history.

Annie, Will, and Ellwood Cooper were appointed executors of the estate, with Hollister's nephew, Edgar, of Fairview Ranch, as alternate.

On August 28, 1886, the petition for probate of the will listed an inventory of the Colonel's worth, totalling $821,436, or an estimated market value in excess of $2,000,000. The Goleta Valley property was appraised at $83,000 for tax purposes. The total estate included, besides the Arlington and Ellwood Hotels, the Lobero Opera House; the Winchester Canyon Ranch; a mortgage on Stearns Wharf which was eventually paid off; the *Morning Press* and its plant; and some 48,656 acres of ranch land in the southwestern corner of Santa Barbara County. (In a dissolution of partnership agreement with Tom and Albert Dibblee in 1882, Hollister deeded them the 48,221-acre San Julian ranch, the partnership continuing only in the co-ownership of the Gaviota Wharf. These ranch holdings remained intact in the Hollister Estate until their sale in 1965 to a Los Angeles syndicate.)

The upper Glen Annie ranch was devised to the Colonel's widow during her lifetime, after which it was to go to his youngest son, Stanley. (Another son, Leonel, had fallen from his pram as an infant and died of a brain concussion in 1873, and was buried north of the Glen Annie house, just outside the Dos Pueblos grant line. In 1907, Annie Hollister had Leo's remains exhumed, and interred beside his father at Santa Barbara cemetery.)

The Lower Ranch, which everyone had taken for granted would go to Auntie Brown, went instead to the black sheep of the family, William. The Bartlett Canyon portion of the ranch was devised to son Harold ("Harry") Hollister. Winchester Canyon went to son John James. Daughter Jennie received $10,000 in cash, which was frozen in a trust "for so long as she shall continue to be intermarried with Robert L. Chamberlain." Even in death, the Colonel could not forgive his daughter for marrying against his wishes.

Pending a verdict on the Goleta Valley property in litigation, Washington James continued to operate the Lower Ranch as usual, but without Auntie Brown's services as housekeeper-manager. That redoubtable woman, realizing the pleasure Annie Hollister would derive from evicting her, moved to 1100 Santa Barbara Street the day after learning she had been cut out of her brother's will.

In August, 1887, Auntie Brown brought suit against the Hollister Estate for $25,000, which she said represented unpaid wages at the rate of $75 a month between December, 1858, and August 1886, during which period she had managed the Colonel's household and invested her personal fortune in the Hollister-Dibblee enterprises. This lawsuit was won handily by Auntie Brown, who paraded such an impressive array of witnesses before the court—including aging Thomas Flint and Llewellyn Bixby—that she could probably have won double her demands. Goleta Valley country folk were delighted; they disliked the imperious Annie Hollister for her overbearing snobbery, and loved hawk-faced Auntie Brown for being "a plain old shoe, like us."

Auntie Brown filed a separate suit to recover her half of the estate, but this case was thrown out of court because the plaintiff did not have a scrap of evidence in writing to prove she had ever loaned her brother a penny during their lifetime.

Annie's triumph was nearly complete, but she did not have long to gloat over her victory. Four years after the Colonel's death, the 14-year Den Estate litigation ended when the State Supreme Court handed down its final ruling in the case.

The Den Estate, in the opinion of Judges MacFarland, Sharpstein and Thornton, was entitled to recover the Glen Annie and Lower Ranch, together with all improvements made thereon.

Assistant counsel P. J. Galpin came down from San Francisco to interpret the court's ruling for Annie Hollister, meeting her in the privacy of her parlor at the Glen Annie mansion. But the language of the court decree was understandable even to laymen:

> Col. Hollister knew of the deed of trust and Den's will [when he bought the property in 1869]. He knew of the want of power of executor Charles E. Huse to sell real estate without an order of the Probate Court. He was warned not to purchase without the sanction of the court, but chose to purchase in spite of this warning.
>
> Col. Hollister was not, therefore, "an ignorant purchaser in good faith." . . . Moreover, Hollister's money was not paid directly to the Den heirs, but to executor Huse, who used the money indiscriminately and partly for other purposes.
>
> Col. Hollister contends that he should have been reimbursed for the value of his improvements on the Goleta Valley land. This court finds that the value of said improvements was not in excess of the rents and royalties earned by said land, and therefore allows no damages.

Attorney Galpin then fed Annie Hollister the bitterest pill she would have to swallow in her lifetime. The victorious attorney for the plaintiffs, Thomas B. Bishop, had just announced that his fee for winning the litigation for the Den Estate, after fourteen years of costly court action, would be the Lower Ranch portion of Glen Annie, which he was going to rename "Corona del Mar," meaning Crown of the Sea. Bishop had already received the magnificent Tecolote Ranch from the Den Estate, and portions of Ellwood Cooper's ranch.

Galpin informed Annie Hollister that Nicolas C. Den was already standing by, waiting to move into Glen Annie mansion, and that the court would allow Annie a reasonable period—six weeks at the most—in which to move her personal property from the premises.

Annie's face contorted with fury. "Mr. Galpin," she said in a venomous whisper, "no member of that greaser Den clan will ever set foot in my house. Never, do you understand? Never!"

After Galpin had departed, Annie informed her father, Samuel

L. James, that she intended to live and die on the ranch. Her father, however, quietly began preparing the town house at Chapala and West Carrillo Streets for his daughter's impending exile.

Annie withdrew to a reclusive isolation at Glen Annie, defying the court order to leave. She admitted no one to the house except her servants and her daughter, Jennie Chamberlain. Finally, Sheriff J. R. Broughton put in an embarrassed appearance at Annie's doorstep. He came armed with a writ of eviction sworn out by T. B. Bishop in behalf of the new owner, Nicolas C. Den. Annie had to get out immediately.

Facing defeat, Annie Hollister promised to comply. Her brother, Wash James, had already taken care of moving personal property out of the Lower Ranch, which T. B. Bishop's new resident manager, Robert Main, would shortly be occupying. Wash James also removed hundreds of yards of portable fencing, an invention of Colonel Hollister's to keep livestock out of his citrus groves. James had no use for the rolled-up picket fencing, but as he put it to friends, "I'd do anything to keep those damned Bishops from getting the benefit of it."

Bishop's men retaliated by opening the corral gates and turning loose Hollister livestock to graze along the county road.

On the fateful afternoon of November 20, 1890, Annie Hollister made her final visit to her Glen Annie home, accompanied by her brother, Wash. She was clad in black mourning, popularized by a grieving Queen Victoria in memory of her consort Prince Albert, a costume Annie would wear until the day she died in the new century.

Hollister's foreman, August Linquest, and a caretaker named Rutherford, were the only persons on hand to greet the deposed mistress of the manor; she had already bid her retinue of household servants a tearful farewell. Annie noticed with mounting fury that Nicolás C. Den's family had already begun unloading furniture and other chattels in the front yard—Annie's precious front yard.

An hour later, a tearful, white-lipped Annie Hollister climbed back into the family phaeton. Wash James clucked to his team and the carriage headed down the road past the Colonel's famous grove of date palms. They had traveled less than a quarter of a mile across the flats when an odor of smoke reached Wash James' nostrils. He twisted around to look back toward the house—and was appalled to see a gout of oily black smoke spewing from under the gingerbreaded eaves on the south gable, followed by an ugly snake-tongue flicker of red flame.

"Annie," Wash James managed to choke out, "*the house is afire!*"

The banished chatelaine of Glen Annie set her jaw like a rock.

"Keep driving," she ordered, "and don't talk to me."

... Within thirty minutes the historic Glen Annie manorhouse was reduced to a seething bed of embers. Linquest and Rutherford could do nothing with their primitive firefighting equipment but save adjoining buildings.

By sundown that November evening, a malignant pall of smoke hung in milky layers over the Good Land. By then the rumor had spread as if on the wings of the wind to every household in the Valley that an embittered Annie Hollister had deliberately put the torch to her mansion in order to prevent the despised "greaser Den clan" from occupying her beloved home.

Detectives and insurance adjusters, summoned by telegraph from Los Angeles, swarmed onto the scene next morning before the ashes had time to cool. After thoroughly sifting the smoking débris, they reported finding no evidence to prove arson, and paid off the loss without protest.

Annie went to her grave in 1909 professing complete ignorance as to how the blaze could have started. Its origin was officially written off as an unsolved mystery. Wash James used to offer the explanation which Annie's descendants in years to come accepted as the gospel truth: "spontaneous combustion" had ignited massive deposits of beeswax known to have accumulated between the walls. That this combustion occurred only minutes after a vengeful Annie Hollister left the premises was, in Wash's straight-faced opinion, a coincidence.

For the next half-century, Hollister's Lower Ranch, henceforth known as the Corona del Mar or, more popularly, the Bishop Ranch, was the largest farming operation in the Goleta Valley, overshadowing the More, Stow, Dos Pueblos, Tecolote and Cooper operations.

Robert Main became ranch manager for Bishop and remained in that capacity for 39 years, under the authority of Frank Bishop.

Nicolás C. Den rebuilt the Glen Annie home on a more modest

scale than before, but soon lost the valuable property through incompetent management and was foreclosed by the Yndart banking interests of Santa Barbara.

Early in the new century the remainder of Glen Annie Canyon took on new owners—Alphonso Den holding title to 179 acres in the north end of the canyon, with another 179-acre tract purchased by James Anderson immediately to the south. In the central heart of the canyon, Bruno Orella, co-owner of Cañada Del Corral rancho, bought 386 acres, with a speculator, Joseph Archambault, buying the remaining 222-acre piece bordered on the south by Hollister Avenue.

Glen Annie became associated with three prominent Italian families, the Cavallettos, Meconos and Pomattos, whose agricultural achievements on the Good Land brought state-wide recognition from soil conservationists and citrus growers. Colonel Hollister's shade would have rested well, had he known into what good hands his lost love had fallen in the Twentieth Century.

CHAPTER XX

The Booming 'Eighties Bring a Railroad

Ask any expert stamp collector what "Goleta, California" connotes in the lexicon of philately, and he will instantly reply "The Kicking Mule!" This curious anomaly of word associations stems from October 11, 1880, when Fred Foster succeeded his father as Goleta's postmaster.

Because the government did not furnish postage-cancelling devices, rural postmasters often made their own out of bottle corks or blocks of wood. Several firms began manufacturing stamp cancellers, among them Klinkner & Company of San Francisco.

One of many designs listed in Klinkner's catalogue was a kicking mule, designed to kick the face of the stamp it cancelled. According to the authoritative philatelic writer, Lee H. Cornell, this was Mr. Klinkner's puerile method of avenging a snub he had suffered when the Post Office Department ignored his request to call his home town "Klinknerville" and named it Emoryville instead.

Fred Foster ordered one of the Kicking Mule cancellers for Goleta. By so doing, he enshrined his obscure village in philatelic catalogues for all time to come. Covers bearing a clear strike of the Goleta Kicking Mule bring high bids at stamp auctions, due to their rarity. Only fifteen specimens were known to exist in 1966. The earliest is dated November 11, 1880; the latest February 11, 1885.

John C. Rudolph inherited the Kicking Mule when he bought out Foster in January, 1882. He was followed by Charles W. Woodbright, who took over Goleta's store and post office on December 11, 1882. Woodbright continued to use the Kicking Mule until 1885, when the government began furnishing postmasters with official cancelling equipment.

The historic Goleta Kicking Mule die was destroyed by the fire which leveled the Goleta store during the winter of 1886. George D. Tillford was postmaster at the time, having taken the job in August.

Upon Tillford's death his widow, Elnora, took over and served until she was replaced by Randolph C. Watson on March 12, 1890.

A short distance east of Patterson Avenue, at what is now 5257 Hollister Avenue, the congregation of the Oakdale Baptist Church saw a dream come true when they erected a church of their own in 1884, the second-oldest temple of worship in the Valley. It consisted of an auditorium and two classrooms, surmounted by a peaked belfry which was a Valley landmark until the church burned down in December, 1955. The lot was donated by B. A. Hicks, whose pioneer home stood next door. It was used as a parsonage until 1909, when a larger manse was built on a lot donated by Frank Simpson on South Patterson Avenue. This parsonage was destroyed by fire in 1930.

In 1916 the "Oakdale" name was changed to Goleta Baptist Church. Additions were made to the edifice in 1922 and 1931. The site is occupied today by the Goleta Valley Foursquare Gospel Church, the Baptists having moved to 300 Magnolia Avenue in 1955.

During the Eighties and Nineties, a vital part of the Valley's religious life was the summer camp meetings held in a magnificent oak grove along Maria Ygnacia Creek. Because the high-arching branches resembled the vaulted ceilings of a Gothic cathedral, people began calling the grove "Cathedral Oaks," and the name caught on.

Cathedral Oaks revival meetings were attended by people of all faiths. Visiting evangelists dispensed hell-fire-and-brimstone sermons at emotion-charged rallies lasting from one to three weeks at a time.

Worshippers who came from a distance by horse and wagon would pitch tents under the oaks and eat and sleep there for the duration of the revival. The climax of each meeting would be the confession night, when sobbing penitents could publicly acknowledge Jesus as their Redeemer and confess their earthly sins while kneeling at what the irreverent younger generation in the Valley called the "slobber rail."

The Booming Eighties Bring a Railroad

Camp meetings are a thing of the past. Woodsmen have almost succeeded in destroying the last of the magnificent Cathedral Oaks as well; by 1966 only half a dozen specimens survived, inside the cyclone fences of the Giorgi Park playground on San Marcos Road.

A gradually swelling population throughout the Eighties produced inevitable schooling problems—overcrowded classes and overworked teachers. By 1883, the Rafaela School had been outgrown and a two-story building was erected at 177 South Patterson Avenue, once again by public subscription, on a two and a half-acre lot northeast of the Methodist Church. The lot was a gift of Isaac G. Foster, who died in 1880 before signing the deed. This formality was taken care of by Foster's widow and heirs in June of 1884.

The acre of ground where the Rafaela School stood, on the south side of Hollister Avenue, reverted to the More Ranch under the terms of T. Wallace More's deed of 1868, which specified the land was for school purposes only. The little red schoolhouse was moved to the vicinity of the present Patterson Avenue overpass, and was used for storage purposes for a few years before being torn down.

The new "Two-Story School," as it was called, had the four lower grades downstairs and the four upper grades upstairs.* The building was in service until 1911, when it was condemned as a firetrap, torn down and replaced by a one-story building on the same location, which was called simply the Goleta School. In 1928, this building was moved to the rear of the present Goleta Union School grounds, where it served as an auxiliary classroom for thirty-two years.

An early-day carriage maker in Ben Pettis' shop was Henry Rich, who changed his name from Henry von Reich in 1857 when he took

---

* Goleta school historian Horace A. Sexton lists the following "upstairs teachers": Frank E. Kellogg, 1884; Fannie H. Thompson, 1886; F. E. Kellogg, 1887; C. G. Meaker, 1890; Mamie Lehner, 1890 (later a county superintendent of schools); John R. Parker, 1890; J. A. Snell, 1904; H. L. Zint, 1906; J. S. Osborne, W. A. Jenkins and Mrs. Freyshold, 1910. "Downstairs teachers" were Miss E. M. Porter, 1884 (formerly a private governess for the Stow family); Isadora Hixon, 1886; Belle Farley, 1887; Jennie Haig (Beck), 1888; Carrie Carr, 1890; Lucile McCarger, 1899; Minnie Kellogg, 1899; Maud Pettis, 1902; Aline Hall, E. B. Hall, M. Haines and Bertha Sears, 1910.

out American citizenship in Seneca, New York. Rich had left his native Germany at an early age to avoid military conscription. At one time he lived on the Jasper Lane place off Hollister Avenue, but on November 15, 1883, he paid J. W. Cooper $3,700 for 30 acres located off present North Kellogg Avenue and Cambridge Avenue. Tax collector Nick Covarrubias got 21 cents an acre on Rich's land, which in 1964 was taxed $64 an acre. Rich removed the oak trees and planted walnuts from Sexton Nursery stock. His son, Hudson, married Lora Lane, daughter of blacksmith Joe Lane, and their son, Chester Rich, was long recognized as one of the county's most active leaders. Henry Rich's great grandson, Robert, is field manager of Calavo, an avocado growers' cooperative.

Samuel Manchester was a prominent Valley rancher who came to the Goleta Valley in 1886 from England. He and his wife, Etta, arrived in Los Angeles from Nebraska by rail, took a steamer to Stearns Wharf in Santa Barbara, and wound up in the Cathedral Oaks district where they built a home. In 1888 they moved to La Patera, where they farmed land south of Encina Avenue extending from Fairview to Kellogg Avenue. Lima beans were the main crop on the Manchester farm. The Manchester children were Clarence, Agnes, Kate (Hendryx), and Paul. During the Spanish-American War, Samuel Manchester was captain of the Goleta Constabulary. He died in 1925, his wife Etta having preceded him in 1900. Paul Manchester's recollections appear in this volume in many places.

Another English family arriving in the mid-Eighties, whose descendants are prominent in modern Goleta Valley, were the Rowes of Plymouth. Herbert William and Eliza Popplestone Rowe had six sons, George, Samuel, Walter, Charles, Russell, and Robert. Rowe was employed by Harry Langman of the Patterson Ranch.

George Rowe married Katherine Pickett, daughter of John and Euphemia Pickett, on November 3, 1888. Their children were Bessie, the widow of Archie Hunt, of the College Rancho in Santa Ynez; Catherine (Mrs. David Wilkins); and George Jr.

Robert Septimus Rowe, after completing his schooling in Goleta, left his father's farm, and in 1900 leased 320 acres in San Jose Canyon in partnership with his brother, Russell, where they engaged in dairying and citriculture. Robert moved to Kellogg Avenue in 1907, four years after his marriage to Genevieve Pensinger, a daughter of

Jacob and Hattie Glass Pensinger of Maria Ygnacia Canyon. Their offspring were Mary Barbara and Robert Pensinger Rowe, the latter a prominent More Mesa orchid grower, former School Board official and active civic leader in the Valley.

In 1918, Robert and Russell divided their ranch, Russell retaining 141 acres of lemon and walnut land. His wife was Ella ("Nellie") Chamberlain, their marriage occurring in 1910. Their son, Norman Rowe, is a walnut grower on Cathedral Oaks Road, and on Baseline Avenue in the Santa Ynez Valley. He married a daughter of John Troup Jr., Jeannie Elizabeth Troup.

On August 21, 1884, the Goleta community was saddened by the passing of its last link with the Hispanic days, Dona Rosa Den Welch, at her town house on Milpas Street in Santa Barbara. The eldest child of Goleta's founding father, Daniel A. Hill, Rosa had borne the ten children of Don Nicolás A. Den of Dos Pueblos. Five years after his death in 1862 she had remarried, to G. C. Welch.

Rosa was buried near her mother, Rafaela Ortega de Hill y Senter, in the pioneer Catholic Cemetery north of Hollister Avenue opposite modern Arboleda Road. Most of the bodies interred there in olden days were transferred, between 1912 and 1915, to the new Calvary Cemetery on Hope Avenue. However, in order for the Church to preserve the tax-free status of its old cemetery and keep the land from reverting to the original donor (the Thomas Hope Estate), a few graves were left *in situ*.

In the absence of any record to the contrary, it must be assumed that the remains of Rafaela Ortega de Hill y Senter and Dona Rosa Hill de Den y Welch still lie in unmarked graves beneath the weeds and litter of the Old Catholic Cemetery—a sadly inappropriate memorial for two women who played such important rôles in the early years of the Good Land. . . .

The year after Dona Rosa died, a Frenchman named John Baptiste Deu opened a saloon and store in one corner of the Birabent House. He was born in 1849 in Haute-Garonne, immigrated to Santa Barbara in 1864, and worked for an uncle, Pedro Baron, whose century-old adobe still stands in Arroyo Quemada, west of Tajiguas.

In 1892 Deu built a larger store, a square, two-story structure at 5859 Hollister Avenue, opposite Birabent's. Deu's Saloon gave La Patera its nickname of "Deuville" for many years; his ornate bar is now a treasured relic at Ted Chamberlin's Los Potreros Ranch near Los Olivos.

During the "Deuville" era, La Patera was looked down upon as a rustic "hick town" by sophisticates from Santa Barbara. The local spit 'n' whittle bunch used to gather around the cracker barrel on the porch of Deu's Store to settle local and world problems. This porch became the arena for La Patera's most celebrated fist fight, starring two elderly farmers named Morehouse and Beal.

The *causus belli* was a dispute as to which man had the more accurate watch, there being a three-minute difference between the timepieces. Hot words soon degenerated into fisticuffs. Finally the two oldsters were eye-poking and whisker-pulling in the deep dust of Hollister Avenue.

Eventually the wheezing belligerents were forced to submit their case to arbitration. There was no way to check the correct time by radio or telephone in those benighted days, and no one had the energy to walk over to the Goleta railroad depot to consult the S.P. chronometer. So neutral referees opened the combatants' respective watches, and found that whereas Beal's timepiece had a 21-jewel movement, Morehouse's turnip had but seven. Beal was duly declared the winner of this battle of the century, presumably on the basis of a TKO.

Deu's Store, called Crissie's Cafe during World War II, was the oldest business building in Goleta when it was razed in 1963.

Southern California's historic Big Boom of the '80s contributed one of the most bizarre chapters to the Goleta saga—that of the ghost town of Naples, on the east mesa flanking Dos Pueblos Canyon.

The Big Boom ranks as the most spectacular real estate promotion in American history. In the Los Angeles Basin, mythical townsites sprouted like mushrooms. Promoters in one classic case tied oranges to Joshua trees far out in the desert, and sold gullible investors "orange groves in bearing." Tourists enjoyed a fantastic rate war between the Southern Pacific and the Santa Fe, which saw one-way fares between Chicago and Los Angeles drop to as low as one dollar. The boom reached its peak in 1887-1888, and its northernmost highwater mark was the Goleta Valley at Naples.

The Booming Eighties Bring a Railroad

Naples was a dream hatched up by a St. Louis lumber tycoon, John H. Williams, and his eccentric wife, Alice Paist Williams, who first glimpsed the Good Land in 1887, from the deck of a passing steamer, and were struck by its resemblance to the Neapolitan coast.

A few weeks later, the Williamses arrived in Santa Barbara to make a personal survey of the Goleta Valley, with the idea of developing a resort city to rival Cannes or Nice. On June 2, 1887, Williams purchased 900 acres on the east side of Dos Pueblos Creek from Greenlief C. Welch, paying him $50,000. From Stephen Rutherford, his Scottish neighbor on the other side of the canyon, Williams bought a thirty-acre parcel which included the historic Den Adobe, which the Williamses made their country seat for many years.

Backed by a syndicate of wealthy speculators with connections in the Southern Pacific hierarchy, John H. Williams made plans to build a fabulous tourist hotel, the Crescent Beach. On the blueprints it rivaled such noted hostelries as San Diego's Coronado, Santa Barbara's Arlington, Pasadena's Raymond and Monterey's Del Monte.

Surrounding the proposed hotel, on the flat mesa extending east of Dos Pueblos Canyon, Williams platted his phantom City by the Sea. Eighteen numbered streets ran east and west, paralleling the beach. Intersecting north-south avenues formed a grid of 250 numbered city blocks. The avenues had exotic Italian nomenclature: Mazzini, Capri, Corona, Milano, Sorrento, Napoli, Florence, Toledo, Pompeii, Lucia, Rafael, Salfatara, Aetna, and Vesuvius. Two streets were named in honor of theatrical luminaries of the day—the Spanish soprano, Patti, and the British sex queen, Lily Langtry. A nation-wide advertising campaign was launched, extolling the virtues of Naples, which was represented as a going concern and the Crescent Beach Hotel as a *fait accompli*. Hundreds of lots were sold to speculators around the world who never came near their land.

The Naples project was conceived in expectation of the Southern Pacific Railroad extending its Coast Division across Dos Pueblos by the early autumn of 1887. A railroad up the coast was no pipe dream; it actually reached Santa Barbara. It even thrust its steel into the Goleta Valley, ending the isolation of its populace whose stagecoach and steamship transportation had been at the mercy of the weather and the tides.

Unhappily for John and Alice Williams, the Big Boom collapsed just one month before the S.P. railroad tracks could reach Dos Pueblos and the site of Naples. The Dream City by the Sea never got off the drawing board. Only one street was ever graded— Langtry Avenue, named for the Jersey Lily. Today it is an oiled road leading to the seldom-used Naples railway siding.

The Southern Pacific's Valley Line had linked San Francisco with Los Angeles in 1876, but construction of the alternate Coast Division stalled at Soledad, in the Salinas Valley, in 1873, due to the financial panic of that year. Work was not resumed until 1886, when rails reached as far south as Paso Robles by the end of October.

Simultaneously with the approach of the Iron Horse from the north, Chinese grading gangs were making fills and cuts, laying crossties and spiking down rails from Newhall Junction on the Valley Line, down the Santa Clara River Valley toward Ventura on the coast.

Great excitement swept La Patera and Goleta residents when a passing stagedriver informed them that trains were serving Santa Paula as of February 8, 1887. Ventura heard its first locomotive whistle on May 18. Within a month workmen were carving a right-of-way shelf around the seaward shoulder of Ortega Hill in Summerland, the last physical barrier on the way to Santa Barbara. Goleta lay just around the corner, and Naples' turn was next!

On the first day of July, 1887, a train reached Carpinteria after a three-hour run from Los Angeles, lopping five whole hours off the stagecoach timetable. A "first train" comprising fifteen sections rolled into Santa Barbara on August 19 and unloaded 5,000 excursionists on a pueblo which itself numbered only 5,000 souls. Among the honored celebrities on hand for the Railroad Celebration was attorney Tom Bishop, whose legal foe, Col. W. W. Hollister of Glen Annie, had been in his grave a little over a year.

Beyond Santa Barbara, the Chinese work gangs laid ties and rails, although they did not ballast the roadbed, on their last lap to the Goleta Valley. The Espee's legal department had already negotiated

Western-style town of Naples, in Dos Pueblos Canyon, with dance hall, hotel, stage station and post office, existed from Seventies to Twenties. Den Adobe behind trees on west rim of canyon in center of picture

Alice Paist Williams, the wealthy eccentric who dreamed of building a resort city at Naples, shown in this rare photograph with the pug dogs she later had embalmed and put in her husband's crypt in Naples' "Haunted Chapel." George Mack, her foreman, at left; he died in 1965, she in 1931

"Haunted Chapel" at Naples was a landmark beside county road from 1898, when it was erected as a memorial to John H. Williams, founder of Naples, until it was wrecked by earthquake of 1925. Only concrete slab floor and Williams' grave vault remain in 1966

Carlo Bottiani

James Jordano Sr.

Mike Durbiano

Mike Cavaletto Sr.

Antonio Pagliotti

G. B. Cavalletto

John Pomatto

Peter Pomatto

James Pomatto

Thomas B. Bishop, who won back two Hollister ranches for Den Estate

John Finley More, the controversial "Monarch of More Mesa," aged 55

Robert Main, Bishop Ranch superintendent for nearly 40 years

David M. Culver, More Ranch superintendent and wharfinger

James G. Williams, who lived in the historic Hill Adobe

This rare snapshot of Marion Peirce's sprinkling wagon will start nostalgic tears coursing down the cheeks of men who remember following wagon down Hollister Avenue

Peter Begg's family posed for this picture in 1902. Seated, l. to r.: Peter Begg; Rosie (Mrs. Fred Irvine); Jessie Grant Begg; Jessie (Mrs. John Gilstrap). Standing l. to r.: Mary (Mrs. Peter Irvine Sr.); John; George; and David. One of Valley's prominent Scottish families

Charles A. Smith family in 1929: standing l. to r.—Sydney; Jim; Charley; Frank; Stanley. Seated l. to r.—Jeannie (Mrs. D. B. Pitts); Charles A. (1857-1947); Barbara Dawson Smith (1862-1947); Barbara (Mrs. Frank Soundy); George (deceased)

The Booming Eighties Bring a Railroad

the 100-foot right of way across the Goleta Valley. Only eight landowners were in the path of the Story Survey: John F. More, of More Ranch; William Begg and Stephen Rutherford, west of San Jose Creek, in what is now the town of Goleta; Titus Phillips, developer of the strip between Hollister Avenue and the Stow ranch west of Fairview Avenue; Ellwood Cooper, of the Ellwood Canyon ranch; Kate Den Bell, of Las Armas Ranch; Louis G. Dreyfus, of Eagle Canyon Ranch; and G. C. Welch, of Dos Pueblos Ranch.

The first railroad into the Goleta Valley did not follow the present alignment, from the main Santa Barbara depot at Victoria and Rancheria Streets to the Bishop Ranch, involving some eight miles as the crow flies. The 1887 route curved northwest as it left Santa Barbara at West Mission Street, crossing what is now La Cumbre Junior High School campus, following contour lines on its way to Hope Ranch. Traces of the old cuts and fills are still visible between Modoc Road and the La Entrada Tract.

Hope Ranch's hilly perimeter was skirted by a level grade now called Vieja Drive. The tracks emerged onto More Ranch, overlooking the Goleta Valley, at the point where Puente Drive meets Via Huerta, on the western boundary of Hope Ranch Park.

On its way across John More's ranch, the tracks hugged the More Mesa bluffs to avoid the willow-lined channel of Atascadero Creek. That portion of the old railroad right-of-way lying west of Orchid Drive is now called Shoreline Drive.

About 500 feet west of the More Ranch Road bridge, near the fork of Maria Ygnacia and Atascadero Creeks, the railroad veered northwesterly in an arrow-straight line across soggy bottomlands where the Shinoda Brothers greenhouses now stand. A twelve-foot high wooden trestle nearly half a mile long led to a curve two blocks south of the present mortuary at 450 Ward Drive. This was the site of the original Goleta depot until 1902.

Horace A. Sexton recalls as a boy driving farm wagons under the long trestle, over what was then a corn field of John More's. By 1965, recurrent winter flooding of the bottomland by rampaging Maria Ygnacia and San Jose Creeks had deposited more than 13 feet of silt over the area, so that farmers' plows now cultivate soil which is higher than the railroad rails of 1887.

The Goleta station was linked with Hollister Avenue by a lane called Depot Road. From the station, the railroad ran westerly in a straight line across the Begg and Rutherford farms, spanned San Jose Creek at what is now the east end of Daley Street, crossed South Fairview Avenue at Daley Street south of the discount department store, met Hollister Avenue at La Patera Lane, and continued westward until it joined the present railroad at Coromar Siding on the Bishop Ranch.

Beyond Coromar the tracks meandered like a snake track (the contractors were being paid by the mile) until they reached an unnamed ravine just west of the boundary of the Ellwood Cooper ranch. Traces of the old cuts are visible today at the north end of Old Glen Annie Road, just west of the new Glen Annie overpass, on the south edge of the present railroad right-of-way.

Railroad construction stopped abruptly at the Ellwood Ranch line in late October of 1887. No one paid much attention to this at the time, but on November 3 an ominous item appeared in the Santa Barbara *Herald:*

We understand from good authority that there is to be a turntable on Ellwood Ranch. If this is true we may expect the railroad to stop there for some time.

Southern Pacific crews completed their culverts and trestles in the Goleta Valley and departed. By year's end, two more depots, identical to the Goleta Station, were under construction. La Patera Station was built on Williams' Flat, west of La Patera Lane and 50 yards north of Hollister Avenue, at what is now the southwest corner of the Defense Research Corporation building. Where Raytheon stands today, west of Robin Hill Road, there was a coaling station and water tank.

At end-of-track, Ellwood Station was built just north of where a telephone company plant is now situated. The access road from Hollister Avenue, one block south, is still called Ellwood Station Road, although the depot was torn down early in the century.

As the *Herald* reporter had feared, a wye and locomotive turntable, symbols of end-of-track, were built at Ellwood. In order to maintain its franchise across the Goleta Valley, the Southern Pacific ran a weekly "Ellwood Special" to pick up freight or passengers. The engineers, or "hogheads" of this little "Hooterville

The Booming Eighties Bring a Railroad 199

Cannonball" train were the idols of a whole generation of freckle-faced Goleta versions of Huck Finn and Tom Sawyer. The engineers' names are almost forgotten now, except by the oldest residents—Jesse Martin, Duncan McDonald, Frank Horner and Dick Bradley.

End-of-track would remain at Ellwood until after the turn of the century, or until the S.P. got around to closing "the Gap" in its Coast Division. What people could not possibly have known, that winter of 1887-1888, was that California's Big Boom, spawned by the Gold Rush, Statehood and the completion of the Overland Railway, had finally burst. Money for expansion was tight, even for a corporate giant like the Espee.

The railroad had faltered to a halt only four miles short of the planned City by the Sea, Naples. This strangled the essential umbilical cord which meant life or death for John H. Williams' Crescent Beach Hotel.

Late in 1888, the Congregational Church of California offered to buy the Naples townsite for a religious retreat, but owners of individual town lots in Naples, scenting a chance to make a killing, upped the prices of $25 lots to $1,000 or more, and the deal died.

Weeds obscured the stakes marking the railroad right-of-way, and the four-block-square city park where John H. Williams' luxury hotel would never rise. Lot owners began to let their taxes fall delinquent. For years, John and Alice Williams redeemed titles at sheriffs' tax sales, holding steadfast to their faith that the railroad would any day resume building the Coast Division, and Naples would become a glorious reality.

In 1888, Stephen Rutherford sold 30 acres of his La Patera ranch, between the Goleta Union School and Fairview Avenue, for a subdivision bearing Goleta's first named streets—Orange, Magnolia, Pine, Rutherford, Gaviota and Dawson—but the economic bubble had already burst. Goleta's first municipal subdivision remained a bean and hay field for many a year to come.

In spite of the shut-down of the railroad, 1888 was considered a prosperous year on the Good Land. Bartlett Canyon boasted the largest walnut orchard west of Santa Barbara, plus the largest berry farm in the county. It was run by Chinese farmers who harvested bumper crops of blackberries, raspberries and strawberries. J. H.

Irwin's apiary in Bartlett Canyon was one of the largest in Southern California. Rancher John Davis built a dining hall and provided tents for free public use.

The Goleta Valley enjoyed its own modest building boom during that summer, with four houses going up simultaneously on ranches belonging to William Rife Coffey, Henry Rich, James Golden and Mrs. Patrick O'Neill.

The heaviest prune crop in Valley history was picked in 1888. Judge W. N. Roberts reported harvesting 100 tons of lima beans off 200 acres, netting him a tidy $8,000 profit, although his ratio of $40 income per acre paled by comparison to what Joe Sexton was getting—$1,000 an acre—from his pampas plumes. Sexton drilled a well on his ranch that summer and ran into such heavy deposits of sea shells and tree fragments at a depth of 340 feet that he quipped "If I run into much more wood down there I'll have to file a timber claim to legalize it." (When it is remembered that Sexton's first well was only thirty feet deep, back in '68, the sinking of the water table under the Good Land can be understood.)

William Begg sold his farm off South Fairview Avenue and moved to the Lompoc Valley that year, receiving $100 per acre. Fellow Scotsman Jim Anderson acquired twenty acres; Francis Simpson forty-three acres; and F. E. Kellogg 100 acres.

Disaster struck More's Landing on March 20, 1889, when a sou'easter wrecked most of the wharf, including the warehouse, which contained forty-four tons of lima beans belonging to John Wall, 500 sacks of corn belonging to John More, several thousand board feet of new lumber, and hundreds of tons of freshly-mined asphaltum.

Henry Allan Smith, a native of Page County, Iowa, who had come west with his family in 1883 in an emigrant train boxcar, was working in the warehouse when the storm struck. Alarmed by the giant waves they saw battering the pilings, the men decided to head for shore. Smith's son, Floyd, of Los Angeles, wrote this account of what happened to his father at More's Landing:

Dad and one of the other workmen each grabbed a 5-gallon tin can of honey which was stored in the warehouse by the Kelley Brothers Apiary of San Marcos Pass. They planned to take the honey to the More Ranch cookhouse, but seeing the wharf breaking up behind them, they dropped the cans and sprinted for shore. It was lucky they did, for the wreckage of the warehouse where they had been at work hit the beach the same time they did, the planks of the wharf deck breaking up under their feet in the last few yards.

Although the opening of the new railroad posed tough competition for the coastal steamships, John More gambled on repairing the facility, and by mid-summer freighters were once more tying up at his wharf.

A rainstorm, said to have been the worst one-day storm in Goleta history, struck the Valley on October 20, 1889, and ruined 900 tons of lima beans in the field. Both the railroad tracks and Hollister Avenue were washed out in the La Patera district.

On November 21, a private lane serving Goleta Valley farmers along the Dos Pueblos ranch line from the La Patera blacksmith shop to the north end of Edgar Hollister's Fairview Ranch was dedicated as a public road, to be maintained by the county. It was named "Fairview Avenue," and became the most important side road in the Valley almost from the first.

A long-vanished Goleta landmark, which played a big part in the community between 1889 and 1907, was Frank Kellogg's dairy and creamery, located on the south side of Hollister Avenue east of Ward Drive. The tall smokestack over the boiler room was visible for miles up and down the Valley. Power to run Kellogg's big churn was provided by a horse walking on an inclined treadmill, before it was replaced by a steam engine. South of the creamery were two milking barns, and corrals for Kellogg's seventy-five dairy cows.

Every morning around nine o'clock, according to Horace Sexton, the Goleta Valley farmers would drive their wagons to Kellogg's Creamery and await their turn to unload their five-gallon milk cans on the platform and pick up steam-sterilized empties in return. Ezra Catlett was Goleta's largest milk producer for many years. Kellogg delivered a wagon load of bulk cream, milk and butter to Santa Barbara markets every day. The invention of the steam-driven centrifugal cream separator enabled Kellogg to handle the milk and cream output of the entire Valley.

The reasons the dairy went out of business in 1907, after being purchased by John More, were related in Chapter XVI.

Another well-known "Kellogg Dairy" came into being in 1902

on the so-called "Potter Farm" at the south end of Kellogg Avenue. It was owned by Frank Kellogg's son, Elmer, who was married to Ezra Catlett's daughter Jessie.

Because Goleta was at the end of a branch railroad for fourteen years, it suffered from infestation by "knights of the road" or hobos, who had to hike the remainder of the way up the coast to reach the other end of the Gap. The unwashed gentry used to pester Goleta housewives for free handouts, until the ladies learned to refer the "Weary Willies" to Frank Kellogg's Creamery, where any man could get a meal—if he chopped firewood for the boiler house.

Paul Manchester tells this amusing true anecdote from Goleta's past:

Two hoboes looked up the Goleta Constable, Oscar Hicks, and said they wanted to get to Santa Barbara but it was too far to walk, adding: "You arrest us and take us to town in your buggy and you get a $2 fee. We get a ride to town, a meal and a night's free lodging." This scheme worked many times. Oscar's kin, Sheriff Tom Hicks also collected a $2 fee for each hobo jailed.

CHAPTER XXI

Genoa to Goleta: Exodus Italian Style

In 1882 an incredible story was going the rounds in the peasant village of Lonate Pozzolo, northern Italy. In America, the story went, even the doorknobs were made of gold!

Mama mia! Twenty-five-year-old Carlo Spezzibottiani knew the story was exaggerated, of course, but he also knew that sooner or later he must immigrate to the New World. There was no future for him in Italy. Every time a peasant died, his land was divided equally among his offspring, and Italian families came large. In the Spezzibottiani family, individual farms had been reduced to postage stamp size. A man could work his heart out trying to make a living on one of them.

So on October 15, 1882, Carlo boarded a freighter at Genoa, and sailed for the Promised Land. On his way across the mosquito-plagued Chagres River Trail on the Isthmus of Panama, he came down with malaria. When he arrived in San Francisco that December, he was still a very sick man. Along with considerable weight, Carlo also shed the "Spezzi" from the spelling of his name.

Carlo Bottiani is an important entry on the roster of Goleta Valley pioneers, because it is the first Italian name to appear there. He was the spearhead of an hegira of poverty-ridden Italian farmers who, like the Scottish exodus ten years earlier, came to *la buona terra* of the Goleta Valley to make a new start.

Remaining in San Francisco long enough to recover his strength, in the spring of 1883 Bottiani took a job herding sheep for a Frenchman named Justinian Caire, who was attempting to establish a French-Italian colony on Santa Cruz Island.

Within two years, Bottiani had saved enough from his meager wages to send back to Italy for his wife, the former Maria Mirata, and his brother, John. He met them upon their arrival in San Francisco, and brought them to live on East De la Guerra Street in Santa Barbara, a town superior in climate and beauty to Italy itself. Shortly thereafter, they were joined by brother Ambrose. Daughters Elisa and Nina were born there in 1885 and 1888, respectively, after which the Bottianis moved out to an adobe in Glen Annie Canyon, where Carlo was employed by the Hollister Estate. In 1891, a baby brother, Angelo, joined the happy and prospering Bottiani household.

In 1890 the Den Estate took over the Glen Annie, and Bottiani went to work for the neighboring Stow Ranch. On January 25, 1892, he paid Sherman P. Stow $1,693 for thirty-seven acres of rich land (sans water rights) lying between San Pedro Creek and the west boundary of Edgar Hollister's Fairview Ranch. This land, the first in the Goleta Valley under Italian ownership, is still Bottiani property.

Carlo died in 1940 at the age of eighty-three. He wore the golden hat of glory; he had lived to see his fondest dreams come true in sunny California. His wife Maria followed him to eternity in 1942, at the age of eighty-five. The old home place is now occupied by Angelo, who in 1925 married Mary Ceriale, of a pioneer Santa Barbara family. Their sons, Carlo and Victor, are prominent Smith Canyon lemon growers.

Alberto Scudelari, of Tremosine, Italy, arrived at Justinian Caire's colony on Santa Cruz Island just as Bottiani was leaving it, at the age of sixteen. He labored on the island for twelve long years. In 1897, while on a visit to Santa Barbara, he dined at Francisco Miratti's Italian restaurant—and fell in love with Mrs. Miratti's sister, Teresa Erbetti, who was working as a waitress to repay the money spent for her steamer passage from Italy.

Alberto married Teresa in 1897, and moved to a dairy farm near Rincon Point, down the coast. Shortly after the turn of the century he was named superintendent of the former Nicolás C. Den ranch in upper Glen Annie Canyon, when it was foreclosed by moneylender Ulpiano Yndart, of Santa Barbara. By 1919, the Scudelaris had saved enough money to purchase 164 acres at the upper end of

Patterson Avenue, extending west to Fairview Avenue, for which they paid $14,000. Here were born Amelia, later to marry Goleta garage owner Fred Acres; Eugene; and Lydia, who married Sheriff Jack Ross.

At first the Scudelaris raised peas, onions and other vegetables, shipping direct to San Francisco by rail. Later they put in walnuts, and a large vineyard with a winery, which they operated until the advent of Prohibition. In 1919, they sold the thirty-acre vineyard for $9,000 and bought a portion of the old Tom Lillard ranch, plus a ranch on San Jose Creek owned by G. B. Cavalletto.

Alberto Scudelari died in 1925, at which time Eugene took over management of the ranch. Teresa died in 1955. The Scudelari heirs sold the last of their Goleta Valley holdings in 1958, one of the few Italian names to vanish from the tax rolls.

Probably the best-known Italian name in the Goleta Valley is Cavalletto, sometimes spelled Cavaletto. The first Cavalletto to make the voyage from Genoa to Goleta was Aventino, from the Piedmonte district of North Italy, who in 1886 opened a famous boarding house on Rancheria Street, the site now occupied by the freeway just west of Wilson School. In 1888, Aventino was joined by his wife, Clementina Pagliotti, and their nine-year-old son, Lodovico, better known as "Coto." Later a second son, Jack, was born. He followed various careers in law, banking and Goleta Valley ranching.

Aventino Cavalletto got his start in the Goleta Valley by buying 300 cords of oak wood from Gus Den's ranch (his woodchoppers were the ones who unearthed the mysterious anchor in the Slough in 1891) for $900 and peddling the wood in town for $2,700.

Young Coto found work with Scotsman Charles Smith, farming land which is now the University campus. He also worked as a mucker in the asphaltum mine there, along with Howard and Harry Sexton, Aleck Taylor, George Phillip, George Simpson and Jim Pomatto. The hoist man at the time, Tom Clancy, later became a justice of the peace.

In 1907, Coto started share-cropping on the Lawrence Orella ranch in central Glen Annie Canyon. Later he subleased some land from the three Pomatto Brothers. In 1913, he and his brother, Jack, took a $15,000 mortgage on 200 acres of land at Coal Oil Point, paying speculator Joe Archambault $5,000 from their farm labors.

A row of cypress trees still marks Coto's eastern half of the ranch (now Isla Vista) from Jack's western half (now the Devereux Ranch). The soil was poor and crops mediocre, but the two Cavalletto brothers made tidy profits when they sold out in 1920. Jack got $60,000 for his 109 acres; Coto $52,000 for ninety-nine acres.

The patriarch, Aventino Cavalletto, died at his Rancheria Street boarding house in 1879. His wife survived until 1935.

Two of Aventino's ambitious nephews from Vesignano, Italy, showed up in 1897. They were Mike, aged twenty, and Giovanni Battista, better known as "G.B.", aged sixteen. They had obtained their passports to emigrate from Italy by swearing they had jobs with their Uncle Aventino in Santa Barbara, California. Actually the boys' first employment was bucking liveoak wood into stove lengths at George M. Williams' ranch in Smith Canyon.

Mike (who started all the confusion of nomenclature by leaving an "l" out of his name) went to work for the De la Cuesta family on Rancho Nojoqui, on the other side of the mountains. Later he returned to Santa Barbara as a milker on the Ontare Ranch. In 1895, having saved his pennies, he returned to Italy to marry his childhood sweetheart, Caterina Cavaletto (no relation).

Back home in the Goleta Valley, Mike leased the historic San Jose Vineyard from the Valley's oldest pioneer, James McCaffery, who had owned it for forty-four years. Cavaletto eventually purchased the property from McCaffery in 1900, and kept the old 1804 mission winery operating until 1918. To protect the ancient mud walls and original tile roof of the padres' *bodega*, Mike Cavaletto enclosed it inside a sheetiron shelter, thereby preserving the oldest man-made structure in the Goleta Valley.* It is presently owned by Mike's son, Joseph.

Mike and Caterina's family consisted of Laura, who married a 1911 emigrant from Italy, Pasquale Borgaro, whose home is located north of Highway 101 at the Patterson Avenue overpass; Frances, who married Angelo Bosio and lived on a San Jose Canyon ranch previously owned by the Pacific Improvement Company; Joseph, present occupant of the San Jose Ranch, who married Selina Giorgi; Peter, who married Selina's sister, Elisa, and lives on the former

---

* Readers are advised that the winery is not open to the public.

Juan Hill ranch at 1026 North Patterson Avenue; L. M. "Cy," who married Laurabelle Rawley, former chief surgical nurse at Saint Francis Hospital; and Louisa, the wife of James Marchiando.

Mike Cavaletto died in 1921, his widow living until 1950.

Mike's brother, G. B., was a more aggressive, outgoing type. He had $1.97 in his pockets when he landed in Santa Barbara from Italy at the age of sixteen, and could not speak a word of English. Within eleven years he had made enough of a stake to marry Katherina Pagliotti on New Year's Day, 1903. Their children were Laura (Mrs. Egisto Giorgi of Santa Barbara); John; Louis, who married Pauline Catherina and lives in Glen Annie Canyon; and George, a prominent attorney who married Margurite "Peggy" Meyers and resides high atop a hill overlooking Glen Annie Canyon and the Valley below.

During G. B. Cavalletto's long lifetime on the Good Land, his fortunes underwent many vicissitudes. Once he had to run a restaurant in Santa Paula to support himself. He bought two horses and hired out to the S.P. railroad as an earth mover around the turn of the century. He leased a portion of Hope Ranch and raised hay on land which is now the barbered greens and fairways of the La Cumbre Country Club golf course. He had a crop growing where Laguna Blanca is now located, and received $25 per acre damages when ten acres of hay were flooded by the water forming the artificial lake.

By 1912, G.B. had prospered to the point where he could afford to buy some of the Good Land. What is now called the Cavalletto "home place" on Stow Canyon Road was obtained from Joseph Archambault, 101 acres for $320 an acre, including the crops and the farmhouse. Although the Italians of the Goleta Valley love the soil with a passionate devotion, and to this day would rather buy land than sell it, G.B. Cavalletto was persuaded to give up forty-five acres to Harry Sexton.

In following years, G.B. added more and more choice Goleta Valley acreage to his holdings. Broad, fertile Glen Annie Canyon was his favorite locale, together with the bottomlands of the old John More ranch. He bought the former Jim Anderson and Dr. Harold Sidebotham ranches in Glen Annie Canyon, which are still in the possession of his heirs.

In 1929, sales of land south of Hollister Avenue were made by the More Estate for as high as $2,700 per acre. When the depression hit, G.B. had the capital to take advantage of cheap prices, and bought two parcels of the More Ranch, comprising 62 and 69 acres, for only $750 and $875 an acre.

One of G.B.'s choicest parcels of lemon land, where the Goleta Valley Community Hospital now stands, witnessed an historic innovation in 1939 when G.B. installed the Goleta Valley's first propeller wind machine to protect his lemon groves from frost damage. Formerly, lemon growers had to depend on smudge pots; the motor-driven propeller of the wind machine could be turned on automatically by thermostatic control. The machine which brought automation to the lemon growers stood about 200 feet south of Hollister Avenue, on what is now the traffic divider island on the extension of South Patterson Avenue.

Beginning in 1931, G.B. Cavalletto launched a program of making gifts of land to his children. To daughter Laura Giorgi he gave eighty acres in Glen Annie Canyon. Son Louis got the old home place on Stow Canyon Road opposite the Goleta Valley Junior High. He later got seventy-one acres adjoining Laura's ranch.

On the west side of Glen Annie Road, on the rolling hills which separate Glen Annie from Ellwood Canyon, G.B. deeded his youngest son, George, 158 acres. He felt the hill land was not as valuable as the level ground he had given Laura and Louie, therefore gave George more of it. Besides, George was away at U.C. studying to be a lawyer, and once a boy passes his bar examination, how can you keep him down on the farm? (The advent of Cachuma water in the mid-1950s transformed Attorney George Cavalletto's 158 hillside acres into one of the choicest lemon and avocado properties on the South Coast.)

Other gifts of land were made by white-haired old G. B. to his children and grand-children in 1942, 1946, 1952 and 1953. George received the More Ranch acreage where the Goleta Valley Community Hospital is located. Laura was deeded twenty-seven acres north of the Borgaro place on Patterson Avenue, which offered dramatic proof of the value of the Good Land: she swapped her twenty-seven acres for 27,000 acres of cattle range north of Spokane, Washington, and got a sizeable sum of cash to boot!

Having disposed of the bulk of his worldly goods for the tax ad-

Genoa to Goleta: Exodus Italian Style 209

vantage of his heirs, venerable old G.B. spent his remaining years in a modest cottage on Hollister Avenue, the site of which is now buried under the south ramp fill of the Ward Memorial Boulevard overpass. He succumbed there of cancer in 1955, just before his eightieth birthday.

Not far behind the Cavallettos came two more important Italian names to the roll call of Goleta pioneers: Jordano and Pagliotti.

James Jordano and his ailing wife, the former Annette Pomatto of Turino, and Mr. and Mrs. Antonio Pagliotti and family, arrived together from Italy in October of 1890. The Jordanos, as related in Chapter XVI, went to live in the dairyman's cottage on More Mesa. The Pagliottis bought the Tom Lillard farm in the foothills north of Fairview Avenue.

Making the Genoa-to-Goleta voyage with the Pagliottis were four children born in the old country: Joseph, who married Carlotta Cavalero; Peter, who married Savina Albertoni; Katherina, who married G.B. Cavalletto; and John, who married Mary Mautino. Later a fifth child was born in Goleta, James Pagliotti, who married Esther Brons. As of 1966, the widows of all four sons were still living.

John Pagliotti got his first job from Superintendent Robert Main on the Bishop Ranch as a walnut picker, receiving $20 a month. Later he worked a thirteen-acre ranch which his parents bought from Sheriff Tom Hicks on upper Fairview Avenue. He died late in 1965, at the age of seventy-nine, from injuries incurred when he fell off a ladder while picking oranges at his home place, which occupied the extreme northwestern corner of Daniel A. Hill's old La Goleta land grant.

James Jordano's wife, Annette, was so entranced by the beauty and climate of the Goleta Valley that in 1889 she wrote her three brothers in Turino and urged them to join her. The three Pomatto Brothers arrived in the Good Land in 1890—John, thirty; James, twenty-three; and Pietro, nineteen. In hunting around for suitable land to lease they were attracted to Glen Annie Canyon, which was beginning to take on the look of an Italian colony. Nicolás C. Den had just taken possession of the northern end of the canyon from the estate of the late Colonel Hollister, through a court order won by T.B. Bishop, his lawyer. Den leased 144 choice acres to the three

Pomatto Brothers, north and west of the Corona del Mar Ranch headquarters, where they established a dairy herd.

Fifteen years later, when Den lost his property through mismanagement to moneylender Ulpiano Yndart, the Pomatto Brothers were able to buy their ranch for $200 an acre. They converted the dairy into a walnut ranch. They lived in the house, still standing in 1966 at 1100 Glen Annie Canyon Road, which had served Colonel Hollister as a fruit-drying plant.

Two of the Pomatto Brothers, James and Peter, married; but John remained a bachelor all his life.

James, through the medium of exchanging photographs and letters, wooed and won Libera Costantino of his own village in Italy. She came to California in 1900 to become his bride, and upon her arrival in Santa Barbara by train was provided with a de luxe room in the town's finest hotel, the Arlington, there to await the arrival of her husband-to-be from Goleta.

After their wedding, James' new bride remained in town to take care of Mrs. Annette Jordano, who was seriously ill. She took care of Mrs. Jordano until the latter's death a few months later.

James and Libera had four children: Dominic, who married Angelina Pignocco and, after her death, Helen Smith, and lives at the old home place on Glen Annie Canyon Road; Margaret, now Mrs. Eugene Miratti; Joseph, who married Sarah Lessett; and Catherine, Mrs. Vince Pollard, who died in childbirth in 1941.

A year following James' marriage to Libera, his younger brother, Pete, married Margaret Mautino of Santa Barbara. They also had four children who made their mark in Goleta Valley affairs.

Dominic, the firstborn, popularly known as Dee, became the Valley's first rancher to fly his own airplane. During the Twenties, Thirties and up to World War II, Dee Pomatto's private landing field and hangar were located on what is now the campus of Dos Pueblos High School, north of El Encanto Heights. Dee also operated the Valley's first amateur radio station, licensed under the call W6PEN. From his "QTH" in Glen Annie Canyon, Dee has talked via shortwave to fellow radio hams all over the world, spreading the name and fame of Goleta's Good Land. These hobbies apparently kept Dee so preoccupied he never found time for courtship and marriage.

The second child of Peter and Margaret Pomatto was Julia, who married Italian-born Benny Scaramuzza, a Goleta food merchant. The third child, John, married Anna Mangan; he died in 1963. The youngest, Margaret, is the wife of William B. Flynn, and follows the career of a kindergarten teacher.

The three Pomatto Brothers continued to live on their Glen Annie farm, which included one of Colonel Hollister's original barns and bunkhouses, until 1916. Then they bought a 368-acre tract on the west side of Glen Annie Road, the former Bruno Orella ranch which had subsequently become part of the Sherman P. Stow Company's operations. They paid $50,000 for the 368 acres in 1916; in 1965, Dee Pomatto sold seventy acres of this ranch for $500,000 as the site of the Dos Pueblos High School and Glen Annie Junior High School.

In 1906, not quite early enough to qualify as Goleta pioneers, came the Durbiano family. Virginio Durbiano, of Turino, arrived in Santa Barbara and went to work for George M. Williams on his Modoc Road ranch. In 1910, his brother, Michael, and wife, Francesca, followed.

Virginio returned to the old country to stay, but Mike Durbiano, after working for Williams for nine years, bought twenty-six acres in the flats immediately east of the John Pickett ranch (where San Marcos High School was built), paying $450 an acre. Here Durbiano raised vegetables, which he peddled to such upper-bracket clientele as Diehl's Grocery, the Arlington, and the Potter Hotel. A housing tract now covers Durbiano's vegetable fields. He also founded the Durbiano Dairy. The Durbiano family consists of Beatrice, Chris, Manuel, James, Mike Jr. and Vincent.

Another prominent Italian family which reached the Goleta Valley early in the new century was Dominic Mecono's, also of Turino. He arrived in 1905, and went to work for the railroad as a day laborer. Later he was a vineyardist on Santa Cruz Island, where he saved enough from his $17 a month wages to send back to Italy for his sweetheart, Cesera Micono.

After their marriage in Santa Barbara, the Meconos moved to the Bishop Ranch, Dominic later going to work for August Linquest on North Patterson Avenue. Still later he farmed land in the Cieniguitas, near the old adobe orphanage erected in 1856 by the Sisters of Charity, now replaced by St. Vincent's School.

The Meconos had five sons: Tony, Frank, John (who was killed in the Philippines in World War II), Dominic and Jimmy. In 1934 the family acquired the 180-acre grazing range belonging to Alphonso Den—a transaction notable in that it marked the last land in possession of a descendant of Don Nicholas A. Den of Dos Pueblos.

Dominic Mecono died in 1955; his widow is still living. The Mecono Brothers have extensive lemon, walnut and avocado groves on their Glen Annie hillsides, north of George Cavalletto's ranch.

Unlike the Italians who colonized further north in Napa, Sonoma and Mendocino Counties, those who settled in the Goleta Valley did not turn to vineyards or wine making on a large scale. One of the most tragic episodes in the history of the Goleta Italian colony involved Olindo Dardi, whose home stood at the present 880 Cambridge Avenue. This ill-starred vintner had lost his wife and two sons during the 1918 epidemic of Spanish influenza, and was raising his surviving daughter, Lina. In 1932, while cleaning his wine vats, Dardi was overcome by fumes. Lina, attempting to get her unconscious father out of the huge vat, was also overcome. Their bodies were found in the vat by neighbors. The premises are now the stables and tack room of lemon grower and horse fancier David Wells.

Primarily farmers, the Italian settlers in the Good Land have transmitted their devotion to the soil to their descendants. Italian names are prominent in the rosters of the Goleta Farm Center, the Farm Bureau, the Four-H Club, Calavo Growers, the Johnston Fruit Company, Goleta Lemon Association, the Agricultural Extension Service and Agricultural Stabilization agencies, the Goleta County Water District and the lima bean and walnut growers associations.

Later Italian families followed the pioneers—such respected names as Miratti, Dal Pozzo, Perello, Giorgi, Prevedello, Corbellini, Bazzi, Manzetti, Ciampi, Mostachetti, and Ferregamo. Although a minority group in population figures, Italian farmers in 1965 were producing nearly half the Valley's agricultural crops.

Italians are traditionally averse to yielding farmland to subdividers. Rising taxes in all likelihood will eventually force them to yield. George Cavalletto says, "the last farming in the Goleta Valley will likely be done by a few stubborn fourth or fifth generation Americans with Italian names. Only death and taxes can do it."

When the inevitable day dawns that the Goleta Valley's last farmer surrenders his fertile acres to the subdivider, and the plow and the planter are replaced by the bulldozer and the concrete mixer, we venture to predict that the farmer will not say "goodbye"; he will say *"arrivederci"* . . ."

CHAPTER XXII

Vanished Industries of the 19th Century

Prior to 1960, the Goleta Valley's economy was primarily agricultural. Walnuts, vegetables, berries, beans, hay and grain predominated in the pioneer era, followed by citrus and avocados after 1930. These crops, now in retreat before the juggernaut of urbanization, will eventually be crowded out of the Valley. They will not be the first victims of "progress" in the Good Land. Before 1900, three major industries flourished, waned and expired: whaling, pampas grass culture, and deep-shaft asphalt mining.

Whaling operations conducted from shore stations, in contrast to the traditional ship-based method, began in 1851 along the Coast from Humboldt Bay to Baja California, with a chain of whaling stations established by a former whaling master named Davenport. These stations averaged 180 kills per day. Two of the camps were located along the Channel—one at Cojo Bay, in the lee of Point Concepción, the other at Goleta Beach at the foot of the UCSB mesa bluffs.

The California gray whale, most numerous species in Pacific waters, migrates north from calving lagoons in the Gulf of California every spring, headed for summer feeding grounds in the remote Bering Sea. In rounding the corner of the continent at Point Concepción, north-bound, the schools swim alongside the kelp beds close to shore. They are often joined by humpback, sulphur bottom, finback and other varieties. From October to January, they swim back to breed in warmer Mexican waters, this time keeping to windward of the Channel Islands.

A UCSB authority, Dr. John Cushing of the Department of Biological Sciences, states that the first whaling company to operate at Goleta Beach did so about 1870, and was composed of Jamaica Negroes instead of the usual Azores Portuguese, with a Captain Van Dorous in charge. This operation was abandoned after nine years, but was resumed by later whaling companies.

Two eye-witnesses to the Goleta shore-based whaling operation, the late J. J. Hollister Sr. and Mrs. Grace V. Greenwell of Isla Vista, gave the writer the following information on this almost-forgotten facet of Goleta Valley life:

Whenever a school of whales was seen spouting and cavorting out beyond the kelp, small boats would set out from Goleta Beach and detonate a charge of dynamite in their midst, usually killing six or eight whales. Eight days later the carcasses would float to the surface, for towing ashore and beaching on a high tide.

Hundred-gallon kettles or try-pots made of cast iron were placed under the beetling sea-caves where the UCSB mesa cliffs had been eroded away by wave action. Woodchoppers were kept busy for years in the springtime, felling oak trees on what is now the University campus and Isla Vista, to provide fuel for the whalers' rendering kettles. The soot stains on the chalky palisades where the kettles stood were plainly visible until covered by the massive earth fill ramp at the UCSB end of Ward Memorial Boulevard.

Flensing crews would strip the thick, yellowish-white layers of blubber from the whales. Chopped into chunks, the greasy blubber would be melted down into pure whale oil in the iron pots. A cooper manufactured sturdy barrels at the spot, into which the rendered oil was poured and left to cool. When closed, the oil barrels were rolled onto barges on the beach and winched out to waiting schooners, which took the oil back to San Pedro for transhipment by rail and/or sail to all parts of the world.

Ezra Catlett, pioneer Goleta homesteader, used to haul supplies to the whaling camp in the early Seventies. The last foreman in charge of the Goleta whaling operation was Vicente Cavalleri, who lived in a rude shack at the west end of the Sandspit during whaling season. His daughter, the aforementioned Mrs. Greenwell of Isla Vista, stated that Cavalleri operated the Goleta whaling station from 1879 until the whale oil industry expired in the 1890s.

Whales practically ceased to migrate northward as a result of

Captain M. Scammon (a government scientist) discovering their breeding grounds at Scammon's Bay in Baja California. Whalers, able to trap their prey at its source, virtually extinguished the California gray whale as a species before the advent of coal oil and electric light reduced the world market for whale oil. The latter found a limited use as fuel for street lighting, in rope-making and leather-working, and as a lubricant for watches.

Whaling was at best a messy and odoriferous business. A whaling camp would certainly be barred as an air pollution menace today. Since only the outer layer of fat was marketable, tons of raw whale meat lay putrifying on the Goleta beach for weeks at a time, until the roundabout area was purged of the fetid stench by tidal action and the scavenging of sharks and seabirds.

No records exist as to how much oil was produced at Goleta over a fifty-year period, but the largest number of barrels of which there is a record was 450 in a single season. A report for the year 1880 indicates that the Goleta and Cojo whaling stations together produced 17,135 gallons of whale oil worth $7,710.

A few of the rust-red, three-legged rendering kettles may still be seen, treasured by their owners as mementos of a vanished era. One is at the Daniel Hill Adobe, 35 La Patera Lane; another is behind the Trussell-Winchester Adobe at 412 West Montecito Street in Santa Barbara. Every few years a storm will shift Goleta's sand dunes and expose a whale rib or vertebra. Except for these skeletal clues, nothing remains to indicate that a large-scale whaling industry once contributed to the payroll of the Good Land.

During the final quarter of the Nineteenth Century, the Goleta Valley was the world supplier of a unique product—pampas grass plumes, which were in brisk demand in London, Hamburg and Berlin for decorating parade horses, military and/or state catafalques, and at grand balls, fairs, circuses and expositions.

Joseph Sexton's Nursery originated the industry in 1872, when he imported seeds of the *Gynarium argenteum*, indigenous to the pampas (plains) of Argentina, and raised several hundred plants. Pampas grass grows in huge clumps, twenty feet wide by fifteen feet high. It had originally been introduced to California by sailors of clipper ships around the time of the Gold Rush. Sexton discarded all off-color varieties, and concentrated on platinum-white plumes.

In 1874, Sexton made an important break-through when he discovered how to differentiate between the sexes of the plants. He learned that if he pulled the immature plumes from their sheaths and dried them in the sun, the male plumes would hang stiff and heavy as oat heads, while the female plumes would fluff up and become gossamer-light and airy as wind-blown sea spume.

As an experiment, Sexton sent samples of pampas plumes to the San Francisco wholesale flower market, and to Peter Henderson Seed Company in New York. The latter firm ordered 300 plumes to test out the European market. The following day Sexton received a telegraphic order to double the shipment and rush it east by express. This was the first lot of pampas plumes ever exported from California, and started a decorators' fad in Europe which in turn spawned a lucrative industry for the Goleta Valley.

Joe Sexton expanded his pampas plantation east of San Jose Creek to 5,000 hills, planted in rows sixteen feet apart, each clump separated ten feet from its neighbor. By the second year, each hill was producing from eighty to 150 plumes. Production decreased numerically as the hills aged, but the quality improved and thus commanded steadily higher prices.

At plume-harvesting time in September, Sexton added twenty extra Chinese coolies to his labor force, housing them in a bunkhouse at the east end of his ranch, behind 5410 Hollister Avenue. The coolies made an exotic sight jogging to and from work in single file, as their ancestors had done for thousands of years on China's restricted hillside trails, jabbering in their nasal sing-song, hands buried up their sleeves, black pigtails bobbing.

The pampas plumes were harvested with a long-handled pruning hook fabricated by Goleta blacksmiths. They were loaded on flatbed wagons and hauled to the open air husking shed near the Sexton barn, on what in 1966 was the Robert Seaton avocado grove. Here a crew composed of school girls and neighborhood housewives slit the green husks open with a stripper invented by Charley Sexton, and carefully pulled out the immature plumes. The discarded green sheaths were hauled back to the fields and plowed under for mulch. The plumes were carried by wagon to three large drying fields (now the playground behind the Saint Raphael Parochial School) and laid out in long double rows to cure in the sun. During the three-day drying period, coolies would go up each row once a day, turning and fluffing the plumes. This spine-cracking task could not be handled by Occidental laborers.

When fully dried, the plumes were loaded like loose hay on a large wagon and hauled to a special barn on the north side of the Sexton ranch, dubbed "the Ark" by Valley residents. Here the plumes were packed in wooden crates, 3,000 to a crate, and kept under pressure until fully packed to a weight of 750 pounds. From the Ark, the crated plumes were hauled to the Goleta railroad depot and freight warehouse, half a mile south of Hollister Avenue, for shipment to New York.

At first Sexton got $200 per thousand for his plumes. He also handled the output produced by neighboring ranchers, on a commission basis. One such pampas grass field grew on the so-called "Chinaman Ranch" operated by the Santa Barbara Produce Company, on the Kate Bell ranch where a large discount department store is now located, at 6865 Hollister Avenue.

Prices declined gradually until 1886, when sales were sluggish at $30 per thousand. Many Goleta Valley growers did not bother to harvest their plumes that year. In the fall of 1887, a boom year everywhere, plumes were back in demand at $40 per thousand; by 1888 they were as high as $60 per thousand.

Sexton's best production years for pampas plumes were between 1890 and 1895, when he was exporting half a million plumes annually. In 1891, Santa Barbara staged the first of its famous "Battle of the Flowers" pageants, honoring a few hours' visit from President Benjamin Harrison. (The idea of a floral parade might have been borrowed from Pasadena's first Tournament of Roses, held in 1890.) For the presidential visit, a large arch was built over State Street at the Figueroa Street intersection. It was completely covered with Sexton pampas plumes, gleaming like spun silver in the sun. Some prankster touched his lighted cigar to the fluffy, tinder-dry plumes, and the whole arch was enveloped in flames in moments. This incident led to a local ordinance forbidding the future use of pampas plumes for public decorations. Shipment of pampas plumes in common carriers was never banned as a fire hazard, however.

Approaching 1900, the pampas plume fad fell off sharply in

Vanished Industries of the 19th Century

Europe, much as did the fad for decorating milady's millinery with ostrich feathers. In 1895, when prices sagged too low for economical harvesting, Joseph Sexton quit the business, but turned over his future orders from abroad to neighbors George M. Williams and C. C. Tinker. They continued to export plumes on a diminishing scale until 1900, when the pampas grass industry expired.

Descendants of Goleta's pampas grass clumps are now seen as plantings in divider strips on the State highway system. Maverick clumps, from seeds carried by birds or the wind, are seen throughout Southern California. Many private gardens feature them. They are also useful as windbreaks, and to hold the banks of creeks in place.

References have already been made to the surface mining of asphalt carried on by the More Brothers along Goleta Beach, starting in the 1850s. This mining was done in a primitive manner and on a relatively small scale, compared to the deep-shaft mining conducted in Goleta by the Alcatraz Asphaltum Company in the 1890s.

The first shaft was dug on Gus Den's Rincon Ranch about six-tenths of a mile northwest of Pelican (Goleta) Point in 1890. It penetrated 200 feet into a surface outcrop of pure asphaltum. The site was approximately fifty feet from the southwestern corner of the Speech and Dramatic Arts Building on the University campus, facing the fish-hook-shaped lagoon to the south and west, which provided a convenient dumping place for mine tailings.

Having had no previous experience with this type of mining, the Alcatraz Company soon realized it had made a mistake in digging a shaft through an exposed ore body as soft and porous as asphaltum. The deposit was rock-hard and glass-brittle when exposed to the air, but a few feet below the surface became plastic and spongy. The deeper the shaft, the more viscid the asphalt. In effect, it was like spooning a hole into a jar of molasses. To get away from the problems of shoring and casing such a shaft, it was decided to sink another vertical shaft through solid shale, 100 feet north of the first shaft. Then, at fifty-foot levels, horizontal tunnels or drifts, lined with heavy planking, could be dug to tap the ore body.

So much brackish water filtered into Number Two shaft during its excavation that for health reasons, work shifts were reduced to four hours maximum. The ceilings of the tunnels were supported by 10 by 10 fir timbers, shipped down from Oregon sawmills and floated ashore at the west end of More Mesa beach. The walls or laggings of the drifts were braced with 2 by 10 planks. Even these heavy supports often snapped like toothpicks under the constant pressure of the shifting asphalt (which nearly everyone in Goleta pronounced "ashfelt" or "asfelt").

Early managers of the Goleta asphalt operation were named Welty and Gillingham. The best-known superintendent was Charles L. Macpherson. Alexander Bell managed the office and handled the bookkeeping. The blacksmith shop, one of the busiest places around the mine, was presided over by Morty Rodehaver, who later became a prominent Santa Barbara auto mechanic. Of numerous hoist operators, the best known were George Willey, who died in 1959 at the age of eighty-two, and Tom Clancy, later a Goleta Justice of the Peace.

During its peak production years, the Goleta asphalt mine employed fifty men, some of them horny-handed veterans of the '49 Gold Rush who were now in their sixties. Since there were only about fifty families living on the Good Land, the Alcatraz Company's payroll was a potent factor in the local economy. Wages at the mine were double those paid to farm hands, although the underground work was not so pleasant. Miners were paid $2.50 for a standard ten-hour shift, while muckers got $2 a day. It was the mucker's back-breaking task to shovel out dirt after a dynamite blast had been set off to fragmentize the congealed tar into workable chunks.

Herbert Roberts, who spent his boyhood in the Goleta Valley and who died in Santa Barbara in 1962 in his ninety-third year, told the writer of a hair-raising adventure he experienced while mucking in the Goleta asphalt mine. He and two others, Bill Bradley and Louis Moore, set fifteen sticks of dynamite in the asphaltum wall, lit the fuse, and then raced to the main shaft expecting to ride the hoist bucket to safety. Unfortunately, a careless boilerman had let his steam pressure drop until there was not enough power to lift the hoist when Roberts signaled the surface to haul away. The three muckers, with barely seconds between them and certain death, scrambled up the shaft's emergency ladder in time to escape flying débris from the detonation.

Roberts described the work at the bottom drift, 550 feet below the ground, as "hot, dirty, cramped, and dangerous." Men often fainted from inhaling toxic fumes, although a fan in the boiler house topside was kept running twenty-four hours a day to circulate fresh air below.

"One time Morty Rodehaver had a pot of fresh mussels roasting over the coals in his blacksmith forge," Roberts recalled some sixty years after the event. "The scamp let the steam from the mussels drift into the ventilating system. The delicious aroma of roasting sea food percolated down to the poor hungry devils slaving away 550 feet below. They almost abandoned their work to come up and eat some of those mussels."*

In its heyday, the Goleta asphalt mine presented a beehive of industry. In addition to three shafthouses, there was a two-story boarding house, machine shops, stables, and a cookhouse presided over by a Fu Manchu-type of Chinese chef of shuddery memory but superb cuisine. Employees paid $4 a week for board and room at the company bunkhouse, and received discounts at the company store for their tobacco, playing cards, soap and other incidentals.

Change-overs in the ten-hour shifts occurred at 7 a.m. and 4:30 p.m. The four extra hours out of each day were utilized for making repairs to machinery or adding shoring timbers, bailing out water seepage which if unchecked could flood the drifts and drown the workmen, and other maintenance operations which could not be carried out below ground while mining was in progress.

Whenever a Goleta farmer had spare time between crops, or when drought or wet weather kept him out of field and orchard for protracted periods of time, he always knew he could make ends meet by taking a job "grubbing ashfelt" at the Alcatraz mine. Such well-known Goletans as Harry Sexton, Coto Cavalletto and others toiled many a week some 500 feet underground. Whenever a new shipment of shoring planks came in by schooner from Oregon, workmen were paid $10 per thousand board feet of timber for stacking the planks on the beach above highwater mark.

Due to the syrupy, migratory nature of asphaltum, there could be no holidays, even on Sundays. Otherwise the miners would re-

---

* Some mussel marginalia: in days of yore, Goletans ate mussels all year round without fear of toxic effects. Today, this is forbidden by health laws.

turn to their jobs below ground to find the drifts clogged with asphalt, which had oozed in through cracks and knotholes. The soft tar also exuded a noxious gas which was heavier than air. When the weather above ground was foggy, air pressures hampered the ventilating blowers. If a miner's lamp candle was exposed to the invisible gas, an explosion and fire could result.

In 1895, two workmen, Charlie Ellis and Bill Burch, drove their picks through a shell of asphalt to puncture a cavity charged with lethal gas, which was exploded by their candles. Both men were killed; their graves lie side by side in Goleta Cemetery. This tragedy led to the prohibition of candles or open-flame lanterns below ground; only "Daveys" or safety lamps were permitted. If a Davey went out for any reason, it had to be sent back to the surface for relighting.

Horses furnished the motive power to run the machinery in the early years. Later a donkey engine was employed. Water came from a well on the Storke Ranch, pumped by hand into barrels by George Sexton, Joseph's brother, who hauled it to the boiler house and cookhouse. Steam from the boiler was condensed and the water stored for re-use.

When the Goleta mine was operating full blast, it turned out sixty tons of 90 per cent pure asphaltum every twenty-four hours. The eighty-pound hunks of solidified tar were loaded onto a fleet of five wagons drawn by four-horse teams, each wagon carrying four tons and making three round trips daily, seven days a week, to the S. P. station at Hollister Avenue and La Patera Lane.

Goleta farmers contracted to do this hauling for 75 cents a ton. A man and four horses could earn $9 a day, which was a princely wage in the Nineties. One rainy night in 1894, the main horse barn near the mine, owned by rancher Charley Smith, was set afire by a hobo smoking in the hayloft. It burned to the ground, cremating 16 fine draft horses trapped in their stalls.

The asphalt, after being loaded onto gondola cars at La Patera siding, was shipped to Newhall Junction on the S. P. Valley Line, from which place it was distributed all over the country. Some of the historic streets of the Vieux Carré in old New Orleans, 2,000 miles away, are paved with tar dug from the deep-shaft mine under the UCSB campus.

Off-duty miners found time for sports. Frank "Peck" Willis organized the first football team ever to scrimmage on Goleta Valley soil. Known as the "La Patera Giants," the team challenged a Santa Barbara eleven whose manager was a young Stanford alumnus named T. M. Storke. The gridiron was a field on the dried-up Estero. The final score was 25 to nothing in favor of Santa Barbara. The La Patera Giants retired, leaving it to the future San Marcos Royals and UCSB Gauchos to retrieve Goleta's gridiron honor.

Number Two shaft, the main producer, was in operation for eight years. A third shaft, complete with hoisting machinery, was dug on the mesa toward Isla Vista. It was of minor importance.

The mine closed down in 1898, not because its orebody was showing signs of depletion, but because the Alcatraz Company could operate more economically from surface tar pits in Brea Canyon on the Sisquoc Ranch, gravity-flowing the molten asphalt by pipe line for forty miles to a refinery at Alcatraz, near Gaviota. Untold thousands of tons of fine quality asphaltum still remain 200 to 600 feet below the University campus, but no traces remain of the surface buildings. Even the old mine tailings have been scattered for use as fill dirt, mostly by the Marines during World War II.

In the late 1950s, UCSB engineers wanted to pinpoint the locations of the still existing network of subterranean shafts and drifts before erecting high-rise buildings. No maps of the mine were available, so several old-timers were called in—Herb Roberts, Horace Sexton, Coto Cavalletto, and Jim Smith. Their memories proved infallible. When the engineers took a test coring at the spots indicated by the oldsters, the ore body was precisely where they said it was. These areas, with potential earth-settling problems, were thus avoided in erecting campus buildings over ground honeycombed by asphalt miners seventy years before.

CHAPTER XXIII

Sexton's Hall: Symbol of the Gay Nineties

Second generation pioneers, in contributing their recollections to this volume, agree on one thing: the Gay Nineties were just that in the Goleta Valley. It was a farming community, unhampered by sophisticated city airs. The horse-and-buggy days were uncomplicated by war and rumors of war. The cost of living was lower than it would ever be again. While the Valley's water supply was failing gradually, serious irrigation problems had not yet developed.

True, sorrow punctuated those happy years. Funeral processions wound their way to the Goleta Cemetery many times during the decade. Important pioneers dropped off one by one. Albert G. Hollister, the Colonel's older brother, died on April 24, 1891, leaving Fairview Ranch to his son, Edgar. During 1892, Annie Hollister lost both her father, Sam L. James, and her brother, Washington, the latter in a hunting accident near Carpinteria. The year 1892 also witnessed the suicide of Jose Lobero, builder of Southern California's first Opera House, whose music was often heard at Glen Annie *soirees*.

German Senter, who had married Daniel Hill's widow, Rafaela, and who was responsible for the rapid subdivision of La Patera lands, died in 1892 at the home of a daughter in Montecito. Lucy A. "Auntie" Brown, the dominant personality of the Hollister family, died in April, 1893, at the age of eighty.

John H. Williams, founder of the ghost town of Naples, succumbed of gout in San Francisco in 1895, his grandiose dreams unfulfilled. His eccentric widow, Alice P. Williams, erected a small stone chapel at Naples in his honor. Standing starkly on the skyline

Sexton's Hall: Symbol of the Gay Nineties

at the east rim of Dos Pueblos Canyon beside the stage road, "the Haunted Chapel" was a familiar landmark for nearly thirty years. A mausoleum at the rear of the square-towered, buttressed Gothic church had a vault for the remains of John H. Williams and Patricia, the infant daughter of foreman George Mack and his wife, Rita. Also entombed there were the embalmed carcasses of two of Mrs. Williams' pet pug dogs.

It was Mrs. Williams' desire to dedicate the memorial chapel with a wedding; but the first two Naples couples to be married after completion of the chapel in 1898—William Rutherford and Jessie Nelson, John K. Wade and Martha Cubin—declined to tie the knot, as they phrased it, "in a dog cemetery." As a result, the little Naples chapel, while intended for the glory of God, was never used as a house of worship. It was still unconsecrated when it was toppled by the earthquake of June 29, 1925.

The dance hall at Naples was a popular gathering-place for Valley young people on Saturday nights, and even for roller skating daytimes. Goleta's most popular dance hall, however, was the upper floor of the general store and post office at Patterson and Hollister Avenues. This structure was so rickety it threatened to collapse whenever a boot-stompin', hand-clappin' square dance got under way.

Nurseryman Joe Sexton, who had five popular daughters in regular attendance at Goleta dances, worried about the safety of the store building. Finally he decided to erect a community social center at his own expense. Thus was created "Goleta Hall," soon renamed Sexton's Hall, located at 5410 Hollister Avenue at the east end of the Sexton ranch. It officially opened on May 16, 1890, with a local talent show—to inaugurate a new era in Goleta society.

Sexton's Hall, painted silver gray, had a unique three-step false front facing Hollister Avenue. The auditorium was 38 by 80 feet in size, and seated 450 for theatrical events. The seats could be folded in gangs of four, and stacked against the walls to clear the floor for dancing. A small balcony seated up to fifty eagle-eyed chaperones. The entry vestibule was flanked by a ticket-seller's booth and cloak rooms.

The stage was twenty-two feet wide and equipped with three sets of flats painted by Goleta's pioneer artist, Frank W. Judd. The flats represented a Victorian parlor, a kitchen, and a woodland scene. The drop curtain, also painted by Judd, depicted a Swiss lake with snow-clad Alps in the background. The proscenium arch was elaborately decorated. Behind the stage were dressing rooms and a kitchen for sociables, lodge dinners and wedding feasts.

Sexton's Hall was the first public building in the Valley to be lighted by artificial gas. Sexton's home-made gas plant was housed in a shack near the hall. Gasoline, shipped to More's Landing in 110-gallon drums, was converted into a vapor which was forced through pipes to the Sexton home and Sexton's Hall by a pump which was powered by a system of weights like those in a grandfather's clock.

Each time a gas jet was turned on, the pressure in the pipes would be reduced, which lowered the weights in the gas house. One winding of the machine usually lasted two weeks, although the Sexton boys made a habit, whenever they passed the gashouse, of winding the machinery. In later years the gas system was replaced by acetylene equipment, similar to that used on early day automobiles.

Sexton's Hall was the scene of varied community activities for more than a quarter of a century. It housed amateur theatricals and vaudeville shows, school commencement exercises, musicales and minstrels. Visiting show troupes presented melodramas, magic acts and song-and-dance turns behind the flickering gas footlights. Actor Leo Carrillo made his theatrical debut on the stage of Sexton's Hall in 1899, doing impersonations which eventually led him to show business stardom.

An oddity of Goleta history was the Valley's first motion picture show. The screen was a bedsheet pinned to the curtain of Sexton's Hall, by an itinerant showman long since forgotten. The year was 1897. The movie had no name or subtitles. A packed house stared with gape-jawed incredulity at the fantastic spectacle of a picture which actually *moved*, however jerkily. Young and old alike sat frozen in the same catalepsy which their enraptured grandchildren would experience sixty years later before a TV set.

"Goleta's first movie only lasted two or three minutes," recalls Maud P. Meyers, of Lompoc, who drove five miles by horse and buggy from her home in Winchester Canyon to attend that unique premiére. "The picture showed a railroad locomotive racing along

Sexton's Hall: Symbol of the Gay Nineties   227

the tracks at high speed, with close-ups of the engineer peering out of the cab window with an expression of utter terror on his face. We never knew why—the film ended there! But everyone in Sexton's Hall got his money's worth from this marvel of the age."

Occasionally the rowdy element from La Patera, or "Deuville," would congregate on the front steps of Sexton's Hall while a dance was going on, looking for trouble, but quickly dispersed when Constable John Pico, a brawny blacksmith, sauntered out the front door.

Funeral services—including those of Joseph Sexton himself in 1917—were occasionally held in Sexton's Hall. The building was used for lodge meetings, as a polling place during elections, and for community gatherings at Hallowe'en, Thanksgiving and Christmas.

Joseph Sexton never broke even from the rentals he collected, but got his compensation from knowing his daughters were close to home instead of taking moonlight rides to the Naples dance hall.

After the advent of the automobile, which gave Valley people the mobility to seek more sophisticated pleasures in Santa Barbara, Sexton's Hall declined as a social center. It was finally torn down in 1920.

The Goleta store and post office burned down in 1891 when Randolph Watson was postmaster. He kept the post office going in his home on Patterson Avenue until a new one could be built, this time on the east side of Patterson. It opened under new management when blacksmith Ben Pettis was appointed postmaster on November 2, 1892. He held the job all through the Nineties and into the new century. In February, 1906, he sold out to Elwood H. Spradlin, who succeeded Pettis as U. S. postmaster.

In 1893, Uncle Ben Owen sold a portion of his ranch on Hollister Avenue to his nephew, William Henry Baker, of Texas, who married Mollie Miller, of Missouri, in 1894. His sister Sally married Edgar A. Hollister, of Fairview Ranch, the following year. The Bakers had three children, William Frank, of Goleta; Dr. Frances Baker, of San Francisco; and Elizabeth, who married Eugene Ford, of Goleta. Baker died in 1935, his wife in 1937. They are buried in Goleta Cemetery.

In July of 1894, a major forest fire broke out in the upper reaches of Winchester Canyon, the worst conflagration since 1856.

It burned out of control for five days, the flames licking down into Ellwood and Glen Annie Canyons. The red tide destroyed century-old trees and threatened to denude the entire south slope of the range.

Foothill ranchers dropped everything to rush fire-fighting crews to the front. No water was available, so backfiring was the only defense. On the afternoon of the fifth day, an ominous black cloud appeared over Santa Ynez Peak. It was mistaken at first for smoke from a fire on the north side of the range, but soon raindrops began falling. Within twenty-four hours the last spark had been extinguished. Aside from a sheepherder's hut and a few corrals, no property damage resulted and the brush had been cleaned out to minimize fire danger for another fifteen or twenty years.

In February, 1895, an historic event occurred with the founding of the Philomathic Club of Goleta "for social intercourse and the mental improvement of its members." This organization evolved into the Goleta Woman's Club in 1904, and became one of the most important social organizations in the Valley.

The ten charter members of the Philomathic Club included Mollie Miller Baker, president; Elizabeth Sevoy Warren, vice president; Jennie Hague Beck, secretary; Serepta Hardcastle Campbell, Emma Rodehaver Cook, Lucy Foster Sexton, Martha Tucker Culver, Elouise Drury Martin, Mrs. James Grant and Mrs. J. H. Bodkin. The ten founders were quickly joined by virtually every farm wife in the Valley. The oldest living member in 1966 was Mrs. Avery Shirrell Pico, ninety.

Among the civic improvements sponsored by the women were a circulating library, which was housed in the homes of members until a Mrs. Porter built "Harmony Hall" on Chapel Street, north of the Fritz Maiers (Elmer Winstrom) residence. She rented this to the club for $15 a year. It was destroyed by fire in the 1925 'quake.

Tucker's Grove County Park was a community project of the Woman's Club, as will be recounted in Chapter XXV. The members were also active in Red Cross, Farm Bureau, school hot lunch programs, conservation, welfare, securing Goleta Beach for public use and inveigling their husbands to build a road to the beach, in their spare time.

Sexton's Hall: Symbol of the Gay Nineties

From the early Seventies the Goleta Valley was predominantly Protestant in its religious faith. The Catholic minority, soon to be augmented by the first appearance of Italian families into the Valley, found itself in a position to establish its own parish in 1896. Prior to that time, the Valley's twenty-five Catholic families had held services in the home of Miguel Pico (still standing in 1966 in the rear of 58 South Fairview Avenue next to Mandarin Drive), or under the backyard grape arbor in warm weather. Masses were conducted once a month by a priest from Santa Barbara Mission.

In 1896, Fr. Polydor J. Stockman, a secular priest, took charge of the Jesuits' Our Lady of Sorrows Church. Under his supervision a tiny frame church was built in La Patera, at the southwest corner of Hollister and Fairview Avenues, for years known as the "Seaside Station Corner." The lot, donated by Mrs. Rafaela Hill, was little more than a swamp, covered by tidewater every winter, which meant the church had to be perched on stilts. Children were known to catch fish from the front steps! Henry Hill and John Pomatto took up a collection to raise the building costs of $500.

The weatherbeaten little St. Raphael Catholic Church, with its square bell tower, was a beloved landmark in La Patera for thirty-four years. In 1908 the Jesuit fathers took charge; twenty years later the Franciscans were back in control, with Rev. Fr. John Otterstadt OFM as temporary pastor.

The church was finally moved to Mandarin Drive in 1930, and remained in use until its demolition in 1964 to make room for an apartment house. The modern St. Raphael's Catholic Church at 5444 Hollister Avenue occupies a portion of the old Sexton Nursery.

In 1896 the walnut growers of the Goleta Valley and the rest of the county tired of being exploited by speculating brokers, who kept prices depressed until they had cornered the market and then sold the walnuts for all the traffic would bear.

Led by Goleta's dynamic Frank E. Kellogg, the walnut growers on the Good Land revolted, deciding to incorporate and eliminate brokerage fees entirely. Goletans dominated the first board of directors of the new Santa Barbara County Walnut Growers' Association which was founded on June 20, 1896. This corporation is the oldest walnut marketing cooperative in California, and possibly the world. It celebrated its seventieth anniversary in 1966, at which time the Valley's walnut groves were fast nearing extinction.

Charter directors included Frank E. Kellogg, W. S. Roberts, S. L. James, G. F. Smith and R. B. Hawley. Other prominent members from Goleta were Jasper Lane, Edgar Hollister, George M. Williams (who was president for twenty-five years), W. W. Hoel, Charles Brocklesby, William Wyles, Charles Emmens and Benjamin Pettis.

The first walnut packing house was built by Kellogg near his creamery, south of Hollister and east of modern Ward Drive. He charged a small fee for bleaching the nuts with sulphur, grading them into two sizes, and sacking them for shipment. Later on chlorine replaced sulphur as a bleach, and three grades of Goleta walnuts—*Diamond, Emerald* and *Suntand*—became known all over the U. S. A few years later a second packing house opened in Carpinteria.

At the time the Association was formed, Goleta growers were getting only six cents a pound for their walnuts. By eliminating the middle man, prices to the farmer jumped ten cents a pound while the cost to the consumer remained the same as before.

In the spring of 1896, the government selected John More's Ranch as the start and finish line for speed trials of the dreadnaught *Oregon*, recently completed at a San Francisco shipyard. In order to be accepted by the Navy, the 350-foot long battleship had to log at least fifteen knots in her speed trials, with a $50,000 bonus payable for every knot in excess of that minimum.

A wooden tripod was erected on the More Ranch at a point midway between Dorwin Lane and Austin Road, with a matching tripod due north in the foothills on the Ezra Catlett Ranch.*

On the morning of Thursday, May 14, 1896, hundreds of people lined the eighty-foot palisades from More Mesa to Refugio to watch the majestic *Oregon* start her westward run. She reversed course at Cojo Bay, forty miles up the coast, and steamed back toward

---

* The pyramidal range marker located at 6587 Del Playa in Isla Vista, at the brink of the cliff, is mistakenly believed by many old time residents to be one of the *Oregon* speed trial markers of 1896. It dates from 1906, when it was established by the U. S. Geodetic Survey.

Goleta with smoke belching from her funnels and a bone in her teeth.

Next day, the nation's press proudly announced that the battle wagon had established a new speed record for her class of 16.78 knots. This speed stood the *USS Oregon* in good stead two years later when she raced around Cape Horn to join the North Atlantic Squadron for duty in the Spanish-American War.

This conflict, which only lasted 114 days between April and August, made its impact on the Goleta Valley, where a volunteer Constabulary numbering more than 100 men, armed with Springfield rifles, was drilled under the command of Captain Sam Manchester. His son Paul, now a resident of Calistoga, informs the writer:

> Every Saturday night the Goleta home guard would don their "Dewey Suits" and march in the school yard on Patterson Avenue just north of Hollister. There were a lot of wild wartime rumors circulating that the Spanish Fleet was going to attack the Goleta Valley, but we felt our Constabulary had the matter well in hand and could repel any invasion.

Short as its duration was, the Spanish-American war claimed a Goleta casualty. Stanley Hollister, the Colonel's youngest son, born on the Glen Annie Ranch in 1873, was a law student at Harvard when Col. Theodore Roosevelt issued his call for Western cowboys to enlist in his famous Rough Riders Regiment for combat duty in Cuba.

Stanley Hollister left Harvard to enlist. He was standing beside Roosevelt during the assault on San Juan Hill when a shrapnel fragment, which grazed Roosevelt's wrist, struck Hollister in the chest. While crawling to a first aid station, he was hit in the leg by a sniper's slug.

Evacuated to an army hospital at Fortress Monroe, Virginia, Stanley was treated by his own family doctor from Santa Barbara, R. F. Winchester, whom Annie Hollister had rushed east to attend her favorite son. Stanley was well on the way to total recovery from his war wounds when Dr. Winchester entrained for home. Upon his arrival in Santa Barbara, he was met by the sad news that Stanley had died of typhoid fever in the interim. His body was returned West for burial beside Col. W. W. Hollister.

In 1903, when Teddy Roosevelt was president of the United

States, while visiting the Santa Barbara Mission, he stopped off to pay a personal call on Stanley Hollister's mother at the home of her daughter, Mrs. Clinton B. Hale, at Laguna and Pedregosa Streets, where he extended his condolences in the loss of her fine son.

Stanley's next-oldest brother, Jim Hollister, was away with the Haynes Party on a gold-hunting junket to the Klondike, and during the year he was gone, was not aware a war had taken place. Jim was accompanied by the former superintendent of the Glen Annie Ranch, August Linquest, who from 1892 to 1896 had also managed the Santa Anita Ranch for the Hollister Estate, west of Gaviota.

The two returned with no gold to show for their year's labors on the Kobuk River north of the Arctic Circle. Jim took up his life-long career as manager of the Hollister Estate cattle ranches. Linquest became superintendent of the County Hospital, a post he filled with distinction for several years before going into farming on his own at the 365-acre Roberts-Casell Ranch, also known as the Goleta Walnut Company Ranch, on North Patterson Avenue. Co-owners of this 256-acre property were J. K. Harrington of Hope Ranch, Horace Platt, a San Francisco attorney, Frank Smith, a Santa Barbara barber, and rancher George M. Williams of Goleta. Linquest, a native of Sweden, purchased the entire stock in the ranch in 1912 after the deaths of Harrington and Platt, both of whom were associated with the Southern Pacific. Linquest retired from ranching in 1921, and passed away in 1928.

The Goleta Valley had its own little "gold rush" the winter preceding the Klondike excitement. A Santa Barbara undertaker, A. H. Emigh, was a prospector on the side. Between burials and embalmings he spent his time scouring the wilderness areas of interior Santa Barbara County in search of rare minerals. Once he claimed to have found a large diamond somewhere in the Manzana country.

Early in 1897, Emigh filed a mineral claim on a quarter section "somewhere in the mountains behind Goleta" (later pinpointed as being in upper Smith Canyon, above the Stow Ranch). The word leaked out, as always seems to happen, that Emigh had struck gold.

Geologists scoffed, explaining that gold occurs in igneous formations such as quartz or granite, whereas the Santa Ynez Range is a layer-cake of sedimentary sandstone: hard, light-colored Tejon formation on the ridge; immediately below it the pink Sespe formation of Oligocene age; still lower the Vaqueros sandstones of the Lower Miocine age, of marine origin; next lower the Temblor or Rincon shales which formed the parent material of the Valley, known as the Zaca or Nacimiento series, transitional in age between the Upper and Lower Miocene.

But Emigh was not aware of these geological verities. He assured the press his auriferous ledge was "inexhaustible"; that it was situated less than a mile from an existing road; and that he could deliver highgrade ore to More's Landing for $5 a ton.

On March 20, 1897, the Santa Barbara newspaper *El Barbareño* reported that Al Pierce had two men sinking a shaft in the Emigh ledge, and would soon ship a few tons of gold ore to San Francisco for smelting. George M. Williams shared the headlines by charging the miners with trespassing across his land in Smith Canyon.

Two months later, *El Barbareño* (which apparently enjoyed exclusive press coverage of Goleta's gold rush) printed the sensational news that Emigh's ore assayed $49.15 to a ton at the smelter. However, since it cost $75 a ton to mine, Emigh's gold rush quickly faded into the limbo of all ghost lodes.

Black gold—petroleum—was the basis for another treasure hunt in 1897, when Steve Rutherford and Frank E. Kellogg financed the drilling of a test hole in a bean field on the Bell Ranch near Las Armas Canyon, where a local geologist, A. C. Cooper, predicted they would strike oil. After drilling to a depth of 1,000 feet, the wildcat was abandoned as a duster. In 1928, the fabulous discovery well Luton-Bell No. 1, which brought in the 100,000,000-barrel Ellwood Oil Field, was drilled almost on top of the Rutherford-Kellogg derrick site, except their drill went 2,500 feet deeper.

After abandoning the Bell Canyon well, Rutherford and Kellogg took their drilling rig to the Naples townsite on Dos Pueblos Ranch, where three wildcat wells were spudded in during the winter of 1900-1901, with Henry Allen Smith as field foreman. Not enough oil was produced to justify further exploration. Forty years later, Signal Oil & Gas Company discovered a rich oil pool under the Channel fronting Naples, by wells which were whipstocked, or slant-drilled, from the sites of the Rutherford-Kellogg derricks. Around the turn of the century, with the crude cable tool rigs available, no one ever heard of intentionally drilling a "crooked hole" to tap an off-shore oil reservoir.

Goleta's crowning historical event of the 1890s was the closure of the fifty-mile gap in the Southern Pacific's coast line between Ellwood Cooper's ranch and the mouth of the Santa Ynez River at Surf.

Starting in 1896, right-of-way agents had begun signing up Goleta Valley landowners for a new short cut between Santa Barbara and the Bishop Ranch, known as the "Hood Survey." In 1887, only six landowners had figured in the Goleta Valley railroad route. For the new and shorter Hood Survey, 31 separate ranches were involved. They belonged to Thomas B. Bishop, George M. Williams, Titus Phillips, Gin Chow, George Hendry, Christian Larson, James Anderson, Edward Towne, Clem Tinker, L. H. Martin, James M. Short, David M. Culver, Frank E. Kellogg, A. J. Boeseke and T. R. Dawe, Joseph and Harry Langman, David Beck, Henry Hill, William S. Brown, T. W. Patterson, the Tecolote Land Company (a subsidiary of the T. B. Bishop Company), Kate Den Bell, Ellwood Cooper, Susan Den Tyler, and Annie James Hollister.

Early in 1898, survey teams rented the old I. G. Foster home as headquarters, while they began driving stakes for a future realignment of the railroad which would eliminate the serpentine curves through Hope Ranch and across the More Ranch to Coromar Siding on the Bishop Ranch. The new alignment, in existence today, cut across the heart of the Good Land a half mile north of Hollister Avenue, roughly paralleling that county road.

Most of the Goleta rights-of-way were purchased without delay. Gin Chow, a colorful Chinese who had emigrated from Canton as a youth in 1873 to become one of Colonel Hollister's houseboys on the Glen Annie, owned twenty-six acres of land lying directly south of Stow's Pond (Los Carneros Lake). Gin Chow, who later became famous as a Lompoc weather forecaster, balked at the highhanded way the S.P. agents were treating him. He tells his own story in pidgin English in the *Gin Chow Almanac*, published in 1932:

> When I farm at Goleta, big corpulation, Southern Pacific, try an take my land for railroad. I fight um. They pay me $400, $500 more than others for right of way. But I had hard time with um. They say

they take it to court in Sacramento. I say, allight, go. I say my land not like hills next door. It worth more. It level. Grow bigger crops. Big corpulation keep bring up price, to get me take. I tell um $1,000 cheapest can make. They say allight, sign. I sign—after friend tell me OK an I get my money.

Further west, at Las Armas Canyon south of Winchester Canyon, Kate Den Bell engaged attorney C. A. Storke to fight a legal battle with the railroad for alleged breach of contract. Louis G. Dreyfus also held up construction across Eagle Canyon to force the S.P. to live up to its right-of-way agreements. Both landowners succeeded in bringing the arrogant "corpulation" to terms in out-of-court settlements.

Finally the haggling and threats of litigation were over, and on March 24, 1899, S.P.'s president Collis P. Huntington gave the go-ahead order and nine carloads of grading equipment and camping supplies were shunted onto sidings at Goleta, La Patera and Ellwood.

Cook shacks and a city of workmen's tents sprang up on the Bishop Ranch. They were shortly joined by the inevitable parasites of railway construction camps, the saloons and brothels under canvas which preyed on the payrolls of the workers.

One bartender whose establishment was located alongside San Jose Creek on the south side of Hollister Avenue, just east of the present Goleta Union School, enjoyed a brisk custom from the S.P. gangs. He applied to the County Supervisors for a license to operate his saloon on a permanent basis.

On the day of his hearing—the saloonman's name was Moretti— a goodly share of the residents of the Goleta Valley, led by Judge R. B. Canfield, crowded the supervisors' chambers to protest the issuance of the license, accusing Moretti of running a disorderly house. They presented a petition signed by sixty freeholders who opposed Moretti. Moretti countered with a petition of his own, signed by La Patera tipplers and winebibbers.

By law, only freeholders living within one mile of the saloon were eligible to sign the petitions. Moretti claimed this meant one mile by airline, not by road, as the teetotaler element claimed. Finally, county surveyor Frank F. Flournoy was called in to decide the issue. He found so many of Moretti's petitioners were railroad transients that the supervisors denied Moretti his license.

Closure of all saloons was vigorously supported by the general contractors for the Goleta Valley segment of the railroad, Col. George Stone and Sam McMurtrie, who had a serious problem in absenteeism caused by drunkenness. Stone & McMurtrie began leasing teams from Goleta farmers at $10 per day. All earth moving for cuts and fills was done by pick, shovel and wheelbarrow, or with crude fresno scrapers capable of hauling only half a yard of earth. Skilled stone mason Tom Pollard, proprietor of the Naples Hotel in Dos Pueblos Canyon, won the contract for building the stone bridges and culverts which are still in existence, such as the one where Hollister Avenue goes under the railroad near Modoc Road.

Advertisements appeared in the three Santa Barbara papers—the *Daily News*, the *Independent* and the *Morning Press*—promising to hire only local help, with no competition from "gringos" or Chinamen. Pay scales ranged from $1.75 to $2 for a ten-hour day; board and lodging was furnished by the contractors at $4.50 a week.

The largest steel construction job on the Goleta Valley leg of the railroad was the 660-foot viaduct at Naples, spanning Dos Pueblos Canyon. This trestle, still in existence, was built from prefabricated parts in five working days, starting April 24, 1899.

The engineer in charge of construction between Ellwood and Gaviota was Jack Carrillo, who in later years designed Kennedy Airport in New York City. His teen-aged brother, Leo, was hired as a stake boy, and soon earned a reputation as an amateur entertainer while boarding with various Goleta families.

Two engineers in the survey crew, who boarded at the I. G. Foster place, Clay H. Beattie and Frank Dearborn, courted and married Edna and Rose Sexton, respectively, the winsome daughters of nurseryman Joe Sexton.

One week during the summer of 1900, when the Goleta sidings were still jammed with flatcars loaded with crossties, rails and other materials, the Southern Pacific shunted its unique "chapel car," complete with a preacher, onto a siding at Goleta Station.

This item of rolling stock was the only one of its kind ever to leave the Pullman Palace Car factory. It was equipped with pews, altar, hymnals, stained glass Gothic windows, and an organ. The chapel car was intended to bring the Word of God to the fast-living sinners who were building the railroads of the West, but around

Goleta those hard-knuckled characters seemed to prefer the conviviality of the bars and bagnios which were doing so much to slow down "Uncle Collis" Huntington's construction timetable.

The God-fearing residents of the Goleta Valley, however, turned out in capacity numbers to attend divine services in the church on wheels during the fortnight it remained at Goleta. The itinerant sky pilot's preachings apparently had little influence for good, however, because shortly after the chapel car left the Valley a disgraceful incident took place at La Patera, which involved the Southern Pacific and the morals of the community.

A freight train was derailed and tipped over on its side when rails spread on an unballasted portion of track between Fairview Avenue and La Patera Lane, near Billy Hamilton's home, now designated as 6260 Shamrock Avenue.

Incredibly, many of Goleta's most respected citizens were transformed into looters. They swarmed to the scene of the train wreck with wheelbarrows, carpetbags, and farm wagons, and began carting away the contents of the capsized boxcars—furniture, liquor, foodstuffs, barrels of beer, drygoods, privately owned trunks, everything they could carry off. Within hours the string of freight cars had been stripped empty. The Southern Pacific, apprised of the looting by telegraph, rushed a squad of trained detectives up from Los Angeles to recover the stolen freight and arrest the thieves.

They were totally unsuccessful in both objectives. Goletans kept mum to protect their neighbors. They also kept their loot.

This untoward behavior on the part of ordinarily law-abiding Valleyites, while in no way to be condoned, can be better understood when viewed in the light of the fact that the Espee's Big Four had long been corrupting the California legislature, disregarding the public welfare for a generation. When Goletans got an opportunity to strike back at the despised "Octopus," as the SP was called, they did so with easy consciences.

Not many of the railroad workers settled in the Goleta Valley when their job was finished. One who did was Patrick Mangan, of Michigan, who bought a farm where San Pedro Creek crosses Stow Canyon Road, in 1966 known as the John Philip place. He married Margaret Hirt in 1904. Their family consisted of John; Anna, who married John Pomatto; William, Rose, Mary, who married Dr. Lee Streaker; Helen, and Margaret. Patrick died in 1945.

No one knows where the actual "last spike" was driven to close the Gap between Ellwood and Bridgeport (Surf), since many construction gangs were spaced along the right-of-way, laying rail in both directions. The first work train to make a transit of the track between Goleta and Surf did so on New Year's Eve of 1900, thereby closing out the old century on a dramatic note.

Going into the Twentieth Century, the Goleta Valley population stood at 500. Everyone predicted that a through railroad would swell that figure many times, and that by 1910 Goleta would be a larger metropolis than Santa Barbara. Whether the crystal ball was clouded remained to be seen.

CHAPTER XXIV

Hello, Central? Get Me the Auto Garage!

The first train from San Francisco passed through Goleta at 10:15 a.m. on January 3, 1901, hauling a two-coach consist filled with Southern Pacific officials. Except for ballasting the roadbed with rock quarried in Cojo Canyon up the coast, construction work was over and the railroad camps disbanded—for which mothers of Goleta's marriageable daughters were grateful.

Heavy rains in February washed out sections of the new trackage, so the first official northbound passenger run from Los Angeles took place on March 31. Crowds of cheering citizens lined the tracks at Goleta and Naples to toss garlands of flowers on the engine cowcatcher as the train passed with bunting flying.

West of La Patera, where the county road paralleled the tracks, the train overtook a Wells-Fargo stagecoach bound for Lompoc. The engineer waved from the cab of his funnel-stacked locomotive and the "jehu" driving the Concord waved his whip in salute. He probably had a lump in his throat, for this was the last time a stagecoach ever rolled along the dirt roads of the Good Land.

When the first southbound passenger train appeared on April 3, 1901, it was flagged down at Dos Pueblos for a rather macabre reason. Alice P. Williams had arranged for six pallbearers to carry her husband's casket from the Naples memorial chapel to the railroad, where they loaded it aboard a baggage car for shipment to Santa Barbara. This gruesome ritual was to fulfill Williams' fondest dream—to ride the first train from Naples by the Sea to Santa Barbara. The next northbound train returned the coffin to Dos Pueblos and it was restored to its crypt. There it remained undisturbed until the earthquake of 1925 wrecked the mausoleum. This necessitated the coffin's removal to Santa Barbara Cemetery, where Alice Williams was to join her husband in 1931.

Yellow, boxlike depots with attached warehouses were built in 1902 for the Naples and Goleta stations. The latter was still in use in 1966, though long since closed for passenger service.

A major outgrowth of the completion of the Coast Division was the opening, in 1902, of a $1,500,000, six-story, 600-room luxury hotel on Burton Mound, near the Santa Barbara waterfront. Builder Milo M. Potter contracted with a Goleta farmer, Elmer Kellogg, to supply him with fresh meat, squabs, vegetables and dairy products. Kellogg's 100-acre "Potter Farm" was northeast of Mescalitán Island; his original home still stood at 749 Ward Drive in 1966.

Kellogg kept 60,000 squabs and 400 little roasting pigs on hand at all times. He fed his hogs Potter Hotel garbage, and silverware dropped into hotel garbage cans by careless bus boys still turns up on the site of Kellogg's pigpens. A herd of 175 blooded cows comprised the Kellogg Dairy.

Milo M. Potter's advertising led the public to believe his hotel owned the Potter Farm in Goleta. Potter did hold a $25,000 mortgage on the ranch at one time, but Elmer Kellogg succeeded in paying it off.

The Potter Hotel's custom declined with the coming of the automobile age, and Potter sold it. Successively renamed the Belvedere and the Ambassador, it continued to lose money. In 1920 Kellogg sold his Potter Farm to W. E. Oakley and A. A. Bonetti, of Santa Maria. In 1921 the Potter Hotel was destroyed by fire. Elmer Kellogg's death occurred a year later.

. . . At the turn of the century, Goleta had a resident doctor, Edgar Campbell, living in the former Koster's cobbler shop, next door to Billy Warren's meat market at what is now 5310 Hollister Avenue. He took over the practise of a Dr. Grail, who seems to have left no footprints on the sands of time. The parents of the red-bearded doctor, Mr. and Mrs. D. W. Campbell, had moved from Illinois to Goleta in 1883, purchasing "The Cairn," a walnut ranch on San Marcos Road. Edgar received his MD degree at Stanford and U.C. In 1900, he married Louisa, a daughter of Philander Kellogg, and left for remote St. Lawrence Island, off the

Hello, Central? Get Me the Auto Garage!

coast of Siberia, to do missionary work among the Eskimos for sixteen years. His successor as Goleta's general practitioner was Dr. W. A. Rowell.

Dr. Campbell was also an ordained Presbyterian minister. Upon his return to Goleta in 1916, he enlisted in the Army Medical Corps, and served in France with the A.E.F. The Campbells had an adopted Indian daughter, Gail, and a girl of their own, now Mrs. Eleanor Barnes, of Goleta. Dr. Campbell died in 1947, his wife in 1950.

In 1902, George M. Williams purchased the historic Daniel Hill Adobe on La Patera Lane, and the 205-acre tract to the west known as "Williams' Flat," from Titus Phillips. At this time the old adobe was deteriorating, the south gable having fallen out. Williams' sense of history prompted him to restore the building. He hired carpenter Billy Hoover to remove the roof, and the termite-eaten ship's mast which Daniel Hill had used for a ridge pole, sheath the adobe walls with clapboards, and add three dormer windows to the attic, to give the Hill Adobe the appearance it has today.

At the time, George Shaw, who lived on the site of the Flight Line Cafe south of Hollister Avenue, was running the Hill place for Williams. Shaw's daughter, Mary, now an octogenarian, was poking around in the attic in 1902 while the new roof was being shingled by Hoover. She discovered three antique brass-studded Spanish trunks filled with yellowed old letters, deeds, newspapers and other souvenirs of the family of Daniel and Rafaela Hill. Some items made very interesting reading, indeed.

Mary selected one of the more titillating letters and took it downstairs to read to Williams' bashful son, James, then aged twenty-one. The letter went into lurid detail concerning an affair a Chinese cook had had with a certain Goleta damsel. Jim Williams was shocked. He raced upstairs, seized the contents of all three trunks, and burned them in the fireplace—destroying irreplaceable historical memorabilia relating to Goleta's first Yankee Don and his large family. Posterity, and certainly this book, are the poorer for Jim's censorship.

James G. Williams married Florence Pollard, daughter of the proprietors of the Naples Hotel, in October 1905. The newlyweds lived in the Daniel Hill Adobe, where their five children were born

—James Jr., George, Thomas, Eleanor and Florence (Mrs. Gordon Thielicke). Eleanor still resides in the old home, keeping Goleta's most historic house in good repair.

The dawn of the Twentieth Century brought subtle, but significant changes to the Good Land and its people. Progress began to accelerate a pastoral tempo of life which had changed but little since the era of the padres and the dons. Just down the road loomed the horseless carriage, to taint the pure air of the valley with its first carbon monoxide fumes. Another appendage of civilization, high speed communication, the telephone, also became commonplace.

It is regrettable that all historical records prior to 1910 have been destroyed by the local telephone company, making it difficult if not impossible to ascertain when the first telephone was installed in the Goleta Valley. More than likely it was the instrument Ben Pettis put in his general store in 1892. Shortly afterward, Frank Kellogg put in the second phone at his creamery. The Goleta telephone wire followed Hollister Avenue to De la Vina Street in Santa Barbara, where it hooked into the system of the Sunset Telephone Company.

Elmer Kellogg, of the Potter Farm, piqued by poor service and telephone company arrogance, built his own private line to town. Later he rejoined Sunset, and his square redwood telephone poles were removed and hauled to the Potter Farm, where they were stacked in a mountainous pile which remained there for many years.

On January 29, 1901, wagon maker George "Fritz" Maiers strung a private telephone wire to link his shops in La Patera and Goleta, a mile apart. Prior to that date, the two villages had never been able to communicate by telephone.

Fritz Maiers' chief claim to fame was as an inventor. The walnut industry had long been held back by the enormous amount of hand labor necessary to hull the nuts. Maiers applied himself to inventing an automated huller to solve this problem for the growers. With the mechanical assistance of Jasper Lane, Maiers built a primitive, hand-powered experimental model mechanical huller, which he tried out at August Linquest's ranch on Patterson Avenue. By 1903, he was ready to patent the huller, an invention which was to revolutionize the walnut industry.

The basic idea of Maiers' Walnut Huller was a set of rotary steel brushes revolving in drums lined with concave knives. Later improved models, driven by gasoline engines or electric motors, were capable of hulling walnuts at the rate of a ton per hour, the equivalent of the labor of thirty-five men.

Maiers' huller was manufactured in Goleta to retail at $350. It sold until well into the 1950s, when competing brands finally replaced the Maiers Huller. Parts are no longer available, so the machine is gradually going out of use.

After enduring several years of shameless exploitation of their monopoly by the Sunset Telephone Company, a group of Santa Barbarans incorporated a rival enterprise, the Home Telephone Company. All stores, and many homes, subscribed to both services, having identical phone numbers. Floyd I. Smith, of Los Angeles, who grew up in Goleta, supplies this quaint bit of telephone folklore:

In 1908 we were a town subscriber of the Home Telephone Company. When my mother wanted to reach her sister, Mrs. Angeline Kellogg Fast in Goleta, who was a Sunset subscriber, she would ring my uncle, a Santa Barbara contractor, who like all local business men subscribed to both services. Uncle Charley would kindly oblige by calling the Fast home in Goleta, then cross receivers and transmitters of the Home and Sunset telephone instruments, holding them together until the conversation had been completed.

The early-day telephone companies refused to extend branch lines to outlying ranches except at exorbitant cost. This forced many subscribers to build their own lines. Ruth Culver Hammond recalls how her father, David M. Culver, joined with neighbors Andrew Hoel and Henry Hill in setting up poles and stringing wire to their homes on South Patterson Avenue, from the trunk line on Hollister Avenue.

As soon as the branch line was in operation, Home Telephone technicians attached drop lines to Culver's private wire, so as to provide service to two neighbors on the west side of the road, E. H. Spradlin, the postmaster, and J. R. Parker, the school principal. Culver promptly snipped the unauthorized extensions asunder. Finally, Home Telephone paid Culver $150 for the privilege of taking over the line.

The Home Telephone Company, with headquarters on Carrillo Street between State and Chapala Streets, installed Goleta's first exchange in Edgar Blakeway's general store in August, 1910, with Ray D. Arnold as night operator. The switchboard had a capacity of 300 subscribers, and included a line running northward on San Marcos Road. By then Home Telephone boasted over 100 subscribers in the Goleta Valley, with an investment of more than $5,000.

Some rural lines carried as many as ten subscribers. There was only one private line, Ellwood Cooper's, in the entire Valley. Telephone wire extended as far west as the Naples post office, and up into remote canyons as far as F. D. Havens' homestead on upper Maria Ygnacia Creek.

Small town switchboard operators belong to a fast-vanishing facet of Americana. They can recognize every subscriber by voice, and Goleta's operators were no exception to this rule. Among the "Hello, Central?" girls of fond memory were Margaret Troup (Mrs. Robert Seaton), Mae Pickett (Mrs. W. T. Lillard), Mary Troup, Mrs. Joseph Langman and Mrs. Al Weatherbee.

According to veteran telephone engineer Joe Dominy, now a resident of Lompoc, the Home and Sunset companies merged into the Santa Barbara Telephone Company around the time of World War I; they were absorbed by the Associated Telephone Company, which became the General Telephone Company in the 1950s.

Goleta's primitive, magneto-powered, hand-cranked telephones were replaced by "common battery" operation in October, 1922. The telephones were invariably mounted on the wall, usually in the farmhouse kitchen, at a height of six feet above the floor. This meant that two generations of housewives had to do their party line "rubbering" on tiptoe. The telephone company justified this inconvenient placement as the only way to keep curious children from taking receivers off the hook, which would immobilize service to every subscriber on that party line.

The first automobile to stir up dust on a Goleta Valley road was a Locomobile Steamer, driven by a George W. Beauhoff of Philadelphia. He and his wife were making a transcontinental tour in 1901. Their very first breakdown after traversing more than 3,000 miles of primitive roads came as they were entering Santa Barbara

Hello, Central? Get Me the Auto Garage! 245

County, at the dry bed of the Santa Maria River. No Goletans were on hand to greet the historic arrival of Beauhoff's horseless carriage to the Good Land. It steamed over the San Marcos stage road and entered the Valley around midnight on March 28, 1901.

The first gasoline-propelled motor vehicles in Goleta ownership were motorcycles, and came in 1904 when Henry Simpson, who worked at the butcher shop, bought himself a second-hand, one-lung Indian "sickle." He was quickly joined on the road by motorcyclists Elbert Hoel, Tom Emmons and Jim Main. Due to their low power, these cycles could only reach a speed of forty-five miles an hour wide open, and that on the hard, sandy beach.

"A motorcyclist's big problem in those days was preventing runaways of buggy teams," Simpson recalls. "It got so bad that whenever I saw a buggy approaching, especially if a woman was driving, I would conceal my motorcycle in the roadside weeds. Then I would take the horse by the bridle and lead him safely by. It seemed the smell of gasoline made the gentlest horse go berserk. In fact it took several generations for horses to become immune to the fear of gasoline."

The first automobile owned by a citizen of the Goleta Valley was a curved dash Oldsmobile, converted from tiller to steering wheel, which mechanic Horace A. Sexton gave to his sister Mariette in 1908, for the convenience of their aging parents, Joseph and Lucy Sexton, neither of whom ever learned to drive.

Out at Naples, Steve Rutherford and John K. Wade rattled about in gasoline buggies. Fritz Maiers bought a Model E Ford with a removable tonneau. The chain-driven, two-cylinder engine was mounted under the seat with the starting crank on the side. Elmer Kellogg drove the Valley's noisiest car, a chain-drive Metz.

Philip Rice, whose ranch adjoined John Pickett's on the west, owned a red roadster which would carry five people, an amazing load. One of the first motor trucks in the Valley was a one-ton Moreland, owned by A. J. Haverland, of Old San Marcos Road. It was popular for hauling groups to school and church picnics at Tucker's Grove, as well as for parade floats on holidays.

Goleta's first Model T Ford was probably Jasper Lane's, which he bought in 1910. Blacksmith Frank Simpson drove a used 1905 Maxwell (the model comedian Jack Benny immortalized on radio), purchased from the noted Santa Barbara author, Stewart Edward White. Other early-day motorists in the Goleta Valley were Andrew Hoel, Charlie Winters, C. C. Tinker, Joseph Archambault and Frank Bishop.

Ernie Vogel opened Goleta's first garage in 1922 at Magnolia and Hollister; his Red Crown gasoline pump, hand-cranked, was the town's first "filling station." He outfitted his repair shop with tools and machinery purchased from the defunct Flying A movie studio at State and Mission Streets in Santa Barbara. Another garage opened in 1922 in one end of Maiers' walnut huller factory, under the ownership of the Acres Brothers, Fred and Frank.

Motoring could be an ordeal on dirt roads rutted and chuckholed by more than half a century of wagon traffic. Drivers setting forth on the hour-long journey to Santa Barbara (not counting time out for patching inner tubes at least once) invariably wore high-necked linen dusters reaching almost to the ankles.

Women passengers shrouded their faces behind heavy veils to escape the stifling dust of summer and the splashing mud of winter. Because of the wretched condition of the roads, speeds of 20 miles an hour were maximum, even under the best of weather conditions.

To combat the dust problem, the County ran sprinkling wagons to wet down the beautiful shady stretch of tree-lined Hollister Avenue with its famous redwood mileposts. This service was provided between Santa Barbara and La Patera until 1912.

Four horses were required to pull a 500-gallon wood-stave tank wagon when fully loaded. The County bought its water from the Pacific Improvement Company, a railroad subsidiary which was developing Hope Ranch. The cost was 25 cents per tank load. Drivers had strict orders to sprinkle only the middle of the road between De la Vina Street and Fairview Avenue. They were not to waste precious water and taxpayers' money wetting down the dust in front of privately-owned property bordering the county road.

One enterprising young tank wagon driver, Paul Manchester, made a *sub rosa* deal with various clients along Hollister Avenue between Goleta and La Patera, whereby he would sprinkle the gutters in front of their business establishments. The grocery paid off in soda pop and licorice sticks; Kellogg's Creamery with a quart of milk daily; Warren's Butcher Shop with a family steak once a week. Manchester's boss was Marion Pierce, who used to pay him $25 a month.

As extinct as the dodo or Goleta's road sprinkler is the meat wagon which once provided door-to-door shopping service for isolated Goleta Valley housewives. Sherman & Ealand, who ran a large butcher shop on State Street and a slaughter house in Sycamore Canyon, opened a branch shop in Goleta, and employed Harry Arthur to cover the meat wagon circuit between La Patera and Naples twice a week.

Shortly before his death in 1959, Mr. Arthur wrote the author:

> My Goleta butcher wagon was drawn by two horses. I carried enough ice to keep the meat fresh during the day-long circuit. My prices per pound were 18c for T-bone steak, 15c for loin steak, 10c for stew meat, chuck roast and hamburger, and 6c for short ribs. We had no such thing as top sirloin or any of the boneless cuts you find prepackaged in today's supermarkets. If anyone bought a beef, I threw in the tongue, heart and tail without charge. I always carried soup bones for Goleta's dogs, and such "inedible" items as fresh liver which I gave as handouts to friendly cats along my route.

Needless to say, Harry Arthur was a hero to the feline and canine population of the Good Land. But he was more than that. He was a Valley fixture, who served as town crier, news commentator, political prognosticator, weather man, and clearing house for the exchange of farmwives' memoranda.

During wet weather, Arthur often had trouble negotiating the muddy back roads, especially the unbridged creeks. He continued to serve the Valley until 1911, when he moved to Portland, Oregon. By that time, automobiles were numerous enough for farmers to drive their wives to Santa Barbara to do their own meat shopping on State Street.

Billy Warren, Goleta's neighborhood meat man, had a pretty daughter named Pearl, considered the "catch" of the Valley. The lucky man who married her on August 1, 1908, turned out to be Fred Stevens. They went up Maria Ygnacia Creek to live at the historic old Indian Orchard, which Stevens had purchased in 1907 from the Ygnacia family—the first time in a hundred years it had not belonged to a Canaliño Indian.

When the Stevens moved in, some forty original orange trees, planted *circa* 1838 by the mission fathers, were still thriving. Stevens removed all but three, which in 1966 were still bearing sweet, if seed-filled fruit. The Indian Orchard was replaced with avocados, lemons, and domestic oranges.

Four children were born to Fred and Pearl—William, Robert, Warren and Elizabeth (Waugh). Fred became a distinguished County Supervisor from the Third District, and also played a key rôle as Goleta's representative in Washington, D.C., during the fight for Cachuma Dam. He died in the summer of 1952. His widow still resided on the Indian Orchard ranch in 1966.

On June 24, 1908, the grocer who had bought out Elwood H. Spradlin's general store, Edgar C. Blakeway, became the new postmaster. He held this position for 20 years. In 1928 his daughter, Mrs. Maude Cunningham, became Goleta's first postmistress. She served until Charles A. Beguhl's appointment on August 12, 1936.

A little-known fact from the Goleta Valley's past concerns the famous naturalist Luther Burbank, who around the turn of the century leased two acres from P. C. Marble, on Yaple Avenue off San Marcos Road. Here Burbank successfully experimented with a spineless variety of cactus to use as cattle feed.

Another almost-forgotten facet of Goleta Valley life concerns the cattle-branding rodeos staged by the T. B. Bishop Company prior to the first World War, at its stockyards near Coromar siding where the present Glen Annie overpass is located.

Bishop owned extensive cattle range in Santa Barbara County, including the Tecolote, Sisquoc and La Laguna ranches. He imported thousands of head of cattle from northern Mexico to stock his range.

According to a former Bishop Ranch superintendent, Ben Hartman, whenever a trainload of cattle arrived on the Coromar siding, Bishop's cowboys would be joined by vaqueros from all over the Valley to brand the steers. Herds, segregated according to brand, were then driven overland by way of Refugio Pass, just as in the

Gold Rush days when Nicolás Den's Dos Pueblos cattle were sent to the northern market.

The rebel general Pancho Villa put an end to Bishop's Mexican cattle purchases in 1917 when the former bandit chief declared war on all *Yanquis* along the border. Thus ended another dramatic and little-known phase of Goleta history which has long since passed into limbo.

CHAPTER XXV

Better Roads, County Parks, and Disaster

By 1912 so many angry voters were breaking auto axles on the Goleta Valley's abominable roads that Third District Supervisor A. W. Conover put pressure on the County to do some improvement work. This was virtually the first attention Goleta roads had received since T. Wallace More reneged on his contract fifty years earlier.

The Valley's central arterial, Hollister Avenue, was a disgrace, despite its eye-pleasing poplars and elms. The only side roads worthy of listing on maps were Fairview, Kellogg, Patterson, San Marcos and Turnpike. All other thoroughfares were mere sandy lanes leading to private farmhouses.

Julius Hatlen, a Norwegian-born resident of Patterson, Calif. (named for speculator J. D. Patterson, of Goleta's Patterson Avenue fame), used to be a teamster for A. K. Langlo on the Bell Ranch. He gives the following eye-witness account of Goleta's first road improvements:

There was a stretch of about a mile and a half of blow sand on Hollister Avenue [near the San Marcos High School] where cars and wagons often got stuck and had to have help to get through.

Finally in the winter of 1912 the Board of Supervisors decided to improve the Goleta road. It turned out this was a good time, for that winter was a dry one. There was a good rain in November, and then it did not rain again until late March. The farmers had given up all hope of raising any crops, so they all applied for and got work on the county road with their horses and hired men.

Where Hollister Avenue went through La Patera, the highway had to be raised two or three feet, because the ocean tides used to come right over the Fairview-Hollister intersection. Much of the dirt for this long fill was taken from a knoll on Fairview Avenue and hauled in dump wagons, two cubic yards of earth to each load. There were dozens of wagons doing the dirt hauling.

There used to be a steep little hill in front of the Bishop Ranch. There we had a new contraption to load the wagons without having to resort to hand shoveling. We had a sort of a bridge, ramps leading up to a deck which had a hole in it. We would drive our wagons under that hole and the teamsters with fresno scrapers would drive over the top and dump their dirt into the wagons below. William Soundy was the man in charge of this operation.

When grading was completed, asphalt-mixing plants were set up at La Patera, where the Sunkist lemon packing plant now stands, and on Modoc Road near Hope Ranch. Hollister Avenue was given its first coat of blacktop, quarried from the prehistoric tar pits in Carpinteria. La Patera Lane was also paved, as was the lane to supervisor Conover's home on Cathedral Oaks Road.

Gone at last was the intolerable dust and mud, but the 1912 paving job was far from perfect. On hot days the asphaltum, laid in too thin a mixture, turned taffy-soft and threatened to entrap vehicle wheels in its gluey grip. Not until the Twenties brought concrete slab construction were Goleta's road problems overcome.

1912 was a vintage year in Goleta Valley history in other respects. That year saw the Woman's Club put on a crash campaign to secure Tucker's Grove as a free park for posterity's enjoyment.

Captain Reasin Penelope Tucker, who owned the land along San Antonio Creek in the northeastern corner of Daniel Hill's original La Goleta Rancho, had died in 1888. His son Charley inherited the land. The centuries-old oaks, sycamores and greenswards along San Antonio Creek above Turnpike and Cathedral Oaks Roads had long been a favorite picnic spot, especially among the Scottish-American settlers of the Valley.

Charley Tucker had many offers to buy the grove from farmers who wanted to chop down the trees and convert the land to agriculture. Charley refused all such offers, maintaining the creekside grove for the pleasure of the public without charge.

Charles Tucker died intestate in 1912. Under the law, his property would have to be sold at public auction—and bargain-hunting farmers turned covetous eyes on the lush acres of Tucker's Grove. Their chance had come at last.

David M. Culver was appointed administrator of the Tucker estate. Realizing that one of the community's most precious assets was in danger of being subdivided for private gain, Culver suggested to his wife, the former Martha Tucker, that her Goleta Woman's Club might launch a campaign to save the grove as a county park. He also enlisted the support of Superior Court Judge S. E. Crow, a wise and good man of great influence in Santa Barbara County politics. Judge Crow circulated quietly among potential bidders for Tucker's Grove, persuading them to withdraw. That Judge Crow was successful in his efforts was due in large part to the climate of public opinion built up by the Woman's Club, who let would-be buyers of Tucker's Grove know the women of Goleta opposed private exploitation of such a playground.

When the public auction took place, only one bid was submitted for Tucker's Grove. It came from George S. Edwards, a Valley rancher and president of the Commercial Bank in Santa Barbara. He offered $3,000 for the 18 acres encompassing Tucker's Grove. The bid was duly accepted.

When banker Edwards attempted to deed the property over to the county for park purposes, the Supervisors, who then as now were traditionally reluctant to take land off the tax rolls, declined to accept the gift on the grounds of insufficient funds.

"Then I will deed Tucker's Grove to the County anyway," George Edwards replied, "and the County can pay me back when it can."

The supervisors had no choice but to accept Edwards' offer.

To celebrate the acquisition of Tucker's Grove County Park, the Goleta Woman's Club staged a barbeque under the ancient sycamores beside the creek, with Judge Crow making the dedicatory address.

"Generations yet unborn will bless your memory," Judge Crow told his audience, "as they enjoy the shady acres of this grove."

Judge Crow's prophecy was true. Taking 1965 as an example, the average summer day census at Tucker's Grove was over 2,000 persons, mostly children. It was necessary to make reservations months in advance for a specific day's use of barbeque pits. Housing tracts and earth-moving operations are changing the face of the Valley in the vicinity of this cool oasis, which through private benefactions is being extended on up San Antonio Creek for miles.

On August 12, 1912, the Protestants of the Goleta Valley organized the "United Church," later renamed the Federated Church, with eighty-five charter members. The former Methodist Church on Chapel Street was used as a place of worship. The pastor, Rev. E. P. Perry, lived in the parsonage next door, which in later years became Judge W. T. Lillard's home. Original officers of of the Goleta Federated Church included A. G. Paulin, E. O. Campbell, Ed Blakeway, Fred Stevens, David M. Culver, William Soundy, and Frank Lane. Sunday School classes met in Harmony Hall, across the street from the church, until World War I ended church activities. The building was purchased by the Goleta Farm Bureau as a community meeting place in 1922.

A purely local event which had far-reaching results took place on August 13, 1913, when a group of valley lima bean growers, led by the dynamic Edgar Stow, met in Sexton's Hall. There they organized one of the County's first farm cooperatives, which they named "The Goleta Farmers, Incorporated," and began selling stock.

Stow was elected president; Clarence P. Day, of the Ellwood Ranch, secretary; Jack D. Cavalletto, treasurer; and other directors were Edgar A. Hollister, Robert Main, James G. Williams, A. K. Langlo, Fred Stevens, Ed Clemmons and John F. More.

On October 10, the directors arranged for a $10,000 loan from the County Bank to finance the building and equipping of a 120 by 150 foot warehouse on Kellogg Avenue, next door to the Walnut Growers' Association facilities.

These were the years when mechanization entered the farming picture in the Goleta Valley, heralding the end of the use of horses and mules for plowing, threshing, and other farm work. The Stow and Bishop Ranches had tractors operating by 1913, followed soon after by the progressive Cooper and Dos Pueblos Ranches. Favorite tractors were the Daniel Best Track-Layer and the Yuba Balltread, forerunners of the modern yellow Caterpillar.

In 1916, it was decided to convert the Goleta Farmers, Inc. into a non-profit cooperative. On July 14, the Goleta Lima Bean Growers' Association was organized, with Edgar Stow as president, W. E. Lingard secretary, and A. K. Langlo, Jack D. Cavalletto, Robert Septimus Rowe and L. D. Hill as directors. Other prominent members included Harry Sexton and John Troup.

During the co-op's first year of operation, Goleta's lima bean crop brought $4.95 per hundredweight to the growers, with the cooperative marketing over 2,600,000 pounds of lima beans.

The Walnut Growers Association, founded in 1896, did a major remodeling job on its warehouse in 1913. To celebrate the opening of the new 110 by 140-foot facilities, a community dance was held, which some old timers believe marked the turning on of the first electric lights in the Goleta Valley, presaging the end of the coal-oil and Coleman lantern era throughout the Good Land.

The unfortunate discarding of early records by local power and light companies, plus a total memory blackout on the part of senior citizens, makes it impossible to fix the exact date of the first electric lighting in the Valley, but 1913 is close.

The walnut industry had remained more or less static, both in acreage and in production, since 1900. An annual crop of 1,100 tons was harvested in 1908; fifty years later, in 1958, the crop had only grown to 1,400 tons, and had reached its peak. The Walnut Association's peak membership, however, was in 1939, with 200 Goleta farmers enrolled in the cooperative.

Frank E. Kellogg resigned as secretary of the Walnut Growers Association in 1916. During his twenty years in office, he had mailed out checks totaling more than $2,000,000 to members.

P. C. Marble was packing house manager from 1910 to 1932, when he became president of the local association to succeed George M. Williams, who had served as president for 25 years. Bill Hollister succeeded Marble in 1933 and served until 1955.

A processing plant which changed from the lime bleaching process to the salt electric process was built in 1918, rebuilt in 1925, and expanded by the addition of fumigation tanks and bulk loading

Better Roads, County Parks, and Disaster

facilities capable of handling twenty tons of nuts per hour in 1955. The plant carried forty workers on the payroll between September 15 and December 15 every year. The plant was destroyed by fire on March 22, 1966.

As oak root fungus became an increasing problem to walnut growers, and lemons came to be more lucrative, the walnut acreage gradually left the Goleta Valley and went over the mountains into the Santa Ynez Valley. This trend continues into the latter 1960s, as housing tracts encroach on the walnut groves.

Catastrophe struck the Goleta Valley on the afternoon of Sunday, January 25, 1914, in the form of a brief but devastating flood. An enormous rain cloud bore in from the southeast, and ruptured its swollen black belly on mountain crags from the Rincon to Dos Pueblos, dumping billions of gallons of water into the canyons, with the greatest havoc being wrought in the Montecito area.

Damage caused by the cloudburst in the Goleta Valley defied description. County surveyor Frank F. Flournoy's survey revealed that every wooden bridge in the Valley had been destroyed. Most of the stone bridges held, one exception being the thirty-foot span crossing Maria Ygnacia Creek at Old San Marcos Road, on the Marble Ranch just north of the Laurel of San Marcos. Not a vestige of that $4,000 span remained, and a 125-foot-wide channel had been gouged out by the rushing waters. The Old San Marcos Road itself was blocked by earth slides and boulders for weeks afterward.

Clarence P. Day, part owner and manager of the Ellwood Cooper Ranch, happened to be in Santa Barbara that afternoon. He found himself cut off from the Goleta Valley unless he walked on the railroad. When he finally trudged the twelve miles of crossties back to Ellwood Canyon, a scene of utter devastation greeted his eyes.

At the "Narrows" up canyon, where 200-foot cliffs come close together, a giant sycamore tree had been uprooted and lodged crosswise between the scarps in such a way as to create a huge dam of débris. When pent-up floodwaters broke this dam, a thirty-foot wall of silt-laden water roared on down the canyon toward the sea, expunging Ellwood Cooper's valuable orchard of Japanese persimmons, which formed a second log jam at a row of eucalyptus trees farther downstream.

Another lake formed; another dam burst. This release of water erased forever Cooper's historic olive orchards, an irrigation system, the engine house, a fine graded road winding through lovely oak parks which were obliterated without trace, and a total of fifteen private bridges.

Persons living on the Cooper Ranch said that the canyon was unrecognizable as it had existed in years gone by.

Above Stow Ranch in Smith's Canyon, an entire lemon grove belonging to George M. Williams vanished like pencil marks under an eraser. Between Goleta and Corona Del Mar ranch, a distance of nearly three miles, Hollister Avenue was buried under one to three feet of mud. The Southern Pacific tracks, while they did not break, were twisted and shoved as much as twenty feet south of the original roadbed alignment.

Goleta Slough, for a few hours, resembled the vast landlocked harbor it had been prior to the massive siltation of 1861. Even as far removed as Dos Pueblos Canyon, the effects of destructive run-off were evident, enough to wash out the twenty-eight-foot wooden bridge west of the Naples Hotel.

No human lives were lost in the Goleta Valley on that tragic January afternoon in 1914, but there were several narrow escapes. The Havens homestead house was ruined by floodwaters driving piano-sized boulders through the structure. The Peter Sabini family, living above the Indian Orchard, escaped drowning by climbing to higher ground when Maria Ygnacia Creek, normally thirty feet wide, spread to a width of 600 feet within a matter of minutes, narrowly missing the Martin Hemmenway home farther downstream.

Uncounted hundreds of chickens drowned during the storm. Floodwaters swept across a corral on Gene Mirratti's place on upper San Antonio Creek and carried a horse three miles downstream. It was rescued from the mud next day in the vicinity of Mescalitán Island. Purchased by grocer Ed Blakeway, the horse lived to pull a delivery wagon for many years.

Since Santa Barbara depended heavily on Goleta for milk and butter, dairy products had to be transported by handcar on the S.P. tracks for several days, Hollister Avenue being cut off by a massive earthslide opposite Nogal Drive, where a stone revetment collapsed.

Men carried meat on their backs from the slaughterhouse to load on John Pagliotti's wagon, transferred by a makeshift footbridge across Maria Ygnacia Creek, and thence to the railroad handcars.

The big bridge on Hollister Avenue near the Kellogg and Sexton homes was damaged so badly as to be impassable.

Two months after the cloudburst flood, on March 23, 1914, the Federated Church manse burned to the ground. The resident pastor, Rev. E. E. Fairchild, and his daughter narrowly escaped death, reminding Valleyites of the fire which destroyed the Troup home in 1902 and killed six-year-old William Troup.

Spurred by this near tragedy, Goleta citizens organized their first volunteer fire department, headed by Ed Blakeway, Frank Simpson, Harry Cunningham and Harry Sexton. A campaign was launched to raise funds to buy a fifty-gallon soda-acid tank, cart and hose. Cunningham distributed handbills up and down the valley, and in a few days $250 had been raised as a down payment on firefighting equipment. Fire Chief John Dugan of Santa Barbara cooperated with technical advice.

It took three months for Goleta's bright-red fire cart to arrive from New York. Cunningham was appointed chief hose man, and preparations were made for a gala public demonstration of the equipment. Boxes, trash, brush and other combustibles were piled up in the Goleta School yard like a school football rally bonfire, and set ablaze. Practically everyone in the Valley turned out to see Goleta's first fire-fighting gear put out a fire. The soda-acid cart was a smashing success.

The cart saw active duty for the next thirty years. Because of its presence in a corner of Simpson's blacksmith shop at Patterson and Hollister Avenues, fire insurance rates dropped a notch. It was not always possible to get the cart to a fire in time to save anything but the lot a house stood on, however. For years it was towed behind a buggy or a spring wagon, a volunteer fireman hanging onto the cart handle because no towing hitch was to be had.

The century's teen-age years also saw the Good Land used as background locations for motion pictures being filmed by Essanay, American Film Company's Flying A studios, and other pioneer production companies which made Santa Barbara an active cinema center from 1910 to 1918, even before Hollywood was in existence.

Especially popular locations for Western serials were the canyons above the valley, and the old stagecoach roads. Goleta's beach and sea cliffs appeared in movies around the world for years, as did some of La Patera's falsefronted Western-style buildings.

Joseph Sexton Sr. died on August 1, 1917, at the age of seventy-five. Sexton's Hall was overflowing with mourners at his funeral. Old cronies Jim Williams, Joe Langman, John B. Pico, W. J. Pettingill, Clement Tinker and Frank Simpson bore his casket to the family burial plot at Goleta Cemetery.

The Sexton Ranch and the "West Place," in what is now the Kellogg tract, were divided among the heirs. Daughter Mariette got the old home. Brother Harry got Sexton's Hall, which he tore down, using the lumber to build the home, still standing at 5410 Hollister Avenue in 1966, on the original foundations of Goleta's first theater.

The war against Kaiser Bill's Germany, starting in 1917, drew a number of the Valley's young men to the colors. The women formed an active Red Cross center at the unused M.E. Church on Chapel Street, where 23 sewing machines were kept busy under the supervision of Ezra Catlett's daughter, Ida, who, incidentally, was the second trainee ever to receive a registered nurse's diploma from Cottage Hospital, in 1895.

Lawrie Rutherford of Dos Pueblos Ranch was among the first local patriots to don khaki and go "Over There" with the A.E.F. He was killed in action at Argonne Forest, Goleta's first casualty in the war to end all wars. When it was all over and Johnny came marching home, the Goleta hero with the most decorations was Fred Olson, later a partner of Chester Rich's in the real estate and insurance business. He was born in Glen Annie Canyon.

Many years and two wars later, the names of Goleta's war dead of 1917-1918 were graven on a granite memorial, donated by John Troup and erected in front of the Goleta Union School. Four doughboys from the Good Land had given their "last full measure of devotion" to defend the cause of liberty. They were:

LAWRIE RUTHERFORD	LESTER F. LIBBEY
WESLEY HOUX	JOHN AMBLER

Better Roads, County Parks, and Disaster

The Goleta post office did not inaugurate a rural free delivery service until 1919. Prior to that time, mail was handled out of the Santa Barbara post office, with carrier Ed Ferl driving his horse and buggy to sixty-four Goleta patrons with sixteen rural boxes.

Goleta's first RFD man was A. P. "Apple Pie" Weatherbee, whose postal-packin' Tin Lizzie was a familiar sight on the Valley's rural roads for 37 years. On his own hook, Weatherbee built up his route from 16 to 250 boxes, by soliciting farmers to install them.

Weatherbee's pioneer mail route started at the post office in Ed Blakeway's store at Patterson and Hollister; went westward to Fairview; north to Stow Canyon; back to Hollister via La Patera Lane; and on occasion, as far west as Naples, where the government withdrew the post office in 1923. Before he retired in 1956, Al Weatherbee had logged 350,000 miles without a single accident.

In 1920 the "Goleta Farm Center" was organized, with Bill Main as president, Jim Williams secretary, and Jim Hollister, Chester Rich and Fred Stevens on the board. A year later a county-wide farmers' meeting was held on the Zanja Cota Indian Reservation near Santa Ynez, at which the Santa Barbara County Farm Bureau was formed. Jim Hollister was charter president. D. T. Batchelder, an expert on animal husbandry, was the first county Farm Advisor. From him, Goleta farmers got free technical assistance on pruning, irrigation, fertilizing, insecticide spraying and other up-to-date techniques. The Farm Bureau sold $10 shares to purchase the old Methodist Church on Chapel Street to use as a meeting hall and community center.

A very interesting chapter could be set down regarding the days of Prohibition in the Goleta Valley, but don't look for it in this book. One bootlegger known only as Old Man Mosher, who operated a blind pig in what became the Plaza de Goleta, was found bludgeoned to death in his shack, but his killers were never apprehended.

Rum-running was another matter. Santa Barbara County's 125 miles of broken coastline afforded seagoing bootleggers many secluded coves in which to land their illicit cargoes—including Goleta Slough, Dos Pueblos and Ellwood beaches, and Arroyo Burro.

One Glen Annie Canyon farmer, now deceased, was offered

$20,000 to store Canadian whiskey in his barn for one night. On the advice of his attorney, Atwell Westwick, the farmer turned down the opportunity, but a neighbor, Carlo Drocco, went into partnership with the bootlegger and claimed to have netted as much as $100,000 in a week. Drocco's cellar, where the booze was cached, was located under the eucalyptus trees at what is now 7020 Del Norte Street, El Encanto. But crime did not pay; Drocco was murdered in that cellar in 1949.

The dawn of the Twenties saw a new status symbol appear over the rooftops of barns and homes in the Goleta Valley—copper antenna wires leading to a new miracle in the parlor, a radio receiver. Overnight, Victrolas began collecting dust while town and country folk alike listened entranced to cacophonic squawks, music and voices issuing from horn-shaped Magnavox loudspeakers.

Crystal sets did not work well at first, owing to the distance to the nearest broadcasting stations in Los Angeles. Santa Barbara's first station, KFCR, went on the air April 1, 1926. It later became KDB, the letters standing for Dorothy Barnes, the wife of the station owner. The KTMS towers, symbol of the new wireless age, did not appear on the west end of More Mesa until 1937.

Throughout the Twenties, on crisp nights Goleta radio fans would clamp earphones over their heads and stay up to all hours fiddling with the vernier dials of their Atwater Kent and Grebe receivers, hoping to tune in such rare DX as KDKA in Pittsburgh. And soon such personalities as Amos 'n' Andy, Fred Allen, Joe Penner and his duck, Lum 'n' Abner, Fibber McGee, Al Pierce and his Gang and Jack Benny became a part of every Goleta Valley household. Television has yet to match that golden era of living room entertainment.

Grain thresher and mobile cookhouse harvesting on More Mesa in late 1890s. More often had four outfits threshing at once

"Ellwood Special" and crew pose for this December 1893 photo on More Ranch at what is now Shoreline Drive at Orchid Drive. This little train served Goleta Valley from 1887 until 1901

The only known photograph of Sexton's Hall, 5410 Hollister Avenue, center of Goleta social life throughout the Gay Nineties. Funerals, weddings, elections, dances, graduations, parties and lodge meetings were held here. Razed 1920 by Harry Sexton

Alcatraz Asphalt Mine which operated during 1890s near present Speech and Dramatic Arts Building on UCSB campus. Shafts went as deep as 500 feet; asphaltum was hauled by wagons to La Patera railroad station for shipment all over the United States

Upper left: Railroad depot built 1902; center left, Harry Arthur and his meat wagon; below, Fritz Maiers with his original walnut huller (Carlton Lane in background) which revolutionized walnut industry. Maiers was a wheelwright and wagon maker by trade.

Rare view of Old Goleta in 1905, intersection of Hollister and Patterson Avenues. From left: Billy Warren's meat market; Dr. W. A. Rowell's office; vacant store on site of 1875 post office; Patterson Avenue; Pettis blacksmith shop; Blakeway's Store and post office; steeple of 1884 Baptist Church. Butcher boy with unidentified girls is Henry Simpson

Hollister Avenue near Ellwood School after 1912 rainstorm

Building the long fill across Winchester Canyon

Grading the new county road, Tecolote Canyon cut, 1912

CHAPTER XXVI

The Fabulous Campbell and Walora Ranches

The *belle epoque* of Goleta Valley high society, in pioneer days, lasted only ten years. This was the period between 1873 and 1883, when Col. and Mrs. Hollister were giving their garden parties at Glen Annie, with an occasional grand ball in the Octagonal Carriage House at the Lower Ranch (Corona del Mar).

Aside from that dazzling decade, social activity in the Good Land was held to a bucolic level for the next forty years. There were country hoedowns at Sexton's Hall, church sociables, school spelling bees and talent shows, the annual Scottish-American picnics at Tucker's Grove, Saturday night dances at Naples, meetings of the Whist Club over a forty-year span, and summer clambakes or occasional grunion hunts on the beach. Good old-fashioned country fun was had by all.

The Hollister and Stow families were venerated as "blue bloods" by their less-pretentious neighbors on the Valley floor. The Ellwood Coopers rarely did any entertaining. The Valley's solid core of middle-class citizens, such as the Kelloggs, Sextons, Troups, Lanes, Rowes, Fosters, Lillards, Smiths, Catletts and their peers, laughingly referred to themselves as "crumbs of the upper crust," but practically speaking, the good people of Goleta, La Patera and Naples put on no high falutin airs and recognized no caste distinctions. Some of Goleta's high school students resented being called rubes, hicks and hayseeds by the "city slickers" in Santa Barbara, but these jibes were more juvenile than justified.

As former Valley resident Lillian Wolking of Healdsburg so aptly phrases it, "Goleta was never fashionable, but always had its own true aristocracy."

Shortly after the outset of World War I, the Blue Book variety of High Society discovered the charms of the Goleta Valley. Oil tycoon Herbert G. Wylie, of Los Angeles, a partner of Ed Doheny of Teapot Dome fame, had realtor A. B. Watkins work from 1914 through 1917 assembling a 4,500-acre block of the old Nicolás A. Den ranch and contiguous homesteads, with Steve Rutherford's farm and the townsite of Naples as its nucleus, and began pouring money into a country estate. Here he bred world-famous Kentucky race horses, Irish jumpers and Percheron draft horses. He made Dos Pueblos the millionaire's showplace which Samuel B. Mosher of Signal Oil & Gas purchased in the early 1940s.

In the Goleta Valley proper, two country estates were founded on a smaller, but in some ways even more lavish scale than Wylie's —the de luxe ranches of retired English army officer Col. Colin Campbell, and a noted eye specialist from San Francisco, Dr. Walter Scott Franklin. These monied gentlemen appeared in the Good Land at about the same time in 1919, and made local investments ranging into millions of dollars.

Col. Campbell, while on His Majesty's military service in India, had met and married a wealthy American heiress, Nancy Leiter, of Chicago. One of her sisters was the wife of Lord Curzon, former Viceroy of India; another sister was the Countess of Suffolk. These royal connections soon had the Colonel moving in high court circles in London. He leased or owned fabulous country estates in Wiltshire, Sussex, Kent and Gloustershire, all of which were converted into country schools following World War II.

Confiscatory taxation of the Colonel's American income finally forced the Campbells to leave England. In October 1919, Colonel Campbell showed up in Santa Barbara. He was scouting America for a location for a country estate to equal those he was having to give up in England.

The hilly area now known as Hope Ranch Park caught Col. Campbell's attention, but the Pacific Improvement Company had just sold it and the nearby Ontare Ranch to a developer, Maurice Heckscher, so the Colonel had to look elsewhere.

Making the acquaintance of Marshall Bond, a prominent Santa Barbara citizen, Col. Campbell drove out to the Goleta Valley to look around. He was struck by the development possibilities of the

The Fabulous Campbell and Walora Ranches

old Alphonso Den ranch at Coal Oil Point, two miles west of Goleta Point. This area was being farmed by Jack and Coto Cavalletto at the time.

Agriculturally speaking, the ranch was probably the poorest land in the Goleta Valley. Long since stripped of its primeval oak forest, the mesa around Coal Oil Point (so named because of the submarine petroleum springs off shore which created perpetual oil slicks on the Channel) was utterly devoid of trees, and had become a wind-scoured expanse of sand dunes. When rainfall was normal, fine crops of hay or lima beans could be produced, but in dry years the ranch was virtually a sterile desert. Wells dug on the property produced salty water, making irrigation impossible.

But the Coal Oil Point area had a large lagoon surrounded by swamps, which in prehistoric times had been connected to the Goleta Slough. Col. Campbell envisioned a future lake for canoeing, stocked with fish and beautiful white swans.

Before returning to London, Col. Campbell had made up his mind to acquire the Jack Cavalletto ranch. He authorized Marshall Bond to purchase 100 acres, and to lease the George Gould property between the *estero* and Hollister Avenue where he could obtain potable water. Jack Cavalletto had purchased the ranch seven years before from speculator Joseph Archambault for $10,000; he sold it to Col. Campbell for $65,000. Dr. Gould received $31,500 for a long-term lease on his 317-acre tract, and well-digging crews started work at the northeast corner, where the west boundary of the present Municipal Airport joins Hollister Avenue.

Back in London, Col. Campbell received a cablegram from Bond informing him that the well drillers were finding indications of oil shale; should they drill deeper? Back came the Colonel's cable: UNDER NO CIRCUMSTANCES STRIKE OIL, WE WANT WATER. Apparently the last thing in the world Col. Campbell desired was a messy old oil field soiling his new country estate!

There had already been a delay in clearing the title to Jack Cavalletto's ranch because the Associated Oil Company had drilled a test well there prior to 1912. This wildcat had tapped petroleum deposits, but they were of such gummy viscosity as to make production unfeasible, and the well had been capped. Cavalletto was not paid off by Bond until the oil leases had been quit-claimed.

Returning to America with a staff of ten servants, his wife and three children—Colin Jr., Mary and Audry—the Colonel ensconced them temporarily at Bonnymede, the beautiful Hammond Estate on the Montecito waterfront. They lived there during the year it took the Colonel to prepare living quarters at Coal Oil Point in Goleta.

Access to the Campbell Ranch was by the old road which led from Hollister Avenue south to the "rincon," or corner, which turned east to serve the ranches of Gus and Alphonso Den. This road was narrow, and in wet seasons a quagmire. Col. Campbell very generously offered to pave the road at his own expense, providing neighboring farmers agreed not to haul heavy loads over the paving.

One domineering neighbor chose to be indignant about this load limit restriction, declaring huffily that Col. Campbell could not use it to reach his private property unless he *did* pave it—and share his paving with the public.

The generous-hearted Englishman refused to be imposed upon. Having unlimited money to spend, he simply bought a fifty-foot strip flanking the old road on the west, where he graded a private drive, blacktopped it, and separated it from the existing sandy road with a divider fence. This was known as Campbell Road. In later years the county took over both roads and removed the center divider. The combined thoroughfare was renamed Storke Road, after pioneer C. A. Storke and his son, T. M. Storke, who owned a 291-acre ranch on the east side of the road extending into the overflow lands of the Goleta Slough.

Beginning at the *rincon*, or right-angled corner, where Storke and El Colegio Roads join, Col. Colin Campbell built a winding, concrete-slab drive more than a mile in length, skirting the lagoon and looping around the knolls where he planned to locate his ornate manorhouse and outbuildings. This scenic boulevard, still in use as part of the Devereux Ranch School of today, was constructed entirely by hand from a mortar box, not with a mechanical concrete mixer.

With his own two hands, Col. Campbell set out rows of eucalyptus and cypress seedlings for windbreaks which now stand tall. What had been a Cavalletto bean field became Campbell's private polo grounds; still later it was converted into a blacktopped landing strip for guests arriving in private airplanes.

Prefabricated houses were erected to serve as a temporary home for his wife and family, barns, garages and other outbuildings. But Col. Campbell was not fated to enjoy the thrill of laying the cornerstone of his manorhouse, nor to break ground for his other enterprises on the ranch. He suffered a fatal heart attack while on a train passing through San Jose in 1924, en route home from Chicago.

Unlike Alice P. Williams of the ghost city of Naples, the Colonel's widow did not let her husband's dream die with him. She knew how deep his love was for the Goleta Valley when his will directed that he be buried in a private cemetery inside a circle of Monterey cypress trees at the very tip of Coal Oil Point, where the crashing surf could sound a requiem throughout eternity. A granite cross quarried in Scotland, ten feet high, marked his last resting place.

Mrs. Campbell devoted herself to fulfilling her husband's grandiose dreams. She poured money into ranch improvements with lavish abandon. The Campbell manorhouse was done in California Colonial Mission style, a bastard motif not fully accepted by many architects. Although cheap adobe brick was used for the walls—for sentimental rather than financial reasons—the manorhouse cost over $500,000 unfurnished, and was unquestionably the showplace of the Goleta Valley up to that time.

On a sunny day in 1925, a fleet of moving vans more than half a mile long threaded its way through sleepy Goleta and La Patera, turned south on Campbell (Storke) Road, and delivered tons of antique furniture, *objets d'art*, linens, silver, crystal and glassware to the Campbell mansion. Most of it was imported from England; some of it from Marshall Field's in Chicago, which was one of the enterprises of Mrs. Campbell's father.

Taking charge of the household in formal English fashion was George Churchill, who had been in the Colonel's employ since 1904, and his wife, Ida, who had "grown up with the Campbell children" as their nurse over in England. Churchill became manager of the Campbell Ranch, as well as majordomo of its household.

The Campbell Ranch became the setting for the most glittering social affairs the Goleta Valley had ever witnessed, throughout the

Roaring Twenties. The most notable *soiree* was a grand ball given for His Royal Highness Prince George, younger brother of the Prince of Wales. A special dance floor was laid on the patio tiling, an orchestra was brought in for the occasion, and the guest list included the cream of the social élite from Montecito, Santa Barbara, Beverly Hills and San Francisco.

Many years later, when the furnishings of the Campbell mansion were sold at public auction, Peter Irvine of Goleta bid in the "Prince George dance floor" and moved it to Oak Park in Santa Barbara. There it is still doing duty for the Recreation Department's Sunday afternoon old-time dances during the summer months.

Mrs. Campbell died abroad in 1932. Her ashes were returned to California for inurnment beside her husband's grave, inside the circle of cypress at Coal Oil Point. Her estate remained in the family for another thirteen years.

The Colonel's personal and real property was put up for sale, with the noted Hollywood auctioneer H. F. Madole in charge. Never had the Goleta Valley seen such an assemblage of Rolls-Royces, Pierce Arrows, Cadillacs and Packards as converged on the Campbell Ranch on the ninth of June, 1941, opening day of the great sale.

There was special interest in the fate of Campbell's personal collection of sterling silver, including extremely rare English pieces handcrafted by silversmiths in the 1600s. It was a shame, the auctioneers remarked among themselves, that the tableware was so deeply incised with the Colonel's C. C. initials that a new purchaser could never buff them off. As it turned out, the C. C. monogram proved an attraction for the eventual purchaser—film comedian Charlie Chaplin.

Among the 2,000 items placed on the block was Col. Campbell's rare first edition of Lawrence's *Seven Pillars of Wisdom*. This prize created heavy competition among the well-heeled book dealers in attendance from as far away as London and New York. The successful bidder was movie star Cary Grant, who at the time was the husband of Woolworth heiress Barbara Hutton. He paid $1,500 for the prized volume.

The 500-acre seaside estate also went on the block, but there were no satisfactory bids forthcoming. By now war clouds were gathering ominously on American horizons, so the Campbell Ranch went unsold—a mansion with seven bedrooms, a mile of private beach frontage, an ornate guest house, employee housing, horse barns, duplex apartments, a steel pier, multiple garages, machine shops, a boating lagoon, the winding concrete-paved boulevard, and garden landscaping which had cost a fortune to create over the years.

Eventually the Campbell Ranch was sold to the Devereux Foundation for school purposes—the same fate which had overtaken the four estates Campbell had been associated with in England—but this had to await the termination of another global war.

Contemporaneous with, and rivalling the Campbell Ranch in opulence and social activity, was the "Walora Ranch," headquarters of which occupied the crown of a 200-foot hill overlooking Stow Canyon Road and Fairview Avenue, a mile and a half north of the airport. The old Albert G. Hollister home, which gave the earlier Fairview Ranch its name in the Seventies, still stood in 1966 at the foot of Walora hill.

Dr. Walter Scott Franklin was the son of pioneers who had come overland to California by wagon train in the wake of the Gold Rush. Walter had graduated from Stanford, studied medicine in Vienna and Berlin, and emerged as one of America's foremost ophthalmologists. His socialite wife, the former Laura Baldwin of San Francisco's *haut monde*, made a dramatic entrance onto the Goleta Valley scene, traveling in a luxurious Pierce Arrow limousine with all the optional accessories, including an ermine carpet.

The Franklins were enchanted with the Good Land, and bought 116 acres of Edgar Hollister's historic Fairview Ranch. They named their country home "Walora," coined from their own names, Walter and Laura.

Contractor George Willey built the long, low, rambling white mansion on the brow of the hill overlooking today's Goleta Valley Junior High School. In 1966 it was still a landmark visible all over the Valley. Now a faded spectre of its glory days, the Walora Ranch mansion, at the time of its construction between 1919 and 1925, was architecturally a generation ahead of its time. It embodied floor-to-ceiling picture windows, pergolaed breezeways, and the split-level floor plans so dear to a later school of "ranchhouse" architecture. The Franklin library, between the east and west wings, was deemed worthy of any palace by awe-struck bibliophiles.

Formal gardens surrounded the manorhouse, with playing fountains, statuary tucked here and there in Forest Lawn splendor, tennis courts concealed behind high cypress hedges, ornamental sun dials, neatly coifed box hedges, and lawns as smooth and velvety as the greens on an exclusive golf course. A large swimming pool became a conversation piece at the Franklin ranch; in 1920 they were a status symbol enjoyed only by the rich. Forty years later, standing on the terrace of Walora Ranch, one can count dozens of swimming pools gleaming like emeralds in the back yards of tract homes.

Whereas the Campbell Ranch on the coast was the scene of parties featuring guest royalty from the Continent, the Walora Ranch was more American in its guest lists. It drew its imposing parade of shiny limousines from the social royalty of Hollywood, Marin County, Pasadena and San Francisco peninsula.

Regular visitors of note included thespian Jack Holt, a relative of the family by marriage; Stewart Warner, the billionaire industrialist; and show business personalities too numerous for listing. Because Dr. Franklin was prominent in State Republican circles, one of his guests in the 1930s was Herbert Hoover, who was President of the United States at the time.

While Dr. Franklin kept token office hours in Santa Barbara every morning, his primary interest in life was his Goleta ranch. At the time he bought from Hollister, the principal crop was walnuts. After ranch manager Charlie Winters left California, Dr. Franklin hired Charlie Troup, of the pioneer Scottish family, to superintend his ranch operations. Troup pulled out all the walnut groves and planted lemons, anticipating a trend which became general in the Goleta Valley by 1930. As a technical consultant, Dr. Franklin enjoyed the services of his dear friend and advisor, Dr. J. Elliot Coit of the U. C. faculty at Berkeley, who paid regular visits to Walora Ranch for many years, conducting experiments in avocado culture.

Extensive grape vineyards, turkey breeding and commercial-scale berry growing were also part of Dr. Franklin's diversified farming program.

Dr. Franklin is fondly remembered as a generous community benefactor in the Goleta Valley. When he installed electric and telephone lines all the way up Fairview Avenue to his hilltop home in 1919, he invited everyone along the route to tie into his service.

In 1938, Dr. Franklin tossed his hat into the political ring as the Republican candidate for lieutenant governor, his running mate being the incumbent governor, Frank Merriam. Dr. Franklin chose the worst possible year to run as a G.O.P.; 1938 was the year Culbert C. Olson won on the "ham and eggs" issue and became the first Democrat in forty years to occupy the Executive Mansion in Sacramento. Subsequently, Dr. Franklin ran for a seat in Congress, was defeated again, and retired from politics.

When Dr. Franklin passed away in Santa Barbara in January, 1946, his widow continued to live at Walora Ranch for many years. Her former chauffeur, Glen Hancock, took over as ranch superintendent until Mrs. Franklin finally sold out in 1961. Bowing to the pressure of skyrocketing taxes and urbanization, she parted with her beloved country estate for a reported price of $977,000— land which had cost Daniel Hill $55! Mrs. Franklin died in 1963.

The year 1925 is of course remembered in the Goleta Valley for the devastating Santa Barbara Earthquake of June 29. While it took no lives in the Valley, it did far more property damage than is generally realized.

Involved in the seismic disturbance, the most severe in California since the San Francisco disaster of April, 1906, were two major fault lines which, unfortunately, underlie the Good Land.

The South Santa Ynez Fault follows the foothills along the base of the mountains from Gaviota to Ventura. In the vicinity of Tucker's Grove, a tributary earth fracture, called the Mesa Fault, branches off in a southeasterly direction, and enters the ocean at the Santa Barbara breakwater. What are called the Mesa bluffs on the west side of the city, where the KEYT television studio stands, is actually a scarp caused by the slippage of the Mesa Fault in prehistoric times.

Shortly after 12:00 midnight on Monday, June 29, 1925, farmers noticed that domestic animals and poultry in Goleta Valley corrals and hencoops suddenly became restless and uneasy. Birds flew crying from their perches in tall eucalyptus trees, for no apparent reason. Seismograph records suggest that they had detected the first warning tremors of the disaster which was impending.

The big jolt struck at exactly 6:42 a.m. Scientists believe the submerged end of the Mesa Fault let loose off shore with a short, cataclysmic jolt which in turn triggered the east-west trending Santa Ynez Fault along the foothills.

The result was a jarring, roaring double shock which in a matter of clock-ticks had killed thirteen persons in Santa Barbara, injured sixty-five, and damaged more than $15,000,000 worth of property.

Early-rising Goleta farmers reported seeing a cloud of dust "lift like smoke" from the entire floor of the valley from Hope Ranch to Ellwood, as the surface undulated to the heavings of the earth's shattering crust far underground. The Santa Barbara *Morning Press* reported "the quake seemed to center, for a wavering moment, in the business section of the tiny village of Goleta."

Mrs. Cora Neeley was lighting a kerosene stove at her home next door to Fritz Maiers' place at 175 Chapel Street, the former Harmony Hall. The quake knocked over the stove and set the kitchen afire. The Neeley home burned to the ground before fire fighters could reach the scene.

Blakeway's general store at Patterson and Hollister presented what the newspapers described as "a decidedly torn-up appearance, with stock off the shelves and counters shifted at wild angles."

The Walnut Association's packing plant near the railroad depot was jarred several feet off its foundations. Up on the hill at Dr. Franklin's Walora Ranch, carpenter George Willey was shingling a new guest house when the earthquake hit. It forced him, in his words, "to hang on for dear life, like riding a bucking horse." At the Colin Campbell Ranch on Coal Oil Point, $25,000 damage was done to the main house, according to custodian George Churchill, mostly because adobe had been used in its construction.

Considerable damage was reported at the Goleta School on South Patterson Avenue. Partial demolition of Tom Simpson's Garage on Hollister Avenue was completed when damaged walls were knocked over by later shocks. Not one brick chimney escaped damage or total destruction throughout the Valley. Brick-veneer walls on an old Hollister-built two-story bunkhouse on the Pomatto Brothers' Ranch, in lower Glen Annie Canyon, fell to the ground. Peter Irvine reported that "everything breakable" in his house at 5045 Hollister Avenue was smashed, and that all the water in a large fishpond in his backyard had sloshed out, stranding fish in an empty pool.

Moderate to severe damage was reported at the homes of George Edwards, Robert Main, Frank Lane, E. A. Rowe, George Donaldson, Frank Baker, Harold Gorman and R. P. Tucker. A concrete-block barn on the Barini farm, and the historic Juan Hill Adobe at 1026 North Patterson Avenue, near the Fault, were totally destroyed.

Extensive landslides altered the geography of the foothill canyons, but no property damage resulted except to fence lines. Out at Naples, the stone chapel was ruined. The coffin of John H. Williams was taken to Santa Barbara Cemetery; Mr. and Mrs. George Mack moved the body of their infant daughter, Patricia, to Goleta Cemetery, and marked the grave with a block of stone from the Haunted Chapel. H. G. Wylie used the dressed stones to build the curving walls and gateway now fronting the main Dos Pueblos ranch house.

By and large, the average frame house in the Goleta Valley survived the quake in good shape. The historic Daniel Hill Adobe, oldest residence in the Valley, survived because it was supported interiorly by its unique three-foot-thick center partition of adobe. Several artesian wells which had long been dry resumed flowing, but this benefit soon tapered off as the water table was restored to equilibrium.

Almost forgotten now were the after-temblors which followed the big shake on Monday—32 on Tuesday, 54 on Wednesday, 22 on Thursday, 36 on Friday and 26 on Saturday. In all, more than 1,000 distinct after-shocks were registered by California seismographs before the nerve-jangling summer of 1925 ran its course, a situation which kept Goleta Valley residents in an understandable state of jitters. Happily, there was no recurrence of seismic disturbances in the Valley until the minor quake of 1952, which did comparatively little damage.

Even earthquakes could not quench the sense of humor of Valley dwellers. One Goleta merchant, before he cleaned up the débris in his store, posted a big sign which read:

> EARTHQUAKE SPECIALS!!!
> *Quaker* Oats
> Milk *Shakes*

Old residents of Goleta are often heard to complain that Santa Barbara has attached its name to Goleta's University campus and Goleta's airport. But the usurpers are welcome, these old-timers agree, to keep their civic label on the Santa Barbara Earthquake of 1925.

CHAPTER XXVII

Black Gold Bonanza at Ellwood Oil Field

Ten days after the earthquake, the members of the new Goleta School Board met at the home of their chairman, Chester Rich. Present were Fred Stevens, Mrs. James G. Williams, Nina Bottiani and Bill Lillard. They were meeting for the first time as trustees of the new Goleta Union School District, comprising La Patera, Cathedral Oaks and Goleta schools.

Such a consolidation had been unanimously approved by a PTA meeting on May 22, 1925, and petitions were circulated to have County Superintendent of Schools Arthur Pope call for a community vote on the unification plan. The electorate overwhelmingly approved the idea at an extralegal election on June 12, 1925. At this time there were 190 students enrolled in the three elementary schools of the Valley.

At their historic first meeting, the trustees obtained options on four school sites; on April 17, 1926, a special bond election was called to raise $22,500 to buy land, and $61,500 for a new school building. The bond issue passed by a vote of 164 to 49, and the trustees immediately purchased the Begg tract, located on the south side of Hollister Avenue just west of San Jose Creek. The plans of Architect Louis N. Crawford were accepted, and general construction work started on December 1, 1926. The cornerstone ceremonies were held on February 26, 1927, and construction was complete by June 1—at which time the contractor filed bankruptcy papers.

The handsome new Goleta Union School had eight classrooms, a fine auditorium with theater stage, offices, and other modern features long lacking in Goleta schools. George Locy became the first principal, followed in 1928 by Hal D. Caywood, who resigned in 1946 to become County Superintendent of Schools.

The former Goleta School on South Patterson Avenue, built in 1908 to replace the old Two-Story Schoolhouse, was moved to the south end of the new school yard. It served as a kindergarten and auxiliary classroom until its demolition in 1957.

The consolidation of the Goleta schools was followed in 1929 by the formation of the Ellwood Union School District, which joined the outlying Den and Tecolote Districts dating from 1889 and 1891, respectively. An attractive new Ellwood Union School was dedicated at 7686 Hollister Avenue, on the old Cooper Ranch, in 1933.

In 1925, La Patera's pioneer blacksmith and constable, John Pico, who had learned his trade from Joe Lane, sold his blacksmith shop at 5960 Hollister Avenue to Jim Smith, the voice of the Goleta Valley's Republican party, and son of a pioneer Scottish family. Smith continued in business there for a quarter of a century before hanging up his leather apron and retiring to the Smith Brothers' Glen Annie Canyon ranch in 1949.

John Pico is fondly remembered as one of the Valley's most useful citizens. In 1902 he had married Texas-born Avery Shirrell Kellogg, widow of Clinton Kellogg, who was injured in a wagon accident near Figueroa Mountain and died of complications in 1898. Pico thus acquired four fine step-children—Eugene, who was later agricultural commissioner; Erma, May and Frank.

After leaving his forge and anvil, John Pico lived on South Patterson Avenue, where he died in 1958. Mrs. Pico turned ninety in 1965, one of the Valley's most spry and charming pioneer citizens.

The mid-Twenties saw many important developments take place in the Good Land. On April 5, 1926, Congress granted the County of Santa Barbara the 24-acre Goleta Sandspit for park purposes, excluding the building of houses thereon, and retaining title to the extreme easterly tip of the Sandspit. The T. B. Bishop Company vigorously protested public ownership of the spit, claiming it was an accretion to Dos Pueblos Ranch which had been patented to Nicolás A. Den's estate in 1877. The resulting lawsuits took a decade to resolve, eventually in favor of the public.

A portion of Alfonso Den's old Rincon Ranch became the scene of a flurry of town-lot subdividing and street dedicating during the middle Twenties. In November 1925, the beach frontage between modern Camino Pescadero and Camino Corto was platted under the name "Isla Vista," or Island View. The following February saw the Ocean Terrace Tract platted east of Isla Vista, as far as the row of eucalyptus trees marking the Gus Den ranch boundary, now the western line of the university campus. In April, 1926, the strip from Camino Corto westward to the Campbell (Devereux) Ranch line was subdivided as Orilla del Mar, meaning Edge of the Sea. However, a complete lack of potable water made the land unsaleable, and it remained a barren pasture for years to come.

"Goleta Center" was the name of a subdivision south of Hollister Avenue, between More Ranch Road and Kellogg Avenue. It was mapped in November, 1927, and also failed to develop. A hog and poultry farm which occupied a swampy strip between South Fairview Avenue and San Jose Creek, south of Hollister Avenue, was subdivided into little forty-foot lots which were sold as low as $10 each. This created a substandard development with shacks, pigsties, chicken yards and junk heaps lining nine short cul-de-sacs named, in north to south order, Daley, Matthews, Olney, Cloer, Carson, Avion, Payaro, Placentia, and Corta Streets. The developer gave this untidy neighborhood the flamboyant title of "Fairfield." But no amount of semantic gilding could camouflage the ugliness or upgrade a soggy terrain which, while ideal for swine to root in, was hardly an area for choice homes, especially when San Jose Creek overspilled its banks in wet winters to make a lake out of the area. Home owners on the Fairfield Tract also had to endure the dubious aroma of "Corral No. 5" from Emmett Gammill's slaughterhouse across Fairview Avenue.

Simultaneously with this development, a Santa Barbara syndicate headed by Harold G. Chase was commencing work on Hope Ranch, one of southern California's most prestigious residential parks, located at the southeastern extremity of the Goleta Valley.

The Twenties saw several important changes of ranch ownership in the Goleta Valley's western foothill sections.

Railroad magnate Frank H. Greene, who had purchased the Ellwood Cooper ranch on March 19, 1915, following the death of

C. J. M. McGill-Crichton in World War I combat, died in 1920, leaving considerable indebtedness. This resulted in the Cooper Ranch being put up for sale at public auction. The winning bid came from Joseph Archambault (known as "Joe Shambow" in Valley parlance) and the Doty Brothers, Julius E., Francis G., Lawrence A. and Russel E., sons of pioneer Julius Doty, who had farmed 200 acres in Las Varas (Doty) Canyon since 1883.

Archambault and the Doty Brothers purchased the Cooper Ranch of 2,200 acres for $275,000, receiving their deed from the Ellwood Ranch Corporation on December 7, 1921. Eventually the Dotys bought out Archambault's interest.

Between July and December 1926, the Thomas B. Bishop Company sold the choice 1,320-acre Tecolote Ranch to investment tycoon and yachtsman Silsby Spalding. Bishop had operated the property (through a subsidiary, Tecolote Land Company) as a cattle ranch for nearly forty years. Spalding and his foreman, William Smith, converted the Tecolote into a fine lemon ranch. A rambling, Spanish-style house was built by the Spaldings, which for sheer opulence outshone the Victorian manorhouses of the Hollisters and Stows and the mansions of Col. Campbell and Dr. Franklin. A notable feature of the Tecolote estate was Mr. Spalding's famous tack collection, since 1959 on display at the Dos Pueblos Orchid Company, and the elaborate wrought-iron fences, gates, and fixtures which artisan Jim Smith, the last of Goleta's old-fashioned village blacksmiths, produced at his forge and anvil.

Farther to the east, that portion of modern Goleta which lies north of Hollister to the railroad, between Fairview and the Kellogg Tract, was subdivided into town lots during the 1927 boom by developers Robert Smith and Frank E. Dow. The north-south avenues were extensions of Orange, Magnolia, Pine and Nectarine, with Mandarin Drive bisecting the subdivision from west to east. This created the present form of the town of Goleta, but it remained more or less stagnant until the postwar boom of the mid-Forties.

What held back the residential subdivision of Goleta during the Roaring Twenties and the Depression Thirties was lack of water. But in 1928, the Good Land was on the verge of a great new boom when a major oil field was discovered at its very doorstep.

Oil had been known to exist in the Goleta Valley for at least 158 years. The outcrops of black tar along the beach from More Mesa to Dos Pueblos Canyon, first reported by Fr. Pedro Font with the Bautista de Anza expedition of 1774, had long given men reason to hope there were extensive oil and gas reservoirs under the region.

The State of California issued its first tidelands oil lease near the mouth of Goleta Slough to one Charles Morrill in 1861. He was sued by Nelson Pierce's "Dead Whale Asphalt Mining Company" for years, but oil rights finally went to T. Wallace More.

In the late Nineties, a part-time geologist named August C. Cooper, who established the first real estate office in Santa Barbara and later sold out to Louis G. Dreyfus, conducted a painstaking survey of the Goleta coastline's petrolic potential. His findings indicated that a dome or anticline was located near the mouth of Las Armas Canyon, on Dos Pueblos property inherited by Kate Den Bell. Cooper showed Mrs. Bell the geologic folds of strata in the earth's crust as exposed on the sea cliffs, and told her he believed an oil pool might be entrapped in the "attic" under this "roof peak" formation. In 1897, as previously related, Stephen Rutherford and Frank Kellogg had drilled a wildcat well to a depth of 1,000 feet without striking oil sand, and gave up.

Kate Den Bell went to her grave in 1926 firmly convinced her heirs would someday strike oil at Las Armas. In 1927, test wells were drilled in Tecolote Canyon by operator E. J. Miley, but while they yielded oil and gas for a time, they began pumping saltwater and were shut in. Oil men in general wrote off the Goleta Valley as a poor risk for an expensive exploration program.

Meanwhile an ambitious young Los Angeles petroleum engineer, geologist Frank A. Morgan, had been studying Cooper's old field notes from the Ellwood area. He decided to do some geologizing himself, using more modern methods. He became as excited over the dome on Kate Bell's ranch (then owned by her daughter, Caroline, wife of Dr. George Luton of Santa Ynez) as Cooper had been thirty years before. For months, Morgan went from office to office of major oil companies in Los Angeles and San Francisco, pleading with executives to risk a paltry $35,000 or so drilling a test well on a structure Morgan had named "Elwood Terrace"—a misspelling of Cooper's first name which still persists in oil circles. However, company after company turned him down cold.

Early in 1928, Morgan had the good fortune to run into Charlie Jones and the Lockhart Brothers, owners of a shoestring outfit known as the Rio Grande Oil Company. These hungry partners made a field trip to Bell Canyon with Morgan. What they saw made them decide to lease the property from Caroline Bell Luton, including oil leases connected with the nearby Miley field in Tecolote Canyon.

But after sewing up the oil leases, Rio Grande found itself strapped for money to drill a well.

Then luck broke in their favor. A few miles up the coast, on the Archie Edwards ranch adjoining Wylie's Dos Pueblos Ranch, another small operator, Barnsdall Oil Company, had just abandoned a dry hole, and was about to move its drilling rig back to Los Angeles.

Barnsdall agreed to drill a test hole on the Luton-Bell lease to a depth of 3,000 feet, providing Rio Grande paid half the drilling costs of $10 a foot, and relinquished a half interest in all their oil leases. Rio Grande agreed, and partnership papers were duly notarized.

Geologist Frank Morgan pounded a stake into a bean field near the spot where Rutherford and Kellogg had drilled their duster to 1,000 feet in 1897, and Luton-Bell No. 1 was spudded in on the first of June, 1928. Within three weeks the well had been drilled 160 feet beyond the stipulated limit, to 3,160 feet, without any significant showings of oil or gas.

Barnsdall's manager, R. F. Broomfield, phoned Charlie Jones of Rio Grande: "We are shutting down the Ellwood well, Charlie—it is getting too deep and needs a string of casing. We see no point in drilling any deeper, and we recommend abandoning the well. If you want to continue drilling, we will rent you our rig for $100 a day—but Barnsdall is pulling out of the deal."

Sorely discouraged, Jones asked Morgan to drive up to Goleta and have a last look at Luton-Bell No. 1 corings before the derrick was dismantled and the draw-works returned to Los Angeles. Morgan and his wife drove up the coast to reach the well around 9 p.m. on a Friday. They found superintendent Dick Burke and tool pusher Bill Hooley waiting with the crew for final orders to abandon.

Morgan looked at the last core in the "doghouse," taken between 3,150 and 3,160 feet. He cracked open the sample on a faulting plane and sniffed—and felt his heart freeze in his chest. His sensitive, educated nostrils caught the thrilling odor of sweet light oil in Temblor Shale, which he knew overlaid the Vaqueros Sands formation which he had predicted would contain oil. This was not the gummy, sulphurous oil of the Monterey Shale above.

Morgan's poker face concealed his excitement from Bill Hooley and the Barnsdall drilling crew. His loyalty was to Rio Grande; there was no reason to let Barnsdall's men know Luton-Bell No. 1 might be only inches away from a momentous discovery.

Picking up samples of coring, Morgan drove back to Los Angeles and arranged a meeting with Charlie Jones and the Lockhart Brothers for early Saturday morning. At this meeting he broke his news, presented his evidence, and recommended that his superiors dissolve their partnership agreement with Barnsdall Oil Company immediately and resume drilling. The big pay-off was near for Rio Grande.

Jones snatched up the telephone and rang Broomfield's office. But it was Saturday, and Barnsdall was closed for the weekend.

"I decided to let the matter rest until Monday morning," Jones reminisced years later. "That was the worst blunder of my life."

For things had been happening out at the Ellwood lease, 100 miles up the coast. That Saturday morning, while the roustabouts were killing time jabbering about aviator Charles "Lucky Lindy" Lindbergh being in Santa Barbara that day visiting with Jack Mitchell, and debating who would win in that night's heavyweight fight between Gene Tunney and Tom Heeney at Yankee Stadium, toolpusher Bill Hooley decided to go into the hole to take a coring and circulate mud. Destiny was riding on that off-hand decision of Hooley's.

The moment the string of tools resumed drilling, history was made for the Goleta Valley. After eight feet the fishtail bit bored through a crust of soft Temblor Shale into oil-soaked Vaqueros Sands. By tapping a high-pressure reservoir at 3,168 feet, the derrick crew found themselves facing the risk of having the gas spew the tool string and casing out of the ground and hurl the steel derrick sky-high. Had it not been for the rugged blowout preventer at the casinghead Christmas tree, Luton-Bell No. 1 would have exploded into an out-of-control gusher.

Barnsdall's chief geologist got on the phone to let Frank Morgan know his faith in the well had been justified. As he hung up, Morgan knew that any chance of Rio Grande dissolving its partnership with Barnsdall Oil was gone forever.

...Luton-Bell No. 1 proved to have been drilled on the very northernmost edge of the Ellwood Oil Field, which was destined to become one of the most productive strikes in California, with a production of over 100,000,000 barrels of 36° gravity crude. The bulk of the formation extended south and west under the ocean floor, beyond the mouth of Tecolote Canyon. Still farther west, undreamed of in 1928, lay yet another submarine pool fronting Dos Pueblos Ranch. Exploration continues to locate new oil and gas reservoirs farther up the Santa Barbara Channel.

Barnsdall-Rio Grande crews fought the gas pressure for weeks. They finally completed the well at 3,204 feet in the Vaqueros Sands. Shortly before completion date on July 26, the owner of the property under lease, Mrs. Caroline Bell Luton, came to the derrick platform with her teen-age son, Bill, who had just finished high school.

"Mr. Morgan," Mrs. Luton said, "I do wish you could tell me whether this well is a flash in the pan or not. Here it is almost the middle of summer, and my husband and I don't know if we can afford to send our boy away to college in September."

"Mrs. Luton," Morgan laughed, "you will not only send Bill to Yale, he'll take a string of polo ponies with him. This well will make you a millionaire several times over, wait and see."

Morgan's prediction was conservative. Luton-Bell No. 1 had a steady flow of 2,400 barrels of crude per day, under control, and during its lifetime produced more than a million barrels. Bill Luton went to Yale that autumn—with a string of polo ponies.

The sensational discovery of Ellwood's black gold bonanza brought in a rush of competing oil companies, lease hounds, wildcat operators, and promoters. Goleta's Good Land for miles in all directions was sewed up in oil leases, most of which proved to be without value. There were the usual cut-throat royalty feuds and boundary disputes, the details of which are far too voluminous for inclusion here. As an example, Barnsdall-Rio Grande had to defend their rights against eighty-seven persons claiming to be illegitimate heirs of Nicolás A. Den, original grantee of the land!

Derricks sprouted like mushrooms along the mesa near the discovery well. All were heavy producers. Wells drilled even a short distance inland were bone dry. Piers of steel and wooden timbers began to jut out over the surf, where oil wells were drilled into the ocean bottom. Clinton A. Langstaff was Barnsdall's production superintendent during the bonanza period.

In November, 1928, Frank Morgan estimated the ultimate recovery from the Ellwood structure would be 110 million barrels, putting it in the category of a major field. Goleta's Good Land had paid off against staggering odds, for the American Association of Petroleum Geologists estimated that one major field has been found in the U. S. for every 968 wildcat wells attempted.

Morgan felt the recoverable reserve of crude could be increased by forty per cent through proper reservoir engineering and conservation practices. However, this was not to be. Rival companies drilled offset wells near the Barnsdall-Rio Grande lease lines, and ran them wide open at 12,000 barrels per day for extended periods. The old-fashioned practice of "drain thy neighbor dry" prevailed, especially in the older eastern end of the field, which, in the opinion of some experts, meant the Ellwood Oil Field was depleted fifty years before it should have been, leaving $100,000,000 worth of oil underground where it could never be recovered.

Among the sight-seers who flocked out to Luton-Bell No. 1 that fall of 1928 was County Tax Assessor Charlie Tomlinson. A year before, the income from the bean crop on this barren mesa had barely covered Luton's tax bill. Now that oil had been struck, the county struck it rich also. Tomlinson's office prepared a tax statement which turned out to be nearly as large as the total net worth of the operating companies.

Upon receiving the bill, Charlie Jones appeared before the County Supervisors, accompanied by a lawyer and a tax expert, and made an impassioned plea for a revision of the Ellwood tax bill.

The Supervisors at that time were Leo Preisker, of Santa Maria; Sam Stanwood, of Santa Barbara; Ronald Adam, of Lompoc; Tom

Dinsmore, of Carpinteria; and Joseph Sexton Jr., of Goleta. Chairman Preisker replied to oilman Jones' recital, "Charlie, I've got news for you. As you know, Santa Barbara is building a new Moorish-style courthouse which will be the most spectacular public building in America. We have decided to give your oil company the high honor of paying what our new county courthouse is going to cost us."

Santa Barbara's ornate County Courthouse, for many years a top tourist attraction, was completed in 1929 at a cost of over $1,500,000. The Ellwood oil tax payments came to more than that amount in 1928.

One of the many oil companies operating at Ellwood was Signal Oil & Gas, headed by Sam Mosher of Signal Hill. Signal's lease was on the western edge of the field, on state land at the mouth of Louis Dreyfus' Eagle Canyon. Later, during World War II, Signal risked $650,000 to acquire the 4,500-acre Dos Pueblos Ranch from H. G. Wylie, in order to acquire upland drillsites facing the Santa Barbara Channel. More than thirty high-producing oil wells eventually lined the shore on the waterfront of the ghost town of Naples, whipstocked under the surf and kelp beds to bottom in a rich oil pool out under the waters of Santa Barbara Channel.*

In the more than three and a half decades since the discovery of oil at Ellwood, production has totaled more than 100,000,000 barrels of crude and 90,000,000 million cubic feet of natural gas. Peak annual production at the field was reached in 1931, with 7,500,000 barrels; by 1935, production stood at 500,000 barrels. Since 1937, production at Ellwood has declined steadily, until by 1966 it was down to a trickle of 600 barrels a day from twenty wells. The maximum number of wells at Ellwood was seventy-nine in 1938. Wells were pumping more than 75 per cent sea water by 1966.

During its heyday, the Ellwood Oil Field had sixteen piers jutting out into the Channel, but as each over-water well was abandoned, owners were required to remove its pier. By 1966, only Signal's pier remained, plus the stubby Mahoney pier at the extreme eastern end of the field.

---

* For further details on the Ellwood oil strike, see *Little Giant of Signal Hill* by Walker A. Tompkins, Prentice-Hall Inc., 1964.

Black Gold Bonanza at Ellwood Oil Field

Oil is only half the Goleta success story; gas provides the other half. Following the Ellwood strike in 1928, the General Petroleum Corporation (now Mobil) leased portions of the More Ranch and began drilling for oil on Mescalitán Island and along the Sandspit. They didn't strike oil, but at 4,533 feet More No. 1 blew in with a roar like a giant blowtorch which could be heard all over the valley, and spewed natural gas into the atmosphere at the rate of sixty million cubic feet per day until it was brought under control.

Standard Oil of California drilled on adjacent land belonging to Harold Chase and Peter Cooper Bryce, with fifty per cent success: one dry hole, one gasser. Shell Oil in 1934 drilled to 6,508 feet in a futile effort to find oil, then plugged back to gas sands to recover their drilling costs.

With a gas field of seemingly inexhaustible proportions on their hands, the operators laid a sixteen-inch pipeline from the More Ranch to Ventura in 1931, and began making deliveries of Goleta dry gas to the Los Angeles area.

More than a gas reservoir had been found under the Good Land. A unique deposit of coarse quartz sand underlay a sealing lid of Miocene shale ranging from 3,800 to 4,200 feet thick, covering an area of 300 acres some 300 feet in thickness, and extending in a sort of elongated figure "8" along the coastline from Isla Vista on the west to More Ranch Road on the east. This sand, estimated to be thirty million years old, was so granular it could absorb 26.2 per cent of its volume in water or natural gas.

Gas experts knew if they could withdraw gas from this sand-filled storage vault, they could prevent seawater from seeping into the formation by injecting gas back underground to equalize the pressure. And the sandy formation could accept twenty million cubic feet of gas per day for a capacity of forty-two *billion* cubic feet of gas. What such a storage capacity above ground would cost to build staggered the imagination.

During 1939 and 1940, the Pacific Lighting Gas Supply Corporation began acquiring surface property above the gas storage vault, which put them very much in the political picture when the Municipal Airport was created.

A permanent compressor station was built north of the KTMS radio towers. Eventually the company owned 294 acres in fee, and leased gas storage rights under an additional 2,046 acres. According to plant superintendent Henry Roades, by 1965 Pacific Lighting's total investment had reached $13,000,000, making it the fourth largest taxpayer in Santa Barbara County.

Now, every time a Los Angeles housewife lights her gas stove she is drawing fuel through 100 miles of pipeline from a lump of quartz sand buried half a mile under ancient Mescalitán Island—certainly one of the most unusual facets of Goleta's dramatic story.

CHAPTER XXVIII

The Depression Years: Airports and Avocados

The fundamental superiority of Goleta's Good Land as a place to live stood out most sharply during the great depression which followed the stock market crash of October, 1929. While belts had to be tightened, NRA, WPA, and CCC were added to the language, living standards dropped and money was tight, none of the Valley's 1,500 residents went hungry or lacked for shelter and clothing.

Through necessity, a radical change occurred in the established agricultural patterns of the Valley. Walnuts and lima beans were phased out in favor of lemons and avocados which, once trees came into bearing, brought high prices in spite of the depression.

At the outset of the 1930s, Goleta's walnut growers were feeling the pinch of competition from Oregon and elsewhere. Oak root fungus, a soil poison left over from Hispanic times when the Good Land was mottled with liveoak groves, helped hasten the decline of the walnut industry. Lemons, pioneered more than half a century earlier by Sherman P. Stow, began to gain a foothold as hard times closed in, so that by 1950 nine out of ten lemon trees had been planted subsequent to 1930.

By tradition, Goleta's lemon growers had harvested, processed and marketed their crops through the pioneer Johnston Fruit Company, founded in 1897. On May 31, 1935, an independent, non-profit, co-operative marketing organization was founded by sixty local growers, under the corporate name of the Goleta Lemon Association. The charter membership included the influential Cavalletto interests and the big T. B. Bishop ranch (but not the Stow Ranch, one of Johnston Fruit's founders).

Some 600 acres of the Valley's choicest lemon groves let the new co-operative handle the picking, hauling and pest control phases of their business. Individual growers did their own cultivating, fertilizing, irrigation and pruning to USDA standards.

Goleta Lemon's charter board of directors, headed by Philip C. Marble, of Maria Ygnacia Canyon, included Bill Main, Egisto Giorgi, Joe Cavaletto, Billy Hamilton, William R. Dickinson, and Robert Rowe. Subsequent presidents were Main, Hamilton, J. Monroe Rutherford and Earl Johnstone Jr.

In the spring of 1936 a major Valley landmark appeared, the million-dollar lemon packing plant on a seven-acre tract across La Patera Lane from the historic Hill Adobe, flanking the S. P. railroad. The operating section of this all-wooden structure could have sheltered a football field under its roof. A 60 by 120 foot mezzanine occupied part of the middle section. The storage section adjoining was a two-story building 120 by 150 feet in size, and provided for 150 carloads of fruit in storage. This space had to be expanded to 425 carloads within a few years, to accommodate the boom in Goleta Valley lemons coming into bearing.

The historic first shipment of Goleta Lemon Association fruit was sold in Chicago in June, 1936, on a very active market, for $9.20 to $9.60 per field box—a dazzling bonanza indeed, considering the dire situation facing American farmers in most parts of the country. There was little fluctuation in the price of lemons during the next three decades, though not at such a high price level.

From the outset the Goleta Lemon Association was affiliated with the California Fruit Growers' Exchange, shippers of world-famous "Sunkist" citrus. Before long, markets all over the globe were ordering the Goleta Valley's various brands of lemons. The top quality Sunkist fruit was shipped under the *Goleta* and *San Marcos* labels; the extra choice fruit was labeled *La Patera*; choice was *Schooner*, *Channel* and *Arboleda* brands; while standards were sold under the *Estero* label.

During the first six months the Goleta Lemon Association was in existence it shipped a total of 306 carloads to the northwest, middle west, and auction markets in Chicago, St. Louis, Boston, and New York. The first overseas shipments were beginning. General manager was Paul Honeywell; his plant foreman was Granvel B.

Caster. By 1943, when Caster became manager, the Goleta plant was shipping 900 carloads of lemons annually.

The varieties which did best in Goleta's various types of soil were the Lisbon and Eureka, budded onto such rootstocks as sweet orange, rough lemon, grapefruit or sour lemon. Trees were producing marketable fruit by the second year and were paying their cultural costs by the fourth season. Peak production came in the ninth or tenth year, and the average Goleta lemon tree paid a profit for at least 30 years—a remarkable testimony to the quality of the Good Land.

The outward effects of the depression, as seen in other parts of the U.S.—soup lines, crime, labor strikes, slum housing—were unknown in the Goleta Valley, except for a "Hooverville" of tents and shanties which spread briefly along the Goleta Sandspit, tenanted by unemployed citizens and undesirable tramps mixed together. The community feared that these men might claim squatters' rights to the Sandspit, which was county-owned and dedicated for public recreation in perpetuity.

In 1932, the county's district attorney, Percy Heckendorf, brought an eviction suit against the Hooverville squatters, who were represented in Justice of the Peace Tom Clancy's parlor courtroom by defense attorney W. P. Butcher. (Both Heckendorf and Butcher became Superior Court judges in Santa Barbara.) The squatters were adjudged to be trespassing on public property, and the unattractive, crime-breeding slum at the mouth of the Slough was eradicated. In 1934 the Goleta pleasure pier was built with WPA labor.

Many of the depression victims found employment in the Goleta Lemon Association packing plant, which had a payroll of up to 350 persons during the harvesting and shipping season, with another 350 employed as pickers and haulers in the field. The spectacular fecundity of the Goleta Valley farmland was evidenced by the fact that from four to seven crops of lemons could be picked annually, compared to only one crop in many localities. Sixty percent of the fruit was picked green and ripened in storage.

Eventually the Goleta plant handled three quarters of the Valley's total lemon production, with some 2,500 acres signed up.

Lemon growers had their headaches, of course. A diminishing

water supply was the most serious threat, and around 1940 the existing water began going bad. Boron began showing up in wells along Patterson Avenue and on the Storke Ranch north of Isla Vista, and only a minute trace of boron was enough to ruin a lemon tree. Other Valley wells showed a high sulphur content.

Oak root fungus, for years the dreaded bugaboo of the Goleta farmer, could now be controlled through scientific fumigation of the soil. Non-toxic oil sprays were used in spring and fall to combat silver mite, red scale, red spider and black scale. Ladybirds, first introduced into California in the 1880s by Ellwood Cooper, were now procurable from the U. S. Department of Agriculture, ending the farmers' dependence on China, as in Cooper's day.

Avocados, a sub-tropical fruit which grows only in certain very limited areas of Southern California, were found to flourish in Hope Ranch and the Goleta Valley, including foothill land so steep it was formerly valuable only for grazing livestock.

Joseph Sexton had made several trips to Hawaii to study the avocado around the time of the first World War. Dr. Horace Pierce of Santa Barbara had avocado orchards bearing on a commercial scale by the middle 1920s, on his foothill ranch above St. Vincent's Orphanage and on land now occupied by San Marcos Gardens.

County horticultural agent Eugene Kellogg (a son of Mrs. John Pico) was responsible for getting such growers as Chester Rich and Billy Hamilton to put in groves of avocados around 1928. Extensive plantings were also made on the progressive Bishop and Stow ranches. Vital scientific research on avocados was done by Dr. Walter Scott Franklin and his consultant, Dr. J. Elliot Coit of U. C., on the Walora Ranch. In Glen Annie Canyon, Louis Cavalletto became an important grower of avocados, and was elected the Goleta Valley's first director of Calavo, the California avocado growers' co-operative founded in San Diego County in 1923. Calavo's 1966 field manager in the Goleta area was Chester Rich's son, Robert.

While the Goleta Valley was never noted as an orange-raising center—its cool sea breezes and soil chemistry being more favorable to lemons—the Bishop, Franklin and Tecolote ranches had impressive acreages of Navels and Valencias totalling from 2,000 to 4,000 trees. Ranchers in the 300- to 1,200-tree bracket included Billy Hamilton, George Gallagher, Joseph Sexton Jr., William Main, P.

The Depression Years: Airports and Avocados

C. Marble, Oliver Runnels, Ernest Sexton, Albert Spaulding, Fred Stevens, A. W. Conover, Roy Rickard, Albert Hill, and James G. Williams. Scores of smaller ranches scattered throughout the Goleta Valley had orange groves of under 300 trees.

When the Johnston Fruit Company discontinued packing oranges to concentrate full time on lemons, Goleta ranchers founded the Santa Barbara County Orange Growers' Association. Dr. Franklin, of Goleta, was president, the directors including Bill Main, Bud McSpadden (a nephew of Will Rogers), Ernest Sexton, Chester Rich and E. W. Hoffman.

While building and subdividing were at a virtual standstill in the Valley throughout the 1930s—lots fronting on the ocean at Isla Vista could hardly be given away, due to lack of water—it was during this stagnant period that "Old Goleta," the settlement which in the late 1860s had had its nucleus at the intersection of Hollister and Patterson Avenues, faded in favor of its rival, La Patera.

The removal of the elementary school from Patterson Avenue to a site west of San Jose Creek in 1927 was the first sign of decay setting in at Old Goleta. Then the death blow came in 1933, when the post office moved from Ed Blakeway's store to 5980 Hollister Avenue in La Patera, two doors east of the corner of Hollister and Orange. This definitely established "New Goleta" at La Patera, leaving the only Hollister-Patterson buildings of importance the 1875 Methodist Church (by then the Goleta Farm Bureau Hall), and the 1884 Baptist Church. Because of the post office, Goleta replaced La Patera as a name on future maps.

Emerging as notable citizens of "New Goleta" were such personages as Jim Smith, last of the village blacksmiths, and a new country judge, W. T. Lillard, who followed Tom Clancy as Justice of the Peace and, with the help of his wife, Mae Pickett Lillard, meted out justice to wrongdoers until he retired in 1956.

The most notable landmark shift in the town of Goleta during the Thirties was the gradual transformation of the sprawling Goleta Slough into a commercial airport. The first airplane ever to chase its shadow across the checkerboard fields and orchards of the Good Land was a flimsy flying machine belonging to barnstorming aviator Lincoln Beachey. At an Air Circus in Hope Ranch in March,

1914, Beachey flew as far down the Valley as Ellwood Canyon, at some 2,000 feet altitude, and then crash-landed in an oak tree near Laguna Blanca after a near-fatal demonstration of looping the loop.

Six years later, in 1920, a fleet of forest fire spotting war surplus biplanes operated from a makeshift airfield on the boggy terrain south of Hollister Avenue between Storke and Los Carneros Roads. These crates, powered with OX-5 engines, were prone to ground-loop end over end when touching down on the soggy turf.

In 1928, two aviators named Gordon Sackett and Royce Stetson landed their light Hisso plane on a cow pasture near Hollister and Fairview, behind the old St. Raphael's Catholic Church. They leased land from the owners, Oakley & Bonetti, so as to open a flying school.

Leo Hanley, county road foreman at Goleta, had William Stronach and Charley Jones take a county road grader and scrape off a makeshift landing strip, entailing the removal of many thickets of age-old willows, running some 3,000 feet southwesterly toward the marshes of the Goleta Slough. This "airport" had but one rival, Earle Ovington's tiny Cosa Loma field near the Samarkand Hills in Santa Barbara, regarded by many fliers as a death trap.

In 1930, chief test pilot Harry Fisher of the General Western Aircraft Corporation of Burbank inspected the new Goleta Airport, and was sufficiently impressed that General Western moved its little factory from Burbank to the W. D. V. Smith property in Goleta.

Several Meteor airplanes were manufactured there, but the financial maneuverings of promoter Louis F. Vremask brought collapse to the firm in 1932. This plane was said to be the first to have a metal rather than a wooden propellor. Many a Goleta citizen took his first airplane ride from Great Western's shortlived flying school at Goleta Airport during the early 1930s.

Then Frederick Stearns II, a stepson of Harold G. Chase of Hope Ranch, established the Santa Barbara Airways at Goleta. He built two small hangars south of Hollister near Fairview, still in use in 1966, and graded two runways. The main strip ran 3,500 feet southwesterly, overlapping the original Sackett-Stetson strip. An alternate runway, partially paved, paralleled Fairview Avenue for 3,200 feet. It was situated immediately west of the Santa Barbara Packing

The Depression Years: Airports and Avocados 291

Company's malodorous eyesore, the slaughterhouse, which Emmett Gammill operated on lower Fairview Avenue for years. Pilots making night landings at Goleta did not need radio signals or lighted signs to tell them where they were—the stockyard effluvium arising from the slaughterhouse told them. Stearns was the first to install radio equipment at Goleta Airport. Carl Putnam's Pacific Seaboard Airlines was the first to serve Santa Barbara customers.

In the spring of 1936, Burton and Jessie Bundy opened their Santa Barbara Flying Service, utilizing two pioneer hangars there, a business they conducted until 1961. United Air Lines inaugurated daily passenger flights to Goleta on October 1, 1936, with more than 1,000 citizens on hand to welcome the first ten-passenger Boeing.

Election year 1936 was enlivened in the Valley by the vehement refusal of Jim Smith to head the local "Republicans for Franklin D. Roosevelt" campaign. Another rugged individualist, C. A. Storke, died on December 6 at the age of 89, closing the book on one of the Good Land's most colorful pioneer figures. His equally aggressive and ambitious son, Tom, took over the Storke interests in Goleta.

In June of 1937, T. M. Storke leased a small plot of land from Miriam More near the western end of More Mesa, where he erected two 258-foot steel towers, spaced 403 feet apart, to support the antenna of a new radio station bearing his initials—KTMS.

There was vigorous opposition from local pilots, who felt the radio towers constituted a navigational hazard in bad weather or after dark, but the Department of Commerce, forerunners of the Federal Communications Commission, ruled otherwise.

On the last day of October, 1937, *News-Press* station KTMS went on the air with 1,000 watts of power, eventually being assigned a permanent frequency slot of 1250 kilocycles. The KTMS towers, later fitted with "top hat" radiators, now broadcast in a directional pattern from Malibu to Morro Bay.

On Thursday, May 19, 1938, in recognition of National Air Mail Week, Goleta's newly-appointed postmaster, Charles Beguhl, handed a sack of mail to a Montecito aviatrix, Miss Bessie Owen, who flew it from Goleta to Ventucopa—the first, and probably the last direct airmail service between those two points. The same day, pilot Burton O. Bundy flew air mail pouches direct from Goleta to

Lompoc, Santa Maria, and Los Olivos, for the first time on record. One of Bundy's aerial escorts was Goleta's flying farmer, young Dee Pomatto, of Glen Annie Canyon.

Modern radio beam signalling systems were installed at the Goleta airport in August, 1939. The following year, the Santa Barbara Chamber of Commerce appointed a committee composed of U. S. Senator W. G. McAdoo, Dwight Murphy, and Earle Ovington to make a survey for a municipal airport site. They recommended the Goleta Slough area.

Philanthropist and art patron Buell Hammett of Montecito, on his own, commissioned real estate broker Roy Metz to quietly track down and acquire title from the owners of lots in the Oakley-Bonetti subdivision, scattered all over the world, with the idea of purchasing the Goleta Slough area for an airport and holding it until such time as the city could afford to buy it.

The McAdoo Committee obtained an option from Harold G. Chase and Peter Cooper Bryce of Hope Ranch Park to purchase 450 additional acres of Goleta Slough for $175,000. The committee estimated it would cost at least $1,000,000 to reclaim the Slough's overflow lands for airport use, which was a figure far beyond Santa Barbara's ability to raise. However, the federal government was establishing a chain of 250 airports around the country on a cost-sharing basis with municipalities, as a defense precaution in the event of war. The Santa Barbara Chamber of Commerce handed the Chase-Bryce $175,000 option to T. M. Storke along with instructions to see what he could do about getting Santa Barbara added to the federal airport program.

Storke departed for the 1940 National Democratic Convention as a delegate from California. Through a fortuitous meeting with an important government official in Chicago, he was able to pull enough strings in Washington to get a federal pledge to construct a modern air terminal at Goleta, if the city provided the land.*

In February, 1941, the voters of the City of Santa Barbara passed a $149,000 bond issue to start the airport ball rolling. The fifty-acre

---

* For the amazing inside details, read Chapter 52 of Thomas M. Storke's memoirs, *California Editor*, Westernlore Press, Los Angeles, 1958.

Goleta "Better Roads Committee" on 1912 inspection tour. Joe Sexton, George Williams, George S. Edwards, Frank E. Kellogg and other prominent local citizens in group. Taken on Hollister Avenue, looking west from Turnpike Road

This truly historic photograph shows Goleta's first automobile, a curved dash "Merry Oldsmobile" (converted from tiller bar to steering wheel by Horace A. Sexton). Joseph and Lucy Foster Sexton in car, parked beside their Goleta home, around 1908. Neither learned how to drive a horseless carriage, however

Right: This 1915 view shows one of the first tractors in Goleta Valley, on T. B. Bishop Ranch. It was built by Holt

Pigeon cotes at Elmer Kellogg's "Potter Farm" kept 60,000 squabs ready for Potter Hotel's gourmet menus. Located at what is now 749 Ward Drive at edge of the airport

The Goleta Valley's first airplane crash occurred on August 3, 1920, at the corner of Hollister Avenue and Los Carneros Road, when pilot of forest service lookout biplane ground-looped on marshy landing strip—but walked away unhurt. Mary Shaw, living nearby, snapped the photo

Goleta's first Volunteer Fire Department personnel pose with fifty-gallon soda-acid cart, purchased by popular subscription in 1914. This was town's only fire protection for nearly thirty years. Left to right: Frank Simpson, Ed Blakeway, Harry Sexton and Harry Cunningham

Goleta Walnut Growers' warehouse was first to get electric lights—circa year 1914

Goleta's first "filling station" and garage was opened by Ernie Vogel near 236 South Magnolia off Hollister, in the year 1920

Intersection of Hollister and Fairview Avenues looking west in 1925 at Catholic Church on corner long occupied by Seaside station. Slough tidewater came under church which stood on stubby pilings

Looking west on Hollister Avenue at intersection of Patterson Avenue in 1925. When post office moved from Blakeway's Store (right) in 1933 to La Patera district, Goleta Village rapidly disappeared

New Goleta Union School as it appeared September 1927. Contractor went bankrupt completing the $65,000 job. This school consolidated La Patera, Cathedral Oaks and Goleta Schools

The Santa Barbara earthquake of June 29, 1925, did heavy damage in the Goleta Valley, but took no lives. Above left, a garage on Hollister Avenue lost part of facade. Upper right, brick veneer fell from bunkhouse on Pomatto Brothers ranch, built by Col. Hollister in 1870s. Below right, the "Haunted Chapel" at Naples, overlooking Dos Pueblos Canyon, was so badly damaged it was torn down and stone blocks used to build existing ranch walls

Earthquake fissures beside Highway near Tecolote Cut are measured by State inspector

Juan Hill Adobe (below) on North Patterson Avenue was principal historic landmark lost in quake

The Depression Years: Airports and Avocados 293

Oakley-Bonetti tract was obtained for $30,000. Pacific Lighting Gas Supply Corporation sold the city surface rights to 528 acres of its gas storage facility for $63,000. The Civil Aeronautics Authority allocated $533,400 for airport construction, and the city exercised its option for the Chase-Bryce land.

Ground-breaking ceremonies for the Santa Barbara Municipal Airport were held on June 9, 1941, staged jointly at a mammoth barbeque by the Goleta Rotary, Goleta Lions, Woman's Club, valley PTA units, and the Goleta Farm Bureau. (The Goleta Rotary Club had been founded June 13, 1936, with Dr. Lee Streaker as its first president. The Goleta Lions Club followed on March 28, 1941, with Stan Pateman as first president.)

Things began to hum around the Goleta Slough. By mid-summer the federal government had appropriated the CAB's allotment for grading and filling the slough lowlands, and another $385,000 for paving the runways. (Within a few months another $84,000 was granted to extend the runways to meet military requirements, making a total of $902,400 in federal funds available for the Goleta job.)

Heavy earth-moving equipment manned by the Army Corps of Engineers began arriving in the early fall of 1941, to begin the herculean task of raising the level of a large portion of the Goleta Slough by nine to twelve feet.

Where could such a mountain of cheap fill dirt be found? In looking around for a source of supply, the Army Engineers spotted Mescalitán Island, and the bulldozers went to work truncating that prehistoric treasure house of Indian relics.

The Santa Barbara Museum of Natural History, realizing this was the last chance archeologists would ever have to rescue prehistoric skeletons and artifacts from Mescalitán, sent curator Phil C. Orr to the island, where he worked at top speed uncovering Canaliño burials for later museum display. If the bones of *conquistador* Juan Rodríguez Cabrillo reposed on Mescalitán Island, they were never found and identified.

By the end of November, millions of cubic yards of earth had been sliced off the flanks of centuried Mescalitán, and spread over the surrounding landscape where airstrips would be paved.

... On the first Sunday in December, a sizeable delegation of history-minded Goleta residents motored out to the Lompoc Valley to attend ceremonies dedicating the new Purísima Concepción Mission State Park. The ruined mission had been restored to its original Spanish appearance by WPA and CCC labor.

At the precise moment that a chaplain was invoking God's blessing on the restored Purísima Mission, some 2,500 miles over the blue horizon to the Southwest, a squadron of carrier-based warplanes, bearing the Rising Sun insignia of Imperial Japan, were leveling off to begin their bombing runs over an unsuspecting Hawaiian target: the U. S. Navy base at Pearl Harbor.

CHAPTER XXIX

Strange Interlude: Sub Attack at Ellwood!

John Hirashima was not among the Goletans who journeyed to Lompoc to attend the Purísima dedication ceremonies. He was a humble, hard-working, highly-respected little Japanese farmer who raised walnuts on land now engulfed by Highway 101 at the Fairview overpass. At mid-day on this Sunday, December 7, 1941, he and his son, Tom, were repairing the roof of their house when they saw a neighbor, Charley Jones, running toward them from his home which stood on the present site of Bray's 101 Restaurant.

"*It just came over the radio!*" Jones was yelling in a frantic voice. "*Japanese warplanes are bombing Hawaii!*"

John and Tom Hirashima went numb. If Japan and the United States were at war, it meant the Hirashimas were enemy aliens. Ironically, Tom's brother, Bill, was a GI at the Army Intelligence School at San Francisco Presidio.

"We felt the world had ended for us," Tom recalled years afterward, when he was the successful proprietor of a Goleta garden supply store. "We might be put in prison, or lose our land—we didn't know what."

History's day that would "live in infamy" ignited a holocaust of anti-Japanese feeling everywhere. "Remember Pearl Harbor" became the watchword of World War II. In the Goleta Valley there were only a few Japanese aliens—the George K. Riusakis at 185 South Patterson, the Honda family who worked at the Walora Ranch, a Japanese chef at Frank Bishop's home, and the Hirashimas. There was the inevitable hysteria about espionage and sabotage, but Goleta's law-abiding Japanese residents created no trouble, nor were they ever subjected to wartime bigotry and persecution. Eventually, in April, they were evacuated by government order to relocation camps in Arizona.

Goletans followed the rest of America in adjusting their lives to wartime austerity. An air-raid siren was installed at Tecolote and Hollister Avenue. Young men left their parental lemon ranches to enlist in the armed forces. A "Victory Billboard" listed 97 Goleta boys in the Army, 60 in the Navy, 39 in the Army Air Corps, 19 in the Marine Corps and one woman in the Army Nurse Corps.

At the outbreak of the war, Goleta was served by a lively little weekly, the *Leader*, published by Frank and Esther Selover. It featured a historical column by blacksmith Jim Smith, who took his pay in a display ad urging his customers to get their farm implements repaired while spare parts were still available.

Spy scares came daily. The Valley still chuckles about one of them. A German alien who lived on the high knoll at 533 North Patterson Avenue, above University Drive, had a spat with his wife one night. She was an air raid block warden. To annoy her, he raised the window blackout shade. She lowered it. He raised it. She lowered it, *ad infinitum*. From the floor of the Valley and to all the ships at sea, the illusion was that of Morse code signals being flashed from a spy's aerie!

Rumors flowered like weeds in springtime. One rumor that was to become a reality shortly was that the Navy was going to take over the Goleta airport and establish a training base for Marine pilots.

Aircraft-spotting stations were built from Tecolote Canyon to Sellar Bullard's Far Horizons Ranch, and on to the hills of Hope Ranch, manned around the clock by civilian volunteers, including such busy and important men as Edgar Stow, Earl Johnstone and Joe Sexton Jr.

Fishermen operating from the Goleta pier were alerted to be on the watch for enemy submarines or surface craft, since a Japanese assault on the West Coast was feared any day after Pearl Harbor.

The Army emplaced a World War I howitzer near the Barnsdall Oil Company plant at Ellwood, and another big gun on the Campbell Ranch at Coal Oil Point. The Coast Guard assigned a patrol boat to the Channel. Supervisor J. Monroe Rutherford became Civilian

Strange Interlude: Sub Attack at Ellwood! 297

Defense chief. The army moved a few GIs into the area and spread them along the coastline for shore patrol, in case the Japanese landed saboteurs by raft.

Such were Goleta's defenses as the war entered its twelfth week on February 16, 1942. During that week, fishermen and shore patrols reported sighting several submarines; their Diesels could be heard at night as they cruised on the surface to recharge their batteries. Not all these subs could be identified as American.

Lieutenant George W. Goman USN, in charge of the Naval Intelligence office in Santa Barbara, on February 16 received a telephone report from a Barnsdall Oil office employee at Ellwood, stating that a big sub had surfaced off the Barnsdall pier, with men clustered around a cannon on deck. Goman notified his superiors in San Diego. No American sub being in the area, two patrol planes were sent north, but by the time they arrived the sub was long gone.

Three days later, the lookout at the Barnsdall plant again reported to Lt. Goman that the same submarine was lying to in the same spot. This time Lt. Goman drove out to Ellwood in time to see the submarine in the act of submerging. Again he reported to 11th District Headquarters in 'Dago. This time he was told "Stop sending us these submarine sighting stories—the coast is full of California gray whales. That is what you're seeing, not subs."

Goman groaned with frustration. "A whale is twenty feet long," he said. "This submarine is 300 feet long."

Several significant things happened during the week. The Coast Guard withdrew its patrol boat on February 22, transferring it south. The Marines transferred a fleet of patrol bombers which had been standing by for emergencies at Goleta airport. The Army pulled out all its men from the coast except a sergeant and two privates, who were stationed at Ellwood oil field. The two howitzers were loaded aboard trucks and hauled to other assignments.

In short, by the Washington's Birthday holiday weekend of 1942, the U.S. had withdrawn all its military defenses from the Goleta area, leaving only the civilian volunteers at aircraft spotting stations.

Monday, February 23, 1942, was a holiday in honor of Washington's Birthday, which fell on a Sunday. President Franklin D. Roosevelt was scheduled to deliver one of his intimate "Fireside Chats" over national radio networks at 7 p.m. Fate had decreed that hour to be the moment in time when Goleta, the Good Land, would keep its most dramatic tryst with history.

Nine out of ten people in the Goleta Valley were waiting at their radio sets for the President to begin his talk, which was on the subject of America's coastal defenses in the event of a Japanese invasion by sea and air.

At that very moment, a few miles out in the Channel, a giant I-series submarine of the Japanese Imperial Navy, the I-17, surfaced in the twilight. Her lookout, signalman Takeo Aiba, stood on the conning tower, focusing his binoculars on the Ellwood oil tanks.

The I-17 was 348 feet long, displacing 1,950 tons. She had a surface cruising range of 16,000 miles at twenty-four knots, and was capable of remaining at sea for three months with a crew of eighty-five men. She mounted a watertight hangar and reconnaissance plane forward of the conning tower. On the after deck was a 5.5-inch cannon. Fore and aft were six torpedo tubes.

The I-17 was under the command of Kozo Nishino, one of the most experienced underwater skippers in the Japanese Sixth Fleet. He had visited Ellwood many times before the war, loading crude oil in a navy tanker. He and his crew had taken part in patrolling Hawaiian waters at the time of the sneak attack on Pearl Harbor; they had stalked an aircraft carrier for weeks. Within the past few days she had torpedoed and sunk two American tankers off the Oregon coast. Now the I-17 had cruised to the Santa Barbara Channel with orders to bombard the Ellwood oil installations near Goleta—Tojo's first mainland target of the war against America!

In plain view of shore observers, who were not aware that the monster was an enemy sub, Nishino steered up the coast a few miles and then reversed course to cruise eastward. No hostile planes were in the sundown-tinted sky. The weather was fair, the sea smooth as glass.

Commander Nishino shouted an order below. Nine ratings swarmed monkeylike up the ladders onto the bridge—the crew of the 5.5-inch deck gun. Lieutenant Nambu, executive officer, maneuvered the sub's rudders by periscope from his station at the base of the conning tower. In the engine room Lt. Commander Yamazaki, the chief engineer idled his propellers to steady the I-17 for the firing to come.

... On shore, Goleta Valley residents tuned in their radios to KTMS or KFI to pick up the opening words of President Roosevelt's Fireside Chat:

My friends . . . Washington's Birthday is a most appropriate time for us to talk with each other about things as they are today and things as we know they shall be. . . .

At exactly 1907 hours, seven minutes after seven p.m., the seafowls feeding along the beach at Ellwood were scattered by an ear-jolting explosion from seaward. A malignant red flash briefly illumined the sky. A projectile made a low arc over the Barnsdall absorption plant and bored harmlessly into a hill on the flanks of Ellwood Canyon, a mile inland, without exploding.

At the Signal Oil & Gas lease on the western rim of the Ellwood Field, superintendent Greg Reay, his wife, and a friend, John Philip, were listening to FDR when they felt the cottage jolt to the concussion of a heavy detonation. They hurried out of doors and stood staring in disbelief at the spectacle of a submarine lobbing shells ashore off the Bankline lease. Reay was sure Signal's gas absorption plant in nearby Hydrocarbon Gulch would be the next target, so he herded his employees into the shelter of a nearby railroad cut before starting fire-prevention procedures.

Barnsdall's production superintendent, Ferris W. Borden, writes:

The sub was firing not far from the Bankline marine loading buoys, which would make the range in the order of one mile off shore. . . . A plot of the hits indicate the prime target was the Richfield tanks near the highway, but no damage resulted. There was no retaliatory action taken by either military or civilian personnel at the time of the shelling.

Borden's last comment nullifies the legend that he snatched up a .30-06 hunting rifle and opened fire on the sub's gun crew.

A short distance down the coast east of the Ellwood Oil Field piers, James Anderson, custodian of the Ellwood Union School, left his radio set to run out and watch the shelling. The sub was so large he at first mistook it for a cruiser.

Meanwhile the soldiers stationed at Ellwood, unable to find a telephone from which to make a report to headquarters, wound up at the Campbell Ranch on Coal Oil Point, where only that day a coastal defense battery, mounted on a concrete emplacement, had been removed and shipped elsewhere.

Mr. and Mrs. George Churchill, custodians of the Campbell Ranch, were advised by the soldiers to leave the premises for their own safety, but refused to desert their posts.

The soldiers were unable to get a telephone message out; the lines were jammed by civilian calls asking the operators what the shooting was all about. To sum up the general situation during the attack—unbelievably poor marksmanship on the part of the Japanese gun crew; military and civilian chaos on shore.

However, one telephone message *did* get outside before the circuits became hopelessly jammed. A civilian contractor, Harold Conklin, was on duty at the lonely aircraft spotting tower at Tecolote Canyon. *Thirteen minutes after the submarine attack started*, at 7:20 p.m., Conklin and his partner, a man named Peirce, dispatched Army Flash No. 82261 to the West Los Angeles Filter Center. Then they relaxed, knowing that in a very short time the sky should be filled with American bombers which would blast the enemy sub out of the water.

Conklin and Peirce waited, and waited. *But no planes came.*

... A short distance east of the overpass where Hollister Avenue (then Highway 101) crosses over the railroad, Mr. and Mrs. Lawrence Wheeler operated a popular roadside restaurant, Wheeler's Inn. Among the customers enjoying the camaraderie of their friends at the Inn that night, while they listened to FDR's Fireside Chat, was Supervisor J. Monroe Rutherford, in charge of the county's Civilian Defense.

With shells whistling overhead, Monroe dismissed the cannonading as coastal defense practice, and went home. He admitted many years afterward "I didn't even know it was a Jap raid until I read about it in the paper next day."

Shortly after Rutherford left, the doors of Wheeler's Inn slammed open and Kenneth D. Roloson of the Santa Barbara *News-Press* circulation department rushed in, accompanied by George O. Wolf.

Strange Interlude: Sub Attack at Ellwood!

"That's an enemy submarine shooting at us!" Roloson yelled. "I climbed up my windmill tower and saw it plain as day!"

Down the coast at the southwestern corner of Hope Ranch, a self-appointed submarine spotter, Mrs. Fredericka Ganes Moffatt, and her husband, a prominent Santa Barbara Clinic endocrinologist, Dr. Paul Moffatt, were eye-witnesses to the drama off Ellwood. The written report Mrs. Moffatt filed with Naval Intelligence that night contained the startling information that she and her husband had seen not one, but *three* submarines lobbing shells into the Valley!

In 1965 Mrs. Moffatt stated for publication in this book:

From all I could learn from careful questioning of nearly everybody who lived along the coast from here to Ellwood, my husband and I were the only two people who actually saw the firing from all three submarines. The Navy knew there were three, but told us at midnight that for the time being, the story was to be that there was only one. . . .

By 7:30 the entire Goleta Valley was buzzing like an upset beehive, as the cannonading continued at leisurely intervals. Another *News-Press* deliveryman, German-born Karl Mueller, was at the Trout Club on the west flank of San Marcos Pass. From his vantage point 1,200 feet above sea level, he counted twenty-nine muzzle flashes in all.

Mueller put in the first call to the city desk of the *News-Press* to report the Ellwood shelling. A bored night editor told Mueller he was "loco" and hung up in his ear. Before many minutes had elapsed, however, the *News-Press* switchboard became well aware that the scoop of the century was taking place up at Ellwood.

Traffic on Highway 101 was moving along briskly without so much as observing dimout, let alone blackout rules. Most of the drivers were listening to the President's talk on their car radios. They were puzzled, but not yet alarmed, by the "fireworks" visible off shore as they approached Ellwood.

Al Weatherbee, Goleta's veteran RFD mailman, was returning with his wife that night from a holiday weekend in San Luis Obispo. As they reached the Ellwood Overpass, a shell missed their car roof by inches, the airwhip almost jerking the steering wheel out of Mrs. Weatherbee's grasp. The accompanying thunder-loud crack of sound made her think she had had a tire blow out, but her husband yelled "That's somebody shooting at us—let's get out of here fast!"

Mrs. Weatherbee braked to a halt at Wheeler's Inn, where a small crowd had collected outside to watch the show. She ran to a telephone and by some miracle got through to radio station KTMS. "That submarine homed in on the red signal lights on your Goleta antenna masts," she told the station engineer. "Turn 'em off!" Before she had time to rejoin her husband in the car, the flashing red beacons on the 258-foot radio towers on More Mesa blacked out.

Another motorist on the road that memorable night was Miss Mary Barnes, of Glendale, now Mrs. Donald F. Allen, of Santa Barbara. She also pulled off the road at Wheeler's Inn to find out what all the explosions were about. Upon being told that a Japanese submarine was attacking, she

> drove as fast as possible through quiet, unsuspecting Santa Barbara, and was not stopped until I reached Ventura. One thing was never explained to me. As I hurriedly left Ellwood, I saw a flare slowly floating down out of the sky in the direction of the mountains to my left. Was that fired from the submarine? Or did someone send it up as a signal to help the Japs?

That question was never answered, officially or otherwise.

By 8:00 p.m. a full blackout was in effect from Monterey to San Diego. Radio stations had signed off the air to prevent enemy ships from using their signals as directional beams. All traffic was being halted on Highway 101 between Gaviota and Ventura to enforce full blackout. Pressed into service at Wheeler's Inn to flag down passing cars were three unsung heroines, waitresses Esther Sexton, Josephine Thompson and Estelle Staneff.

The shelling ceased around 7:45 p.m. The submarine, while it did not submerge, vanished into the mists off Dos Pueblos, bound for the open sea. Navy radiomen manning a shortwave monitoring station at Pt. Arguello intercepted a coded report purporting to be originating from a Japanese submarine and directed to Emperor Hirohito in Tokyo. It boasted that they had left Santa Barbara "a seething mass of flames, with wild panic visible on shore."

There were no flames, but of panic there was plenty. No amount of postwar Pentagon whitewash can gloss over the fact that both the military and civilian defenses of Ellwood were found shamefully wanting that memorable night of February 23, 1942.

What had happened to the 7:20 p.m. telephone report which Harold Conklin had flashed to the Filter Center in West Los Angeles? Land-based planes should have answered that call within forty minutes at the outside. Yet it was not until around 10 p.m., almost three hours after the first shot was fired by the sub, that a squadron of U.S. planes began dropping flares over the waters off Ellwood.

The planes had come from an air base near Bakersfield. Their flares turned night into day, even illuminating the canyons and ridges on the Channel Islands thirty miles away. But by this time Kozo Nishino's giant submarine was comfortably out at sea. When dawn finally broke on February 24, the Ellwood area swarmed with military personnel. Lt. Goman, who with his assistant, Lt. Francis Price Jr., had spent a hectic night out at the oil field, recalled twenty-three years after the event:

Around noon next day a large artillery detachment came in and camped on the grounds. They made a great display as though they were arriving just in time to save the day. They remained there a day or two, and then were moved to another semi-permanent site nearer Goleta. I read later that the officer commanding the detachment had been commended for his action in connection with the shelling—though he arrived on the scene 17 or 18 hours after it was over!

Needless to say, the Navy brass no longer chided Lt. Goman for mistaking California whales for enemy submarines.

In broad daylight, experts assessed the damage caused by the submarine bombardment and found it to be minuscule. Four out of five shells fired had proved to be duds. Their casings were plentifully inscribed with Japanese ideographs, as if in an effort to convince people they had been delivered in anger by the enemy.

Rancher Jack Hollister found a dud shell on a hill above Winchester Canyon which, if it had had a trajectory one foot higher, might have scored a direct hit on his home further inland. (Years later, during the 1955 Refugio Fire, mysterious explosions in the brush behind Winchester Canyon, on the John K. Wade homestead, were believed to have been caused by dud shells from the 1942 attack, duds which had rusted unnoticed in the thick brush until set off by the intense heat.)

A lemon worker picked up another unexploded shell in Tecolote Canyon and tossed it in the bed of his pick-up truck. At noontime he took it in to the ranch and gave superintendent Bill Smith the fright of his life. All recovered unexploded shells were picked up by trained demolition crews, defused and flown back to a naval ordnance laboratory in Maryland for examination.

Total damage from the attack was finally assessed at $500. This included a cracked reduction gear casing on an oil well pump at Luton-Bell No. 17, and a splintered catwalk railing. A nearby sheet-iron shed, and the plank decking and timbering of the Bankline pier, were peppered with steel fragments. GIs on guard duty did a land-office business picking up bits of shrapnel and peddling them to the throngs of sightseers who lined Highway 101 for days after the attack.

Dairyman Russel Doty of Ellwood Canyon had his entire milking crew panic and desert for the purlieus of their native land, Oklahoma. This left him with a labor problem in rounding up milkers to relieve the swollen udders of his valuable dairy cows.

Two days after the Ellwood raid, the United Press monitoring station in San Francisco recorded and translated this broadcast from Radio Tokyo to the Japanese people:

The U. S. War Dept. officially announced that Santa Barbara, California, was devastated by enemy bombardment, admitting that a Japanese submarine suddenly appeared on the waters 20 miles (sic) west and shelled military establishments in the neighborhood of Ellwood. The U. S. is not publicizing this damage, however, for fear of the impact on the minds of the public.

Many brave Santa Barbarans fled from California, even without benefit of scary publicity, leaving their property to be sold for whatever it would bring. Some of the biggest real estate bargains on record were picked up by alert buyers after the 1942 raid.

According to records of the Japanese Imperial Navy, examined by American intelligence officers after V-J Day, 1945, this is what happened to the submarine I-17 after she "left Santa Barbara in flames": She spent the next fortnight preying on Pacific shipping

Strange Interlude: Sub Attack at Ellwood! 305

between Cape Mendocino and San Francisco, then sailed back to her home base at Yokosuka, arriving there the end of March, 1942.

Later the I-17 went on a tour of the Aleutians, after which Commander Nishino left her to accept another post. This was lucky for Nishino, because his submarine's next tour of duty, to the Solomon Islands, ended in disaster. On August 19, 1943, the I-17 was destroyed off Noumea, New Caledonia, in a running surface battle with a New Zealand minesweeper and two shore-based U.S. Navy planes. Six Japanese crewmen were rescued after the I-17 went to the bottom. From them, U.S. Naval Intelligence interrogators were able to piece together details of the Ellwood bombing of February 23, 1942, as related in these pages.

In October, 1956, President Charles S. Jones of the Richfield Oil Company, told the Channel City Club this interesting story:

The Battle of Ellwood actually began in the early 1930s, when the tank ships of many nations used to take on oil there. It was our custom to meet the captain of each ship, bring him ashore, and extend him our hospitality. On one occasion we welcomed a Japanese Captain [Kozo Nishino] and with great ceremony escorted him ashore. . . . Our guest fell into a great patch of prickly pear cactus growing near the beach trail. It was one of the most excruciating moments I can remember. Of course it cost our Japanese skipper an unbearable loss of face.

He left us in a polite but grim mood, but ten years later he returned, as Captain of the enemy submarine which shelled the very scene of his humiliation. . . .

Mr. Jones was not aware of another bizarre sidelight to his story: the cactus clump had been planted by Kate Den Bell in 1920, with the half-joking remark to her kinfolk that if they would drill an oil well where the cactus grew, they would strike a gusher. This prophesy came true two years after her death.

Mrs. Bell's sentimental son-in-law, Dr. George Luton, caused a welded iron fence to be put around the cactus clump to protect it from oil field trucking. It was into this spiny thicket of *nopal* that Kozo Nishino tumbled, to start one of the most incredible chain reactions in the annals of World War II.

Kate Bell's cactus patch, and Dr. Luton's iron fence, were still in existence in 1966, thirty-eight years after the oil strike.

So ends the strangest chapter in the history of the Good Land.

Or is it ended? Should we neatly tie the ribbons on a story so filled with coincidences and far-fetched solutions, a story which leaves so many nagging questions unanswered? For example:

How could the Japanese gun crew have missed a point-blank target 25 times, unless they were missing on purpose?

Why were a majority of the shells duds—were they supposed to be?

How could an enemy sub dare remain in plain sight for forty minutes—unless it knew there was no danger of counter attack?

A telephone message about the attack reached military headquarters thirteen minutes after the firing began. Why did it take nearly three hours for American planes to reach the scene?

Why were the Coast Guard patrol boat, the U.S. Army guard, the Navy patrol bombers at Goleta airport and the Coast Artillery's heavy guns removed from the Ellwood area just before the attack?

Was it more than mere coincidence that the submarine attack came precisely at the time when FDR was addressing the nation by radio concerning the need to step up the war effort?

These and other unsolved riddles could be explained if one could accept a simple hypothesis: *that the submarine was not Japanese, but American.*

A sizeable number of responsible Goleta citizens who were eyewitnesses to the 1942 raid believe this startling theory, even though they know they can never prove their case. They point out that the hoax could have been planned as a dramatic, harmless way to wake up the lethargic American public to the fact that we were in a shooting war, at a time when war bond sales were lagging, blackout restrictions were being winked at, and Civil Defense was bogged down in play-soldier red tape.

The Goleta Valley eye-witnesses who suggest in private that the submarine was American are, it must be admitted, in the minority. The consensus has always been that Fate chose Goleta, the Good Land, to be the target for the first enemy naval bombardment of the American mainland since the War of 1812. So be it. This researcher does not profess to know the answer. But he does agree there is a shadow of a doubt as to what *really* happened at Ellwood that wild night in February 1942.

CHAPTER XXX

From Marine Base to State University

Under the whiplash of a shooting war which had come much too close for comfort, construction work on the Goleta airport was stepped up to a round-the-clock operation. The old slaughterhouse on the west side of Fairview Avenue below Hollister was removed, and an endless train of bulldozers and earth-movers raised the ground level with nine feet of fill dirt, the familiar skyline of Mescalitán Island shrinking proportionately.

In January, 1942, the Goleta Sanitary District was formed, to provide sewage disposal for the 1,500 persons residing in a territory between Fairview and Kellogg Avenues, from the railroad to two blocks south of Hollister Avenue, plus the "Fairfield" tract where the old hog farm had been turned into a sub-standard subdivision.

Almost immediately the new Sanitary District suspended its plans, having been reliably informed that the U. S. Navy was going to lease the airport from the city for a Marine pilot training base.

Meanwhile the women of the Good Land did their share for the accelerating war effort by setting up a completely-equipped Disaster Center in the Farm Center Hall on Chapel Street. Dr. Lee Streaker conducted classes in first aid. Ruth Culver Hammond opened a casualty station with a stand-by staff of registered nurses on 24-hour call. Mrs. Lodovico Cavalletto, the former chief surgical nurse at St. Francis Hospital in Santa Barbara, outfitted a surgery room with a professional operating table, autoclave and anesthesia equipment. Miss Mariette Sexton donated seven beds. The American Red Cross supplied bedding, linens, bandages and medicines. Volunteer sewing groups were supervised by Rose Sexton Dearborn.

Practice runs were made in conjunction with Santa Barbara Civil Defense, where "casualties" furnished by the Goleta Boy Scouts were picked up in outlying areas, correctly tagged by teams of gas-masked disaster corpsmen, and transported by farm trucks to the Disaster Center for first aid treatment. Happily, the volunteers were never called upon to treat actual war casualties.

On June 14, 1942, the first contingent of civilian contractors arrived in Goleta to start construction of the new Marine Corps Air Station. A railroad spur was built to handle the heavy influx of materials and machinery; tenants on the T. B. Bishop property on the mesa overlooking the Slough were evacuated elsewhere.

The Navy had unlimited manpower, money and materials at its disposal, resulting in a crash program of construction during the latter half of 1942 which saw miracles accomplished.

The city leased the airport to the Navy for $2,600 a year (a rental which was never paid, by the way) at a time when that facility consisted of 580 acres of land, two small hangars, a new $40,000 United Airlines terminal, and four 4,000-foot runways which would have to be lengthened to 4,500 feet to make them suitable for military aircraft.

Because of the marshy terrain on the west side of the Slough, the operational and housing areas of the new air base had to be widely separated—a factor which was to completely reshape the future of Goleta after the war, by transforming it into a University center. The control tower, maintenance shops, hangars and related military operational buildings were built along both sides of Hollister Avenue, west of Fairview. The barracks, mess halls, chapels, post exchanges, theaters, laundry, administration buildings and other housing facilities for a small city had to be located on the old Gus Den ranch, on the mesa near Goleta Point.

A total of 103 temporary wooden buildings were constructed by the end of the year. They included twenty-nine barracks for a complement of 1,800 enlisted men, and ten barracks for 250 officers. A few taxpayers complained about "country club frills" such as an Olympic-sized swimming pool and deluxe appointments in the Officers' Club as being inappropriate extravagances during wartime, but the Navy ignored civilian critics. It was an open secret in the Marine Corps that the air station at Goleta was the plushiest assignment any gyrene could draw, with posh "rest homes" for combat-weary officers awaiting them on nearby Montecito's fabulous estates.

The enlisted men on the Goleta base also got a break, receiving the proceeds from a $10,000 lemon crop harvested annually on the Storke Ranch, which the Navy had acquired. This money went into various Company funds to provide athletic and recreational equipment, to stock libraries, and otherwise contribute to the morale of the non-commissioned officers and men on the post.

By the time the Marine base was officially activated on August 13, 1942, contractors had built a complete sewer system and disposal plant, and telephone and electrical systems for a city twice the size of Goleta itself.

Navy engineers were dismayed to find that the city airport's main north-south airport runway lay in a direct line with the three-story section of the Goleta Lemon Association's packing plant on La Patera Lane. This, the Navy brass declared, would never do; training planes could not take off or land at the north end of this runway with such a dangerous obstruction in the flight path. Lemon Association manager Granvel Caster was notified that his entire sprawling complex would have to be bodily moved out of the way —at an estimated cost of $1,500,000. Fortunately, some unsung guardian of the tax coffers came up with the simple idea of paving a parallel runway west of the existing one, thereby avoiding the Lemon Association obstacle, and at a cost of "only" $500,000. This was done, and fortunately so, inasmuch as the lemon packing plant burned to the ground a few years later.

Before they were finished, Marine engineers had laid 5,500,000 square feet of asphalt runways over what had been worthless swampland, turning a centuries-old eyesore into a community asset. The government's total investment in the Goleta Marine Air Station was over ten million dollars.

Formal commissioning of the facility took place on December 4, 1942, less than a year after the sneak attack on Pearl Harbor. An advanced echelon of Marine Base Defense Aircraft Group 42 arrived on January 11, 1943, and remained in Goleta for the duration of the war. Construction of the base was designated as officially complete on May 15, 1943.

Marine Base Defense Aircraft Group 48 was activated at the

Goleta station on August 3, 1944, and throughout the autumn months the squadrons carried on a heavy schedule of practice glide bombings, torpedo runs, rocket firing, gunnery runs, navigational flights and ground courses in synthetic and instrument training. On October 21, Goleta air station was named headquarters for Marine Carrier Groups to train pilots for anti-submarine and combat air patrols from Navy and Marine aircraft carriers.

A crane was built on the Goleta pleasure pier, from which was suspended the fuselage of an old bomber. A pilot and two crewmen, fully dressed and wearing parachutes and Mae West life jackets, would board the fuselage which would then be dropped from a height of fifteen feet into the water. With less than sixty seconds in which to escape the sinking hulk, the men had to inflate a life raft and abandon ship—a lesson which later saved lives in South Pacific combat. Trainees were also dropped from the crane to the water to simulate parachute landings in the ocean.

Goleta postmaster Charles A. Beguhl went into the Navy on July 1, 1944, with Loren "Butch" Howell named acting postmaster. He served until Beguhl's return from the service in September, 1946.

Training accidents killed an undisclosed number of embryo pilots who crashed in the brush-choked canyons and ridges of the Santa Ynez Mountains, in the waters off shore, and in Goleta itself. The worst single mishap occurred on January 2, 1945, when four pilots died in a midair collision between two torpedo bombers off Goleta Point.

The younger local matrons organized a U.S.O.-type organization to provide entertainment for the off-duty marines, including a coffee and doughnut canteen on Hollister Avenue. Mrs. Dee Pagliotti was the first president of this group, which evolved into the Goleta Woman's Service Club after the war. By the 1960s it was among the most active civic organizations in the Valley, largely replacing the activities of the pioneer Woman's Club, whose aging members turned more and more to social meetings rather than service projects.

In November, 1944, an event of considerable historical import occurred with the organization of the Goleta County Water District, one of five such districts tied in with a Department of the Interior reclamation project involving the proposed building of a flood control and water storage dam on the Santa Ynez River. In February, 1945, Fred Stevens was elected chairman of a board of directors which included Ben Hartman, Frank Baker, Bill Hollister and Chester Rich. Boundaries of the Water District ran from the Santa Barbara city limits on the east to the Ellwood School District (a north-south extension of Ellwood Station Road, between the beach and the upper foothills). The following October 17, the boards of the county's four Water Districts joined with Santa Ynez and Santa Barbara to select a future damsite. They agreed on a place called "Cachuma".

... The Signal Oil & Gas Company under Samuel B. Mosher bought the 4,500-acre Dos Pueblos Ranch from H. G. Wylie early in the war for $650,000. Supervisor J. Monroe Rutherford was superintendent of the ranching operations. The primary objective behind Signal's acquisition of the historic Nicolás A. Den ranch was to give Mosher's company upland drilling sites so his whip-stocked wells could "stick straws in the cider keg" of the vast newly-discovered Dos Pueblos oil reservoir under the Channel. The second of Mosher's thirty-odd oil wells was accidentally set on fire by a welder's torch on September 24, 1944. It erupted a 200-foot geyser of flame for more than a week before it was brought under control, with a loss of over fifty million cubic feet of gas and 3,500 barrels of crude oil. The flaming well was a spectacular sight for passing travelers on nearby Highway 101 and the S. P. railroad.

Beyond Dos Pueblos, on the Archie Edwards ranch, 300 Nazi prisoners of war were kept in a camp under the supervision of Bill Hollister, of Goleta. They were used to harvest local farm crops. In 1966 the barbed wire barricades, ten-man hutments and machine-gun tower of the old POW camp could still be seen from the highway.

An important by-product of the war years in the Goleta Valley was the development of dry-land tomato farming, a crop which commanded premium prices during the war. Sam Mosher cultivated a hilltop on his new ranch and netted a profit of $100,000 from non-irrigated tomatoes.

Although well past its peak production years, Goleta's famous Ellwood Oil Field was a potent asset to the allied war effort.

When the war ended with the dropping of the first atomic bomb on Japan, in August 1945, joy was mixed with sorrow in the Goleta Valley. Twelve of the Good Land's finest had been sacrificed on the altar of Mars. Their names joined those of World War I's casualties on John Troup's granite War Memorial in front of Goleta Union School. One of them was Troup's own son.

"Lest we forget," the publishers of this history, Post 55 of the American Veterans of World War II (Amvets), take solemn pride in saluting the memory of Goleta's war dead, several of whom were descendants of the Valley's earliest pioneers:

BETTY PAULINE STINE	JACK B. RICKARD
JOHN R. TROUP	JOHN MICONO
W. FRANKLIN BAKER	ROBERT DUREN
FRED C. McCLOSKEY	WILLIAM HARSHBERGER
DAVID LOVE	MANUEL DELGADO
CALVIN W. CLOER	CLARENCE SILVA

Goletans knew the war was over when, on October 10, 1945, a legion of heavy machinery commenced construction on the new two-lane highway between the Hollister Wye and Tecolote Creek (Ellwood Wye). Construction was completed January 17, 1947, at a total cost of $1,138,989, not including right-of-way.

On March 1, 1946, the Marine air base went on a caretaker basis. Spiders and mice moved into the barracks and shops and PXs. Dust gathered in the Olympic-sized swimming pool. Two months later, on May 1, the Navy declared the facility surplus and turned it over to the War Assets Administration—a move which was to have a profound significance to the Goleta Valley's future.

Miss Helena T. Devereux of Philadelphia, who since 1912 had pioneered in the field of teaching the slow-learning or emotionally-disturbed child, purchased the Murphy Estate in Montecito in 1945 as the site of her first Devereux School campus in the West (she had twenty campuses operating in the East).

Finding that the Montecito site was not large enough, Miss Devereux engaged the Harold Chase agency to search for a more suitable location. They found exactly what she was looking for at Coal Oil Point, west of the Goleta Marine base—the former Colin Campbell ranch, which had been shut down since 1941.

Col. Colin Campbell, the wealthy Englishman who bought the Coal Oil Point ranch (right) and made it into a showplace

At right is the Campbell mansion, cost $500,000, now part of Devereux Ranch School. Heavily damaged in 1925 earthquake

Left: Hollister Avenue looking west from Turnpike Road in 1924; below—R. W. Sherman, Barnsdall geologist, with Frank A. Morgan (right) who discovered Ellwood oil field. Discovery well Luton-Bell No. 1 derrick in background

Goleta in 1938, as viewed from air looking northeast (above, John Gorin photo) and southwest (below, Burt Bundy photo). Note empty spaces now occupied by Isla Vista; hayfield where Kellogg Tract is now located; empty land between Hollister Avenue and the foothills. Runway is the one built by Stearns

On October 1, 1936, United Air Lines inaugurated daily passenger service to Goleta airport, using ten-passenger Boeing "air liners". Large crowd greeted first arrivals

Above, 1941 flood, Fairview at Hollister; left, Ellwood oil field piers; below, minor damage inflicted by Japanese submarine raid of February 23, 1942

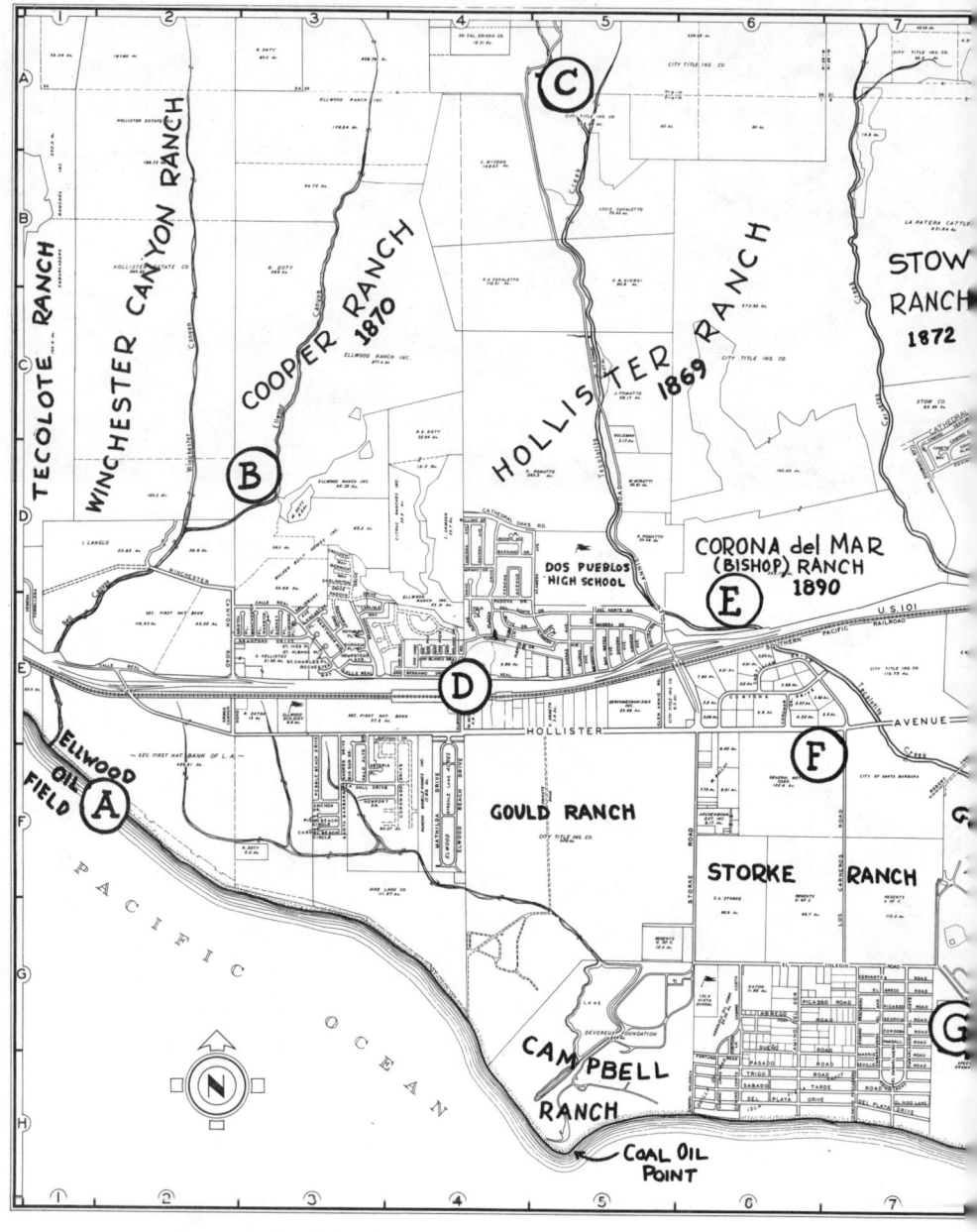

A—Scene of Japanese submarine attack, 1942
B—Site of Ellwood Cooper's olive mill, 1872
C—Site of Hollister's Glen Annie manorhouse, 1872
D—Site of SP railroad end-of-track, 1887 to 1901
E—Location of Colonel Hollister's "Lower Ranch", 1872-1890
F—Site of Goleta Valley's first airplane crash, 1920
G—Site of Alcatraz Asphalt Company deep shaft mine, 1890s
H—Emigh's Gold Mine one mile northeast of circle
I—Daniel Hill Adobe, the oldest home in Goleta Valley
J—Stagecoach route leading to Slippery Rock, 1868-1892
K—Site of La Patera Village, founded 1870

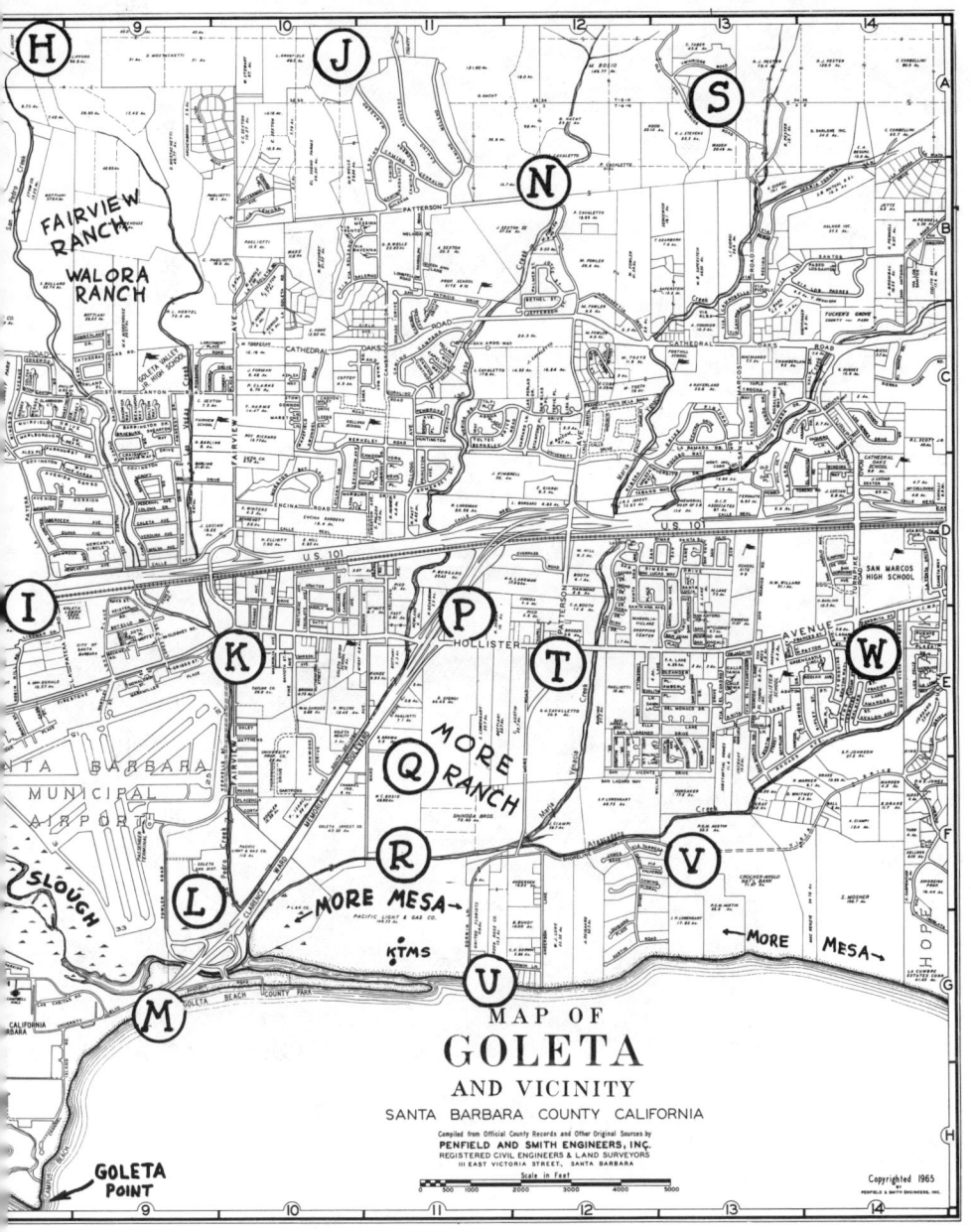

L—Mescalitán Island, Indian rancheria in 1542 and 1769
M—Site of old Goleta whaling camps, 1850-1900
N—Mission padres' 1804 winery, San Jose Vineyard
P—Site of Joseph Sexton's Nursery, founded 1869
Q—Site of Goleta's original railway station, 1887-1901
R—Benjamin Foxen's shipyard of 1828 (not authenticated)
S—Indian Orchard Ranch, orange trees planted 1838 still alive
T—Site of original Goleta town, established 1868
U—Site of More's Landing and asphaltum deposits, 1874
V—Dotted line indicates 1887-1901 S.P. railroad alignment
W—Location of pioneer Abel C. Scull ranch, established 1863

Original Sunkist packing plant built by Goleta Lemon Growers' Association in 1936 at the La Patera Lane railroad crossing west of Fairview Avenue

Incendiary fire after midnight on January 26, 1950, totally destroyed packing plant shown in top photograph. Loss added up to $1,500,000

By January 1, 1951, present Sunkist plant was ready to go, on former location. Lower left is Daniel Hill Adobe of 1850, oldest residence in Goleta Valley. Lemon plant is one of the largest of its kind in world

Thomas M. Storke
California editor

Dr. W. S. Franklin
of Walora Ranch

Bill Hollister
County Supervisor

Dr. Ian Crow, Supt.
Goleta Union School

William T. Lillard
Country Judge

J. Monroe Rutherford
County Supervisor

Jack Hollister
State Senator

Fred Stevens
County Supervisor

Daniel G. Grant
County Supervisor

Earthquake of July 1952 shook up lemon packing plant

Flood of December 1952 caused boating on South Fairview Ave.

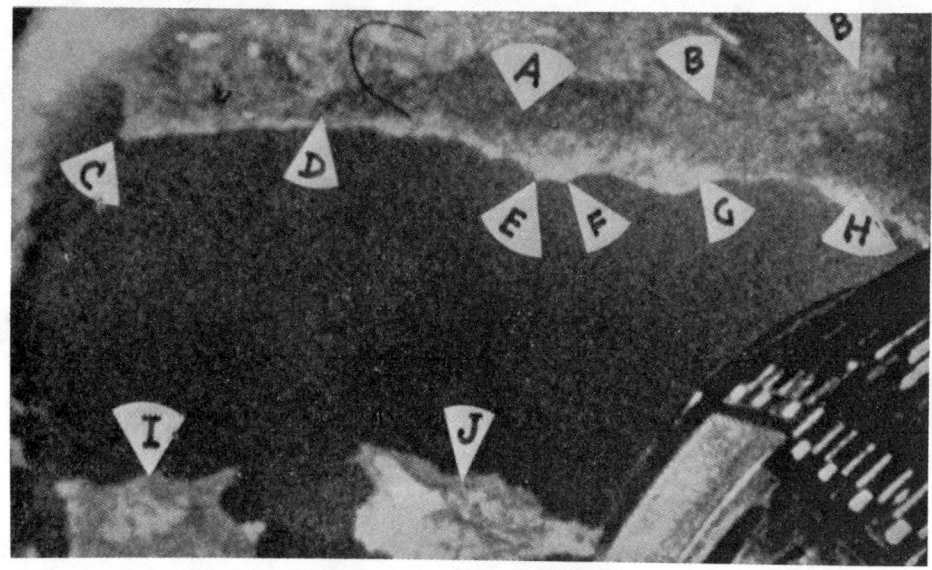
Goleta's community history can boast a portrait taken by an astronaut from 100 miles overhead! On June 9, 1965, James McDivitt took this NASA picture from cabin of Gemini IV. Landmarks include: A—Goleta Valley; B—Coyote Fire area; C—Pt. Concepcion; D—Gaviota Pass; E—Coal Oil Point; F—UCSB campus; G—Santa Barbara; H—Montecito; I—Santa Rosa Island; J—Santa Cruz Island. Space craft shows at lower right. Channel in center of picture, Santa Ynez Valley at upper edge.

From Marine Base to State University

For the fantastically low price of $100,000—less than one-fifth of what Mrs. Campbell had spent on her house alone—the Devereux Foundation purchased the entire 500-acre ranch and all its improvements. In September, 1945, the custodians of the estate, Mr. and Mrs. George Churchill, turned over their keys to a dynamic young Devereux administrator from Philadelphia, Joseph F. Smith. He went to work immediately to convert the former millionaire's rural estate into a school for the rehabilitation of emotionally-disturbed youngsters. Contrary to general belief, it is not a school for the exclusive benefit of children of the wealthy; many students are from low-income families, with the $600 monthly tuition provided by scholarship funds.

Devereux School at Goleta opened within a few days of Smith's arrival, with a staff of thirty-five for an enrollment of forty-five. This amazing parity between staff and student body is a hallmark of the Devereux School system; in 1965, for example, there was a staff of 172 for an enrollment of 175.

The average child spends eighteen months at Devereux. Those who complete their training receive a diploma of graduation from Santa Barbara High School.

The Campbells' private burial ground on Coal Oil Point constituted a cloud on the ranch title. To remove it, the Campbell heirs consented to transfer the remains of Col. and Mrs. Campbell to Chicago, allowing the tiny graveyard to revert to ranch ownership. The ring of cypress trees and the tall cross of Aberdeen granite were still *in situ* as late as 1966.

A steel pier jutting seaward from Coal Oil Point, left over from an unsuccessful oil exploration program in pre-war years, could not be maintained for pleasure use, and was removed per State law.

In January, 1947, the new Highway 101 north of the railroad was opened to traffic, siphoning a tremendous flow of cars away from Hollister Avenue. The business men of Goleta became concerned that the town's economy would suffer. They had no kind of cohesive booster organization, and the village was unincorporated.

During 1947, to meet the need for an organized promotional and advertising program, the Goleta Valley Chamber of Commerce was formed, with Oliver Crismon as president, Stanley Pateman as secretary, and sixteen dues-paying members.

On August 17, 1947, the federal government turned the airport back to the City of Santa Barbara, worth about $9,000,000 more than when it had been leased in 1942. The city took pains to remind the Navy that it had not received any of the agreed rental of $2,600 per year, but the Navy ignored the duns.

Goleta Valley had been represented through the difficult war years at the County level by Third District Supervisor J. Monroe Rutherford. Early in 1948, Rutherford incurred the disfavor of *News-Press* publisher Tom Storke, whose editorial support was considered tantamount to election by many candidates. After Storke's publication of several critical appraisals of his handling of the Supervisor's office, Rutherford in a moment of discouragement announced that he would not be a candidate for reelection.

Rutherford's friends Chester Rich and Hal Caywood persuaded William Hollister, of Goleta, a grand-nephew of Colonel Hollister's, to run for Supervisor. No citizen had better qualifications for the office. He was an overseas veteran of World War I; his capable wife, Kathryn, was a member of the pioneer Kellogg family. He had helped build and install the new walnut plant in 1919. For many years he had been assistant to Walnut Association manager Philip C. Marble. He had been president of the Goleta Farm Center in the depression years, and since 1933 had been general manager of the Walnut Growers' Association.

During World War II, Bill Hollister had served as Civil Defense coordinator for the district between Santa Barbara and Gaviota, as well as managing the POW camp on the Edwards ranch. He was chairman of the County Water Board, and on the original board of directors of the Goleta County Water District.

Bill Hollister agreed to be a Supervisorial candidate, and the campaign began. Then, a few weeks before election, J. Monroe Rutherford changed his mind and announced he would run again. By now, Hollister's campaign was in high gear, with Tom Storke's support. On the eve of election day, the *News-Press* delivered the *coup de grâce* to Rutherford's chances of re-election by publishing a long, blistering editorial accusing Rutherford of trying to "serve two masters" because he was the manager of Dos Pueblos Ranch, a subsidiary of the Signal Oil & Gas Company, which owned nearly one-sixth of the assessed value in the Third Supervisorial District, and paid nearly one-sixth of the taxes.

Rutherford must find it difficult [opined the *News-Press*] to keep an unbiased attitude toward his employer ... who pays him a manager's salary that is much larger than the tax money he is paid for being supervisor ... when oil interests conflict with farm and home interests. ...

When the ballot box was opened the following day, Bill Hollister was the Goleta Valley's new Supervisor. He would remain so until he retired from office for health reasons fifteen years later.

Shortly after his defeat at the polls, J. Monroe Rutherford relinquished the management of Dos Pueblos Ranch to Ray C. Ault. In later years, Signal's board chairman, affable Sam Mosher, became one of Tom Storke's closest personal friends. They served at the same time as Regents of the University of California, representing the Santa Barbara campus.

It was in the closing months of the fateful year of 1948 that the Good Land suddenly turned a sharp corner in its destiny. The War Assets Administration offered the deactivated Marine base, with all improvements, to the Regents of the University of California for use as a college campus.

For several years past, prominent Santa Barbarans had been working diligently to persuade the State Legislature and the Regents of U. C. to admit Santa Barbara State College, formerly a teachers training normal school founded in 1891, to the State University system. State Senator Clarence Ward and State Assemblyman A. W. "Bobby" Robertson, prodded by Tom Storke, Pearl Chase and other Santa Barbara civic leaders, had carried on the fight for a Santa Barbara branch of the University of California. Now Uncle Sam was offering a ready-made nucleus for a campus, equipped to accommodate 3,500 students—a miniature city complete with housing, a telephone system, a sewage system capable of also handling Goleta's 1,500 population, an electric power and light system—yes, even an Olympic-sized swimming pool!

The Regents did not stampede to accept the offer, however. They took time to make a painstaking oral examination of this gift horse. In their wisdom, they foresaw knotty problems in converting a former military base into a working State university.

The problem of water supply was expected to be solved by the Cachuma Project, which the coming of peace would accelerate. Present access roads from Highway 101 were grossly inadequate. The proximity of a commercial airport was enough to make University planners groan.

Meanwhile, Santa Barbara State College was bursting the bounds of its fourteen-acre campus on the Riviera, and was contemplating a cross-town move to the 110-acre Leadbetter Hill site overlooking the harbor (later to become the City College campus).

On February 15, 1948, U. C. President Robert Gordon Sproul informed the *News-Press* that the Board of Regents was considering the acquisition of the Goleta Mesa portion of the Marine air station.

Finally it happened... and Goleta would never be the same again.

On June 1, 1948, the War Assets Administration awarded the former training base to the University Regents, with actual custody to take place four months later. (A story has circulated for years that the Regents paid the WAA one dollar to legalize the deal. Uncle Sam was hardly *that* generous; he actually charged U. C. *ten* dollars.)

Thus, by the proverbial stroke of a pen, what had been a sleepy trading center for a Valley of citrus farmers awoke one June morning to find itself classified in the same category with Berkeley, New Haven, Cambridge.

Overnight, bucolic Goleta had become a *university town!*

CHAPTER XXXI

Cachuma Triggers a Population Explosion

Goleta was like a naive farmer's daughter, unready to don the academic robes placed upon her shoulders by the coming of a college campus. Commented a *News-Press* feature writer:

> The Goleta that has been known as the ugly duckling of Santa Barbara County is about to sprout fine new feathers and spread her wings toward a development unparalleled in her history. . . .

When the college came, Goleta stood as the end product of a Topsy-like growth of seventy-five years standing, sans zoning or planning of any kind. The town's most loyal supporter sensed that the metamorphosis from grub to butterfly was going to be slow and painful.

Esthetically, Goleta's business district was a monstrosity. Jerry-built establishments, mostly one-storied, conformed to no discernible standards of architectural merit. A few modern, well-designed business structures stood out from their unlovely neighbors as conspicuously as gold teeth in a jaw full of decayed molars.

Sporadic attempts were made to incorporate Goleta, without success. A community promotional project known as the Magnolia Festival petered out for lack of patronage. There had never been much empathy between the wealthy lemon growers and the townspeople. Efforts to annex Goleta to the City of Santa Barbara only tended to rouse resentments of long standing. The Valley complained, with reason, that Goleta's light was always being hidden under Santa Barbara's bushel. The unkindest cut of all came when the new institution on Goleta's mesa was named the University of California, Santa Barbara College—later UCSB.

The college had chosen an inauspicious year to locate in Goleta. The Valley's economy, still geared to agriculture, was in the doldrums owing to a sustained drought period which threatened the citrus, avocado and tomato industries. Santa Barbara had to pass ordinances making it a misdemeanor to water lawns or wash cars. Two deep water wells at the airport turned salty when the Goleta Valley water table dropped from twenty-four feet to forty-eight feet during 1948.

But help was in sight: a federal reclamation dam was to be built on the Santa Ynez River for the benefit of the South Coast. In 1940, Santa Maria's Leo Preisker and Santa Barbara's ex-Senator T. M. Storke had met in Washington, D. C., to confer about such a plan with Oscar Chapman, chief of the Reclamation Bureau. Since 1944, the County Supervisors had been working on the new "Cachuma Project."

After a long and bitter fight with county residents hostile to the dam, on November 22, 1949, the voters overwhelmingly approved a contract whereby the government would build Cachuma Dam, a connecting Tecolote Tunnel and a South Coast Conduit, to be paid for by the users of the water over a fifty-year period. This election unlocked the door to the future progress of Goleta, the Good Land.

Meanwhile the daily pageant of human life marched on. Major crime was almost unheard of in the Goleta Valley, but in December, 1949, the community was shocked by the brutal murder of bootlegger's accomplice Carlo Drocco, at his ranch home on the southeastern corner of what was soon to become El Encanto Heights subdivision.

Eight months later, an auto thief named Louis Grijalva confessed the killing, but hanged himself in his jail cell before the law could punish him. Drocco's $70,000 estate was awarded to his business manager, Mrs. Matilda W. Maryatt of Santa Barbara (who had drawn up the will for her illiterate client) rather than Drocco's kinfolk in Italy, who unsuccessfully sued to break the will.

On the night of January 26, 1950, a firebug burned the huge

Goleta Lemon Association packing plant to the ground. The $1,500,000 loss was exceeded only by the Potter Hotel fire of 1921. Stunned citrus growers feared the Association would never recover; but plant manager Granvel B. Caster leased unused facilities from Johnston Fruit Company in Santa Barbara, and kept the crops moving.

By April a new, ultra-modern Sunkist plant was being built, its 182,000 square feet of floor space making it one of the largest in the world, with a storage capacity of 450 carloads of fruit. It was ready for operation January 1, 1951. Advances in automation reduced the labor force from 350 to 125; modern methods boosted the plant's capacity to nearly 2,000 carloads annually.

Anticipating a post-war influx of new people to the Valley, the Goleta Sanitary District, back in business after its wartime hiatus, went to work to acquire the Marine base sewer lines and disposal plant, which could service a population of 4,500. The War Assets Administration had deeded the sewerage facilities to the U.C. Regents with one string attached: the college and the municipal airport were to have priority in their use. The Goleta Sanitary District could use the surplus, providing the community paid for the necessary sewer lines.

On February 5, 1950, a $225,000 sewer bond issue carried by a wide margin. An eleven-acre site on the north half of Mescalitán Island—a site occupied by a Canaliño village in 1542, and bulldozed flat in 1942—was purchased from Pacific Lighting Gas Supply Company. Work started on a $2,000,000 sewage disposal plant designed for a population of 15,000.

The new sewerage system was built as a joint undertaking by the Goleta Sanitary District and the University of California. Later, the Isla Vista Sanitary District, the City of Santa Barbara (airport) and the County (general hospital) acquired capacity in the district's treatment facilities.

At the time the plant was started, Diego Terres was president of the Sanitary District, Stan Pateman was secretary-manager, and directors were Fred Catherina, J. Murray Durham, C. W. Cloer, I. S. Austin and Ronce Hughes.

Ground was broken for the $14,000,000 earth-fill Cachuma Dam on August 16, 1950. There was considerable political opposition to the project in the Congress, which prompted Goleta to dispatch a capable lobbyist to Washington in the person of Fred Stevens. At the county level of government, Supervisors T. A. Twitchell of Santa Maria and C. W. Bradbury of Carpinteria spearheaded the fight to keep Cachuma appropriations in the federal budget from year to year. Back home, a Citizens' Committee of 3,000, headed by Donald Welch of Santa Barbara, solicited funds to carry on the fight for Cachuma. Chester Rich was in charge of raising money in the Goleta Valley.

Anticipating a boom, the downtown business men of Goleta were making slow but steady progress in improving the appearance of Hollister Avenue. During 1950, paving was laid from the Goleta Union School to Fairview Avenue, boosting property values to $75 a front foot. (By 1965 the same frontage was worth $600 a front foot.) Flood control, always a major headache in the vicinity of the Slough, resulted in the deepening and straightening of Maria Ygnacia and San Jose creeks, but did not prevent serious flooding during the rains of 1952.

In January, 1950, the University Regents announced plans for a Goleta campus envisioning a liberal arts college with a maximum enrollment of 3,500. The first construction work was to convert Marine barracks into classrooms and student quarters. The first two permanent buildings, the Library and the Science Building, costing $2,000,000, were started in 1952.

The Regents were still confronted by the unsolved problem of how to channel traffic to their new seashore campus. Fairview Avenue had only been paved as far south as the United Air Lines terminal, which would revert to city ownership in 1967. There was a country lane leading from Highway 101 to Isla Vista, an area now undergoing a building boom in anticipation of the college opening. But even in combination, these two approaches were inadequate to handle the load.

The Regents' first choice for an access road to the campus was merely an extension of Pine Avenue in Goleta. It would extend southward to Shoreline Drive, hook around the remnants of Mescalitán Island, and slant up to the Goleta mesa on an earth-fill ramp.

Actual work on this route began in 1950, but in 1952 the County Supervisors, perhaps angling for State aid, announced that the county budget would not permit the building of the University access road.

Neither Senator Clarence B. Ward nor Assemblyman Stanley Tomlinson favored putting the University under obligation to the State Highway Commission. A sharp conflict developed between the immediate needs of the college, and the thinking of the County Supervisors. The result was a two-year hiatus during which nothing happened at all.

On February 8, 1952, a blind old man of eighty died at the geriatrics ward of the County General Hospital. A pauper, his death would have gone unnoticed had it not been for the fact that he was unique in history: the last survivor of the Canaliño Indian tribe which had flourished 12,000 strong when the Spaniards came in 1769.

Tomás Ygnacio de Aquino, born in 1871 at the Indian Orchard Ranch owned by his family in Maria Ygnacia Canyon, would have been buried in Potters Field and forgotten, had it not been for the compassionate hearts of the then owners of Maria Ygnacia Ranch, Mr. and Mrs. Albert C. Ruddock of Montecito. The Ruddocks paid for a shroud and casket for "Tio Tomás," and arranged with the Franciscan fathers at the Old Mission to entomb The Last Canaliño in the Friars' Vaults.

Another death occurred in 1952 which saddened hearts all over the Goleta Valley. On October 27, Captain Edgar Hollister, a Marine Corps fighter pilot, was shot down in Korea. The son of William and Kathryn Hollister, winner of the Silver Star and the Purple Heart, Captain Hollister was the Good Land's only casualty of the Korean Conflict. (Coincidentally, the Valley's only loss in the Spanish-American War was also a Hollister—Edgar's cousin Stanley.)

The year 1952 saw two events on the debit side of the ledger —an earthquake centered on the San Andres Fault near Tehachapi, which damaged thousands of boxes of lemons in storage at the Goleta Sunkist plant, and winter floods which saw Maria Ygnacia and San Jose Creeks go on their worst rampage since 1941. Residents of homes on South Fairview Avenue had to be evacuated by rowboat.

On the credit side, 1952 saw the Goleta County Water District contract with the federal government for $2,800,000 with which to build sixty miles of pipeline during the next two years. The District at this time acquired the services of a dynamic young secretary-manager, Don P. Johnston, to guide its affairs during the particularly critical years facing the Goleta Valley.

With the University scheduled to open at Goleta for the autumn semester 1954, in 1953 the top echelons of the County, City and University governments met and reached agreement on an access route to the seashore campus. It roughly followed the old 1887 railroad right-of-way along Vieja Drive, spanning the old More Ranch via Shoreline Drive; thence to and across the University campus to an exit on Highway 101 near the present Ellwood Wye.

This so-called Eastern Approach met with instant opposition from the upper-income bracket residents of Hope Ranch Park. Main support for the route came from a Citizens' Committee whose avowed purpose was to prevent University traffic from being fed into busy Highway 101 anywhere west of the city. The chairman and spokesman for the Committee was T. M. Storke's son Charles A. Storke II, co-editor and publisher of the *News-Press*.

The situation took a turn for the worse in the summer of 1954 when the Airport Commission suddenly closed the access road to Isla Vista on the grounds that traffic would disrupt newly-installed instrument landing equipment at the airport. The Commission substituted Robert Troup Road, farther west, and a crash program got under way to grade it in time for the opening of the college.

The University of California, Santa Barbara College, which was soon to change its title to the University of California at Santa Barbara when it became a full-fledged member of the U.C. family, opened its doors to 1,725 students in September, 1954. The faculty numbered 152.

Moving the 74,122-volume library from the Riviera to Goleta was a triumph of logistical ingenuity. The books were packed in Goleta Lemon Association field boxes and conveyed to the second-floor library stacks by means of a shingle conveyor borrowed from a roofing company.

Early in 1955, Senator Ward and recently-elected Assemblyman James L. Holmes introduced bills in the State Legislature calling for nearly $900,000 in State funds to build the Eastern Approach access from La Cumbre Overpass to the campus.

The bills went into committee and would probably have remained there had not fate intervened: on May 9, 1955, Senator Ward died, unexpectedly.

A few days after the funeral, freshman assemblyman Jim Holmes was awakened in the middle of the night by what he described as a "divine inspiration": he would propose naming Santa Barbara's new university access road the "Clarence Ward Memorial Boulevard."

Holmes achieved a masterful stroke of political finessing. If Ward's colleagues rejected this memorial tribute to a deceased Senator, they would close the door on similar posthumous awards for themselves. Thus, with reluctance, the Legislature approved a measure to build UCSB's access road with state funds. On June 9, 1955, Governor Goodwin J. Knight signed the bill into law—to the delight of his close friend T. M. Storke of Santa Barbara, whom Knight appointed to the U.C. Board of Regents a few months later.

Assemblyman Holmes admitted privately that the original bills would never have become law had Ward lived, due to the late Senator's outspoken opposition to the state's participation in the project.

Ward's successor was J. J. "Jack" Hollister Jr. of Winchester Canyon.

In the early autumn of 1955, calamity threatened the Goleta Valley—the worst forest fire in a century ravaged the Santa Ynez Mountains from Refugio Pass to San Marcos. The conflagration started just after midnight on September 6, 1955, in an outbuilding on La Chirpa guest ranch in upper Refugio Canyon. By daybreak the blaze was raging out of control and sweeping eastward.

Like molten lava spilling out of the canyons to seaward, the Refugio Fire vaulted Highway 101 west of El Capitan in several places, damaging the railroad and knocking out electric and communications lines. Ham radio operators helped the Forest Service maintain communications as more than 2,000 men, including 600 Marines from Camp Pendleton and 300 Zuñi Indian "hot shots," were rushed into action.

Flames denuded the chaparral jungle from the ridges which divided Dos Pueblos, Eagle, Tecolote, Winchester, Ellwood, Glen Annie, Stow, Bartlett, Catlett, San Jose, Maria Ygnacia and San Antonio canyons. Sixteen homes and as many ranch structures were destroyed before the holocaust was finally brought under control, near the San Marcos highway, on September 15.

The total acreage burned over, 84,770, including 30,260 acres of private land, exceeded by 17,000 acres the land area involved in the Coyote Fire of 1964 above Santa Barbara and Montecito. The Refugio Burn did an estimated damage of $2,137,000, with suppression costs set at $960,000.

Before the winter rainy season set in, grass was seeded on the burned area from airplanes, with Goleta Valley ranchers, particularly Dos Pueblos and the Bishop holdings, sharing the cost.

In January, 1956, a representative of the Aerophysics Development Corporation of Santa Monica arrived in the Goleta Valley on an historic errand: to find housing for the employes of his firm, which was moving from Santa Monica to a multi-million-dollar research center located at 6767 Hollister Avenue, opposite the Bishop Ranch.

This move presaged Goleta's emergence into the electronics research field, and was bolstered the following December by news that the government was activating Camp Cooke, north of Lompoc, into a missile base that would rival Cape Canaveral. (Two years later it was renamed Vandenberg Air Force Base.)

Out of these events of 1956 evolved Goleta's first big modern housing development, Kellogg Park, on the open field where Joe Sexton once raised calla lilies and inaugurated the Valley's first irrigation. In March 1957, with the backing of a San Francisco bank, the developer poured slabs for 118 new homes between Kinman and Tecolote Avenues.

The Aerophysics plant (later Curtiss-Wright and by 1960 the

Defense Research Laboratories of General Motors) focused the eyes of planners on the new westward movement of Goleta Valley progress. Reflecting this trend, in 1957 manager Don P. Johnston announced the annexation of "Goleta West", 6,800 acres, to the Goleta County Water District, thus extending the District boundary to El Capitan. Two years later a $1,600,000 water line was laid nearly eight miles from Glen Annie to Las Llagas Canyon, west of Dos Pueblos Ranch.

A new Donnybrook flared up over which of five proposed access routes was the most feasible for the new University approach. They ranged in cost from $1,200,000 for the Isla Vista-Ellwood Wye route, to $3,600,000 for the longer Eastern Approach from La Cumbre Overpass.

The State Highway Commission wearied of the local bickering. Not noted for allowing such trifling distractions as public opinion, redwood groves or historical sites to impede their desires, on April 25, 1957, the Commission adopted an eastern access and declared it a freeway. This "stub" alignment left Highway 101 near the Patterson Avenue overpass, cut a 160-foot swath across the floor of the Valley to truncated Mescalitán Island, and so by earth-fill ramp to UCSB mesa.

A howl of protest went up from all sides. Chairman Bill Hollister of the County Board of Supervisors called it "of all the routes proposed, this is probably the worst." Next day editor Charles Storke leveled an editorial blast at the Commission in the *News-Press*:

> [This route] will be a menace to the lives of the students and other motorists, long before the University reaches maximum enrollment. . . . Student cars by the thousands will pour onto busy Highway 101, instead of having a direct, safe route into Santa Barbara. . . . The State Highway Commission is riding rough-shod over the wishes of the people.

Storke had plenty of support. The University Regents voted unanimously to "protest vigorously" the route choice. Sixteen Goleta organizations calling themselves the Goleta Co-ordinating Committee on April 29 voiced their united opposition. A county delegation appeared before the Highway Commission on May 23, and succeeded in getting the stub alignment rescinded.

Meanwhile, still another controversy was incubating. The City of Santa Barbara made a move to annex its Municipal Airport in Goleta so as to collect sales taxes from business transactions taking place on airport property then in the county. At first, the city had hoped to link itself to the airport by a corridor running along the mountains, but this involved too many private land owners. Then *News-Press* reporter Tom Kleveland suggested to Charles Storke "if not by land, why not by sea?" A similar corridor could be run off shore just as well, thereby making the city and the airport "contiguous" by legal definition.

Kleveland's idea excited Charles Storke, who conferred with the late Francis Price Sr., a prominent lawyer, and others. Santa Barbara had recently obtained an "oil sanctuary" out to the three mile limit, to protect itself against unsightly oil well platforms along a fifteen-mile stretch from Ortega Hill to UCSB. It was suggested to Mayor Jack Rickard that the city annex this 45 square miles of water—more than the area of the city itself—and thus achieve contiguity with its Municipal Airport in Goleta. Rickard decided to act.

The plan did not appeal to Montecitans, who visualized Santa Barbara controlling their beaches or annexing Montecito bite by bite. They appealed to the State attorney general, Pat Brown, who instituted *quo warranto* proceedings to invalidate the oil sanctuary annexation.

The city was only temporarily blocked, however. It came up with a unique "horizontal annexation" of the water only, waiving mineral rights to the ground under the ocean (in order to placate the Pacific Lighting Gas Supply Company, which feared the city might be in a position to tax them in the event of annexation), and re-submitted their plan in 1960, featuring an off-shore corridor 300 feet wide and 37,000 feet long which joined city and airport. This plan, formulated by city attorney Stanley Tomlinson, proved acceptable—almost identical to the original scheme suggested by Tom Kleveland. The State moved quickly to plug the legal loophole, however, to circumvent any repetition of this gerrymandering procedure in future.

Returning to the University access problem: on October 9, 1957, Senator Jack Hollister protested that no decision for an eastern route should be made until objections raised by the Goleta Harbor

Association against bridging the harbor inlet had been cleared up. Because Hollister was a State Senator, his protest carried weight.

News-Press editor Charles A. Storke angrily nominated Hollister for a "Hats-Off Award for Obstructionism," branding him in a signed front page editorial as

> the most obstructionist Senator in the history of this County. We doubt if history will produce an equal. Too bad. There was a time when the name Hollister commanded respect. .*

Not since the Twenties, when Reginald Fernald of the *Morning Press* and "Old Man" Storke of the *Daily News* had traded bitter editorial diatribes until they collided head-on in a libel action, had the public taken such a keen interest in their local newspaper's opinions.

On October 23, 1957, the Highway Commission in a surprise move re-adopted its eastern stub route, only six hours after Supervisor Bill Hollister and Mayor Floyd O. Bohnett of Santa Barbara led a delegation to Sacramento to appeal for a decision in favor of the La Cumbre Overpass or Eastern Approach.

Again there was a public clamor against the Highway Commission. The planning department said "they have fouled up our planning for the area." Bill Hollister reiterated "it's the worst route they could have selected." The County Farm Bureau took a strongly-worded stand against the route; so did the Goleta Valley Chamber of Commerce.

But the outrage of the citizenry was to no avail. The State paid out $748,205 to acquire rights-of-way across such historic soil as Joe Sexton's Nursery and the old More Ranch, and construction began on Ward Memorial Boulevard.

After being partially open for some time, the Boulevard was formally completed on August 6, 1963, at a cost of $3,021,555—thereby terminating the bitterest feud the Goleta Valley had seen since the Hollister-Bishop litigation of the Seventies and Eighties.

---

* Ironically, when Jack Hollister won re-election in 1960, it was with *News-Press* endorsement. But by that time, Charles A. Storke II had abdicated to Mexico City to enter the advertising business, a move which led to the eventual sale of his family's newspaper and radio interests to end a dynasty which had begun with T. M. Storke's purchase of the old Santa Barabara *Independent* on January 1, 1901.

To back-track in time: in June of 1953 Cachuma Dam was finished. However, its outlet to the Goleta Valley, the 6.5-mile, seven-foot diameter Tecolote Tunnel, was not ready until June 1956. As early as 1952 the Goleta County Water District had taken delivery on the tunnel's seepage water (which was excellent for lemons, but contained too much sodium for use by cymbidium growers).

Total cost of the Cachuma Project was $44,000,000. South Coast ranchers now had a reservoir capable of storing 206,000 acre-feet of water, enough to last eighteen years at current levels of use.

In May, 1956, the Goleta Union School District, now under the capable administration of Dr. Ian Crow, added its first new elementary school in nearly thirty years—Cathedral Oaks School at 300 North Turnpike Road.

In the fall of 1958, residents of the Good Land paused to pay tribute to Judge W. T. Lillard and his wife, Mae, upon their retirement after serving the Goleta-Hope Ranch Judicial District since 1934. Judge Lillard's successor on the bench was Joseph Lodge.

Over the years, some 30,000 persons had paid traffic fines at Bill Lillard's bar of justice at 5744 Hollister Avenue. Violators included such celebrities as William Randolph Hearst, Billie Burke, Robert Taylor and Mrs. Jack Dempsey. Judge Lillard's dogeared docket book listed 1,500 small claims cases and nearly 500 civil suits, not one of which was ever reversed on appeal. The Judge also united some 800 couples in marriage during his years in office. His Honor's sons, Gene and Bill, were probably Goleta's most famous athletes, both enjoying successful careers in big-league professional baseball. Judge Lillard died April 4, 1966.

Approaching the new decade of the 1960s, the Good Land found itself on the threshold of the Space Age and an entirely new way of life. Agriculture was doomed, said the prophets of the new order, although one postwar industry—orchid growing and hybridizing—thrived so well in the Goleta Valley's smog-free climate that the Chamber of Commerce was moved to adopt "Valley of the Orchids" as an official slogan.

More Mesa became a center for the growing of orchids and roses, but the main impetus of the new industry resulted from oil tycoon

Samuel B. Mosher founding the huge Dos Pueblos Orchid Company at his historic ranch ten miles west of Goleta. Mosher's operations were put on a commercially profitable basis by his manager, orchidist Margaret Clinch McGann. When Mosher married Mrs. McGann in September, 1965, one of the groom's miscellaneous wedding gifts to his bride was title to the Dos Pueblos Orchid Company—the largest operation of its kind in the world.

Three historical events, which occurred independently of each other but which were all closely inter-related, combined to bring a new way of life to the Goleta Valley:

(1) the establishment of a State University campus at Goleta;

(2) the availability of unlimited water from the Cachuma Project;

(3) the activation of Vandenberg AFB as a major missile center. These three factors were responsible for Goleta, the Good Land, becoming "ground zero" for a spectacular population explosion commencing in 1960.

CHAPTER XXXII

Progress: From Mescalitán to Megalopolis

Goleta's post-war trickle of newcomers, slowly gathering momentum throughout the 1950s, became an avalanche by the 1960s. First to feel the overwhelming impact were the public schools, the post-office, the utility companies, and the highway and road system.

The Valley's first Junior High School, La Colina, built at 4025 Foothill Road, was filled to its capacity of 1,000 students the day it opened its doors in 1958.

A year later, in September, 1959, a dream came true for Goleta Valley parents with the completion of beautiful new San Marcos High School at Turnpike Road and Hollister Avenue, at a building cost of $3,826,000. Simultaneously the Catholic High School opened a new campus near La Colina, named for Bishop Garcia Diego.

That same autumn of 1959, two new elementary schools opened in the Goleta Valley, Isla Vista at 6875 El Colegio Road, next to the Devereux Ranch School, and Fairview, at 401 North Fairview Avenue.

Housing developments began to sprout like mushrooms at various places on the valley floor. South of San Marcos High School, on the historic Scull Ranch of 1863, hundreds of new tract homes lined a grid of curving streets which formed asphalt beaches for a sea of composition-shingle and shake roofs.

The first major subdivision in the valley was El Encanto Heights, 368 homes costing $3,500,000, on Colonel Hollister's old Lower Ranch, west of Glen Annie Canyon Road adjoining the freeway. Walnut Park sprang up where Captain R. P. Tucker's ranch had been. Everywhere one looked, housing tracts appeared, blending like raw eggs in a skillet.

By 1960, more that 1,000 new homes, worth over $17,000,000, were ready or under construction, enough to house 3,000 newcomers.

An early index of the population rise was the postal receipts of the Goleta Post Office. It had served 3,500 patrons in 1950; by 1965, the total was passed 17,000 and rising sharply. Postmaster Ben Wells got along with nine employees in 1957; by 1966 he had forty.

The Goleta post office achieved First Class status in 1952, the year it reached $40,000 in stamp sales. Five-year postal receipt statistics hold a measuring stick up to Goleta's phenomenal growth: $24,000 in 1950; $50,000 in 1955; $125,000 in 1960; and $390,000 in 1965.

Back in April, 1949, when Loren "Butch" Howell became Goleta's first uniformed postal carrier, he rang 283 doorbells twice a day. By 1965, the number of houses had skyrocketed to 7,848, requiring the services of four foot-carriers and fourteen mounted carriers. The public used to mail 1,800 letters a day, and receive 4,500, in 1956; in 1965 the totals were 4,500 letters mailed, 35,000 received per day!

The Goleta post office moved from 5782 Hollister Avenue in November, 1962, to a new rented building on Plaza de La Goleta at 420 South Fairview Avenue. At long last it appeared the Goleta post office had enough room—but with the community growing at 25 per cent per year, a move into larger quarters was inevitable. The only alternative would be to establish branch post offices in outlying subdivisions such as the one Goleta post office operates at the Gaviota store.

Bill Hollister retired as Supervisor in 1960 due to failing health (he died in 1962) and was succeeded by an ex-Marine sergeant and Hope Ranch avocado grower, Daniel G. Grant. Grant served as first chairman of the Local Agency Formation Commission, and as chairman of the Santa Barbara County Flood Control and Water Conservation District he signed the contract with the State for the importation of Feather River water to Santa Barbara County. Grant was re-elected in 1964.

After a three-year lull in school building, Goleta's burgeoning population called for a new elementary school for every 600 new homes. In May, 1962, Hollister School was built at 4950 Anita Lane, south of Hollister and west of Turnpike Road. The following November, Kellogg School opened at 475 Cambridge Avenue, north of the freeway.

Two more elementary schools came into being the following year—La Patera, third Goleta school to bear that name, at 555 La Patera Lane on the old Stow Ranch; and Foothill, at 711 Ribera Drive between Turnpike Road and Patterson Avenue. The Catholics built a parochial school where Joe Sexton had once raised pampas plumes, St. Raphael's, opening in September 1963 with 335 students and nine teachers. El Camino School at 5020 San Simeon Drive, on San Marcos Road, was built in 1965. Goleta's public school enrollment jumped from 1,925 in 1960 to 4,802 in 1966.

The University was also booming. The Regents' original maximum enrollment figure of 3,500 was reached in 1960; by the fall semester of 1965 enrollment had ballooned to 9,750, and plans were being made for an eventual enrollment of 15,000.

Over 2,000 students lived in on-campus dormitories, while over 6,000, including married couples, lived in adjoining Isla Vista (or "Sin City", as it was dubbed by the college crowd). Less than one-fourth of the student body came from homes in the Santa Barbara area.

One of the most rapidly-growing phases of UCSB was the Graduate Division, with 929 students working toward advanced degrees in 1965. UCSB was offering the M.A. in twenty-six fields and the Ph.D. in thirteen fields. Two professional schools opened, in Engineering and Education. An Institute of Environmental Stress was established in 1964. A highly sophisticated Computer Center and Educational TV department also kept pace with Goleta's mounting importance in the realm of electronic and allied research.

The total capital investment on the Goleta campus had exceeded $43,000,000 by 1966. By 1969, some forty-two separate construction projects costing over $72,000,000 were scheduled for occupancy.

This fantastic decade of growth at UCSB took place under several chief campus officers. Dr. J. Harold Williams, Provost since

1946, retired in 1955. His successor, Dr. Clark Keubler of Ripon College, withdrew from the field of education less than a year later. Two deans, Dr. Elmer R. Noble and Dr. John C. Snidecor, served as Acting Provosts until Dr. Samuel B. Gould arrived from Antioch College in 1958, at which time his title was changed to Chancellor. When Dr. Gould resigned in 1962 to go into educational television work in New York City, his successor was Dr. Vernon I. Cheadle, from U.C.'s campus at Davis.

As housing tracts continued to devour Goleta's lemon and walnut lands, the esthetic beauty of the Good Land deteriorated apace. Developers were not required by law to provide playgrounds for the children who would live in the tracts, forcing them to play in the streets as if they lived in the tenements of Brooklyn or Harlem. The primary target of the average bulldozer seemed to be trees. The magnificent Moreton Bay Fig at New Horizons, second largest in the county, planted by George Washington Hill 80 years before, was slated for destruction before public opinion intervened. Even worse than the uprooting of trees was the rape of hillsides with homesite pads in some foothill areas.

Only by night does the urbanization of the Good Land delight the eye of the beholder. When viewed from West Camino Cielo or the south slope of San Marcos Pass highway, the lights of Goleta's sprawling subdivisions magically resemble the twinkling stars of the firmament swept together into the black bowl of the valley, with here and there square patterns like diamonds glittering on black velvet trays. The crowded 101 freeway becomes a moving tape of color, white on one side, ruby on the other, flowing in opposite directions through the heart of the Good Land—quite literally the bloodstream of a new way of life.

Any area of boom growth inevitably draws its share of swindlers and fast-buck operators, and the Goleta Valley proved no exception. Sloppy workmanship, inferior building materials, and other evasions of building codes created development scandals from time to time, which the *News-Press* vigorously investigated and brought to public attention.

The most notorious Goleta land scandal was a whopper. It involved the historic Tecolote Rancho, previously owned by Don

Nicolás A. Den, the Sturges Brothers, Tecolote Land Company, and Silsby Spalding.

On the last day of July in 1959, two Los Angelenos, H. Roy Steele and Irwin H. Harris, paid Mrs. Deborah Spalding Pelissero $945,303.69 for the 1,320-acre ranch. Steele and Harris used money put in escrow by Los Angeles Trust Deed & Mortgage Exchange (LATD), which dealt in ten per cent interest on mortgages. The pair's advertising pitch promised an elaborate yacht marina, or Embarcadero, on the beach frontage. Not since John H. Williams' fictional City by the Sea, Naples, had such glowing promotional brochures been published in the Good Land.

Using the names Embarcadero Ranchos, Inc., and Embarcadero, Inc., Harris and Steele made 628 deeds of trust on lots having no legal description, which they peddled to unwary LATD investors. A highly controversial "Embarcadero Municipal Improvement District" was created, thanks to assistance in Sacramento from Tecolote Ranch's next-door neighbor, Senator Jack Hollister of Winchester Canyon, who was intrigued by the promoters' grandiose plans for a yacht marina.

Harris and Steele, controlling officers of the Embarcadero Municipal Improvement District, voted $3,874,000 in general obligation bonds for sewer, water, and general improvements on the property. Bonds totalling $1,207,000 were sold to hundreds of gullible investors. A $5,000,000 bond issue for a marina was voted on the ocean-front property, but never sold.

When LATD toppled into bankruptcy, the Tecolote Ranch developments went down with it. Senator Hollister died of a stroke as the scandal was breaking, his last days of life made miserable by the realization that Harris and Steele had exploited his senatorial influence for their gain.

Harris and Steele went on trial in Los Angeles Superior Court. After a costly seventeen-week-long litigation they were found guilty, on July 26, 1962, of thirty-two felony counts, involving their mishandling of funds of the Embarcadero Municipal Improvement District. The development corporations filed in federal bankruptcy. The holders of deeds of trust were also left holding the bag. In 1965 Harris and Steele won an appeal on a microscopic technicality in the transcript. At the opening of their new trial in March,

Progress: From Mescalitán to Megalopolis 335

1966, Harris and Steele pleaded guilty to two counts of grand larceny totalling $23,000 and one count of falsifying records of the Embarcadero Corporation. Judge Kathleen Parker set September 22, 1966, as the date for a probation hearing and sentencing.

During the first half of the 1960s, the economic structure of the Goleta Valley showed a marked shift from primarily agricultural to residential-industrial. Twenty-eight manufacturing firms, ranging from one-man shops in wooden buildings built for the Marines around the airport, to huge modern plants employing up to 700 people, were located in and around Goleta, although at first there was a tendency for them to use the better-known mailing address of Santa Barbara (a trend which was declining by the mid-Sixties).

All these were "smokeless industries," for the Good Land is subject to the same temperature-inversion phenomenon which has made smog such a blight in the Los Angeles Basin. Goleta's factories manufactured a wide range of items: asphalt, precision magnetic recording heads, business forms, aircraft, beautician's fixtures, electrical ceramics, surfboards, electronic components, plastic model kits, food dispensers, electric signs, meteorological instruments, hydraulic valve devices, truck bodies and wrought-iron furniture, precision parts for guided missiles, wire and cable products, plastic bottles, aerial photographs, toys, nameplates—the variety seemed endless.

Units of such corporate giants as General Motors, Raytheon, Edgerton, Germeshausen & Grier, Hughes Aircraft, and Bausch & Lomb, established "think shops" in the valley. Other large firms include Defense Research Corporation, Applied Magnetics, Joslyn Electronic Systems, and Ratel, Inc. The latter was brought as a pioneer in this field by G. E. Archenbronn, who served as Goleta's representative on the County Planning Commission during the most critical period of the boom.

What was all this doing to the large ranches, which one brief generation ago had dominated the economy and thinking of the Valley?

At first the big ranchers hoped to band together to stave off the encroachment of urbanization. As early as 1956, Gary Van Horne had the Stow Ranch zoned A-1-X, exclusively agricultural, hoping to keep taxes at a level where La Patera Ranch could remain open.

Van Horne got his agricultural zoning, but no tax stability. Stow's neighbor to the west, the 4,100-acre Corona del Mar Ranch, was sold in the spring of 1957 to Chicago financier Henry Crown. Frank Bishop, who had managed the destiny of the huge property since 1922, died in 1953 and the T. B. Bishop Company's attorney, Allan Chickering, of San Francisco, had managed the ranch in cooperation with James Hall Bishop Jr. In 1958, Andrew Brydon became ranch manager for the new owners.

In 1959, Crown's Exchange Building Corporation engaged William L. Pereira & Associates to prepare a master plan for the future development of the $2,500,000 ranch, a plan which included industrial parks near Hollister Avenue, golf courses in the foothills, and a Carmel-type upper-class residential development. At about the same time, to the east of the Stow Ranch the Conover, Hamilton, Ravenscroft and Louis Cavalletto properties, bordering the west bank of San Pedro Creek between the freeway and Stow Canyon Road, were zoned for housing—and Van Horne's taxes on the La Patera Ranch began to mount accordingly.

Unable to buck "progress", the Stow Ranch sold 156 acres from La Patera Lane to Los Carneros Creek, between the freeway and an extension of Cathedral Oaks Road, where a new upper-income-bracket subdivision was launched above Los Carneros Lake (the old Stow Pond). La Patera Cattle Company continued to operate the remaining 700 acres of the historic Stow Ranch for agriculture.

Things were humming at the new offices of the Goleta County Water District, which had contracted to purchase a minimum of 260,500 acre-feet of Cachuma water over a 35-year period starting in 1960, at a rate of $25 per acre-foot for 33,000 acres of ranch land and $35 per acre-foot for 4,124 acres zoned as "municipal" land. Eastward, portions of the Water District overlapped new annexations to the City of Santa Barbara, where property owners found themselves subject to double taxation for services rendered. This touchy situation was expected to be solved eventually by the new LAFCO, or Local Agency Formation Commission.

The town of Goleta, reporting a 122 per cent population growth between April, 1960, and October, 1965, was also booming, al-

Progress: From Mescalitán to Megalopolis

though far from being ready to enter a "City Beautiful" competition.

A town which for some eighty years had had only three churches, now had twenty-three churches serving fifteen different denominations.

Where the pioneer Rafaela School had stood near Hollister and Patterson Avenues in 1875, rose the new non-profit, doctor-owned, 102-bed Goleta Valley Community Hospital.

Goleta had fifteen physicians and surgeons, twelve dentists, two optometrists, four chiropractors, three attorneys, and two mortuaries. There were five banks, one savings and loan institution, two finance company offices, a weekly newspaper, a branch library, three movie theaters, eight parks and eight playgrounds, two mammoth discount department stores and several shopping centers.

The civic leaders of the Goleta Valley during this post-war boom were many. The community "Man of the Year" and "Golden Deed" Awards identify typical outstanding citizens and civic organizations. The first such award went for the year 1948 to blacksmith Jim Smith, whose retirement in 1949 marked the end of an era for the town. Other winners included:

1949, Fred Stevens; 1950, Hal Caywood; 1951, Goleta Lions Club; 1952, Robert P. Rowe; 1953, Kay and Elmer Winstrom; 1954, Sen. J. J. Hollister, Jr.; 1955, Clyde Conover; 1956, Goleta Amvets Post 55 Auxiliary; 1957, Garrett Van Horne; 1958, Loren "Butch" Howell; 1959, Goleta Union School District Board; 1960, Woman's Service Club; 1961, Earl G. Johnstone, Jr.; 1962, Eugene C. Sexton; 1963, Charles W. "Chuck" Begg; and 1964, William and Marcia Sommermeyer.

By 1963, La Colina Junior High's soaring enrollment forced it to go on double sessions. The Board of Education paid $264,777 for the cheapest campus site it could find, 24.5 acres of the old Fairview (Walora) Ranch north of Stow Canyon Road and west of Fairview Avenue. Here rose the Goleta Valley Junior High School, completed by the end of 1964 at a cost of $2,457,000.

A second senior high school for the Goleta Valley, scheduled to open in February 1967 in lower Glen Annie Canyon north of El Encanto Heights, was originally designated as "Ellwood Mesa High

School." A storm of public disapproval arose over a name which had no historical or topographical significance, resulting in its being changed to "Dos Pueblos High School"—which will pose a problem for a future School Board when yet another high school is required in the Dos Pueblos district, six miles farther west.

When the contractors' bids were opened late in 1965 for the Dos Pueblos High School, the lowest bid was $1,000,000 above the architect's estimate of $3,848,000. An angry controversy involving taxpayers, the Board of Education and the alleged incompetence of the architect became a stalemate, but increasingly overcrowded conditions at San Marcos High forced the School Board to authorize start of construction at the higher cost figure early in 1966.

The future Glen Annie Junior High School was slated to share the seventy-acre campus with Dos Pueblos, which would be the Valley's first four-year high school.

"Tomorrow rubs elbows with the past in the Goleta Valley," wrote county planning director Richard S. Whitehead in 1965, "but only for an instant; there is no static condition in this valley of opportunity."

To prepare for a tomorrow that would see an estimated 146,000 people crowding onto 22,000 acres of the Good Land, the County of Santa Barbara in 1962 authorized a firm of planning consultants to draw up a General Plan as a blueprint of the shape of things to come.

The General Plan for the Goleta Valley allotted 15,242 acres for homes, with lots ranging from 870 square feet to three acres. Open space, including parks, green belts, water bodies, athletic fields, cemeteries, and playgrounds, would occupy 1,437 acres. (It is significant that *no acreage was listed for agricultural use.*)

Freeways, expressways, airport facilities and secondary roads would occupy another 2,398 acres. Community features such as schools, the university, a civic center, hospitals, historical sites, and a sewer plant, were allocated 1,438 acres of space. Industry received 1,021 acres; commercial zoning, 491 acres. This blueprint, taking care of 146,000 population, called for quadrupling 1960 service facilities.

Three major traffic arteries ran east and west: Hollister Avenue,

Progress: From Mescalitán to Megalopolis

Highway 101, and Cathedral Oaks Road, funneling together at Ellwood Wye. Beautiful 18-hole golf courses were spotted on the Bishop Ranch, Ellwood Canyon, and other Valley points. A marina for small boats was placed on the site of the old Potter Farm in the lee of Mescalitán Island, and possibly a second marina on Devereux Ranch. Most of the beach frontage west of Goleta Point, exclusive of that owned by UCSB, was earmarked for public park use.

Anticipating monumental traffic jams in an area squeezed between non-expandable borders of mountain wall and ocean surf, the General Plan foretells rapid transit systems on the existing S.P. tracks, whisking passengers from Gaviota to the Rincon at 100 miles per hour. If this proved inadequate to handle the passenger load, the General Plan suggests monorail trains flanking the Highway 101 right-of-way.

But these projections were of the future. The present was breeding its own problems. The municipal airport broke all previous passenger-carrying records in 1965 with Pacific Air Lines and United Air Lines accommodating 124,729 passengers, plus 1,765,129 pounds of air mail, first class mail, air express and air freight—an increase of 41 per cent over the previous year.

Pacific announced that as of July 1, 1966, it would be landing pure jet Boeing 727 ninety-passenger airliners at Santa Barbara. This set City Hall to talking about extending the runways to accommodate the big 707 jets, along with a new airport terminal to cost $2,000,000.

Such talk fanned into flame long-smouldering embers of past resentments in the Goleta Valley. Hundreds of Goleta homes would lie under the approach paths of eardrum-cracking, sonic-boom jet aircraft. Certainly, a modern jet airport only eight short miles from De la Guerra Plaza would be wonderful for Santa Barbara to advertise; but it could blight vast residential areas in the Good Land. As always, complained many Goletans, arrogant Santa Barbara was exploiting the Valley, treating Goleta like a poor country cousin.

Native Goletans had potent support for their anti-jet sentiment. Several years earlier, Chancellor Gould of UCSB and planning consultant William Pereira had confided to Richard Buffum, publisher of Goleta's weekly newspaper *Gazette-Citizen*, their belief that the municipal airport would increasingly become a nuisance and a hazard, as well as a block to the intelligent growth of the community.

Buffum commented editorially on this subject in late 1965:

> Santa Barbara's political acquisition of some 570 acres of airport property stands as an unprecedented monument to legal sharpness. It still rankles oldtimers here, and does much to explain some Goletans' resentment of the city's ramming jet noises down our eardrums. Many have claimed . . . that the airport is a serious deterrent to the logical and orderly growth of the Goleta Valley into a desirable residential-commercial-educational-recreational community.
>
> It seems to us that eventually the airport, because of surrounding high-grade development and the protests of home owners, would be forced to move, possibly to the Santa Ynez Valley where, it is claimed, flying conditions are more favorable the year around.

While the General Plan envisioned high-speed helicopter shuttle service to and from Santa Ynez Valley, it made no specific recommendation to move the airport from Goleta. It did point out that "surrounding developments will make extension of the runways to handle large jets difficult. It is unlikely that such extensions are either desirable or practical."

Aldous Huxley, on a lecture tour, sized up the Goleta Valley situation by saying "the day will come when Goleta will be just another bead in a long, long chain extending from San Diego to San Francisco."

The public official closest to the changing picture of the Good Land, county planning director Dick Whitehead, sounded a warning:

> By the year 1980 the residents [of the Goleta Valley] will no longer be able to enjoy the green vistas of lemon and avocado groves; they will have been replaced by houses . . . [But] with foresight and attention to planning details, the Goleta Valley can be transformed in the next few years into one of the finest residential and educational communities in California. . . .

The transition of the traditionally pastoral Goleta Valley into a research and education center for the Space Age will entail heartbreaking experiences for many persons, especially those whose roots are sunk three or even four generations deep into the Good Land. A typical Valley rancher summed it up this way to the writer:

Progress: From Mescalitán to Megalopolis 341

"I cannot endure the thought of selling this ranch. My father was born here in 1882. I was born here in 1909. I raised my family here. But the income I can expect from an acre of lemons leaves me little after I pay my taxes. As the housing tracts close in around my land, those taxes will catch up with my income. What do I do then? A developer from San Fernando Valley has offered me more cash for my ranch than I could hope to make in twenty years of hard work. What choice do I have?"

The rancher's eyes narrowed sardonically as he watched a flock of birds arranging themselves on his television antenna, like so many quarter-notes on a musical staff. "I remember when I was a kid", he mused wistfully, "when wild ducks rising off the Slough could black out the sun. Now the ducks and geese are gone and even the swallows are thinning out. All in my lifetime. It is a sad thing to see."

... But these are the nostalgic yearnings of an older generation. A new breed of pioneer is taking over the Goleta Valley—pioneers in as true a sense as were the pioneers of '49 and '69. In time their numbers will exceed those living in Santa Barbara. They bring college diplomas to their jobs. When they gather socially they chat about computers and slide rules and interplanetary travel as off-handedly as Goletans of another era met around the cracker barrel on the porch of Deu's Store to discuss fertilizer, chicken feed and the price of beans. The newcomers were not around when the Goleta Valley was a green and pristine Eden, so they do not miss the beauty progress has taken away.

The future belongs to them, and they know it. They are not so blasé that they cannot find inspiration in the vista of purple mountains marching majestically toward the sunset. Their thrill at beholding a sublime metal-blue seascape is only slightly diminished by the intrusion of marine oil well platforms off shore.

... January 20, 1965, marked the one hundredth anniversary of the death of Daniel A. Hill, an event which started the transition of the Goleta Valley from the old Mexican grants to small farms. Even on that late date, the Goleta Valley still retained much of its pastoral charm, although the bulldozer was fast taking over.

The newcomers who were filling the open spaces and who would be raising their children here, still had a chance to keep their Valley beautiful, providing they took militant steps to close ranks against selfish developers who would deface the lovely hill slopes with building "pads"; providing they insisted on removing adequate park, playground and green belt space from the tax rolls; provided they resisted the senseless destruction of trees, topsoil and other God-given assets.

It will be a difficult struggle, this unending feud between greed and beauty. But it will be worth winning. The preservation of the Goleta Valley as a superior place to live now rests squarely in the hands of its young, latter-day inheritors. There is still time for them to hold the line against commercial exploitation of esthetic values, but that time is short . . . so terribly short. With united dedication to the common cause, the new dwellers of the Good Land can keep their valley as attractive as it was 200 years ago, when a gray-robed Franciscan friar, Juan Crespí, recorded white man's first appraisal of this richly-blessed homeland:

> *This whole country . . . is extremely delightful.*
> *It is all a Good Land . . .*

Index

airplanes, first: 289, 290, 291
airport annexation coup: 326
airport, municipal: 272, 290-293, 296, 297, 307-310, 314, 316, 319, 326, 340
anchor found in Slough: 1, 2
Anderson, James, family: 173-174, 188, 207
Anza expedition of 1774: 11, 13
archaeological activity: 139-141, 307
Archambault, Joseph: 122, 188, 206, 246, 263, 276
artesian wells: 143, 144
Arthur, Harry, butcher wagon: 247
asphalt industry: 57, 132, 160, 219-223, 277
Atascadero Creek: 14, 57, 60, 62
automobile, first in valley: 244, 245
avocado industry: 248, 285, 288, 318, 340

Baker, William H., family: 227
Baptist Church, pioneer: 110, 190, 289
Barnsdall Oil Co.: 278-296, 299
Bartlett Canyon: 56, 98
Begg family: 171-175, 178, 197, 198-200, 337
Beguhl, Charles A.: 248, 291, 310
Bell, Kate Den: 36, 114, 161-163, 172, 174, 197, 234, 235, 277, 305
Birabent (Jean M.) House: 104
Bishop Ranch: 234, 235, 248, 251, 274, 276, 285, 288, 324, 336, 339
Bishop, Thomas B.: 161-170, 174, 176, 180, 188, 196, 209, 234, 248
Bishop Hollister suit: 162-170, 179-188
Blakeway, Edgar: 244, 248, 253, 256, 257, 259, 270, 289

Bottiani, Carlo, family: 203
Bouchard raid of 1818: 17
Brown, "Auntie": 54, 85, 87, 88, 182, 224
Bundy Flying Service: 291, 292

Cachuma Dam: 248, 311, 316, 318-320, 328, 329, 336
Campbell, Col. Colin: 262-267, 313
Campbell, Dr. Edgar: 240
Campbell Ranch: 262-270, 275, 300, 312, 313
Canalino Indians: 2-10, 12, 14, 23, 321
Carneros Creek: 14, 60, 65, 71, 80, 83, 106
Carrillo, Leo: 226, 236
Cathedral Oaks named: 190; school, 137-138
Catlett, Ezra, family: 72, 94, 137-230, 258
cattle drives, Goleta Valley: 50, 248, 249
Cavalletto family: 188, 205-209, 212, 221, 223
Cemetery, Goleta: 5, 47, 112, 121, 122, 148, 174, 176, 177, 222
Chinese labor in Goleta Valley: 84
Chow, Gin: 234, 235
Coal Oil Point: 114, 160, 205
Cochera Tract: see La Patera
Conover, A. W.: 250, 251
Constabulary of 1898: 192
Cooper, Ellwood: 113-122, 162-167, 171, 173, 179, 182, 183, 185, 187, 197, 224, 234, 244, 255, 256, 261, 275, 276, 288
Corona del Mar ranch: 83, 185, 336, (see Bishop Ranch)
county road work: 59, 246, 250, 251
Culver, David M.: 151, 155, 157, 234, 243, 253

Dardi asphyxiation: 212
Den, Nicolás A.: 36-38, 47, 50, 65, 80, 82, 160, 177, 180, 184, 185, 188, 204, 212, 249, 274, 281, 311, 334
Den, Dr. Richard S.: 36, 39, 50, 65, 80, 82
Deu (J. B.) store: 193, 194
Devereux Ranch (school): 8, 12, 62, 264, 267, 312, 313, 339
Dorotea (schooner) 26
Dos Pueblos grant: 2, 9, 14, 31, 33, 34, 40, 51, 60, 223, 239, 262, 271, 274, 280, 282, 302, 314, 315, 324, 325, 327, 338
Dos Pueblos High School: 337, 338
Dos Pueblos Orchid Company: 276, 329
Doty Brothers: 122, 276, 304
Drocco, Carlo, murder: 260, 318
drought of 1864: 65-69
Durbiano family: 211

Eagle Canyon: 60, 282, 324
Earthquake, 1925: 225, 228, 240, 269-272
Edwards, George S.: 73, 112, 175, 177, 252
electric lights, first: 254
El Encanto Heights: 83, 260, 318, 330, 337
Ellwood Canyon: 9, 35, 80, 87, 113-114, 115, 255
Ellwood Oil Field: 233, 277, 282, 298, 299, 311
"Ellwood Special" train: 198-199
Embarcadero land scandal: 333-335

Fairfield Tract: 275, 307
Fairview Avenue: 40, 71, 75, 106, 201
Fairview Ranch: 87, 224
Farren, Patrick, family: 99
Fast, Salathial: 72, 111, 112
Federated Church: 253, 257
Fernald, Charles: 71, 163-166
Fires: Glen Annie, 186-187; lemon plant, 318; Refugio, 303, 323, 324; 1894—227, 228
fire department, first: 257
floods: 1861—62-63; 1914—255-257; 1952—321
Foster, I. G., family: 75-77, 84, 102, 105, 111, 132, 234, 236
Foxen, Benjamin: 18, 26, 27, 44, 109
Franklin, Dr. Walter S.: 262, 267-270, 288
Franklin Ranch: see Walora Ranch
Frémont, John C.: 37, 41-48, 95, 105

garage, first in Goleta: 246
gas wells, More Mesa: 283, 284
gold mine, Emigh's: 232, 233
gold rush period: 49, 50
Goleta, origin of name: 1, 18, 26
Goleta County Water District: 310, 311, 314, 322, 325, 328, 336
Goleta Farm Bureau: 253, 259, 289, 293, 327
Goleta Farm Center: 259, 314; Inc., 253, 254
Goleta Lemon Association: 251, 286, 287, 309, 319, 322
Goleta Center (tract): 275
Goleta Sandspit: 17, 26, 274, 283, 287
Goleta Sanitary District: 307, 319
Goleta Slough: 1-8, 10, 18, 27, 34, 256, 290, 292, 293, 341
Goleta Union School: 257, 270, 273, 289, 328, 330, 332, 337
Goleta Valley C. of C.: 313, 327, 328
Goleta Valley Jr. Hi School: 267, 337
Goleta weekly newspapers: *Leader*, 296; *Gazette-Citizen*, 339, 340
Goleta Woman's Club: 228, 251, 252, 293, 310
Goleta Woman's Service Club: 310, 337
Glen Annie Canyon named: 81
Glen Annie Jr. Hi School: 338
Grant, Daniel G.: 331

Harmony Hall: 228, 253
Havens, Francis: 244, 256
Hendry family: 171-172, 174, 176
Hicks family: 73, 96
Hill Adobe: 28, 52, 68, 71, 73, 103, 106, 121, 126, 143, 216, 242, 271, 286
Hill, Daniel A.: 20, 31-48, 52, 58, 69, 70, 132, 133, 149, 159, 193, 209, 241, 268, 341
Hill, Rafaela Ortega: 20, 24, 25, 52, 70, 106, 123, 124, 224, 229, 241
Hirashima, John, Tom: 295
Hollister, Albert G.: 87, 106, 224, 267
Hollister, Stanley: 231, 232, 321
Hollister, Col. W. W.: 53, 54, 57, 65, 79-91, 113, 114, 120, 121, 123-125, 145, 162-170, 171, 179-185, 188, 196, 209-211, 224, 231, 234, 261
Hollister Avenue: 4, 47, 73, 85, 109, 250, 251, 256, 313, 338
Hollister, Sen. Jack: 303, 323, 326, 327, 334, 337
Hollister, W. N. (Bill): 254, 311, 312, 314, 315, 321, 325, 327, 331

Index

Homesteads in foothills, 92-100, 244, 256
Hope Ranch Park: 275, 289, 301
Huse, Charles E.: 64, 65, 71, 72, 79, 80, 86, 160-164, 185

Indian Orchard: 63, 248, 256
industries, smokeless: 335, 340
irrigation, first: 124, 126
Irvine family: 159, 175, 177, 178, 266, 271
Isla Vista created: 275

Japanese families, 1941: 295
Johnston Fruit Company: 127, 128, 129
Jordano family: 154, 209

Kellogg family: 110, 116, 143, 143, 147-149, 150, 151, 157, 159, 174, 191, 200-202, 229, 230, 233, 234, 240, 242, 245, 254, 274, 288, 314
"Kicking Mule", the: 189, 190
Kinevan, Patrick: 133
Koster's cobbler shop: 109
KTMS radio towers: 260, 283, 291, 302

La Colina Jr. Hi School: 330, 337
La Goleta grant: 38, 40, 51, 71, 72, 78, 106
La Joven Angustias (ship): 17, 18, 26
La Patera: 34, 35, 52, 71, 97, 102, 106, 227, 229, 235, 237, 250, 257
La Patera School: 138, 139, 332
Lane family: 103, 104, 230, 242, 245
Langman family: 75, 109, 244
Larkin, Ysabel birth: 28
Larson, Christian family: 127
last Canalino Indian: 9, 321
"Laurel of San Marcos": 135
lemon industry: 248, 268, 285, 287-289, 318, 319, 333, 340, 341
Lillard family: 94-96, 134, 135, 148, 154, 205, 209, 253, 273, 289, 328
Lima Bean Growers Association formed: 254
Linquest, August: 187, 232, 242
Lobero, Jose: 81, 90, 224
Luton-Bell No. 1 (oil well): 233, 278-281

Maiers, George "Fritz": 228, 242, 243, 245
Main family: 173, 174, 186, 187, 209
Man of the Year awards: 337
Manchester family: 231, 246
Marble, Philip C.: 98, 135, 248, 254, 286, 289, 314

Maria Ygnacia Canyon: 13, 14, 60, 67, 105, 109
Marine air station: 307-310, 312, 316, 319, 335
McCaffery, James: 53, 63, 68, 74, 99
McGowan, Judge Ned: 55, 56
Mecono family: 188, 211
Mescalitán Island: 2, 6, 7, 67-69, 140, 141, 151, 155, 158, 207, 293, 307, 319
Methodist Church, pioneer: 253, 289
Mexican War: 40-48
Modoc Road, how named: 108
More, Alexander P.: 51, 151, 155-157, 160
More, John F.: 147, 150-159, 177, 182, 187, 197, 200, 201, 207, 253
More's Landing (wharf): 131, 132, 151, 155, 200, 201, 233
More Mesa: 10, 18, 40, 150, 159, 260, 283, 291, 302
More, T. Wallace: 51, 53, 59, 60, 63, 69, 84, 86, 101, 107, 121, 126, 131, 132, 137, 139, 148, 149, 150, 158, 159, 191, 250, 277
Morgan, Frank A.: 277-281
Mosher, Samuel B.: 262, 282, 311, 329
motion picture, first: 226

Naples: 136, 194-196, 199, 224, 225, 233, 235, 236, 239, 241, 244, 245, 256, 259, 261, 265, 271, 282, 334

orange growing in Valley: 288, 289
orange trees, first: 248
orchid industry: 328, 329
Owen, Uncle Ben: 97, 227

Pacific Lighting Gas Supply Corp.: 153, 283, 284, 293, 319, 326
Pagliotti family: 205, 207, 209
pampas plume industry: 146, 214, 216-219
Patterson Avenue named: 75
Patterson, J. D.: 74, 250
paving, first road: 251
Pennsinger, Jacob: 99
Pettis, Ben: 103, 227, 230, 242
Philomathic Club formed: 228
Pickett, John, family: 136, 147, 148, 173, 192, 211
Pico's Blacksmith Shop: 227, 274
Pomatto family: 177, 188, 205, 209-211
population explosion: 329, 336, 338, 340
Portola Expedition of 1769: 3-9
post office: first, 132; 225, 227, 259, 289, 331

"Potter Farm": 240, 339
Powers, Jack: 55, 56
prehistoric inhabitants: 5, 6
Prohibition era: 259, 260
pumpkins, giant: 142

Rafaela School, 103; Cemetery Association, 112
railway construction: 196-199, 234, 235, 236, 238, 239
Rancho del Ciervo: 46, 95
revival meetings, old-time: 190
Rich, Chester: 192, 273, 288, 314, 320
Rio Grande Oil Co.: 278-281
Ross, Sheriff Jim: 177
Rowe family: 148, 192, 193, 337
rural free delivery, first: 259
Rutherford family: 171, 172, 186, 187, 195, 197-199, 233, 245, 258
Rutherford, J. Monroe: 286, 296, 300, 311, 314, 315

San Jose Creek: 14, 47, 57, 60, 74, 94, 102
San Jose Vineyard: 53, 74
San Marcos High School: 4, 40, 47, 61, 67, 148, 250, 330, 338
San Marcos Road: 135, 173, 175
Sangster family: 176
Santa Barbara Mission: 6, 10, 12, 14, 17, 37, 39, 51
Scottish immigration to Valley: 171-178
Scottish-American picnics: 178
Scudelari family: 204, 205
Scull, Abel C.: 67, 71, 97, 105
Senter, German: 105, 123, 124, 224
Serra, Padre visits: 12
Service Clubs: Goleta Lions, 293; Goleta Rotary, 293
Sexton, Joseph, family: 74, 78, 101, 119, 124, 137, 143-147, 150, 155, 173, 176, 191, 192, 197, 200, 201, 205, 207, 216-219, 221-223, 225-228, 236, 245, 254, 258, 282, 288, 289, 296, 307, 324, 332, 337
Sexton's Hall: 225-227, 258, 261
Shewan, "Sandy": 176, 177
Signal Oil & Gas Co.: 233, 262, 282, 299, 311, 315
simoon of 1859: 57, 58
Simpson family: 173, 200, 205, 245
slaughterhouse: 275, 307
Slippery Rock: 134, 135
Smith family: 171-173, 176-177, 205, 223
Smith, Jim (blacksmith shop): 274, 276, 289, 296, 337

stagecoaching era: 61, 133-137
Stevens, Fred: 247, 248, 253, 259, 273, 289, 311, 320, 337
Storke, C. A.: 121, 150, 156, 157, 234, 264, 291, 327
Storke, Charles, II: 322, 325-327
Storke, Thomas M.: 264, 291, 292, 314, 315, 318, 322, 323, 327
Stow, Edgar: 253, 254, 296
Stow Ranch: 125-129, 155, 173, 187, 204, 285, 288, 335, 336
Stow, Sherman P.: 123-128, 172, 210, 285
Stronach family: 176
Sturges Brothers: 72, 91, 162, 164, 167, 169, 170
Submarine attack on Ellwood: 297-306

Tecolote Canyon: 61, 169, 276, 288, 333, 334
Tecolote School: 139
Tecolotito Creek: 14, 54, 60, 65, 80, 83
telegraph, first: 105
telephones, first: 242-244
Towne, Edward family: 109
tractors, first in valley: 253, 254
trains, first: 198, 239
Troup family: 174, 175, 193, 244, 254, 257, 258, 261, 268, 312
Tucker family: 109, 251, 252, 330
Tucker's Grove: 12, 40, 228, 245, 251, 252, 253, 261, 269
Turnpike Road: 74, 134
Two-Story School: 191

underground gas storage: 283, 284
UCSB (University of California at Santa Barbara): 140, 160, 161, 174, 178, 205, 214, 215, 219, 222, 272, 308, 315-320, 322, 325, 326, 329, 332, 333, 338, 339
USS Oregon speed trials: 230, 231

Van Horne, Garrett: 128, 130, 335, 336

Walnut Growers Association: 229, 230, 253, 254, 270, 314
walnut huller, Maiers: 242, 243, 246
walnut industry: 230, 254, 255, 268, 333
Walora (Franklin) Ranch: 267-270, 288, 295, 337
Ward Memorial Boulevard: 320-327
wedding, first in valley: 104, 105
Welch, G. C.: 72, 105, 172, 193, 195, 197
Welch, Donald: 320
well drilling: 143, 144

whaling industry, Goleta: 214-216
wharfage rates, More's Landing: 132
Williams, George M. family: 108, 230, 232-234, 239, 241, 254, 256, 259, 289
Williams, James G.: 241, 253, 259, 289
Williams, John H. and Alice P.: 195-196, 224, 239, 240, 265, 271, 334
Winchester Canyon: 9, 14, 18, 87
Winchester, Dr. R. F.: 87, 89, 162, 179, 180, 231
World War II days: 295, 296, 307, 311, 312
World War dead, Goleta: 258, 312, 321
wreck, first railroad: 237
Wylie, Herbert G.: 172, 262, 271, 278, 282, 311

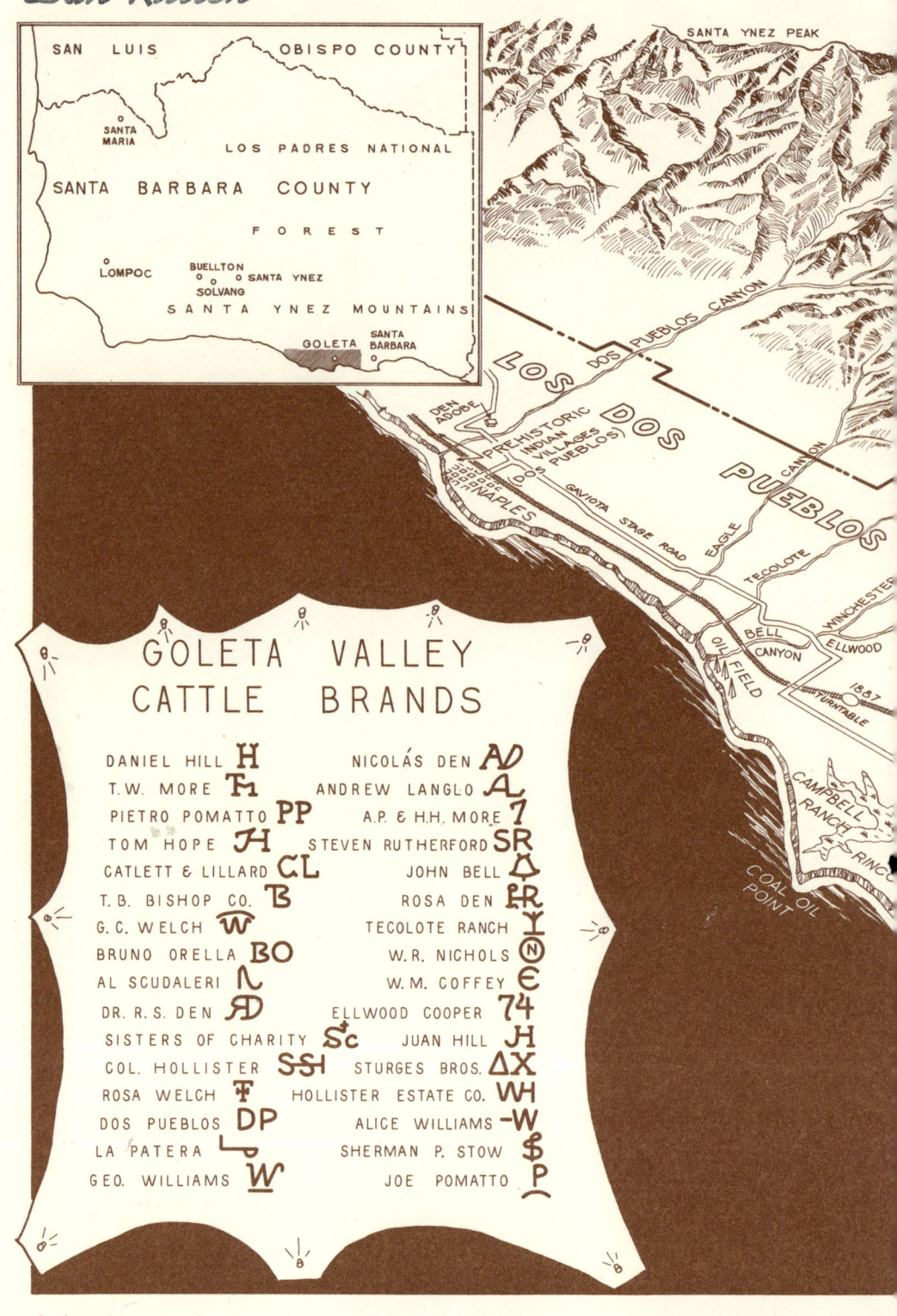